Michael Oakeshott

The Concept of a Philosophical Jurisprudence: Essays and Reviews 1926–51

Edited by
Luke O'Sullivan

imprint-academic.com

This collection copyright © Imprint Academic, 2007

The moral rights of the author have been asserted
No part of any contribution may be reproduced in any form
without permission, except for the quotation of brief passages
in criticism and discussion.

Published in the UK by Imprint Academic
PO Box 200, Exeter EX5 5YX, UK

Published in the USA by Imprint Academic
Philosophy Documentation Center
PO Box 7147, Charlottesville, VA 22906-7147, USA

ISBN 978-1845400309 (cloth)
ISBN 978-1845401801 (pbk)

A CIP catalogue record for this book is available from the
British Library and US Library of Congress

Michael Oakeshott, *Selected Writings*

Volume I (2004):
What is History? and other essays
edited by Luke O'Sullivan, 978-0907845836

Volume II (2006):
Lectures in the History of Political Thought
edited by Terry Nardin & Luke O'Sullivan, 978-1845400934

Volume III (2007):
*The Concept of a Philosophical Jurisprudence:
Essays and Reviews 1926-51*
edited by Luke O'Sullivan, 978-1845400309

Volume IV (2008):
*The Vocabulary of a Modern European State:
Essays and Reviews 1952-88*
edited by Luke O'Sullivan, 978-1845400316

Contents

Preface vii

Introduction 1

1 Review of J. Needham (ed.), *Science, Religion, and Reality* (1926) . 37
2 Review of A.C. Bouquet, *The Christian Religion and Its Competitors To-day* (1926) 40
3 Review of E. Griffith-Jones, *Providence – Divine and Human* (1926) 41
4 Review of T. Whittaker, *The Metaphysics of Evolution* (1927) 42
5 Review of R.B. Perry, *General Theory of Value* (1927) 43
6 Review of R.W. Sellars, *The Principles and Problems of Philosophy* (1927) 44
7 Review of F.J.E. Woodbridge, *The Realm of Mind*; A.A. Jascalevich, *Three Conceptions of Mind* (1927) 45
8 Review of A.G. Widgery, *Contemporary Thought of Great Britain* (1927) 46
9 Review of C. Gore, *Can We Then Believe?*; E.G. Selwyn (ed.), *Essays Catholic and Critical*; W.R. Bowie, *The Inescapable Christ* (1927) 48
10 Review of P. Gardner, *Modernism in the English Church* (1927) . . . 50
11 Review of J.S. Mackenzie, *Fundamental Problems of Life* (1929) . . . 51
12 Review of P.S. Belasco, *Authority in Church and State* (1929) 54
13 Review of J. Martet, *Clemenceau* (1930) 57
14 Review of J.C. Powys, *The Meaning of Culture* (1930) 58
15 Review of G.E.G. Catlin, *The Principles of Politics* (1930) 61
16 Review of K. Feiling, *What is Conservatism?*; L. Powys, *The Pathetic Fallacy* (1930) 63
17 Review of H. Rashdall, *God and Man*, ed. H.D.L. Major and F.L. Cross (1930) 65
18 Review of G.G. Atkins, *The Making of the Christian Mind* (1930) . . 66
19 Review of H.H. Farmer, *Experience of God* (1930) 71
20 Review of L.P. Smith, *Afterthoughts*; F.H. Bradley, *Aphorisms* (1931) 73
21 Review of L. Britton, *Hunger and Love* (1931) 76
22 Review of J.B. Pratt, *Adventures in Philosophy and Religion* (1931) 77

23 Review of H. Driesch, *Ethical Principles in Theory and Practice* (1931) 78
24 Review of F.J. Sheen, *Religion without God*; K. Heim, *The New Divine Order*; E. Holmes, *Philosophy without Metaphysics* (1931) 80
25 *John Locke* (1932) 82
26 Review of F.J.C. Hearnshaw (ed.), *The Social and Political Ideas of the Age of Reaction and Reconstruction* (1931) 87
27 Review of M. Ruthnaswamy, *The Making of the State* (1933) 88
28 Review of J. Macmurray, *Interpreting the Universe* (1933) 89
29 Review of C.R. Morris, *Idealistic Logic* (1933) 90
30 Review of L. Chestov, *In Job's Balances* (1933) 91
31 Review of M. Grant, *A New Argument for God and Survival* (1934) 94
32 Review of L. Curtis, *Civitas Dei* (1934) 96
33 Review of O. Gierke, *Natural Law and the Theory of Society* (1934) 97
34 Review of H. Levy and others, *Aspects of Dialectical Materialism* (1934) 100
35 Review of A.N. Whitehead, *Adventures of Ideas* (1934) 105
36 Review of C.D. Burns, *The Horizon of Experience* (1934) 108
37 Review of G. Michaelis, *Richard Hooker als politischer Denker* (1934) 109
38 *Thomas Hobbes* (1935) 110
39 Review of H.G. Wood, *Christianity and the Nature of History*; J.C. McKerrow, *Religion and History* (1935) 122
40 Review of E.F. Carritt, *Morals and Politics* (1935) 124
41 Review of M.B. Foster, *The Political Philosophies of Plato and Hegel* (1935) 126
42 Review of A.W. Tilby, *Right: a Study in Physical and Moral Order* (1935) 128
43 'History and the Social Sciences' (1936) 129
44 Review of W. Brock, *An Introduction to Contemporary German Philosophy* (1936) 135
45 Review of N. Berdyaev, *The Meaning of History* (1936) 137
46 Review of C.C.J. Webb, *The Historical Element in Religion* (1936) . 138
47 Review of F.H. Bradley, *Collected Essays* (1936) 140
48 Review of B. Pfannenstill, *Bernard Bosanquet's Philosophy of the State* (1936) 143
49 Review of L. Strauss, *The Political Philosophy of Hobbes* (1936) . . . 145
50 Review of K. Mannheim, *Ideology and Utopia* (1937) 147

51	Review of F. Birch, *This Freedom of Ours* (1937)	149
52	Review of M. Roberts, *The Modern Mind* (1937)	151
53	*The Concept of a Philosophical Jurisprudence* (1938)	154
54	Review of R.G. Collingwood, *The Principles of Art*, ed. T.M. Knox (1938)	184
55	Review of J. Marshall, *Swords and Symbols* (1939)	187
56	Review of K.B. Smellie, *Reason in Politics* (1939)	189
57	Review of E.F.M. Durbin, *The Politics of Democratic Socialism* (1940)	191
58	Review of G. Wallas, *Men and Ideas* (1941)	195
59	Review of B. Croce, *Politics and Morals* (1946)	196
60	Review of R.G. Collingwood, *The Idea of History* (1947)	197
61	Review of W.A. Orton, *The Liberal Tradition* (1947)	200
62	Review of J. Bowle, *Western Political Thought* (1947)	201
63	*Contemporary British Politics*. Review of J. Parker, *Labour Marches On*, and Q. Hogg, *The Case for Conservatism* (1947)	203
64	Review of H.D. Lasswell, *The Analysis of Political Behaviour* (1948)	220
65	Review of L. Whistler, *The English Festivals* (1948)	222
66	Review of J. Lavrin, *Nietzsche* (1948)	224
67	Review of W.T. Jones (ed.), *Masters of Political Thought*, (1948)	226
68	Review of K.B. Smellie, *Why We Read History* (1948)	228
69	Review of S. Campion, *Father, a Portrait of G.G. Coulton* (1948)	230
70	Review of V. Bulwer, *Bulwer-Lytton* (1948)	233
71	Review of G. Bryson, *Man and Society* (1948)	234
72	Review of M. Ginsberg, *Reason and Unreason in Society* (1948)	235
73	Review of R.B. Perry, *Puritanism and Democracy* (1948)	236
74	Review of C.E.M. Joad, *Decadence* (1948)	238
75	*Science and Society* (1948)	240
76	Review of J.D. Mabbott, *The State and the Citizen* (1949)	248
77	Review of E.F. Williams, *The Triple Challenge* (1949)	260
78	Review of F. Sternberg, *How to Stop the Russians without War* (1949)	262
79	Review of G.C. Field, *Principles and Ideals in Politics* (1949)	266
80	Review of E. Whittaker, *The Modern Approach to Descartes' Problem*; S.M. Jacob, *Notes on Descartes' Règles*; P. Valéry, *Descartes* (1949)	268
81	Review of H. Selsam, *Socialism and Ethics* (1949)	271
82	Review of E. Dudley, *The Tree of Commonwealth*, ed. D.M. Brodie (1949)	275

83	Review of A. Koestler, *Insight and Outlook* (1949).	277
84	Review of O. S. Wauchope, *Deviation into Sense* (1949)	280
85	Review of W. G. de Burgh, *The Life of Reason* (1949)	283
86	Review of W. Carington, *Matter, Mind, and Meaning* (1949).	285
87	Review of T. Gilby, *Barbara Celarent* (1949)	287
88	Review of J.D. Bernal, *The Freedom of Necessity* (1949)	289
89	Review of D.G. James, *The Life of Reason* (1949).	292
90	Review of J. Lindsay, *Marxism and Contemporary Science* (1949)	295
91	Review of H. Butterfield, *The Origins of Modern Science* (1949)	297
92	Review of J. Burnham, *The Coming Defeat of Communism* (1950)	306
93	Review of J.R. Watmough, *Cambridge Conversations* (1950)	309
94	Review of J. Plamenatz, *The English Utilitarians* (1950).	311
95	Review of J.W. Gough, *John Locke's Political Philosophy* (1950)	313
96	Review of R. Filmer, *Patriarcha*, ed. P. Laslett (1950).	315
97	Review of G. Ryle, *The Concept of Mind* (1950)	317
98	Review of J. Godley, *Tell Me the Next One* (1950).	319
99	Review of W.M. Urban, *Beyond Realism and Idealism* (1950)	321
100	Review of E.W.F. Tomlin, *The Great Philosophers* (1950)	323
101	*Mr Carr's First Volume.* Review of E.H. Carr, *The Bolshevik Revolution* (1951)	325
102	*The B.B.C.* (1951)	334
103	Review of T. Wilson, *Modern Capitalism and Economic Progress* (1951).	345
104	Review of J.H.S. Burleigh, *The City of God*; R.H. Barrow, *Introduction to St Augustine* (1951)	348
105	Review of T.H. Marshall, *Citizenship and Social Class* (1951).	352
106	Review of N. Machiavelli, *The Discourses*, ed. L.J. Walker (1951).	355
107	Review of G.J. Renier, *History, Its Purpose and Method* (1951)	357
108	Review of C. L. Morgan, *Liberties of the Mind* (1951)	359
109	Review of G. Santayana, *Dominations and Powers* (1951).	362
110	Review of D.W. Brogan, *The Price of Revolution* (1951).	364
111	Review of R.E. Money-Kyrle, *Psychoanalysis and Politics* (1951).	367
112	Review of D. M. Pickles, *Introduction to Politics* (1951).	369
Indexes		371

Preface

Preparing the third and fourth volumes in the series of Oakeshott's *Selected Writings* for publication posed copyright problems not raised by the first two volumes, which consisted entirely of material from the Oakeshott archive at the London School of Economics. Volumes one and two therefore only required permission from the British Library of Political and Economic Science. Obtaining permission to reproduce the material in volumes three and four, however, involved negotiating with around twenty different parties.

In some cases—where, for example, a journal or magazine had changed hands, or was now defunct, or a book had long been out of print—this proved problematic, as it was not immediately obvious where the copyright lay. The editor is obliged therefore to Gabrielle White, Permissions Assistant at Random House Archive and Library, for investigating the status of the material in the *Cambridge Journal*.

In the majority of cases, however, a copyright holder was found, and given the total absence of a budget for obtaining the rights to reprint the material included in this volume and its companion, it is gratifying to be able to record that in every case the owners of the rights were prepared either to accept a significantly reduced fee or in some cases even waive their fees altogether.

So far as the material in this volume is concerned, I am very pleased to be able to thank the following individuals and institutions for their willingness to accept less than their regular fee and for consenting to republication: Sophie Buchanan on behalf of *The Spectator*; Toby Lichtig on behalf of the *Times Literary Supplement*; Linda Nicol on behalf of Cambridge University Press, for permission to use material from *Philosophy*; Julia Pieri on behalf of Express Group Newspapers, for permission to use material from the *Evening Standard*; and Gemma Puntis on behalf of Oxford University Press, for permission to use material from the *Journal of Theological Studies*, *Mind*, and the *English Historical Review*.

For their generosity in agreeing to waive their fees altogether I am particularly indebted to: Helen Burton at the department of Special Collections and Archives, Keele University Library, for permission to use material originally published by the Le Play House Press; Professor Rudolf Hanka, Chairman of the Cambridge Review Committee, for permission to use items from the *Cambridge Review*; Dr Robin Leavis on behalf of the estate of F.R. Leavis, for permission to use material from *Scrutiny*; and Anna Towlson of the London School of Economics, for permission to use material originally published in *Politica*.

Once permission to use the copyrighted material had been obtained, of course, it was necessary to raise the funds to pay for the rights. I am grateful to the British Academy for the award of a Small Research Grant which was sufficient to cover the costs involved in purchasing the reproduction rights for both volumes. This assistance was all the more welcome as the editor was without an academic affiliation for a significant portion of the period during which this volume and its companion were in preparation. Thanks are also due to Professors Robert Grant and Terry Nardin, who lent their support to the grant application.

Imprint Academic, publishers of the *Selected Writings*, have continued to play a vital role in the success of the series; their ongoing support is a major contribution to Oakeshott studies.

Finally, I would like to thank my family for their continued support as I suffered the vagaries of an academic career. Without their help this volume would never have been completed. My wife Olga also deserves my thanks for her assistance with the proofs, which saved me from some heinous errors. All those remaining are of course my own.

London and Singapore, 2007

Introduction

This volume collects all of Oakeshott's essays and reviews published between 1926 and 1951 and not previously republished elsewhere.[1] Together with its companion for the years 1952 to 1988, it will make the vast majority of these pieces easily accessible for the first time. The laborious experience of consulting them in their scattered state provided the initial impetus for collecting them into book form, but more than convenience is involved; these writings supply valuable continuity between Oakeshott's relatively small number of published books.

There were only four major works; *Experience and Its Modes* (1933), an early philosophical treatise; *Rationalism in Politics* (1961), a collection of largely previously published essays, mainly on political theory; *On Human Conduct* (1975), a definitive restatement of themes in the previous two works; and *On History* (1983), another late work, mainly devoted to the nature of historical understanding. But as Oakeshott himself put it, 'the mind... is always in motion', and his early, middle, and late books were all written in very different styles.[2]

Consequently, the relationships between them have been disputed. But as Auspitz has noted, '[Oakeshott's] changes did not come all at once. They began to appear piecemeal in his essays and reviews.'[3] From the first, he was regularly reviewing books on subjects reflecting his own interests: theology, philosophy (including metaphysics and ethics), history and historiography, and political theory. He also reviewed a variety of literary and topical works. Collectively, they provide valuable contextual material to complement his books, which were sparing in their references and tended to address arguments rather than persons.

Furthermore, taken together, the reviews are a distinctive record of the development of the humanities and social sciences in England over a good portion of the twentieth century; they tell us about the changing times through which Oakeshott lived, as well as about his own intellectual development. And quite apart from such academic considerations, many are exemplary specimens of the reviewer's craft that remain entertaining to read even if many of the books they dissect have been forgotten.

---

[1] For these previously published essays and reviews see M. Oakeshott, *Religion, Politics, and the Moral Life*, ed. T. Fuller (New Haven: Yale, 1993), and M. Oakeshott, *What is History? and Other Essays*, ed. L. O'Sullivan (Exeter: Imprint Academic, 2004). A full list of the contents of these volumes is online at http://www.michael-oakeshott-association.org/bibliography.htm.

[2] #91: *The Origins of Modern Science*, p. 297. (NB. Footnotes in this format refer to selection numbers and page numbers in this volume.)

[3] See J.L. Auspitz, 'Modality and Compossibility', in *The Intellectual Legacy of Michael Oakeshott*, ed. C. Abel and T. Fuller (Exeter: Imprint Academic, 2005), p. 10.

Some of the longer reviews became essays in their own right, like those in the short-lived *Cambridge Journal* that Oakeshott established on his return to Cambridge after the end of World War Two. Others were not reviews at all, but a contribution to a debate, such as the little-read piece on 'History and the Social Sciences' from 1936, or an effort to develop his own thinking, like 'The Concept of a Philosophical Jurisprudence' from 1938. This latter essay is the longest in the volume; it was both a summing-up of the state of jurisprudence and a statement on the nature of philosophy, and as such it gives the volume its title. Its place in his thought has been much disputed, for reasons we will examine below, so its appearance here ought to be particularly welcomed by Oakeshott scholars.

Oakeshott once remarked that 'it is impossible to be profitably critical without having a point of view'.[4] This claim implies that the various pieces published here express viewpoints of his own, suppressed or explicit. Ideally, then, one would like an overview of what these were, but few readers will peruse a volume such as this from start to finish. The remainder of this editorial introduction is therefore the best place to ask what emerges when writings that were never intended to be put together are treated as a unity.

I: Religion

In the mid-1920s, theologians and philosophers were digesting the implications of the nineteenth-century geological and Darwinian revolutions when the theories of quantum mechanics and relativity emerged. Oakeshott's first ever review was of *Science, Religion, and Reality*, an attempt to come to grips with these developments. Edited by Joseph Needham, another member of Oakeshott's Cambridge college, Gonville and Cauis, it had some eminent contributors. They included the former prime minister Lord Balfour, the experimental physicist Arthur Eddington, and the anthropologist Bronislaw Malinowski. Needham actually thanked Oakeshott in the Preface for his assistance, but the two men drifted apart in the 1930s, as Needham intensified his Christian and Marxist commitments while Oakeshott abandoned from his youthful sympathies for religion and socialism.

In 1926, however, Oakeshott shared Needham's interest in the effect of science on Christian belief. Oakeshott's approach was always to try to insulate the two from one another by arguing that in effect they were talking about different things. The scientific conception of the universe 'consisting solely of physically measurable relationships' was distinct from the 'practical' view of life found in religion. He consistently protested against any confusion between them. There could be no scientific proof of the exis-

---

[4] #89: *The Life of Reason*, p. 292.

tence of God, and any attempt to fit the notion of miracle into a scientific account of natural phenomena was 'naïve'.

Science could not be said either to prove or disprove the claims of Christianity. With respect to the question of miracles, for example, '[i]t is impossible to attach any relevant meaning to the notion of [a miraculous] event which "violates natural laws" when these laws are conceived as statistical generalizations'; the transformation wrought in physics by quantum theory had clearly influenced Oakeshott's conception of a scientific 'law'.[5]

Even if Christianity could be preserved in principle by arguing that scientific criticisms of it were irrelevant, there were historical as well as scientific issues to deal with.[6] Oakeshott was if anything more concerned with the impact of historical than of scientific scholarship, declaring that 'the most pressing feature of our theological thought' is 'the exact bearing upon Christianity of the modern historical criticism of the New Testament'. The revolution in Biblical criticism appeared to have left literal or dogmatic belief in Christianity in tatters. The only solution was to separate Christian belief from historical as well as scientific knowledge; the critical perspective on the past and the past required by religious practice were entirely different.[7]

The religious past was a practical matter, so could only be judged by practical criteria; any other form of criticism committed the error of *ignoratio elenchi*.[8] This phrase later cropped up repeatedly in *Experience and Its Modes* as part of Oakeshott's argument for the mutual independence of the various modes, but first emerged in this theological context. Indeed, the arguments as well as the terminology of these early discussions of religion became crucial to *Experience and Its Modes*.

The claim that the distinctive presuppositions of different forms of experience made them irrelevant to one another was later extended to include history and philosophy, but began here, in the context of these religious debates. The price of this manoeuvre, though, was the admission that 'the time has ... passed when it is any longer profitable to attempt to "prove" the existence of Providence or Purpose'.[9] Put another way, the 'truth' of Christianity became entirely a matter of its pragmatic efficacy in generating a community of believers and perhaps of its poetic success in conveying an ethic.

Oakeshott's position marked him as an Anglican 'Modernist', and left no room for the accommodation with Roman Catholicism sought by the 'high church' wing of Anglicanism. The Catholic position entailed the very conflict between religion and history that he was anxious to avoid; it con-

---

[5] #31: *A New Argument for God and Survival*, p. 94.
[6] #2: *The Christian Religion and Its Competitors To-day*, p. 40.
[7] #46: *The Historical Element in Religion*, p. 138.
[8] #19: *Experience of God*, p. 71.
[9] #3: *Providence – Divine and Human*, p. 41.

ceived of Christianity as 'something static, made, and not even in a process of being understood', and dismissed any 'doctrine or practice which does not conform to this definite and positive religion' as 'un-Christian'.[10]

But Modernism too could harden into the dogmatism of seeing a religion as a set of doctrines. The fundamental question here was how Christianity could change while retaining its identity. For Oakeshott, Christianity was really 'something which has always existed and must always exist—a striving to make theology give some answer to "the force and patience of the present time"'.[11] It was impossible to distinguish the essential from the inessential in the development of Christianity, and there was no essential core, such as 'the mind of Jesus', that had remained unmodified throughout history.

Christianity then became no more and no less than 'the deposit of its constituent centuries'.[12] Oakeshott rejected the suggestion that the history of Christianity was simply that of a perverted departure from an original 'feeling of pity or compassion' towards a system of institutional control based on fear.[13] He was even more scornful of the idea that 'Christianity (or anything else) can be discredited by recounting its history'; it was, in effect, what he later called a confusion of the historical and practical modes.

Thus, as well as assisting Oakeshott to formulate his philosophy of modality, his early theological reflections led him to articulate an important principle regarding historical identity. '[T]he identity of a historical phenomenon cannot be preserved by mere adherence to a fixed original datum, because (a) there can be no identity without a real change of some sort, and (b) there is no fixed original datum for us to adhere to.' As a corollary, '[i]f there has been change and development there must also be an identity, for without an identity there can be no change.'[14] These principles later played an integral role in his critical philosophy of history.

It was probably in this theological context that Oakeshott first used the phrase 'a world of ideas'. Being a world of ideas was something he later declared was an essential characteristic of any mode of experience, but here he was talking specifically about the historical identity of Christianity when he wrote that, '[i]n the development of a world of ideas a former stage, as such, is always lost in a later.'[15] By 1933 he had generalised this into the view that any form or 'mode' of experience was a dynamic whole; the theoretical worlds of experience of philosophy, science, and history no

---

[10] #9: *Essays Catholic and Critical*, p. 48.
[11] #10: *Modernism in the English Church*, p. 50.
[12] #18: *The Making of the Christian Mind*, p. 66.
[13] #16: *What is Conservatism?* and *The Pathetic Fallacy*, p. 63.
[14] #19: *Experience of God*, p. 71.
[15] #18: *The Making of the Christian Mind*, p. 66.

more stood still than did the practical world to which religious belief belonged.

While Oakeshott believed that all religion must involve some kind of relationship to the past, it did not justify 'the importance which traditional Christianity has attributed to past events'. But he never followed up his own suggestion that 'the only adequate defence' of Christianity 'would be in terms of a philosophical view of the nature of time and its relation with eternity, and a philosophical theory of belief'.[16] The religious standpoint was becoming an increasingly marginal one in philosophical circles; Russell was among those leading its rejection.[17]

Oakeshott restricted himself to distinguishing Christian speculative philosophies of history from the critical concept of historical understanding.[18] Speculative Christian histories distinguished certain events on the grounds of their pivotal role in the divinely ordained process 'to indicate their eternal significance'. But from the critical point of view, no event could be singled out as pivotal simply as such; its importance was entirely relative to the series of events under consideration. The criterion of significance, eternal or otherwise, was a practical one with no part in historical understanding as Oakeshott understood it.

II: Historiography and Philosophy of History

Much contemporary social science also struck Oakeshott as at least implying an all-embracing theory of human history that traduced the bounds of critical historical thinking. Sociologists, for example, were self-consciously attempting to transpose the biological theory of evolutionary adaptation into an interpretation of the human past as a process of development 'towards democracy, peace, and a world economy'.[19] Insofar as this kind of rationalistic optimism was present in social science, Oakeshott opposed it.[20] But it was not the only source of pseudo-scientific social science. He was also hostile to any positivistic philosophy which treated physical science as the only form of all valid explanation.

Yet Oakeshott was not hostile to sociological science as such. Scientific knowledge in the broad sense was 'always in the form of universal generalizations', and he saw nothing illegitimate in the attempt to 'discover and establish generalizations about the life and conduct, or some particular aspects of the life and conduct, of societies'. The roots of this enterprise lay partly in the attempts of eighteenth-century Scottish philosophers like Hume and Smith to erect 'a science of man and society based upon the

---

[16] #46: *The Historical Element in Religion*, p. 138.
[17] #24: *Religion without God*, p. 80.
[18] #39, *Christianity and the Nature of History*, p. 122.
[19] #39, *Christianity and the Nature of History*, p. 122.
[20] #75, *Science and Society*, p. 240.

newly elaborated empirical methods of physical science'; an impeccable genealogy.[21]

Some contemporary sociological work could strike Oakeshott as 'brilliant'; he praised T.H. Marshall's famous study of the genesis of the civil, political and social rights making up modern English citizenship, *Citizenship and Social* Class. Inevitably, however, it was a piece of *'histoire raisonné'* that resulted in 'less than a concrete picture' because of the nature of the sociological perspective. The sociological treatment of the human past required that 'each event or situation must be transformed into an instance of a general rule'; events consequently lost the exclusive status as differences that they had when treated historically.

Oakeshott also greeted Mannheim's *Ideology and Utopia* as an 'acute and valuable' book, despite some acerbic remarks about its 'turgid' style and 'alarming terminology'. He found in it a congenial kind of contextualism; Mannheim's 'sociology of knowledge' was 'an examination of the political and social ideas of an epoch or a community from the standpoint of their genesis and context in the culture of the community in which they find place'.[22]

Social change according to Mannheim was the result of conflict between ideologies, or 'mental fictions which are accepted by those who are anxious to stabilize the social order in which they find themselves', and utopias, 'ideas ... which represent our desire to replace our existing social order by another'. Crucially for Oakeshott, these two groups of ideas were not dependent in any simple way on a material base. If Mannheim had gone too far in attempting to 'prove the inadequacy of all so-called "classical logic" and all non-sociological approaches to human knowledge', he had still produced an 'extremely suggestive work'.

Nor was Oakeshott automatically hostile to psychology. He received Money-Kyrle's argument in *Psychoanalysis and Politics* that 'human behaviour is irretrievably ambivalent, alternating in love and hate' in a way that ultimately generated 'two forms of ... moral conscience' as 'candid' and 'moderate'. These dispositions in turn corresponded to two styles of politics, 'the one authoritarian and the other "humanistic"'. If this Freudian viewpoint resulted in some over-simplification, Oakeshott nevertheless accepted the aim of psychoanalysis – a 'redemption of mankind by greater self-knowledge' which aimed to confine 'conflict to realities' – as a plausible one.[23]

Oakeshott was also sympathetic to Koestler's *Insight and Outlook*, a search for the 'psychological common denominator' in all creative activity, including science and moral conduct as well as art.[24] Koestler claimed to have found it in the idea of the sudden 'simultaneous association of two

---

[21] #71, *Man and Society*, p. 234.
[22] #50, *Ideology and Utopia*, p. 147.
[23] #111, *Psychoanalysis and Politics*, p. 367.
[24] #83, *Insight and Outlook*, p. 277.

habitually incompatible contexts'. To reach this conclusion Koestler relied, as did Money-Kyrle, on the idea of 'two opposed tendencies in emotional behaviour', one 'self-assertive (aggressive-defensive)' and the other 'self-transcending (integrative)'.[25]

There is even a possibility that Oakeshott learnt something from these psychological works. At least, both relied on a notion analogous to one he sometimes adopted in his later writings, in which modern political history and theory are explained in part as a tension between two contrasting approaches to government ultimately traceable to two contrary dispositions within the European character or personality.

In 'History and the Social Sciences' Oakeshott aimed to distinguish the critical historical attitude from the positivistic and practical views of history that he believed were conflated in the model of social science advanced by the economic historian M.M. Postan, a fellow member of the Cambridge history faculty. Oakeshott began by asserting that there were a variety of ways of thinking about the past, none of which was 'preeminent', but argued that to call all of these 'historical' ways of thinking about the past invited confusion.[26]

Firstly, the specifically historical type of view of the past was unique in being based exclusively on the use of evidence. Mythical, traditional, and religious views of the past, or even the 'imagined or fancied' past of historical fiction, might make use of evidence, but they were not exclusively based on or bound to it. Secondly, and relatedly, the historical view of the past was not a 'relevant' view. The relevant past is the significant past; the past that has been 'influential in deciding the present or future fortunes of men'. 'Significance' focuses on the ethical or moral importance of the past for us, on its goodness, rightness, or legitimacy.

Such practical attitudes to the past were indispensable, but they were not characteristic of the exclusively historical view that focussed exclusively on understanding one or more events as an outcome of earlier events. Historical understanding was the appreciation of 'differences', which positively required 'imagination'. It implied 'the perpetual recreation of lost worlds' that were themselves always constructed as 'changing identities'. The historical past was a dynamic, not a static, construction.

Nor could the historical concept of an event be made analogous to the scientific concept. As we saw above, Oakeshott considered that natural science aimed at 'a statistical generalization' in which an event was a discrete 'point-instant'. It conceived the world in 'the most abstractly universal manner possible', seeking 'to generalize the world under the category

---

[25] #83, *Insight and Outlook*, p. 277; see also M. Oakeshott, *On Human Conduct* (Oxford: Clarendon Press, 1975), pp. 278, 325.
[26] For the Postan debate see also L. O'Sullivan, *Oakeshott on History* (Exeter: Imprint Academic, 2003), pp. 109–10.

of quantity'. By largely accepting the positivist account of physical science, but denying that historical events were reducible to the quantitative terms characteristic of purely physical events, Oakeshott devised a neat strategy for disarming his opponent.[27]

The physical world knew nothing, strictly, of 'the past' at all. '[F]or the historical way of thinking, the position of an event or situation in the past, and its pastness, are both essential aspects', but 'the world of scientific generalizations is a world ignorant alike of past and future as such; it ... recognizes time only within its own world as a method of relating its concepts'. Nevertheless, Postan's historical work was not to be judged by the positivistic theory of history he advanced; Oakeshott allowed that the practitioner of an activity may still perform it well while being ignorant or even mistaken about the nature of its presuppositions.

All Oakeshott objected to in the end was the claim that psychological, sociological, or economic explanations were 'scientific' in exactly the same way as the physical sciences:

> [T]here cannot be a science, in the strict sense, of human affairs ... but it does not follow that the scientific enterprise and the approximation to a social science that has been achieved ... are wholly without legitimate influence upon the way in which we think about the ends to be pursued in human affairs ... it is impossible to separate absolutely ... that sort of learning from experience we call 'science' and that sort of learning from experience which is involved in judgments of value. And one of the important oblique effects of the scientific enterprise has been to make necessary a reform in the way in which the ends pursued in society are stated, and consequently the way in which they are thought about.

Oakeshott could even accept speculative philosophy of history as a vehicle for discussion of social ends, so long as it was not confused with history proper. He gave a qualified welcome to Berdyaev's *The Meaning of History*, a pessimistic vision of 'European man ... emerging from modern history exhausted and with all his creative forces spent'. Berdyaev had provided an 'original and intelligent ... diagnosis of the present condition of European civilization' alongside 'a set of moral judgments which determine the relative value of human ideals and activities'.[28] This only underlined, though, that the present and future, and not the past, were the ultimate focus of all speculative philosophies of history.

Collingwood's *The Idea of History*, on the other hand, was unmistakably a contribution to the critical philosophy of history. Subsequent research has shown Knox's posthumous edition of Collingwood's papers on 'the character and possibility of historical knowledge' to be less definitive than supposed in Oakeshott's declaration that it represented 'all that is recover-

---

[27] See E. Podoksik, 'The Scientific Positivism of Michael Oakeshott', in *British Journal for the History of Philosophy*, 12 (2004), 297–318.
[28] #45, *The Meaning of History*, p. 137.

able'.[29] Nevertheless, posterity has generally endorsed Oakeshott's verdict that Collingwood was then 'ahead of every other writer' on the subject, and Oakeshott himself definitely agreed with Collingwood's claim that 'history had come to take its place beside natural science'.

It is not clear, however, that *The Idea of History* actually endorsed the goal of historical interpretation Oakeshott ascribed to Collingwood, of 'understand[ing] a writer more profoundly than the writer understood himself'. Oakeshott had earlier advanced this interpretative ideal as the goal of Hobbesian studies, and later ascribed it to Nietzsche, but it does not fit well with Collingwood's notion of re-enactment as the aim of understanding an author exactly as (not better than) he understood himself.[30] It really reflects Oakeshott's own belief that history offered a kind of understanding of events *necessarily* unavailable to the individual, or indeed the society, concerned.

Oakeshott's major criticism of Collingwood was that he assimilated all knowledge to historical knowledge, and consequently implied a 'radically skeptical philosophy'. Collingwood himself would not have accepted this, though he had argued that history and philosophy merged at their boundaries — something that Oakeshott never believed. Moreover, Collingwood was also more convinced than Oakeshott of the power of history to make a positive contribution to the conduct of practical political affairs. Despite these important differences, Oakeshott considered his argument 'profoundly thought out and brilliantly expounded'.[31]

Smellie's attempt to explain *Why We Read History* gained a less than enthusiastic reception, though Oakeshott complimented him on his 'urbanity and sense of style'.[32] He thought Smellie's work illustrated that 'the contemporary interest in history is centred upon the use to be made of it, upon the dogma it can be made to prove'. The practical concern with the future ensured 'we pervert history to our purposes'. He reprimanded Smellie for approving Lord Acton's injunction to '[j]udge ... character at its worst', something that he had been opposing at least since *Experience and Its Modes*.[33]

In fact, Oakeshott was by no means immune to allowing his own prejudices to colour his view of the past. Still, his shortcomings in this regard do not undermine the force of the qualitative distinction between historical and practical views of the past. However necessary it is for legal or political decisions to pass ethical judgment on the past, historical propositions were not statements about the rightness or goodness of what had been

---

[29] #60, *The Idea of History*, p. 197.
[30] #38, *Thomas Hobbes*; #67, p. 110; *Masters of Political Thought*, p. 226.
[31] #45, *The Meaning of History*, p. 137.
[32] #68, *Why We Read History*, p. 228.
[33] M. Oakeshott, *Experience and Its Modes* (Cambridge: Cambridge University Press, 1991 [1933]), p. 158.

done. That historians had to recognize the presence of ethical and moral beliefs in the words and actions of their subjects was axiomatic, but an entirely different matter.

Oakeshott also emphasized the impractical imaginative pleasures of historical reading. The 'historical masterpiece ... arouses no extraneous passions and releases us from the burden of history as the intellectual and moral preface to the contemporary world', which is what, politically speaking, it always must be. The joy of reading a history of the Popes, he remarked, lay in the fact that it was 'fascinating' rather than 'important'. He entirely agreed with Butterfield's rejection of 'Whig' history, or the 'finding significant in the past only that which led subsequently to positive achievement', and admired *The Origins of Modern Science*, which emphasized the mediaeval roots of the early modern revolution in scientific thought, for having avoided this temptation to 'read the story backwards'.[34]

E.H. Carr's history of the Russian revolution, however, had failed to avoid that pitfall. Despite a 'profound, perhaps unrivalled, knowledge' of his sources, Carr's identification with the Bolshevik cause had become so complete that he frequently lost his historical perspective. His treatment of the history of Soviet Russia was 'almost a replica of St Augustine's attitude towards the history of the Roman Empire'; in other words, part of an inevitable unfolding of world history.

We have already noted Oakeshott's view of history as 'the art of understanding men and events more profoundly than they were understood when they lived and happened', and thus revealing a meaning in events 'which was not their meaning for those who participated in them'. Carr's uncritical adoption of the terminology of the actors in those events only interfered with this goal; the historian, like the novelist, ought not to identify himself too closely with his subjects. [35]

There was an admitted difficulty in that '[t]he historian has no vocabulary of his own; he is obliged ... to use the language of morals and politics', but the only solution was to 'be wary of its implications', including the tendency to reduce individuals entirely to types. Despite his scrupulousness over 'simple fact' and willingness to highlight 'disingenuousness in the arguments of the Bolsheviks', Carr's work lacked this 'critical attitude'; he tended to see the actors in the events of 1917 simply either as 'revolutionaries' or 'bourgeois' and 'to measure them by their own standards'.

It was not only Carr who failed to keep the historical and the practical perspectives on the past separate. At the end of the period covered by this volume Oakeshott clearly felt that both philosophers and historians still had an uncertain grip on this distinction. The positivistic concept of histor-

---

[34] #91, *The Origins of Modern Science*, p. 297.
[35] #101, *Mr Carr's First Volume*, p. 325.

ical fact remained in evidence, and the goal of history continued to be conceived of as practical; it was to fulfil 'the "social purpose" of recalling to a society its past experiences'.[36] For Oakeshott, this excluded all historical subjects with no obvious contemporary relevance, and involved an implicit denial of the intrinsic imaginative fascination of the past.

III: Culture

Oakeshott's insistence on the importance of imagination was not intended to reduce history to an aesthetic spectacle, but he always valued literary and artistic imagination highly. In John Cowper Powys, author of *The Meaning of Culture*, he found a kindred spirit. Oakeshott took Powys to be exploring three possible views of culture, identifying each through the contrary concept involved. The first concept of culture contrasted it with ignorance, and associated culture simply with the accumulation of fact. This 'passion for amassing a vast quantity of knowledge' was the least satisfactory notion of culture, and Oakeshott's comments on a character in the novel *Hunger and Love* suggest he regarded it as characteristically modern.[37]

More satisfactory was the contrast between culture and anarchy associated with writers like Matthew Arnold and T.S. Eliot who identified culture with the assimilation of the best literary and artistic works. This view was superior to the first in that it 'seems to have some answer for death; it is not the hopeless pursuit of an ever-retreating aim'. In Powys' view, however, there was something beyond even reconciliation to mortality, and Oakeshott concurred. It was a kind of Epicureanism, expressed in the contrast between culture and despotism, and analogous to religion in being a 'way of life'. Despotism here was being in permanent thrall to the future, resulting in an inability to value 'not the fruit of experience, but the flower—something we know only in a present enjoyment and cannot garner'.

This sense of culture was particularly relevant in 1930, when the one thing that the various struggling ideologies shared was the subordination of the individual to some future good. Even in England, where the threat of ideological politics was smaller than in continental Europe, the capitalist preoccupation with consumption involved mortgaging oneself to the future in a way inevitably detrimental to happiness.

The threat posed by modernity to culture was the theme of Robert's *The Modern Mind*, which argued that 'during the last three centuries or so ... poetry, and religion, whose language is poetic, have lost at the expense of a

---

[36] #69, *Father, a Portrait of G.G. Coulton*, p. 230.
[37] #21, *Hunger and Love*, p. 76.

logical and matter-of-fact attitude to mind and use of language'.[38] But in 1937 Oakeshott, though he later expressed a profound cultural pessimism in two re-tellings of the Tower of Babel story as a metaphor for modernity, wanted to qualify Robert's view. Insofar as such a loss of poetic sensibility really had occurred, it was an exaggeration to single out the rise of scientific thought as the only factor responsible. The 'relationship of science and religion', as we saw, was 'not one of direct antagonism' for Oakeshott; 'the one never denies what the other asserts'. Treating religion in terms of analogies drawn from politics or business was just as likely to prove harmful as taking a scientific view of it.

Oakeshott found serious difficulties with the notion of modernity as decadent. There were clearly elements of Joad's thesis that decadence was 'the valuing of experience for its own sake, irrespective of the quality of the experience, the object of the experience ... being left out of account'[39] that Oakeshott would have agreed with. But in applying this notion to particular periods or persons, the arbitrary character of the judgements involved became clear. Amongst the signs of decadence were 'the craze for speed ... art as self-expression ... the eighteenth century, selfishness, the present day, Debussy ("because he produces on me a lowering effect") and Virginia Woolf'. There was surely some humour in Oakeshott's remark that while Joad 'thinks that the *douceur de vivre* disappeared in 1914', he himself 'should have put it at 1906' — when he was five. In his late forties, Oakeshott still resisted a completely pessimistic view of the world; his verdict was that Joad 'doesn't understand the charm of fashion, and any man who has no sympathy for this is likely to find the human race both puzzling and more stupid than it really is'.

One of the greatest threats to a civilized cultural life in the modern world was a simple lack of leisure. Oakeshott was delighted by Whistler's *The English Festivals*, hailing it as 'charming and profound'.[40] The meaning of observing festivals was to recognise and appreciate 'the rhythm of the natural and the civilised year, making of it a microcosm of the wheel of life'. But festivals were fragile as well as durable traditions, threatened not only by war but by many of the other changes in British life in this period, including the mass adoption of radio and television.

Oakeshott, no lover of either urban life or technology (witness his remark that 'the indiscriminate competitive exploitation of the internal combustion engine has transformed our manner of life without demonstrably improving it'), wrote a lengthy essay on the B.B.C. following the 1949 report of the Committee on Broadcasting. By this time, television as well as radio broadcasts were well-established, but Oakeshott did not treat

[38] #52, *The Modern Mind*, p. 152.
[39] #74, *Decadence*, p. 239.
[40] #65, *The English Festivals*, p. 223.

the arrival of the small screen as particularly noteworthy. He focussed instead on arguing that the B.B.C., 'a Corporation self-dedicated to the improvement of mankind according to a recipe of its own', was abusing its status as a monopoly by carrying out an 'enterprise of evangelization' in a manner that smacked of 'self-righteousness and priggishness'.[41]

The B.B.C.'s monopoly amounted to 'a far-reaching experiment in universal education conducted by persons whose activities are ... virtually uncontrolled'. In a thinly concealed contrast with France, Oakeshott treated 'the easy acceptance of the B.B.C. by a nation which for so long has avoided an authoritative Academy of Letters and a unified system of school or university education' as symptomatic of a creeping rationalism, liable to encourage 'one of the less good products of contemporary education: the extensive mind, curious, interested, pseudo-sympathetic, preferring many contacts to few intimacies, preferring fact to thought ... the quiz mentality'. In other words, the least satisfactory type of culture.

Oakeshott suspected that the proliferation of broadcasting would inevitably have an effect on the quality of the material, if only because 'the opportunity of turning on the tap corrupts the listener in the same manner as the ready supply of tinned food corrupts the cook'. Yet the B.B.C.'s monopoly was less of a problem than its sense of moral mission. Given the importance of the idea of economic competition in later twentieth-century conservative thought, we should note in particular his remark that 'there is little evidence that competition itself produces diversity—rather the reverse. We enjoy a variety of newspapers, but wherever there is genuine competition there is less diversity (except in opinion) than makes no matter'. What was most needed was not more competition but less paternalistic central direction.

This sense that cultural life was undergoing a crisis had only been exacerbated by the war, and was reinforced at the philosophical level; Oakeshott believed Nietzsche had provided 'a profound and imaginative diagnosis of a crisis in European culture'.[42] Such admiration was still unusual in the late 1940s, when scholarship, as he observed, had only just begun to extricate Nietzsche from 'the exaggerated reverence of his injudicious admirers ... and the protests of the injured', and the association with National Socialism had not yet been undone. But it is a point of similarity between Oakeshott and other major English philosophers of the later twentieth century, such as Bernard Williams.[43]

Oakeshott could certainly adopt a Nietzschean (or at least romantic) tone on occasion, once declaring that the 'only two subjects worth discuss-

---

[41] #102, *The B.B.C.*, p. 334.
[42] #66, *Nietzsche*, p. 224.
[43] 'By the end of the twentieth century, most avant-garde English intellectuals found themselves probably closer to Nietzsche than anyone else': K. Ameriks, *Kant and the Historical Turn* (Oxford: Clarendon Press, 2006), p. 46.

ing' were 'love and death'.[44] He certainly shared Nietzsche's belief that a liberation from the 'commonplace' was a condition of first-rate authorship. In a discussion of the decidedly Nietzschean subject of aphorisms he pronounced that the unity of such a collection could only come from 'the reactions of a single mind to its various experiences'.

Where authors failed to achieve something uniquely their own, these collections would inevitably be failures. But a personal view of experience had to be the very opposite of dogmatic; it required the author to be 'satisfied with the delights of conversation without requiring indisputable conclusions', and to avoid the 'vulgar, mawkish, and sentimental'. The idea of conversation, an important theme in Oakeshott's work after 1945 as a metaphor for the contingent relationships between the various forms of experience, surfaced here as early as 1931.

Oakeshott was under no illusions about the difficulty of producing great art. In comments with a teasingly autobiographical ring (though no unfinished novel has yet turned up among his papers), he remarked that 'there is nothing like writing a novel for revealing one's emotional limitations'. In fiction 'all the concealments at the disposal of the historian, the scientist, or the essay-writer are discarded and the mind is thrown back upon its essential self and stands or falls by what it can create'.[45]

The same could be said of philosophy; and given Oakeshott's Nietzschean sympathies and strong interest in literature, it is unsurprising that he regarded style as being as important as substance in a comprehensive interpretation of a philosophical work. Certainly, the presence of any contradiction in a text was 'a lapse to be observed', but 'the concern of the literary man is as much with the quality of mind as with the actual argument'.[46] Only 'the mere philosopher' regarded 'style, mood, intention, and emotional spring' as 'irrelevant'.

IV: Philosophy

In the inter-war era the Absolute Idealism that partly inspired Oakeshott's early thought was in retreat. Having been an orthodoxy from roughly 1875 onwards, it was now attacked on both sides of the Atlantic. One of the first philosophical works Oakeshott reviewed was a *General Theory of Value* by Ralph Barton Perry, a former student of probably the best known of the American Idealists, Josiah Royce. But Perry had become more impressed by another of his teachers, the pragmatist William James, and increasingly emphasized knowledge derived from common sense and natural sci-

---

[44] #20, *Afterthoughts and Aphorisms*, p. 73.
[45] #56, *Reason in Politics*, p. 189.
[46] #89, *The Life of Reason*, p. 292.

ence.[47] Perry's 'new realism' and the 'critical realism' of another American, Roy Sellars (father of Wilfred, who eclipsed him in philosophical fame), were typical of the change in direction; both argued for materialism rather than Idealism.

Oakeshott's review of Woodbridge's *The Realm of Mind* is further evidence of the arrival on the international scene of American philosophy after 1918. He complained that 'The relation of mind and body and of minds with one another is taken as a fact to be stated, not a problem to be solved', and was rather dismissive of the book.[48] In fact, Woodbridge's work was attempting a kind of Aristotelian naturalism that aimed to bypass the whole problem of mind-body dualism, and Oakeshott did not really do Woodbridge justice in making him sound like a naïve defender of a common-sense belief in an external world.

Still, there was no disputing Widgery's verdict in *Contemporary Thought of Great Britain* that 'Idealism counts for little at the present time'.[49] Oakeshott found Widgery's theism as unsatisfying as Widgery found Idealism, but he accepted philosophy was no longer dominated by a single orthodoxy. He did take issue with Widgery's desire for philosophy to have a social purpose, however; to give such a role to philosophy blurred the boundary between critical thinking and dispensing practical moral advice.

Ethical Principles in Theory and Practice by the German biologist turned philosopher Hans Driesch committed exactly this error in Oakeshott's eyes. Driesch had merely presented his own opinions on 'sex, marriage, war, education, property, patriotism, birth control, etc' dressed up as the inevitable conclusions of his own speculative philosophy of history.[50] Similar criticism was levelled at John Macmurray, the Grote Professor of Mind and Logic at London University, who left the impression that 'all thought is for the sake of action', and that the only aim of philosophy was to solve practical difficulties. Macmurray's belief that a future 'scientific psychology' would perform the main task of interpreting thought, seemed to Oakeshott to make philosophy redundant.

Of course, Idealism did not disappear instantly. It retained some appeal throughout the inter-war era, though Oakeshott's discussion of Bradley's *Collected Essays* made no mention of it. He located Bradley's work on psychology and ethics within the tradition of an 'English analytical school' whose earlier members included Bentham and James Mill rather than within an Idealist context.[51] Normally, Bentham and Mill senior are labelled as utilitarians having little in common with the later British Ideal-

---

[47] #5, *General Theory of Value*, p. 43.
[48] #7, *The Realm of Mind and Three Conceptions of Mind*, p. 45.
[49] #8, *Contemporary Thought of Great Britain*, p. 46.
[50] #23, *Ethical Principles in Theory and Practice*, p. 78.
[51] #47, *Collected Essays*, p. 142.

ists, and Bradley and Sidgwick were undeniably implacable philosophical opponents when it came to ethics, but in Oakeshott's mind such divisions were clearly not insurmountable. However, Oakeshott did review some late Idealist works, including Morris's *Idealistic Logic* and Wauchope's *Deviation into Sense*, that made clear he still regarded 'objective idealism' as 'a very respectable doctrine'.[52]

Oakeshott accepted that '[i]t is the business of philosophy continuously to renew itself',[53] and acknowledged that the 'modern technique of mathematical and symbolic logic' pioneered by thinkers such as Frege, Russell, and Whitehead had 'opened up new fields'.[54] Nevertheless, he saw no need to simply abandon the older logic and always remained sympathetic to scholastic thought, at least in its proper context. He praised the historical perspective that could make the *Summa Theologica* appear 'as an intellectual adventure and not ... a kind of staff-college doctrine', and Gilby's book on medieval philosophy inspired him to some more general reflections on the relationship between logic and philosophy.

There was, Oakeshott believed, an important contrast between 'the science of logic', concerned with 'the good manners of argument', and dialectic, which is 'between two and is a cooperative effort to trace disagreement to its source'. Both were indispensable to philosophizing, but they were distinct. The 'business' of logic is 'not with the truth of our conclusions but with their conclusiveness'; it aimed to 'get rid of formal defects in our thinking, to avoid a bungled argument', by pointing out '[i]ncorrect statements, recklessness in enumerating contradictories, illicit inference from negatives to affirmatives', and the like.

But in dialectic it was possible to 'call upon myth and analogy ... recognize that even equivocation can be benign and that all circles are not vicious'. So, while logic was 'an indispensable rudder', it was also in a sense subordinate; 'the game is not played for the benefit of the referee', and 'the friendly opposition in disputation ... is as ready to understand a clumsily expressed argument as to counter with the distinctions necessary to put it right'. That said, Oakeshott acknowledged 'dialectical as well as merely logical fallacies, sophisms, sham arguments, false or strained analogies'. These were 'more subtle offences against good taste in disputation, to be exorcized by a sympathy for rational argument rather than by the application of a clear rule.'

Oakeshott did review a work by Whitehead, who had made a major contribution to the analytical philosophy of logic in *Principia Mathematica*. Faced with *Adventures of Ideas*, however, Oakeshott employed the tactic so beloved of analytic philosophers faced with works in another style, and

---

[52] #29, *Idealistic Logic*; #84, p. 90; *Deviation into Sense*, p. 280.
[53] #38, *Thomas Hobbes*, p. 110.
[54] #87, *Barbara Celarent*, p. 287.

affected not to understand it. As a contribution to speculative metaphysics he found in it 'some profoundly thought-out ideas and many brilliant *aperçus*', but claimed he was simply unable to comment on Whitehead's overall philosophical doctrine.[55]

The analytic approach was not the only philosophical movement sweeping through Cambridge in the 1930s. Marxism was also very popular, and from the first, Oakeshott was largely hostile. He declared the essays in *Aspects of Dialectical Materialism* a nonsensical collection of disturbingly dogmatic uniformity.[56] Marxism had become an 'official philosophy', displaying an orthodoxy more appropriate to a 'religious creed' than a philosophical doctrine. Indeed, Marxist thought presupposed a scheme structurally analogous to Christian apocalyptic; it was interested in the past only as a revelation of the conditions of future emancipation. The 'esoteric' character of Marxism also ensured anyone objecting would 'unavoidably ... find that what he has been objecting to is not the true doctrine, but merely one of the numerous "distortions" which the authentic philosophy has suffered'.[57]

However, Oakeshott did not have the same attitude to Marx. Although he described Marx's teaching as 'cloudy and dogmatic', and even questioned whether Marx was best thought of as a philosopher, he also acknowledged some of Marx's thought on history as 'profound', and his work as 'full of ingenious ideas'.[58] He named Marx with Nietzsche and Weber as a founder of a 'tradition of great vitality in the recent history of social investigation'; hardly a contemptuous dismissal.[59] Moreover, any Marxist prepared 'to be critical ... and to seek the value in the work of others of a different persuasion' could expect a fair hearing; Lindsay's *Marxism and Contemporary Science* won praise for its 'subtlety and fair mindedness'.[60]

Oakeshott was less interested in philosophical affiliations than in avoidance of triviality. He did not laugh at the attempt 'to construct a philosophy of psychical research' into paranormal phenomena inspired by the positivism of Bertrand Russell and A.J. Ayer, observing that the 'neutral monism' it recommended at least 'removes in principle the difficulty of understanding how mental and material ... systems may influence one another, how minds may interact' and perhaps even 'how minds can survive death'.[61] Only those whom he felt were not doing philosophy in the right spirit aroused his ire. 'Philosophical fun', he remarked, 'is a special-

---

[55] #35, *Adventures of Ideas*, p. 105.
[56] #34, *Aspects of Dialectical Materialism*, p. 100.
[57] #51, *This Freedom of Ours*, p. 149.
[58] #51, *This Freedom of Ours*, p. 149.
[59] #50, *Ideology and Utopia*, p. 147.
[60] #90, *Marxism and Contemporary Science*, p. 295.
[61] #86, *Matter, Mind, and Meaning*, p. 285.

ized taste; and when it is devoid of wit there are few who do not find it tiresome'.[62]

Collingwood's *The Principles of Art* did not win praise for its close adherence to the thought of Hegel (or anyone else), but for its careful use of language. The right approach was 'to make certain that we know how to apply' a word, in this case 'art', 'where it ought to be applied and refuse it where it ought to be refused'. Oakeshott, though sometimes associated with the 'linguistic turn' of the 1950s when ordinary usage became of intense interest in Anglo-American philosophy, was already consistently emphasizing the philosophical importance of an exact use of language in the 1930s.

While Oakeshott stressed that 'every notable discovery involves the destruction of hitherto accepted knowledge, and has to overcome the inertia of what is already established', he did not think that the task of philosophy was completed by such destruction.[63] In true philosophy, 'destruction is followed by construction', and it was thus incumbent on Collingwood to provide a positive notion of what art is. But in the end, whether or not readers found themselves in agreement with Collingwood's thesis that art proper has 'two characteristics: expression of emotion and imagination', mattered less than the opportunity 'of following a masterly discussion of … fundamental questions'.

In Oakeshott's reviews, a conception of philosophy emerges in which reasoning is an end in itself and the rewards of thinking through a problem are intrinsic. While he was prepared to allow that a 'modest dogmatism … belongs to all bold and lucid thinking' in philosophy, he rejected all sceptical doubts about the value of reason as such.[64] For example, he took Chestov to task for having made 'a philosophy out of misology'.[65]

The only way that Chestov had been able to reach his conclusion that the history of European philosophy revealed 'an unexamined prejudice in favour of what is reasonable' was by conflating Reason and scientific rationalism on the one hand and science and common sense on the other. But a belief in philosophical reason was not a commitment to a mechanistic view of physical science, and a valid judgment did not have to be 'ecumenical'. The 'possibility of judgments which are universally valid in no sense depends upon there being anything whatever universally believed', and '[w]hat is reasonable and mere normality (what is satisfactory to common sense) are not the same thing.'

Oakeshott could sympathise with Chestov's desire to defend spontaneity in art and life, and preserve art's ability to jerk us out of everyday existence. To say that 'Everything for Dostoevsky is abnormal, fresh, *sui*

---

[62] #22, *Adventures in Philosophy and Religion*, p. 77.
[63] #75, *Science and Society*, p. 240.
[64] #84, *Deviation into Sense*, p. 280.
[65] #30, *In Job's Balances*, p. 91.

generis' was an unobjectionable critical verdict, but it was 'true of every artist; it is just what art means'. But there was no need to reject reason and philosophy (or science and common sense, for that matter) to value spontaneity. Oakeshott's defence of reason deserves emphasis because his post-war polemics against rationalism sometimes wrongly lead critics to think that like Chestov, he was hostile to reason as such. What Oakeshott was criticising, however, was the view that *only* reason in its narrowest sense was important;[66] human irrationality was ineliminable, but not necessarily destructive. '[T]o behave rationally is not necessarily to be without anxiety, love, hate, inner conflict, or potential conflict with others'.[67]

Rationalism for Oakeshott was linked with a certain philosophical interpretation of the nature of scientific inquiry, one with deep historical roots in the Cartesian project of a 'universal science or general philosophy'. Its modern heirs included those philosophers who regarded their central task as following out the implications of mathematics and natural science. He had no issue with mathematics and natural science being important philosophical concerns, but he did object to them being made its only concerns, or the exclusive foundations of the unity of knowledge, as some suggested.[68]

This sensitivity to scientific Rationalism may well have been so pronounced because Oakeshott was gradually emancipating himself from a philosophical variety of it. In his earliest works, under the influence of Plato and Spinoza as well as Hegel, he had treated philosophical definition as the only fully satisfactory form of thought, but later increasingly emphasized the need to discriminate between different kinds of thinking that stood on an equal footing. To that extent Oakeshott was in sympathy with the philosophical project Collingwood and others called a *speculum mentis*, a 'mirror of the mind', in which the different departments of thought were reflected. But he was never very inclined to attempt to construct a disciplinary hierarchy of the sort Collingwood and others had attempted, and became even less so over time.[69]

Certain passages in *Experience and Its Modes* from the early 1930s still favoured the idea that philosophy was a more satisfactory form of thought than all others, but Oakeshott never attempted, for example, to show in quasi-Hegelian fashion how practice was superseded by history which in turn gave way to science which ultimately produced philosophy. The various forms of theoretical and practical thinking he identified had an equal status, with the exception of philosophy, which somehow escaped the need for the presuppositions to which the others were subject. If there was

---

[66] #72, *Reason and Unreason in Society*, p. 235.
[67] #111, *Psychoanalysis and Politics*, p. 367.
[68] #80, *The Modern Approach to Descartes' Problem*, p. 268.
[69] #85, *The Life of Reason*, p. 283.

a hierarchy here, it was a pretty flat one, with philosophy simply standing over everything else.

It has sometimes been claimed that Oakeshott never really changed his view of philosophy, because in both his earlier and his later writings he espoused a conception of philosophy as the ceaseless questioning of presuppositions. While this notion of philosophy is indeed present throughout his work, this claim ignores both the later abandonment of his early emphasis on definition as the outcome of philosophical reasoning and the fact that in his earlier writings he tended to feel, at least in some moods, that definition was not the only characteristic of philosophy but also made it superior to other forms of thought, as distinct from simply different to them.

Oakeshott had still not fully emancipated himself from the idea of philosophy as the comprehensive definition of concepts by 1939, and the tensions it produced are visible in *The Concept of a Philosophical Jurisprudence*. This piece, an attempt to identify the conditions for a satisfactory theory of the nature of law, represents Oakeshott's last major statement on the nature of philosophy before the war. Consequently, its place in the development of Oakeshott's thought has been constantly disputed.

There is no reason to expect all the various parts of a philosopher's work to fit neatly together as if they were all pieces of some grand design. But on one interpretation, *The Concept of a Philosophical Jurisprudence* is particularly anomalous; the one place where Oakeshott favoured the idea of a hierarchy of forms of explanation which he always eschewed elsewhere. Taken in isolation, certain passages do seem to support this view. For instance, he said explicitly that a philosophy of law 'will be one explanation of law in a hierarchy of explanations', and that '[i]t has the authority to create this hierarchy by supplying a universal criterion by which the adequacy, the relative completeness of all explanations may be determined.'[70]

When these statements are placed in context, however, it becomes clear that Oakeshott made no real attempt to rank the various types of non-philosophical explanation of law he distinguished during the course of the argument: analytical, historical, psychological, sociological, etc. He wanted only to establish that the philosophical explanation of law must be more satisfactory than any other form, and this is identical with the approach found in *Experience and Its Modes* and other early writings in which the relative merits of other forms of thinking were not at issue once their inferiority to philosophy had been demonstrated. The talk of a hierarchy thus turns out to be misleading.

The piece nevertheless remains important, even if it does not constitute the major and inexplicable departure that it has sometimes been presented as, because it sheds light on some of the key features of Oakeshott's con-

---

[70] #53, *The Concept of a Philosophical Jurisprudence*, p. 176.

ception of philosophy. For one thing, his discussion of theories of law exemplifies what might be called the hermeneutic affinities of his thought. The hermeneutic theory of a circle of meaning insists that no statement is intelligible in isolation; any given utterance must be placed in the context of the world in which it was made to be correctly understood. Moreover, the understanding that results is subject to the same kind of condition; it can only be meaningfully criticized when the reasons that led to it are appreciated.

Thus, Oakeshott stressed that any particular statement about the law ultimately implied a broader theory about its nature; he also advanced the general principle that

> text and interpretation are one and inseparable ... what we call 'the text' is itself an interpretation, a meaning, for which (in interpretation) we substitute another, different or more extended, interpretation or meaning. Theory, explanation, interpretation are attempts to find and expound the meaning *in* what is given, and what is given and its meaning are not two things ... but one.[71]

In the inter-war years Oakeshott was alive to developments in German as well as British philosophy. He raised no objection to the selection of Husserl, Dilthey, Max Weber, Nietzsche, Kierkegaard, Jaspers, and Heidegger as the most influential German philosophers since 'the last great orthodoxy—Hegelianism'. While he believed that some members of that list—Kierkegaard and Nietzsche in particular—had 'no counterpart in English thought, the main problem confronting both English and German philosophy was the same. It was "[w]hat, in this age of science, is the real task of philosophy?"'[72]

Part of the answer lay in understanding (and practising) philosophy historically. By this one should not understand the attempt to reduce philosophy to history, as Collingwood wanted to do in his later work. Rather, Oakeshott believed that our understanding of philosophy should be sensitive to the time and place in which it was written. This position was intended to avoid a number of dangers, one of which was the idea of a *philosophia perennis*, of philosophy as uncovering timeless and universal truths. But another, related, error was the progressive approach, a view of philosophy as 'a gradually developing body of doctrine'.

The history of philosophy, as Oakeshott understood it, displayed no unbroken continuity; philosophers from different periods could not simply be read as if they were 'all talking about the same thing'.[73] He was dismissive of most philosophy textbooks, finding them 'at best ... dully informative, at worst merely confusing and misleading', especially when compared to 'the great classics of philosophy' which belonged to 'another

---

[71] #53, *The Concept of a Philosophical Jurisprudence*, p. 155.
[72] #44, *An Introduction to Contemporary German Philosophy*, p. 135.
[73] #100, *The Great Philosophers*, p. 323.

and brighter world'.[74] The best introduction to philosophy was still 'Plato's *Republic* ... not because its doctrine is acceptable but because it reveals a master at work', and the 'range of a subject is usually better displayed in arguing an interesting case than in summarizing the views of x, y, and z'.[75]

In philosophy, just as in art and history, Oakeshott placed a high value on imagination. Philosophical imagination was what most impressed him about Santayana's *Dominations and Powers*,[76] and he considered it the mark of a great philosopher.[77] But he was not defending an aesthetic irrationalism as the correct standard for the evaluation of philosophical works; only to 'think in metaphors and not to restrain one's fancy must always be defects in a philosopher'. Rather, he related imagination to 'the conception of a comprehensive theory'. A philosopher was imaginative insofar as he had achieved a complete system, embracing the whole of physical and human nature.

Though Oakeshott thought such imagination 'comparatively rare ... in English philosophical writing' (Hobbes was his only example), at least two English works that appeared in the immediate post-war era struck him as extremely valuable. The first was Ryle's *The Concept of Mind*, conventionally located within the analytic tradition. Ryle famously attacked what Oakeshott called the 'hypothesis ... which, perhaps more than anything else, distinguishes modern from ancient philosophy ... that every human being has a body and a mind (or is both body and mind)'.[78]

Oakeshott seems to have been prepared to accept ontological monism, but he considered Ryle's version of it was in danger of being too reductionist, because it retained the old materialist language of body which would presumably have to be abandoned alongside the old way of conceiving mind; he felt Ryle had been too confident in talking of a 'physical world'. Moreover, he felt Ryle's account of Idealism as 'the "reduction" of the material world to mental states and processes' was an 'unfortunate abridgment', no doubt because it seemed to identify Idealism exclusively with the subjective strain associated with Berkeley.

The idea of a category mistake which Ryle used to attack this dualistic hypothesis proved hugely influential, however, and is now frequently encountered in fields far beyond those in which it was originally employed. It may well be, too, that Ryle was the inspiration for Oakeshott's later use of the term 'categorial error' as denoting an inappropriate confusion of different ways of thinking that we saw he attacked in his inter-war writings as the logical fallacy of *ignoratio elenchi*.

---

[74] #44, *An Introduction to Contemporary German Philosophy*, p. 135.
[75] #114, *Introduction to Politics*, p. 369.
[76] #109, *Dominations and Powers*, p. 362.
[77] #38, *Thomas Hobbes*, p. 110.
[78] #97, *The Concept of Mind*, p. 317.

Be that as it may, Oakeshott hailed *The Concept of Mind* as 'philosophical writing of the highest class'. He was similarly enthusiastic about Urban's effort to get 'beyond realism and idealism', which he thought indebted 'to both Rickert and Alexander'. Urban sought to reconcile Idealism (the belief that 'the known cannot be independent of the knower') and Realism ('the belief that what is known must be an antecedent reality').[79] The proposed solution rested on the argument that neither Idealism nor Realism 'is a belief concerning fact; both are beliefs about the meaning of knowledge', and that therefore the conflict between them was dialectical rather than empirical.

There was, Urban concluded, a 'harmony between Idealism and Realism in such concrete enterprises of knowing as the physical and social sciences, history, and *Geisteswissenschaft*'. This was not dissimilar to Oakeshott's own post-war position; with respect to the nature of historical understanding, for example, he argued in effect that historians might treat evidence in realist terms, but that philosophically speaking the historical past was entirely ideal, with no objective existence independent of the community of historical readers and writers.

V: Politics

The changes in political philosophy mirrored philosophy at large; Idealism was increasingly deprecated, though works were still being written in this vein.[80] For example, in 1929, John Mackenzie, a student of Edward Caird and Henry Jones and a friend of McTaggart, published *Fundamental Problems of Life* which treated society as a metaphysical reality and the purpose of the state as the realisation of a Common Good that in turn required the existence of co-operative groups. This notion of the Common Good (regarded by Oakeshott as a descendent of Rousseau's General Will) struck him as fundamentally ambiguous. He complained that it was unclear, in Mackenzie at least, whether the General Will and the Common Good were moral or metaphysical notions.

Nevertheless, in 1936 Oakeshott was still prepared to assert that the 'Idealist theory of the State is the only theory which has paid thoroughgoing attention to all the problems which must be considered by a theory of the State', and that Bosanquet's *The Philosophical Theory of the State* 'remains (with all its defects) the most comprehensive account of this theory'.[81] At the same time, he believed that it 'has yet to receive a satisfactory statement'. His later political thought can be read partly as a reconsidera-

---

[79] #99, *Beyond Realism and Idealism*, p. 321.
[80] #49, *Bernard Bosanquet's Philosophy of the State*, p. 143.
[81] #49, *Bernard Bosanquet's Philosophy of the State*, p. 143.

tion of this problem of the relationship between the individual and the group as it had been handled within the Idealist tradition.[82]

If Oakeshott was unhappy with the received Idealist tradition, he was still less happy with what was succeeding it. Catlin's *Principles of Politics* proposed making political theory into a science 'in the strict sense in which chemistry is a science'. At the heart of this project was a quantitative approach based on economics, though Oakeshott observed that 'the book contains few references to statistics and statistical generalization ... the most hopeful method of constructing this science'.[83]

Catlin's project rested on an empirical individualism; a single person was the bearer of a single will, and thus regarded as an ultimate unit of political decision with preferences that could be counted in the form of votes. In fact, Oakeshott was not hostile to the quantitative approach as such, at least in the 1920s; he went so far as to say that '[a]ny attempt to develop a genuinely quantitative study of politics deserves encouragement'. What he objected to was Catlin's 'clinging so closely to the economic analogy' for politics.[84]

Oakeshott and Catlin did have something in common, however: an interest in Hobbes, on whom Catlin had written a short introduction.[85] Both were part of a 'revival of interest' in Hobbes traceable to the later nineteenth century. By the inter-war period this revival had become a 'flood' which has never really ceased. Oakeshott later played a significant role in it by editing the Blackwell edition of *Leviathan* and authoring a number of essays. The essays have been superseded as scholarship, but they pioneered a then novel but increasingly popular 'liberal' reading of Hobbes (suggesting controversially that 'Hobbes ... had more of the ground of liberalism in him than even Locke'), and remain useful evidence for the development of Oakeshott's own thought.[86]

Oakeshott nevertheless cautioned against too narrow an emphasis on Hobbes' contemporary relevance.[87] A philosophical reading of a philosophical text was compatible with, indeed required, 'a genuinely historical attitude'. The historian could offer a 'detailed consideration of the actual meaning of a philosophical text, regardless of its present significance or of any view we may hold about the truth or error it contains' that was at once a necessary part of the enterprise and the source of 'inspiration for fresh

---

[82] #11, *Fundamental Problems of Life*, p. 51.
[83] #15, *The Principles of Politics*, p. 61.
[84] #15, *The Principles of Politics*, p. 61.
[85] G.E. Catlin, *Thomas Hobbes as Philosopher, Publicist, and Man of Letters: an Introduction* (Oxford: Basil Blackwell, 1922).
[86] Oakeshott's revised introduction to *Leviathan* is republished in M. Oakeshott, *Rationalism in Politics*, 2nd edition, ed. T. Fuller (Indianapolis: Liberty Press, 1991). Four other essays were republished as *Hobbes on Civil Association* (Oxford: Basil Blackwell, 1975). For a detailed study see I. Tregenza, *Michael Oakeshott on Hobbes* (Exeter: Imprint Academic, 2003)
[87] #38, *Thomas Hobbes*, p. 110.

thought'. A crucial part of this historical enterprise was making clear that philosophical works cannot merely be treated in terms of their conclusions; what a given author thought, and why he thought it, were 'inseparable' in Oakeshott's view.

The trend in the history of science in this period was to emphasize the mediaeval background of the seventeenth century, and the same was true in Hobbes studies, which stressed the continuity 'in politics, religion, and philosophy' with earlier centuries. This historically oriented approach produced a metaphor for Hobbes's philosophy as a 'palimpsest', a manuscript that has been written over many times. This metaphor is applicable to all philosophy, and requires that any philosophical work must be viewed as an accretion, as composed of a number of layers.

At the same time, the metaphor does not exclude originality. Every philosopher may add a new layer of their own, and a truly great philosopher may still be original. Hobbes's writings really had been 'a profound revolution in European thought', but his originality did not lie in his conclusions; rather, it was the reasons he gave for them.[88] These made him 'the most profoundly philosophical individualist in the history of political theory' and 'the first great theorist of the political world in which we live'.

Oakeshott's Hobbes was a theorist of the rule of law. Far from the Hobbesian ruler relying on force to strike terror into its subjects and control them accordingly, sovereignty had strict limits; it concerned only 'the control of men's actions', meaning that both 'the intellect and the conscience are excluded'. There was nothing in Hobbes of the Platonic belief that government was responsible for the right ordering of the soul; it was partly for this reason that Oakeshott was inclined to see Hobbes in a liberal light. Thus, despite hailing *The Political Philosophy of Hobbes* as 'excellent and timely', he could not endorse Strauss' view that 'the distinctive innovation of Hobbes is ... his rejection of law and his substitution of right or claim as the principle from which the State is to be deduced'.[89]

The relevant consideration here is the kind of individualism on which Hobbes based the state. Contemporaries distinguished between a 'hedonistic ethical' type of individualism, in which freedom is defined by the will of the individual, and a 'universalistic' theory focussed on the common good. Hobbes was conventionally regarded as espousing hedonistic individualism, but Oakeshott regarded this as a mistake; 'the true nature of Hobbes's individualism has yet to find its expositor'. In 1935 he offered the suggestion that 'Pride, and not Fear, is the master-conception of this political philosophy'.[90] Of course, pride excluded making immediate grat-

---

[88] #38, *Thomas Hobbes*, pp. 138, 110.
[89] #49, *The Political Philosophy of Hobbes*, p. 145.
[90] #38, *Thomas Hobbes*, pp. 117.

ification the highest good, but it also precluded submerging the individual in communal association.

Oakeshott's 'liberal' reading of Hobbes had ramifications for his philosophical and historical views on politics in the post-war period. Historically, it prompted him to focus on the fact that modern governments were more powerful by an order of magnitude than their mediaeval and early modern counterparts. But this growth in the power available to governments had also had consequences for political philosophy. Philosophers had moved away from a consideration of problems of authority to problems associated with the use of government power that bore no direct relation to questions about the sources, nature, and limits of governmental authority.

A central problem in theories of authority is the nature of obligation. To Oakeshott's mind, the liberal democratic tradition had equivocated over this issue; Locke, for example, had tried to give obligation a dual basis in both natural law and consent, but had only confused matters.[91] He therefore welcomed Carritt's attempt to deal with obligation in *Morals and Politics*, which he described as trying to do 'for political philosophy what other writers, like Moore, Broad, Prichard, and Ross, have been doing ... for ethics in general'.[92] But Oakeshott was unconvinced by Carritt's attempt to show that political obligation was a species of moral obligation, presumably because it too failed to shield political obligation from reduction to something else.

That liberal democracy must include some notion of political obligation was necessary if it were to rest on a commitment to the rule of law as distinct from mere force. While Oakeshott knew that the maintenance of authority inevitably involved an element of force, and conceded that Machiavellian analyses of power had their place, he always resisted philosophical attempts to identify law and authority with mere coercion.[93] Here he agreed with the last great representative of Italian Idealism, Benedetto Croce, who described political action in the abstract as simply 'action guided by the sense of what is useful and directed towards a utilitarian goal'. To this extent politics was indeed intelligible in exclusively Machiavellian terms. Yet 'political action is never self-sufficient but always exists in the wider world of the moral consciousness', so that 'policy is always unavoidably related to some moral ideas'.[94]

Oakeshott was in complete accord with Croce over the impossibility of an absolute separation of morality and politics, but what may surprise those who only know Oakeshott as a 'conservative' from his essays in *Rationalism in Politics* is his sympathy for the socialist ethical critique of

---
[91] #67, *Masters of Political Thought*, p. 226.
[92] #40, *Morals and Politics*, p. 124.
[93] #55, *Swords and Symbols*, p. 187.
[94] #59, *Politics and Morals*, p. 196.

capitalism. Although Oakeshott found Selsam's *Socialism and Ethics* suffered from an 'ignorance of history', and levelled against it the familiar charge that socialism had become a form of religion, he also declared the book 'worth while'.[95] Selsam had used both Marx and Spinoza as foundations for a naturalistic ethics according to which the state exists to satisfy human needs and desires. This did not convince Oakeshott (he thought all such attempts were doomed), but he nevertheless found some virtue in Selsam's analysis of capitalist society.

Nor would one expect to find the supposedly 'conservative' Oakeshott writing that 'the social democratic position ... is one that must have great inherent attraction for many people' in England; yet he expressed admiration for Durbin's 'lucid and intelligent analysis' of 'State organised private monopoly capitalism' in *The Politics of Democratic Socialism*, and shared Durbin's alarm at the central control of the economy that was becoming the norm. What he did not share, of course, was the suggestion that an alternative form of planned economy (exemplified by Russia) was the answer.

Oakeshott was convinced that 'a shooting war is no solution' to the emerging cold war conflict, but he disagreed completely with the argument that the way to avoid nuclear conflict was to be 'more progressive than the Russians'.[96] To support 'democratic socialist planning' in Europe and elsewhere removed the reason for opposing Russia in the first place. 'If Russia is "progressive", God help us all if the USA were to become more progressive', was Oakeshott's considered verdict on the 'utterly unconvincing thesis that if you want to stop a Russian you must become a Socialist'.

The Communist threat provoked Oakeshott's only recorded foray into media punditry. A retiring man, the experience of seeing a photo of himself in the *Evening Standard* next to the headline 'MAN WHO TOOK LASKI'S JOB ATTACKS THE COMMUNISTS' likely put him off any further ventures.[97] Nevertheless, the piece gives some interesting insights into the changes Oakeshott believed the war had wrought on the British political climate. 'Up to about 1939', he declared,

> it was possible to ... be a Communist ... from a variety of motives, none of them entirely foolish or deplorable. The Russian Revolution, like the French, could appear as the dawn of a glad day. And in the time of Hitler's rise or the Spanish Civil War one might join the party out of the generous impulse to side with the down-trodden.

The rise to international prominence of Stalin's Russia had changed this situation. Communism now stood 'for the subjugation of the world, including the peoples of Russia, to the oligarchy which now rules in Mos-

---

[95] #81, *Socialism and Ethics*, p. 271.
[96] #78, *How to Stop the Russians without War*, p. 262.
[97] #92, *The Coming Defeat of Communism*, p. 306.

cow'. It was simply 'Russian imperialism'. The correct response, however, was not to promote a countervailing and equally ideologically-inspired 'American imperialism' that could result in an armed clash. It was to try to remove the menace without further war; 'our aim must be to assist in overthrowing that oligarchy by working upon the weaknesses of the regime'.

However correct it was, the socialist critique generally struck Oakeshott as a case of the pot calling the kettle black. Both socialism and capitalism saw the good life as 'nothing other than the enjoyment by more and more people of more and more everything'. Both relied on 'the plausible ethics of productivity', an ethic which had become 'one of the most damaging moral superstitions of our time'. The dominance of economic concerns in modern politics threatened individual freedom from both left and right.[98] Freedom here meant the ability to exercise 'independent judgment and moral choice'. It was not to be identified with either security or prosperity: 'an excessive desire and hope of security is an emotion which has long since invaded and overrun European life and politics'.

Security and prosperity were undeniably goods; but they were not the same as the ability to choose for oneself; what socialism offered was the role of a recipient rather than a consumer. Freedom was further threatened by 'the gross pressure of numbers which goes to compose a morally worthless public opinion, and the moral delusion that when we have discovered how to do something we are well advised to do it'. The only alternative in a productivist society, whether socialist or capitalist, was between a 'tyranny of the majority' (Oakeshott actually used Mill's phrase), in which '[t]he desires of the masses (in so far as desire is allowed to appear at all) are to be the standard for everyone', and a 'tyranny of those who determine the need, the "scientists"'. 'Of the two, any sane man would no doubt choose the former; but it is a desperate alternative.'[99]

Oakeshott singled out Orwell's totalitarian satire *1984* as an example of the kind of 'precise and microscopic imagination' and 'ironic vision' that he found equal to the task of examining this modern predicament. The liberal tradition that he had found so unsatisfactory in the inter-war period now became a tradition of liberty 'coeval with our civilization' and 'in danger of being destroyed'.[100] Having survived the ideological assault of National Socialism, post-war liberalism now faced the threat of being eaten by one of its own children, the abstract rationalism to which it had given rise and which had influenced left and right in equal measure.

Oakeshott's strident criticisms of the Rationalist supporters of central planning meant contemporaries sometimes accused him of taking aim at a straw man, and he certainly went too far in describing post-war British

---

[98] #103, *Modern Capitalism and Economic Progress*. See also #25, *John Locke*, pp. 345, 82 respectively.
[99] #108 *Liberties of the Mind*, p. 359.
[100] #61, *The Liberal Tradition*, p. 200.

government as tyrannical and as a despotism.[101] Nevertheless, one should take into account the radically utopian mood that followed the end of the war. Some writers really were prepared to make very radical claims that would surely have sounded very alarming to almost anyone who did not share their beliefs.

Oakeshott found himself reviewing works by authors claiming that 'the political arrangements of a society ... should be based wholly upon the discoveries of scientific research'; that 'the fundamental problem of government is one that can be treated by exact biological methods';[102] that socialism in Britain would have arrived when the majority of working people were employed in the public sector, and that this system, if implemented internationally, would produce world peace;[103] that 'within democratic socialist planning the individual can be given a larger social justice, a greater security, and a more complete freedom than under capitalism';[104] and that through a combination of scientific and Marxist methods, 'it would be possible to set up and get working within a few months a comprehensive, productive and distributing mechanism for the whole world'.[105]

Yet Oakeshott was not hostile in principle either to a 'more equalitarian' or a 'more prosperous' society. He believed Lloyd George had already introduced measures tending in this direction. He also accepted that Britain was 'a society recovering from war', and that the current system needed 'maintenance and reform'. But he was convinced that Attlee's Labour government and the ideas of its supporters were departures from British law and custom.[106] Oakeshott was no economist, so it is impossible to extract more than the most general alternative proposals from him; but instead of proposals for 'the curtailment of private enterprise', he wanted to see taxation of income and capital overhauled. In particular, he would have welcomed 'a thorough investigation of the morals and economics of bequest and inheritance'. Monopolies 'impervious to the criticism of the market' also needed to be more carefully regulated, whether they were monopolies of capital or labour.[107]

In economics as elsewhere, Oakeshott was keen to warn against dogmatic orthodoxies. Popular Keynesianism treated economic institutions as 'pieces of machinery held in stock, to be shuffled about, selected and rejected, brought or kept in use or put by for another occasion', but it was

---

[101] #64, *The Analysis of Political Behaviour*, p. 221.
[102] #75, *Science and Society*, p. 241.
[103] #63, *Contemporary British Politics*, p. 204.
[104] #77, *The Triple Challenge*, p. 261.
[105] #88, *The Freedom of Necessity*, p. 290.
[106] #103, *Modern Capitalism and Economic Progress*, p. 346.
[107] #63, *Contemporary British Politics*, p. 204.

important to remember that they were ultimately 'ways of being active'.[108] The same held true, of course, for institutions of all kinds, including political ones. An institution was not a pile of bricks and mortar, but a way of doing things that had come into being over time; it was not something that could be erected overnight.

This Burkean attitude to institutions is one reason Oakeshott has been classed as a conservative, but he found most contemporary statements of conservative doctrine almost as flawed as socialism. The conservative opposition of a philosophy of natural law to the socialist 'philosophy of the mandate' struck him as 'perhaps the least convincing of the current formulae of current moral criteria'. It might offer an escape from 'the absurdity of attributing absolute authority to the will of a temporary majority', but it was unsatisfactory for at least two reasons. It was 'too abstract to offer much practical guidance' and second, it was 'merely an external limit'. Both Burke and Hegel had demonstrated the necessity of a community being able to criticize its political life according to standards that were intrinsic to it: according, in other words, to its own constitutional tradition.

The natural law tradition tended to regard legal rights and duties as limitations on or interferences with an original freedom, but (perhaps following Hobbes) Oakeshott rejected this position. Human beings were not naturally free, at least in the sense of being possessed of rights and responsibilities; freedom was an historic achievement. 'The "private individual" … is an institution, a social, indeed for the most part a legal creation.'[109] Any failure of conservatism to appreciate this point made it more liable to accept the rationalist approach to planning as just another form of limitation or interference, and not as something different in kind.

Natural law, of course, was not the only basis for conservatism. Conservatism, like any other 'historical phenomenon' (including Christianity), was no more than the product of its changes, and if there was an 'essence' to it, it lay in a continuity that did not exclude change.[110] Even when the problematic foundation of natural law was excised from conservative thought, however, it remained liable to be unduly satisfied with what had already been achieved and to regard what had gone before as better than what was currently in existence.

In opposing socialism, conservatism needed to offer not reaction, 'but something quite modestly better than the present'. In communicating a political programme to the public, it was important that the limits of political action were made clear; 'the most a politician can do is to ensure that some, and these by no means the most important, conditions in which the

---

[108] #103, *Modern Capitalism and Economic Progress*, p. 345.
[109] #76, *The State and the Citizen*, p. 248.
[110] #16, *What is Conservatism?* and *The Pathetic Fallacy* , p. 63.

good life can exist are present'. To hope for more than this from politics presupposed a change in human nature. Unfortunately, the conservative response seemed not to be to try to reverse the trend towards centralised state intervention greatly accelerated by the war, but to adopt the same predilection for central planning observable on the left.

In the post-war era, Oakeshott began demanding a revision of the terms in which politics was understood. In particular, the terms 'left' and 'right' obscured tendencies shared across the political spectrum; the demotion of parliament 'to the position of an executive body for carrying out the items of a programme determined ... by an irresponsible body', and insensibility to formal and procedural considerations. This critique was a precursor to his later notion of an 'enterprise association', or the idea of the state as an association in terms of a common purpose willing to disregard any rules not directly instrumental to the purpose being pursued. For the socialist and the fascist, the existence of a parliamentary opposition seemed pointless, 'an expensive luxury, a piece of wastefulness'. Yet the maintenance of the rule of law required an opposition 'to oppose, to criticize, to expose foolishness, corruption and mismanagement wherever they lie hidden'.

Indeed, Oakeshott saw a large part of political activity as preventative; power had a tendency to constantly find new centres in which to concentrate, and the true politician (of any party) aimed to counteract this trend. Left unchecked, power tended to corrupt its wielders and reduce the degree of freedom in society by upsetting the established legal order which provided an important source of predictability in conduct. Somewhat paradoxically, law acted as a 'method of social integration' by creating a framework within which each individual could 'exercise ... the springs of human enterprise ... the only source of happiness'.

Against this background, J.D. Mabbott's *The State and the Citizen* in 1948 was hailed by Oakeshott as the most important work since Bosanquet's *Philosophical Theory of the State* in 1899.[111] Mabbott not only saw the need to limit the authority of the state, he grasped that the basis for doing so could not rest on natural rights or on moral motivation. Moreover, Mabbott had understood that the unity of the state was not generated by 'a general will or a corporate self'. Oakeshott entirely agreed that this 'dangerous mythology' (which had often, as we saw, been espoused within the Idealist tradition) prevented a proper understanding of the historic, institutional nature of individuality.

However, Oakeshott did object to Mabbott's effort to protect activities such as art and religion by arguing that they were 'non-social' in the sense that they were 'beyond the reach of any association to procure', and they could only be preserved and protected by state action, not produced by it.

---

[111] #76, *The State and the Citizen*, p. 248.

Mabbott did not take account of the fact that 'there can be no such thing as a non-social action or activity in the sense of a concrete action performed or activity pursued which is devoid of social consequences and owes nothing to society'.

The fact that an activity like art 'has no practical end to serve does not deprive it of social consequences'. The same was true of religion: '[n]either the language of the poet nor the idiom of worship ... is private.' Oakeshott acknowledged that any attempt by the state to achieve 'direct legal control of artistic, scientific, or religious activity (beyond the control, often very material and going very deep, inherent in the civil and criminal law)', would destroy these activities, but they were still only 'free' because of the existence of the state in the first place; they were not 'naturally' free activities.

Another work that struck Oakeshott as of major importance was Brogan's *The Price of Revolution*, which he called a 'tour de force'.[112] Most political theory consisted either of 'vulgar realism', or 'the exploration of necessary relations between a collection of abstract nouns', both approaches that obscured the actuality of political situations: '[W]e first raise the dust and then complain that we cannot see. Half of human activity becomes incomprehensible to us, and the rest is misconceived'. Brogan had avoided these faults by taking a carefully defined theme — 'the history and significance of violent change (political and technological) in the modern world'.

Brogan's argument was that since the late eighteenth or early nineteenth century, 'we have been living in an age of revolution'. Yet revolution was an inefficient and 'uneconomical' means of political change; the 'cost is to be counted not merely in the good that they destroy (that is often exaggerated), but in the very elementary goods (such as order and decency) which they endanger, and in the displacements of society which they cause ... which go on revealing themselves for generations'.

This conclusion was irresistible to Oakeshott, for whom gradualism was a central article of political faith. At the same time, it was not grounds for despair; Oakeshott welcomed Brogan's ability to 'avoid the contemporary habit of exaggerating our situation into a kind of cosmic tragedy — a Predicament', and he shared Brogan's view that what was important in politics was 'not being deceived about our situation and doing our best in almost unendurably "interesting" circumstances'.

VI: The History of Political Thought

One way of avoiding being deceived about our political situation was to be historically informed. The history of political thought could not suggest

---

[112] #110, *The Price of Revolution*, p. 364.

any positive courses of action, but it could dispel ignorance and illusion. The best historian in this respect was one who 'keeps severely to the matter in hand ... and writes with brevity, precision, and lucidity'.[113] What irritated Oakeshott most was the superficial general survey.

The effort of Curtis, the Round Table founder, to find a 'guiding principle' for politics in world history (which he duly located in the idea of a commonwealth) met with short shrift.[114] Curtis saw a more or less unbroken development of the democratic ideal from ancient Greece onwards; he believed that Jesus had expounded its principles, and that Edward I had tried to put it into practice. This unsophisticated indifference to historical change displayed 'more courage than judgment' in Oakeshott's view. But he found the same fault in professional scholars.[115]

For example, Bowles' *Western Political Thought* had been

> constructed round a sort of fixed skeleton of constants, themselves immune from change. The 'European mind' is something to which this history happens ... Something called 'science' or 'the scientific attitude' emerges, disappears and re-emerges at irregular intervals; but itself suffers no detectable change.

Bowle had written of 'the main stream of European civilization', Oakeshott remarked, as if it were 'being turned on and off by a celestial controller'.

Towards the end of the period covered by this volume, however, Oakeshott detected a notable increase in the quality of research on the history of European political thought. The 1950s saw the appearance of some scholarly editions that were to prove very long-lived, and that greatly advanced the study of the Renaissance and early modern periods.[116] Moreover, work had progressed on a much earlier period, the 'complicated and overwhelmingly important first four centuries of the Christian era'.[117]

The relationship between Christian religious ideas and political thought forms a recurring theme in Oakeshott's reviews. The earliest work on the history of political thought he reviewed was on seventeenth-century England, a period in which politics and religion were 'indistinguishable'.[118] He credited its author Belasco with some sharp observations, in particular that 'the Toleration Act does not mark the birth of religious toleration, but establishes for the first time, with the connivance of all Protestant Churches, the right of religious persecution of the state'. In his later writings Oakeshott always emphasized that the Reformation resulted in a

---

[113] #37, *Richard Hooker als politischer Denker*, p. 109.
[114] #32, *Civitas Dei*, p. 96.
[115] #62, *Western Political Thought*, p. 201.
[116] #106, *The Discourses of Niccoló Machiavell*; #96, *Patriarcha*, pp. 355, 315, respectively.
[117] #104 *The City of God and Introduction to St. Augustine*, p. 348.
[118] #12, *Authority in Church and State*, p. 54.

massive transfer of religious authority to the state that had been inimical towards individual liberty.

When Plamenatz described Hobbes, who from Oakeshott's point of view was one of the most important defenders of individual liberty, as a utilitarian, he did not protest.[119] However, he did not share the enthusiasm of one of his predecessors as Professor of Political Science at the LSE, Graham Wallas, for utilitarian thought.[120] Oakeshott typically saw both Bentham and Mill as ambiguous figures because of the tension between their consequentialism and the rule of law, though there was a gradual softening of his attitude towards Bentham over the years.[121] He may also have thought that neither Bentham nor Mill were as self-conscious as they might have been about the theological origins of Utilitarianism; he commented that Paley provided a clear 'example of the way in which the hedonistic foundation of Utilitarianism was developed from the Natural Law theory by positing the happiness of mankind as the evident will of God'.[122]

Utilitarianism, and indeed democratic thought in general, was a product of an optimistic 'Enlightenment ... confidence that from tolerant discussion' the truth would emerge.[123] This was the strand of Enlightenment thought which had produced Rationalism. But there was another source of democratic thought that lay in 'scepticism (doubt not only concerning the power of human intelligence to arrange a satisfactory state of society, but also concerning the whole idea of a permanently good society)'. Clearly, it was this latter strand of democratic thought with which Oakeshott himself was most in sympathy, and the idea of the ambiguity or division within democracy was a constant preoccupation of his post-war work.

It was already visible, however, in some of Oakeshott's inter-war writings: for example, his critique of Lockean liberalism. Built on a commitment to freedom and property, it espoused values which any political philosophy favouring the rule of law would endorse; at the same time, its stress on science and progress had contributed much to a later rationalism prepared to over-ride these commitments in the name of the common good. It lacked the absolute commitment to individualism that Oakeshott demanded; he contrasted Montaigne's 'radical, Epicurean' type of individualism, which he himself clearly favoured, with Locke's more insipid variety.

We noted above that despite the exaggerated criticisms of democracy, parliamentary government, and discussion Oakeshott made as part of this critique of Lockean liberalism as 'absurd and exploded', he rediscovered

---

[119] #94, *The English Utilitarians*, p. 311.
[120] #58, *Men and Ideas*, p. 195.
[121] Bentham and Mill were 'admirable writers (or at least one of them) but unsafe guides': #51, *This Freedom of Ours*, p. 149.
[122] #56, *Reason in Politics*, p. 189.
[123] #73, *Puritanism and Democracy*, p. 236.

the virtues of democracy and parliamentary government when they were seriously threatened by the volkish ideology of national socialism, with its claim to embody the will of the superior racial group. From the national socialist point of view, the clash was between a decadent Western individualism and a dynamic German nation; for those who opposed national socialism, the battle was between freedom and a particularly perverted notion of group personality.

This problem of the relation between the individual and the group was one of the themes of Gierke's *Das Deutsche Genossenschaftsrecht*, an influential product of late nineteenth-century German historiography. In 1934 there appeared a translation of the section on the period 1500-1800 by Ernest Barker, the first Professor of Political Science at Cambridge. For Gierke society had an independent, metaphysically real, existence that was prior to the state and independent of it, and his story of the early modern and Enlightenment period purported to show how the growing individualism of modern Europe had been destructive of society's communal associations. He regarded Hobbes in particular as responsible for introducing an atomising conception of the state that was a threat to any cohesive form of society.

In England, the rise of German nationalism meant that any positive account of group personality was increasingly regarded with suspicion, and Hegel in particular was often viewed as having attempted to reassert the reality of group personality. This was an interpretation with which Oakeshott disagreed, so it is no surprise he considered English Hegel scholarship to be 'maddeningly disappointing' in this period, with noble exceptions.[124] He rejected the idea that the *Philosophie des Rechts* was part of an early nineteenth-century 'Age of Reaction'; it 'belongs so obviously to the Age of Reason ... that its inclusion [in an Age of Reaction] is almost absurd'.[125] In 1939, he felt that the best guides remained Bradley and McTaggart, both of whom had by then been dead for some time. This perhaps rather overlooked the work of Edward Caird (and indeed Robert Flint), but it is true nevertheless that the number of valuable books on Hegel in English prior to the 1970s was small; Popper's *Open Society and Its Enemies* remains a classic example of a text commendable for its commitment to liberal values but worthless as a guide to Hegel.

Oakeshott's earliest political writings displayed some sympathy for Idealist and pluralist theories of the reality of group personality, but by the end of this volume he had completely rejected them as strategies for limiting the power of the state and maintaining the rule of law, his two most important political goals. His later writings on political philosophy and on

---

[124] #56, *Reason in Politics*; #41, *The Political Philosophies of Plato and Hegel*, pp. 189, 126, respectively.
[125] #26, *The Social and Political Ideas of Some Representative Thinkers of the Age of Reaction and Reconstruction*, p. 87.

the history of political thought should be read as repudiations of it. In political philosophy, he consistently argued that the only reality groups could have was legal, and that all forms of personality, both individual and group, were historic and artefactual. In the history of political thought, individualism was a positive achievement, and the existence of social groups gave no grounds for placing corporate welfare before that of the individual.

A Note on the Texts

Unlike the previous two volumes in the series, this third volume consists entirely of previously published material, meaning that obtaining a good text was generally unproblematic. Assembling the various essays and reviews was greatly facilitated by the existence of the comprehensive bibliography maintained by the Michael Oakeshott association.[126] Photocopies were made and either transcribed by the editor or electronically scanned using optical character recognition software and checked for accuracy. Obvious errors in spelling and punctuation in the originals have been silently corrected, and to assist the reader, fuller bibliographic details have been provided.

---

[126] See note 1, above.

One

Science, Religion, and Reality

This book, consisting of ten essays by various hands, has already attracted considerable and deserved attention. Its subject is one of perennial interest, and it achieves the by no means easy distinction of making what I take to be a genuinely significant pronouncement. It is fortunate in being introduced by Lord Balfour who 'sets the problem' with great clearness. The rest of the book falls naturally into two parts, the first three essays being historical, and the last six devoted to an exposition of the respective spheres and claims of science and religion.

Dr Malinowski opens the discussion with a valuable essay on Magic, Science, and Religion, drawing his material chiefly from a first-hand study of native life in Melanesia. He points out that magic, science, and religion each play a distinct part in the life of primitive man. Scientific knowledge is definite though limited; and it is never confused with a belief in magic, which is invoked only when knowledge fails. 'It is most significant that in the lagoon fishing, where man can rely completely upon his knowledge and skill, magic does not exist, while in the open-sea fishing, full of danger and uncertainty, there is extensive magical ritual to secure safety and good results' (p. 32). In Dr Malinowski's view, religion is necessarily, though not primarily, public, and yet the 'social' and the 'religious' are not to be confused as so many anthropologists have done. It is never found in conflict with science. Magic is 'a practical art consisting only of means to a definite end to follow later one religion [is] a body of self-contained acts being themselves the fulfilment of their purpose' (p. 81). Dr Singer writes with his usual learning on the history of science in its relations with the various religions and ecclesiastical powers from the great age of Greece to the end of the eighteenth century. And Professor Aliotta of Padua, in what is in some respects a rather confused essay, treats of the final stages of the

---

Review of Joseph Needham (ed.), *Science, Religion, and Reality* (London: Sheldon Press, 1925). First published in *Journal of Theological Studies*, 27 (1926), 317–19.

struggle in the nineteenth century. It is never quite clear to the reader whether he is speaking of 'naturalism' or of 'science', and modern pragmatism is repeatedly taken as offering a critique of the scientific method, whereas it usually represents itself as a theory of knowledge – a very different thing.

Professor Eddington, writing on the Domain of Physical Science, gives an altogether admirable account of the method and aim of modern physics, which is applicable in principle to all the sciences. The scientific conception of the universe is the most abstract of all conceptions, it is of a universe consisting solely of physically measureable relationships, and physical science is a closed system created for the study of those relationships. Comparing this essay with Prof. Hobson's Gifford Lectures we may note a marked agreement in the main outlines of the picture. Dr Needham's essay on Mechanistic Biology and the Religious Consciousness is in part a criticism of the neo-vitalist theory of biological life and in part a historical survey of the various theories of life and their relationship with religious and ecclesiastical opinion. He himself, with the majority of biologists (though there are distinguished exceptions), is a mechanist. The interest in the historical part lies chiefly in his thesis that in the past religious minds have shewn an instinctive attraction for some sort of vitalistic theory of life, but that, on the whole, it should be doubted if 'even from a narrowly apologetic point of view, it [is] wise to nail the colours of religion to the precarious mast of neo-vitalism' (p. 235). I would suggest that religion is not scientifically required to nail its colours to *any* biological mast. This essay seems to confuse, in its various 'philosophical' arguments, the main point that the so-called mechanistic and vitalistic theories of life are purely methodological hypotheses applied only to an abstracted aspect of organic phenomena, and not theories of the nature of life at all. Things can be mechanically described which cannot be defined in terms of mechanism. Science does not set out to give such a definition; and it is a matter of method to be decided among biologists (on purely biological grounds, not in any sense 'philosophical') whether the vitalistic or the mechanistic hypothesis is the more pragmatically useful and productive (cf. p. 17).

Dr Oman's contribution on the Sphere of Religion contains the exposition of his view of the nature of religion which his contributions to this journal have indicated.[1] Religion can be understood fully only by the religious (p. 262), and the failing of many of the theories of religion hitherto put forward is that they have been formulated, often on sound enough logical principles, but without any true conception of the nature of the subject in hand (p. 265). Religion deals with environment in a practical and not a theoretical manner, 'by way of feeling and value' (p. 283). It stands in its own right, resting upon the sense of the Holy, which is stirred only by

---

[1] Cf. *Journal of Theological Studies*, 25 (1924), 275.

what is valued as 'sacred' – the 'sacred' meaning a valuation of absolute worth which cannot be expressed in, or reduced to, any less absolute terms (p. 289). Religion and Psychology are dealt with by Dr William Brown, who reviews and appreciates various psychological theories chiefly relating to mystical experience. He distinguishes between the philosophical and the psychological treatment of religion, and recognizes that the latter is not required to, and cannot, do justice to questions of validity. Professor Webb's essay on Science, Christianity, and Modern Civilization, shorter than the others, grapples with the difficult question of the 'philosophy' of Christianity. It has much to say of interest, but there is missing from it any consideration of the most pressing feature of our theological thought, noted by Aliotta (p. 155), viz. the exact bearing upon Christianity of the modern historical criticism of the New Testament.

The Conclusion by the Dean of St Paul's is first a judicial summing up of the foregoing essays, and secondly an unequivocal statement of his own views on the relationship of Science and Religion. The conflict, he says, still exists, but is not inherently necessary in the subjects. 'A religion which does not touch science, and a science which does not touch religion, are mutilated and barren. Not that religion can ever be a science, or science a religion; but we may hope for a time when the science of a religious man will be scientific, and the religion of a scientific man religious' (p. 348).

The title 'Science, Religion, and Reality' embodies the only serious defect of the book. The ultimate relation between any human activities is, as Lord Balfour says (p. 16), a question of metaphysics; and, while the importation of the 'Reality' into the title suggests that we are to be offered a treatment of the ultimate nature of the relation between science and religion, the contents of the book are, wisely enough, largely confined to a historical, scientific, and theological discussion, and philosophy enters only by the back-door of biology.

Two

The Christian Religion and Its Competitors To-day

These four lectures and the epilogue are inspired by a double purpose; for with his analysis of various competing interests, Dr Bouquet is able to give us some hints of his view of what the Christian religion is, and this adds greatly to their value. Since they are in the nature of an *exposé* of some of the false gods of our time we cannot expect them to exhaust their subject, but the competing interests which Dr Bouquet has chosen are none of them men of straw: he has selected them with discernment and brings to his judgments considerable practical experience as well as wide reading and a balanced enthusiasm. They are Secularism, or no religion; Pantheism; Traditionalism; and Relativism, or the belief that Christianity will yield to something truer. Secularism is a clumsy critic, rarely troubling to distinguish religion from the name; it is a kind of 'stark insensibility' whose many forms agree in being ways in which we 'lay waste our powers', and fail to satisfy the religious sense which is part of nature. Pantheism may 'explain the world', but it lacks practical power for the direction of life. Religion is, after all, nothing if not practical, and the real value of the historical element in Christianity is best explained in terms of this necessity. Even so, it is doubtful whether this forces us to go so far as to say that 'the Christian religion champions the essential reality and uniqueness of all events, and the reality of time' (63).

That the current mode of presenting Christianity will remain unchanged few will think probable, and the view put before us is that we should have less to fear from any change which may occur if we learnt to think of religion, the church, and the ministry in terms of their more fundamental features. It is not another religion which is the chief competitor with Christianity at the present time, but the worship, in some form, of the world, that is, no-religion.

Review of Rev. Alan Coates Bouquet, D.D., *The Christian Religion and Its Competitors To-day. Being the Hulsean Lectures for 1924–5, etc.* (Cambridge: Cambridge University Press, 1925). First published in *Journal of Theological Studies*, 27 (1926), 440.

Three

Providence – Divine and Human

This is a conscientious attempt to deal with the doctrine of Divine Providence 'under evolutionary categories'. 'The validity of the essential Christian doctrines is taken for granted', and we are conducted through the various departments of the physical universe, in each of which the workings of purpose and providence are pointed out. Part of the book is taken up with a restatement of the conventional view of the 'providential order', and the rest with displaying the scientific evidence for a teleological view of the universe. The main problems considered are those connected with purpose and evil, and the universe is regarded throughout as the 'conditioned will of God, not His free personal activity'. There is a second volume to follow in which human history is to receive similar treatment. We may, perhaps, doubt whether the time has not now passed when it is any longer profitable to attempt to 'prove' the existence of Providence or Purpose. Rather we should ask, 'what kind of a Providence can we believe in?'

Review of Ebenezer Griffith-Jones, D.D., *Providence — Divine and Human. A Study of the World-Order in the Light of Modern Thought*, vol. 1 (London: Hodder and Stoughton, 1925). First published in *Journal of Theological Studies*, 27 (1926), 440–1.

Four

The Metaphysics of Evolution

The greater part of this book consists of critical and historical essays and notices reprinted from either philosophical journals or volumes previously published. The earliest takes us back to the first years of *Mind*, the most recent is from the 1925 volume of that journal; but Mr Whittaker claims that the title expresses the main thought, being one of his most permanent interests, of all the essays. In spite of the fact that the author's chief motive is 'to arrive at something positive through criticism,' the interest which they satisfy is, for the most part, historical. His excursions into Classical Greek, Hellenistic, Mediaeval and Renaissance philosophy show a life spent among the writers of those times, and his own views appear chiefly as incidental to these explorations.

Review of Thomas Whittaker, *The Metaphysics of Evolution, with other essays* (London: Williams and Norgate, 1926). First published in *Cambridge Review*, 48 (1927), 230.

Five

General Theory of Value

As philosophy passes more and more under the misleading influence of the natural sciences it adopts their principle of *divide et impera* and is becoming increasingly cut up into exclusive fields, each with its warning to trespassers; all of which is making it increasingly difficult to see the wood for the trees. One of the more modern and more useful of these divisions is the Theory of Value, which is designed to consider a problem which cuts across older categories such as ethics and aesthetics. The problem is, What is the nature of all determinations of value?

In this formidable work Prof. Perry gives us no more than the *allgemeine Teil* of his theory of Value, and there is a second volume to follow called *Realms of Value*. The aim of philosophy, he says, is 'to bridge the gap between common-sense and science,' but the result seems to give some countenance to the definition of philosophy as 'a fussy acquaintance with things in general.' The argument is that value is ascribed to objects in respect of the interest taken in them, and by far the larger part of the book is taken up with a minute analysis of interest, leading us into biology, neurology, psychology and sociology, and in fact amounting to a natural history of interest, though its logical structure is all that is relevant to the discussion of Value. This tends to make the book somewhat tedious reading. But the more interesting, because the more relevant, chapters are the first five, in which value is defined in terms of interest, and the last three, where the structure and implications of value judgments are considered.

Review of Ralph Barton Perry, *General Theory of Value: Its Meaning and Basic Principles Construed in Terms of Interest* (New York: Longmans, Green and Co., 1926). First published in *Cambridge Review*, 48 (1927), 230.

Six

The Principles and Problems of Philosophy

The aim of this book is to afford an introductory text book of philosophy which shall give students 'a *feel* for philosophy' rather than mere information: a very worthy endeavour. It is evidently written with an eye to the teaching system of American universities, and for all we know will be found to fill the requirements of that system admirably. The form it takes is a survey of as much of the whole field of philosophy and pseudo-philosophy as can be got into 500 pages; and, for its purpose, seems to us both too long and too much taken up with 'philosophical' jargon. But the notion of an elementary text book of this kind for the use of beginners is the product of a mistaken way of approaching the subject, and this one is not likely to be more disappointing than others. In addition, the book is intended to be a contribution to philosophy; Prof. Sellars is a 'critical realist.'

Review of Roy Wood Sellars, *The Principles and Problems of Philosophy* (New York: Macmillan and Co., 1926). First published in *Cambridge Review*, 48 (1927), 429.

Seven

The Realm of Mind and *Three Conceptions of Mind*

We may all envy Professor Woodbridge for his simple philosophical creed, the two main articles of which seem to be that 'a modern metaphysician must be analytic and empirical,' and that we are 'given' certain 'obvious natural facts,' one of which—'that the material world is a fact'—he even goes so far as to say is 'too obvious.' From this basis, by arguments which cannot be stated shortly, he arrives at a variety of conclusions; that 'mind is not properly a being, but a realm of being,' that this realm possesses a logical structure which our thinking discovers and may be called 'objective mind,' and that since many minds are also given they must somehow be related. But he has a short way with such problems. The relation of mind and body and of minds with one another is taken to be a fact to be stated, not a problem to be solved. 'It seems quite gratuitous for metaphysicians to belabour the problem how two minds can read the same book, when it is daily solved by librarians.' It does not often occur to Professor Woodbridge that to be content, in this way, to take things as 'facts' is the negation of philosophy.

Dr Jascalevich is a disciple of Professor Woodbridge. His book consists of an historical study of three conceptions of mind—those of Aristotle, St Augustine and Descartes. His aim is to show how each of these writers is 'an interpreter of a contemporaneous mentality' and to show them also as contributing to a general movement which he calls 'the denaturalization of mind in history.' The value of his comparison is, however, somewhat limited by the fact (which he admits) that, whereas Aristotle treats the mind as a psychologist, both St Augustine and Descartes approach it as a problem in metaphysics.

The price of these books seems somewhat out of relation to their size and value; both would have been more fittingly published in paper covers.

Review of Frederick James Eugene Woodbridge, *The Realm of Mind. An Essay in Metaphysics* (New York: Colombia University Press, 1926); and Alejandro A. Jascalevich, *Three Conceptions of Mind: Their Bearing on the Denaturalization of Mind in History* (New York: Colombia University Press, 1926). First published in *Cambridge Review*, 49 (1927), 93.

Eight

Contemporary Thought of Great Britain

Mr Widgery has written a well-informed and thoughtful book on a subject which presents not a few difficulties and ambiguities. In the main, it is a review of contemporary British thought about the universe, which includes not merely what may be strictly called philosophy, but also the kind of 'free speculation' in which certain scientific and other writers are apt to indulge, and the thought about the universe which takes the form of a so-called philosophy of life, such as that to be found in the writings of Thomas Hardy, the value of which lies rather in the intensity and passion with which it is felt than in its ultimate coherence. And it might have added to the clearness of the picture had these been distinguished at the outset.

The first chapter deals with thought of the third kind as exemplified in such writings as those of Hardy, Chesterton, and Wells. Under the heading of Naturalism we are given an account of some of the contemporary 'scientific' speculations about the universe, but perhaps it might have been shown more clearly how a man may have a naturalistic attitude to the universe without elevating it into a philosophy and that the death of naturalism as a philosophy has by no means involved its death as an attitude.

In Mr Widgery's opinion the philosophical doctrine called Idealism counts for little at the present time. Pragmatism has failed to take its place, and, although he sees little sign of any 'dominant movement' in contemporary thought, he is inclined to regard what is called Realism as the philosophy which possesses the most vitality. In the penultimate chapter, called Theism, an interesting set of writings is discussed, but with certain exceptions these leave the impression of being so many escapes which their authors have discovered when wearied with the inconclusiveness of thinking.

Review of Alban Gregory Widgery, *Contemporary Thought of Great Britain* (London: Williams and Norgate, 1927). First published in *Cambridge Review*, 49 (1927), 156.

At no time in reading this book do we feel our fingers on the very pulse of the present, and indeed one of the conclusions we are encouraged to draw from this account of contemporary thought is that, although still alive, it has no such pulse. But, in spite of its rather atomic method, the book is not without its glimpses of a comprehensive view. Contemporary thought is anti-dogmatic and empirical, it is occupied in the main with details and is eclectic in character. In a book of this size there are necessarily sides of contemporary thought which receive but scanty treatment, and here both aesthetic and so-called social philosophy are left more or less untouched. But, although Mr Widgery's constant demand that a philosophy should be also a 'philosophy of life', 'dominating the minds and guiding the lives of the people', is, I think, a little misleading, his readers will carry away a picture of contemporary thought, certainly significant, and perhaps as clear as circumstances allow.

Nine

Can We Then Believe? *Essays Catholic and Critical,* and *The Inescapable Christ*

Bishop Gore has planned his latest volume to be a summary of three earlier books which went under the title of the *Reconstruction of Belief*. This, like his other works, impresses us with his sincerity and real belief in all he writes, so that we can never be wholly out of sympathy with him. But this hardly lessens the difficulties of his position. What he gives us here is not so much a theology as a series of descriptions of religious beliefs which are represented as Christianity. Constantly the language in which he writes is that of religion and not of theology, and the sanctions to which he appeals — power in human life, the certainty which comes with accepted belief — are religious and not theological. Questionable as many of his statements of detail may be — for Dr Gore seems often more certain than facts will sometimes allow — the chief dissatisfaction with which the book leaves us lies in the seeming arbitrariness of many of its more fundamental arguments and distinctions which often relieve one element in our experience only at the cost of another.

The main position of *Essays Catholic and Critical* is somewhat similar to that of *Can We Then Believe?*, but there is lacking in this larger work the simplicity — almost naiveté — which characterizes Dr Gore's attitude. It is impossible to give an account of the various essays which compose this volume, but it is, perhaps, worth while to indicate its general tendencies. Christianity is conceived of as something static, made, and not even in a process of being understood; it is a 'definite, historical, and positive religion'. Consequently 'the Church is not primarily a society for spiritual or intellectual research, but a society of which it belongs to the very essence to

---

Review of Charles Gore, D.D., *Can We Then Believe?* (London: Murray, 1926); Edward Gordon Selwyn, M.A., B.D. (ed.), *Essays Catholic and Critical* (London: S.P.C.K., 1926); and Walter Russell Bowie, *The Inescapable Christ* (London: Murray, 1926). First published in *Journal of Theological Studies,* 28 (1927),

put forward the emphatic claim to be the bearer of a revelation'; and Christian Theology is simply Christianity rendering its own life and truth explicit or, at most, a process of deducing the implications of Catholic doctrine. *Any* doctrine or practice which does not conform to this definite and positive religion is 'un-Christian', and any theologian who does not first accept it is 'non-Catholic'. These judgments necessitate some standard, and it is found in the authority of 'revelation, in the form of the message of the Gospel' as interpreted by 'a genuine consensus of competent and adequately Christian minds' or 'the general Christian consciousness'. This view seems to carry with it a general readiness to judge scholarship by its results, and to conclude that it is faulty when it does not come to 'catholic' conclusions. Sometimes also we are presented with ill-examined or even false alternatives, as when we are bidden choose between the Dominical institution of Baptism and the Eucharist, and 'the hypothesis of a fortuitous origin', or between the rejection of the mystery hypothesis of the origin of the Eucharist and 'the end of historic Christianity as we know it'. No sort of discussion is allowed of the exact theological value of Dominical institution, which, whatever our views, can hardly rest satisfactorily on mere assumption. History, at best, we are told, gives no more than 'a very high degree of probability', but the difficulty of basing the whole value of this absolute religion upon a probability of any sort does not seem to have been fairly faced. There are many points of interest in the volume, but I cannot but think that it loses force owing to the fantastic nature of some of its arguments — when, for example, we are asked to believe *that* a thing is true while it is admitted that the question of *what* it is, is still open (pp. 101, 114, cf. *Can We Then Believe?* p. 165). We miss from this collection of essays any clear consciousness that Christianity is a difficult thing to *understand,* and a still more difficult thing to explain at once unambiguously and coherently.

Although Dr Bowie disclaims any intention of presenting a 'compendium of theology', he is moved by a genuinely theological impulse, a desire to find *a* meaning in the religion of Jesus Christ, and a meaning, above all, which is intelligible to the present day. A theology, whether or not in the end it turn out to be true, must at least be reasoned and coherent, and the value of Dr Bowie's book lies very much in the fact that he has seen this more clearly than most.

Modernism in the English Church

Dr Gardner has given us an interesting sketch of Modernism to-day in theology and in practice. But, although he tells us that it is 'a tendency rather than a school', his view of it is not altogether without ambiguity. A 'consensus of Modernist opinion' is contemplated as possible (though not actually extant), and Modernism is even spoken of as a 'religion'. We leave the book with the impression that Modernism is somehow connected with particular tenets, but with no sense of it being something which has always existed and must always exist — a striving to make theology give some answer to 'the force and patience of the present time' — and, indeed, we are told that before 1800 there is small trace of any such tendency. In Dr Gardner's view the only sound philosophy upon which Modernism can be based is 'activism or pragmatism'.

Review of Percy Gardner, *Modernism in the English Church* (London: Methuen and Co., Ltd, 1926). First published in *Journal of Theological Studies*, 28 (1927), 316, 316–18.

Eleven

Fundamental Problems of Life

The reader will remark, and probably welcome, two general characteristics of this book before he has got very far. First, Professor Mackenzie seems to aim at finding some meeting-place for the extremes of modern political philosophy, and in this his book may be compared with Mr Hsiao's *Political Pluralism*. Such a meeting-place may be a mere compromise, or it may include and supersede the extremes; and in so far as Prof. Mackenzie has been successful in this matter the meeting-place he discovers is of the latter kind. And secondly, the general view of life to which the reader is introduced is one achieved under the influence of Goethe and Carlyle; and in this matter the author seems to speak to us with the voice of the past — our generation is not, on the whole, much given to quoting these authors.

The sub-title describes the book as *An Essay on Citizenship as Pursuit of Values*, and the argument may be briefly stated as follows: After considering in the First Part the general nature of value, we reach the conclusion that human life consists in the pursuit of values — not, characteristically, in their attainment. Or, if there be attainment, then it is the achievement of a finer sense of the values to be pursued. Where, then, is the wholeness of life to be found? Religion, it is true, gives us a sense of the whole we aim at, a foretaste of completeness, but this sense does not become a concrete experience unless we see that all values contribute to a Common Good. Values may be intrinsic or instrumental, but they are values only in so far as they find their place in this Common Good. This has been recognized by many writers, but it does not follow that the 'actual or effective will of a community' is always directed to this end, and the problem is to discover the means by which the Common Good can become the object of the effective will of a society. And we are told that the means we are seeking is to be found in Co-operative Creation, creation by a co-operative group as opposed to the mere individual and the crowd. Readers of Miss Follett's

---

Review of John Stuart Mackenzie, *Fundamental Problems of Life*: *An Essay on Citizenship as Pursuit of Values* (London: George Allen and Unwin, Ltd, 1928). First published in *Journal of Philosophical Studies*, 4 (1929), 264–6.

books will be familiar with this idea, but Professor Mackenzie discusses it in detail in a long chapter called 'Co-operative Groups.' The Common Good, his argument continues, implies a Commonwealth. And the three main aspects of this are Cultural, Economic, and Political; which he discusses in relation to Rudolf Steiner's work on the *Three-fold State*. In each of these aspects he finds the conception of a common good, compounded by the pursuit of values, intrinsic and instrumental, and achieved by means of co-operative creation. The book ends with a consideration of the problem of a world commonwealth, and some remarks on marriage, the family, population, and education.

The book naturally raises many points of interest, into all of which it is impossible to enter here. And the three I choose are probably not the most important. (i) In a chapter on the Value of Truth the author discusses the theories of 'correspondence' and 'coherence,' and though he concludes that the coherence theory is, on the whole, the better, he says that the correspondence theory at least offers an adequate explanation of historical truth. This is an instance of a meeting of extremes, and it seems to me that the compromise suggested is confused and consequently misleading. 'Correspondence' must be seen as an inadequate form of 'coherence,' or vice versa, before a true meeting is achieved. One or other must be *aufgehoben*. And the same is true of the effort to find a meeting-place for the so-called Pluralist and Absolutist theories of politics, which, I think, are contradictory only so long as Pluralism is taken to be more, and Absolutism less, than it is. (ii) In discussing the conception of a Common Good, Professor Mackenzie compares it with the older conceptions of a General Will and a Group Mind. A great many modern writers seem to me to go wrong in taking the General Will to be a psychological idea, whereas it is fairly clear from Rousseau, and quite clear from Hegel, that they regarded it as an ethical, or even metaphysical, conception, and consequently in no way connected with the Group Mind, which is essentially psychological, where it is not merely a legal fiction. 'General' *means* rational or real with Hegel, and '*toujours droit*' with Rousseau, and the subsequent confusion is, for the most part, the work of their critics. And so the idea of a Common Good, as a modern translation of an old phrase, is possibly less misleading than the General Will, but is certainly open to the same objection that its language is moral, not metaphysical, and consequently liable to be misunderstood. It depicts a process in terms of change or development, and the necessary identity which change implies is lost sight of. (iii) In the chapter on Co-operative Groups there is some consideration of the State, as one among other groups which make up society, and the author follows Mr McIver in taking the State to mean 'an independent, or largely independent, political organization established and recognized in a particular country or region.' (p. 185). The only objection to this procedure is that it leaves us without a word for the distinctively moral aspect of human societies. If we call the State what Hegel named the Civic Community, there is no word left for what for what he called the State, except Commonwealth, which has other associations. And since this has resulted, in some quarters (though not with Professor Mackenzie), in a denial of the supremacy and even of the existence of this aspect, such a use of the word 'State' seems to me more misleading than it is sometimes considered.

On practical questions the book is eminently sane and moderate — indeed, the reader sometimes finds himself wishing for a more definite, if less well-balanced, statement of opinion. It is a book full of the thoughtful consideration of a man who has kept well abreast of the modern literature of politics, and is as alive to the new as he is conversant with what is old. One particular for which most readers will be grateful to Professor Mackenzie is the justice he is able to do Bosanquet, by a quieter and more dispassionate estimate of his politico-philosophical writings than some of his critics have achieved.

Twelve

Authority in Church and State

The main subject of this book, which covers a wide and miscellaneous field of topics in a rather unsystematic manner, is the practical problem of authority in Church and State in seventeenth century England. And, for the greater part, it is taken up with an exposition and criticism of the ideas of the early Quakers on this subject. But, at the same time, 'the book seeks, however modestly, to serve as an introduction to the problem of Authority in Church and State', that is, the problem in a wider and more permanent sense. And this gives it a dual character: it is an historical survey and an account of the author's own position.

The first concern of the reader will be to ascertain how Dr Belasco joins these two interests, for it is clear from the beginning that he intends them to have a logical connection. Apparently he unites them in his belief that a knowledge of past history is a *sine qua non* to solving present problems: the present stands on the past logically as well as chronologically. How far, and in what sense, this is true is a difficult question, and we ought not to allow ourselves to be misled by the current assumption that it is unlimitedly true in every sense. But, putting aside the general question, there are two dangerous paths into which this belief may lead a writer: it permits a hasty and facile identification of present with bygone situations and problems, and it encourages vague and unhistorical generalizations about the past. And Dr Belasco, though he has felt the seduction of both these paths, has perhaps found the second the more fascinating.

For example, the word Quaker evidently signifies for him two separate things which, however, he does not always distinguish. Sometimes he takes the Quakers to be representatives of a kind of general mystical attitude, admitting the validity of no external authority whatever, which turns them from historical persons (few of them made such extreme claims) into an abstract point of view; and at others, they are an historical religious sect 'intimately related to the conditions of their age' (42). Thus,

---

Review of Philip Seth Belasco, *Authority in Church and State* (London: George Allen and Unwin, 1928). First published in *Journal of Theological Studies*, 30 (1929), 426–8.

he tells us in consecutive sentences that Fox was the founder of Quakerism, and that it existed in England long before Fox raised his voice; at one moment the Quaker spirit means any assertion of the unlimited authority of conscience, any insistence that the letter kills, and at another Quakerism is placed in the historical sequence of ideas which first transferred Divine Right from the Pope to the King and later to the individual conscience, and is therefore seen to belong in origin essentially to the seventeenth century. In these circumstances, then, the reader will, I think, do well not to pay close attention to the connexion Dr Belasco finds between the two sides of his book.

So far as the book is an historical study of the relations of Church and State in seventeenth century England, it has much to recommend it, though there are defects along with merits. Dr Belasco appears sometimes to make an attempt to separate, and then bring together again, politics and religion; but in this century they were so far indistinguishable as to make any suggestion that they can be set over against one another misleading. Frequently, also, the history is a little too simple, as when he says that 'in the Commonwealth period, Englishmen achieved a certain measure of freedom' (45). But often he has a more subtle view to put, and his observation that 'the Toleration Act does not mark the birth of religious toleration, but establishes for the first time, with the connivance of all Protestant Churches, the right of religious persecution of the State' (228), is altogether admirable. In dealing with the Quakers in general the author gives a sympathetic and well-documented account of their practical attitudes towards the civil and ecclesiastical power, but I think he is mistaken (at any rate on the evidence he adduces) in supposing that this attitude — even in the case of Penn — ever amounted to a thorough-going theory. The Quakers questioned a great many of the assumptions of politics and organized religion, but they took without criticism 'the commonly accepted practical virtues of Christianity' ('conscience', indeed, meant very little else than the free operation of this particular moral attitude), and for all their freedom of outlook on political and ecclesiastical questions, they certainly encouraged moral obscurantism. The last section is taken up with a defence of William Penn's attitude towards James II's religious policy, which is ably conducted and is in many ways the best part of the book.

On more speculative matters Dr Belasco cannot be said to go very deep. His interest is exclusively in practical questions, and indeed the problems of Authority and Sovereignty have for him, as they had for most of the writers he examines, no other than a purely practical bearing. He has no use for any but a pluralistic theory to explain a pluralism of opinion. And he is much influenced by the New Individualism of certain contemporary political thinkers — an individualism which appears to differ from the old only by being warmed up to satisfy a new generation.

On the whole the book seems accurate, except in a few minor details: Descartes is said to come after the Quakers (14), but Barclay is spoken of as 'referring to the Cartesians' (36); and Burnet is made Archbishop of Canterbury. But its most awkward feature is the difficulty the reader experiences (owing to the style of exposition adopted) of ascertaining whether an argument is the author's own, somebody else's, or merely hypothetical.

Thirteen

Clemenceau

This book consists, in the main, of conversations between Clemenceau and his secretary M. Jean Martet, who is an Eckermann rather than a Boswell. Clemenceau became a legend before his death, and the legendary Clemenceau is so engaging a figure that it would be absurd to complain of this account of him and his opinions. The conversations begin in 1927 when Clemenceau remarks, 'I am not ill, I am just dying.' And though for the most part they deal with war-time and post-war affairs, his earlier life comes in for some discussion. The legendary Clemenceau is a strange contradiction: an Epicurean—not a scholar—who has been drawn into politics. *Au Soir de la Pensée* introduced him to the English public as a man of wide, if miscellaneous, intellectual interests: this book shows him an undaunted man of action, a man of violence and of one idea, who can hate his enemies with the utmost intensity and love his friends with moderation. But he is always willing to retire from the political arena to his cottage in La Vendée—or, while still in Paris, into a kind of inner Vendée of sardonic merriment—and declare that 'looked at from Vega, the greatest statesmen do not seem to deserve so much hate.' In these moods, and in this book they seem to predominate, he never tires of expressing his love for the great age of Greek life and art, his contempt for Rome, and his belief in the decadence of modern Europe. 'Roman architecture,' he remarks, 'gains greatly by being in ruins.'

It is an interesting book, and has several interesting illustrations. Like most of us I suppose, Clemenceau looked his best 'at 10 years of age.'

Review of Jean Martet, *Clemenceau*, tr. Milton Waldman (London: Longmans, Green and Co). First published in *Cambridge Review*, 51 (1930), 332.

Fourteen

The Meaning of Culture

It seems that three different notions of culture have gone to shape our civilization. And, while it is impossible to reconcile them, there are few periods of our history when they have not been operative together. The first is the notion of culture as the indiscriminate acquisition of knowledge of whatever sort or kind: the pathetic, febrile eagerness for encyclopaedic information. This notion is, I believe, congenial both to youth and to old age. It is instinctive in youth, the natural condition of which is activity ill-distinguished from external achievement: in old age it is calculated, because often the only superiority old age can claim is sheer quantity of experience and, since it may be expected to make the most of what it has, its inclination will be towards a quantitative view of culture. Nevertheless, it is, I believe, a fanatic, breathless view, totally out of harmony with the real conditions of human life: it has no answer ready for death. The opposites here are Culture and Ignorance. The second is the notion of culture as the acquisition of 'the best that has been thought and known in the world.' This is naturally associated with the name of Matthew Arnold, and seems to lie behind many of the literary opinions of Mr. T. S. Eliot. It is a selective view, and appears to offer some escape from the purposelessness and anxiety of the other view. In literature we are bidden read 'the classics', in life follow a path beaten by 'great men'; art consists of 'the masters' — who are, so to speak, born old. This view seems to have some answer for death; it is not the hopeless pursuit of an ever-retreating aim. And here the opposites are Culture and Anarchy.

These two notions of culture, dominated by a stronger sense of the past and the future than of the present, lie together at the root of our civilization; their voices have been loudest, their influence predominant. But there is a third view, which begins by throwing over altogether the notion, common to both the former views, of culture in terms of acquisition. It proposes neither a quantitative, nor (in the usual sense) a qualitative, but a

---

Review of John Cowper Powys, *The Meaning of Culture* (London: Cape, 1930). First published in *Cambridge Review*, 51 (1930), 367–8.

personal criterion for culture. Behind it lies an improvident desire for freedom, integrity: like Montaigne, it is 'besotted unto liberty.' Nothing is essential but an integrated self whose purpose is not to remember, adopt or assimilate, but to live a life contemporary with itself. The past and future are nothing to it except in so far as they come alive in the present. The sense of mortality, which, I suppose, every notion of culture must meet, in this case leads, neither to feverish activity, nor to a desire for a 'classic' permanence, but to a determination to find an altogether extemporary satisfaction in life. What is valued is not the fruit of experience, but the flower — something we know only in a present enjoyment and cannot garner. Death is not outrun; it is denied, dismissed. This notion opposes Culture to Despotism; and, I suppose, may not improperly be associated with the name of Epicurus.

Mr Powys' book is an exposition of the meaning and implications of this third notion of culture. 'The essence of culture,' he says, 'is the conscious development of our awareness of existence.' Culture does not show itself among men as something acquired and noteworthy; it does not, in order to flourish, require to 'show' itself at all. And where it is confronted with opposition, it can afford 'to use the weapon of ironical submission,' for it can sustain no irreparable defeat so long as it refuses to compete with 'the world.' It is the determination, and all that this involves, 'to abide by one's own taste — though naturally with many ironic reserves.' 'The least possible amount of culture, when what it does is to set free and round off the natural movements of the individual psyche, is better than the greatest possible amount of it when it hangs heavy and stiff upon the outside of one's skin.' Culture is, then, a way of life, a religion. It does not imply that we consider our own path the noblest or the wisest, but simply that we know it to be our own and value it as such. Culture desires to avoid, not 'specific errors,' but any hint of tyranny.

The book is written with distinction, and there is no doubt that it embodies the experiences of a peculiarly sensitive mind. But, as an exposition of this notion of culture, it appears to me in some respects defective. It moves round the idea, but its grasp is not always sure and the elusive prey escapes. For example, this view of culture can tolerate no separation of pursuits or interests, everything is seen to subserve a single end, and Mr Powys insists upon this. But his book is divided into two 'parts' — The Analysis of Culture, and The Application of Culture — and twelve chapters — e.g. Culture and Literature, Culture and Religion, Culture and Poetry, Culture and Happiness — and in so far as these divisions are insisted upon they introduce another and quite extraneous view of culture. It seems to me that his form of exposition disagrees with what he wants to say. This, perhaps, is not very important; but if we could do without *talking* in a way contradictory of our real view, we should be less in danger of *thinking* in this way. Then again, Mr Powys sometimes falls into a way of speaking which belongs, not to his view of culture, but rather to the view which opposes culture to anarchy. He speaks of 'the classics', 'good books', 'important things'; whereas whether a thing is important, or a book good depends (in his view) not on the intrinsic character of the thing or book, but upon the person with whom it comes in contact. And there is a hint now and again of a desire for that spurious intellectual cosmopolitanism which affects to be equally at home with all literatures and equally sympathetic to all religions. We ought, I think, to notice these things, because an allegiance to a particular view is uncertain until we have thrown overboard all that conflicts with it. And this, I think, Mr Powys has not quite achieved. At times, also, he lapses into exceedingly commonplace advice on what to read and how to look at pictures which, in a writer of less distinction and sincerity, would appear to come perilously near to Mr Arnold Bennett's worst 'How to live on twenty-four hours a day' style. And his chapter on Culture and Painting is little better than a rag-bag. However, these are faults mainly of exposition, and if the book had been thrown into a less imposing, less atomic form, all that is commonplace in it (and there is very little) would, I think, have fallen away from sheer lack of place or relevance. And we should be left with a book on the level of its best chapters— those on Culture and Nature, Culture and Love, and Culture and Human Relations—full of uncommon insight.

The value of the book seems to lie partly in its appropriateness to the present time. It presents a view of culture which, indeed, depends upon no particular circumstances and which, on the whole, meets more difficulties than it raises, but, what is more, it meets some of the difficulties which are peculiarly our own. This is not the place to consider how far an attempt to follow it out would lead to a way of life very different from our present way. Mr Powys sees clearly enough that there is, to say the least, no pre-established harmony between his notion of culture and the modern world, but I should like to have found in his book some more positive discussion of whatever relation there is. As it stands, culture seems to offer an effective escape, but behind its happiness hovers always, in crass contradiction, the confused and gloomy background of life as it is passed by 'the world.'

But I must not appear ungrateful. The book has the rare merit of being entirely free from any infection of sentimentality; and, though it cannot be said to have performed for its notion of culture what, for another notion, *Culture and Anarchy* performed, it is certainly worthy of its theme.

Fifteen

The Principles of Politics

This is an attempt to make political theory into a science 'in the strict sense in which chemistry is a science.' It begins with a discussion of the character of science and of previous attempts at the construction of a political science, and reaches the admirable preliminary conclusions that such a science must not be afraid of being abstract, and must free itself from all pretension of founding a science of history or of predicting historical events. Prof. Catlin is conscious, also, that a political science must, somehow, be quantitative, but he does not develop this idea, and the book contains few references to statistics and statistical generalization, which (I should have imagined) would be the most hopeful method of constructing this science.

'Politics' is the scientific study of 'the act of social control or of government, in the broadest sense of that word.' And 'the will,' or 'the individual as a will,' is taken to be the unit of political science: 'for politics the will is an atom.' But beyond this, Prof. Catlin appears to prefer an economic to a chemical analogy. The individual, we are told, desires a system of 'control' which guarantees him security: he is a 'consumer,' not of economic goods, but of security. This he obtains by 'supporting' some 'security-producing authority.' And here it is possible to introduce a genuinely quantitative conception: 'in so far as this transfer of support from one security-producing authority to another takes place by the acts of individuals, it is not only quantitative but admits of actual measurement.' The unit of measurement is 'the vote.' This is, of course, 'an artificial measure; it is token-money. It stands for one conventional unit of "support".' And so on. The State is 'an organization of persons to maintain the effective production of a given type of political goods.' And, 'the economic law of decrease of profits in proportion to increase of prices beyond the limit of marginal utility has its parallel in the political field in the curve of effects resulting from increased doses of force.'

Review of George Edward Gordon Catlin, *The Principles of Politics* (London: George Allen and Unwin, 1930). First published in *Cambridge Review*, 51 (1930), 400.

How far all this, and other things in the book, will appear intelligible to a reader unacquainted with Professor Catlin's earlier work, *The Science and Method of Politics*, I cannot say. It is not, I think, likely to appear less fantastic. Any attempt to develop a genuinely quantitative study of politics deserves encouragement, but I do not myself see the necessity of clinging so closely to the economic analogy. And for the rest, I have found it peculiarly difficult to ascertain what exactly Prof. Catlin's views are. It is a large book with, on an average, two inches of footnotes to a page. It might, perhaps, be described as a systematically tangential discussion of the idea of a science of politics. I have failed entirely to discover a connected argument running through it, and have been compelled to conclude that Prof. Catlin's learning (which is evidently great) is better than his judgment.

Sixteen

What is Conservatism? and *The Pathetic Fallacy*

Both these are excellently and vigorously written books, both are short; and together they discuss two questions of considerable contemporary interest. They stand apart because, while Mr Feiling believes in Conservatism, Mr. Powys considers Christianity a moribund religion. But, what is more interesting, they stand together because they are faced by the same problem, that of historical identity.

Conservatism is an historical phenomenon, and as such it must be supposed somehow to have changed and yet to have remained the same. Mr Feiling makes it his business to attempt a description of 'the continuing spirit of Conservatism' (in virtue of which he considers it to 'remain the same'), and also to discuss why it has never been realized completely in history and what steps might be taken to achieve its realization now. He insists equally on identity and change. The essence of Conservatism, it appears, is a belief in quality, inequality (as a fact to be faced), energy and permanence, and 'reciprocity is the essence of Conservative justice.' The programme is, briefly, to stop listening to our 'elder statesmen' and 'to face the facts as we find them.' And if, when he concludes that 'our cause survives only by continued absorption of liberal ideas,' we are tempted to enquire, In defending Conservatism, have you not transformed it? He would quite properly reply that it is not he, but history which has transformed it. There has been change, but since there has been continuity also, identity has not been lost. The main defects of his view, genuinely Conservative defects, appear to me his undue satisfaction with what has already been accomplished in the way of establishing equality of opportunity, and his belief that 'the founders of Conservatism' were better than their successors.

Review of Keith Feiling, *What is Conservatism?*, Criterion Miscellany, No. 14 (London: Faber and Faber, 1930); and Lllewlyn Powys, *The Pathetic Fallacy — a Study in Christianity* (London: Longmans, Green, and Co., 1930). First published in *Cambridge Review*, 51 (1930), 512.

Christianity, like Conservatism, must be supposed to have changed and yet to have remained the same. Mr Powys, however, insists upon it remaining the same without changing — and this is the main ground of his contention that it is moribund. For the rest, it appears to be based upon the belief that all religion is a product of fear and is a mere interference with 'a clear and enlightened vision of life.' The original essence of Christianity, for him, seems to be a feeling of pity or compassion. But 'from the beginning Christianity has been perverted.' And his book is, for the most part, an account of this perversion. A view of anything, however, and specially of a religion, which regards its history as a tale of mere perversion, appears to me to be based upon a fundamental misconception: in an historical phenomenon, change cannot be merely dismissed. And the notion that Christianity (or anything else) can be discredited by recounting its history is, I should have thought, as much out of fashion as it is out of logic. 'Your father was a serf, mine was a chemist. And what do you propose to conclude from that?' says a character in the *Cherry Orchard*. But, in spite of his weak arguments, Mr Powys seems to me to have more of the 'stomach of truth' in him than many modern apologists for our religion.

Seventeen

God and Man

Dean Rashdall was not among those who think it boring and unnecessary to convince other people; he was, indeed, an instinctive controversialist, and he believed in controversy because he believed controversy promotes truth. In short, although his general attitude was sincerely speculative, his mind had in it a hard streak (absent from the minds of the greatest philosophers) which permitted him the joys of advocacy. As a philosopher and theologian his chief weaknesses were his inability to forget, or put aside, the practical aim of a moral teacher, and his inability to escape from the language of a belief, the substance of which he had rejected. He was, however, a subtle, systematic (if cautious) thinker, unwilling to cover up the deficiencies of an argument by an appeal to 'experience', or to close an argument with the assertion that the 'human intellect' could go thus far, but no farther.

All these characteristics are illustrated in this third volume of his collected papers. There is great variety in the subjects discussed. And besides those which deal with such topics as Immortality, Theism, the Trinity, and Justice, there are three or four historical essays on mediaeval theologians.

Review of Hastings Rashdall, *God and Man (Papers and Sermons)*, ed. H. D. A. Major and F. L. Cross (Oxford: Blackwell, 1930). First published in *Cambridge Review*, 52 (1930), 39.

Eighteen

The Making of the Christian Mind

Professor Atkins describes his book as an attempt to trace the development of the Christian mind. He maintains that there has been 'an essential development' which has made Christianity 'richly different from what it was at the beginning'. The chapters follow one another in what appears to be intended for a chronological order, and each represents a new phase in the making of the Christian mind. The making of creeds is followed by the organization of a church, the mystical mind succeeds the sacramental mind, until the 'rediscovery of the mind of Christ' by the 'humanitarian mind' of the present age 'completes the long cycle' (315). But the history of Christianity, as indeed the author appears at moments to recognize, has not been so simple as this; nor perhaps may we claim that this latest age has completed the process. Each chapter, then, represents not so much a new phase in the development, as the emphasis of an element present from the beginning. Thus, arriving at the Church half-way through the book, what we are shown is not something which did not exist before, but a fuller development of what existed from the beginning. And this half-chronological, half-expository scheme of the book makes it less coherent than it might have been had one or other plan been excluded.

Of the historical aspect of the book I can say little. There are some passages of insight; but the author is perhaps a little facile in his explanations and too ready to let us into the real 'secret' of this or that. It is peculiarly free from obvious party bias, but not, of course, entirely free from the broad assumptions which the membership of a particular church carries with it. What interests me more, however, are the presuppositions which lie behind the plan of the book, and it is because these are not concealed (though I can scarcely suppose them to have been fully thought out) that the book deserves attention. They are important because they are the kind of presupposition which lies behind any history of Christianity. And the

---

Review of Gauis Glenn Atkins, *The Making of the Christian Mind* (London: Heinemann, 1929). First published in *Journal of Theological Studies*, 31 (1930), 203–8.

chief merit of this book is that the author has recognized their existence, while its chief defect lies in his failure to see them clearly.

Professor Atkins starts with the thesis that the history of Christianity shows an 'essential development', and his book is mainly concerned to trace the 'fact basis' of this development. But behind this lies a question which must find some sort of answer: What is the character of this development? If the Christian mind has changed, in what sense is it still Christian? Is it still Christian because, underneath the change, it has always adhered to some essential core of truth, or why? In more philosophical language, Where does the identity of Christianity lie? This problem of identity is not so acute with some other religions as with Christianity. With them there has often been little change of surrounding civilization and little internal development; Christianity, however, has suffered both extensively. But that scarcely excuses Professor Atkins for giving us not one answer, but five (perhaps six), each inconsistent with any other, and all save one inconsistent with the main thesis of the book.

(i) His first answer is this. 'The historic Jesus is the source which, through changing form and circumstance, have (*sic*) kept it Christian' (22 n.). But if all that has changed is 'form and circumstance' our problem does not arise, for in no sense can there be said to have been an 'essential development'. 'The Reformation went deep, but it did not reach the historic foundations of Christian faith' (116): it 'did not radically change the Christian mind' (265). This I take to mean that, inasmuch as it was a 'back to Jesus' movement, it still adhered to the source which alone could 'keep it Christian'.[1] In this mood, then, Professor Atkins identifies the Christian mind with the mind of Christ, which again is not distinguished from what he takes to be the mind of the historic Jesus (316). Christianity is simply 'Jesus' religion' (45). 'Essential Christianity' is the Sermon on the Mount; and to depart from the Gospels is the surest way of leaving Christianity (253, 275, 315–316). 'Back to Jesus' is the road to Christianity (315, 317). And the mind of Jesus or 'Jesus' ethic' has proved itself strong enough 'to survive [unchanged?] any change in temporal condition' (37). This, however, seems to me not only a contradiction of the main thesis of the book, but also a denial of most of what Christianity has usually been taken to mean. Christianity cannot be simply 'Jesus' religion' because, at present, it involves ideas or beliefs *about* Him and about His death.

(ii) Professor Atkins's second mood is similar to the first, but distinguishable from it. 'Where Christianity has, in any period, grown too external and in the way of being lost in some form, it has corrected that by being recalled to the reality of the inner life; or again, the process has been exactly reversed. And yet every correction has been always along the line

---

[1] Yet on p. 272 he remarks that 'catholicity of spirit is the very essence of Christianity', and that it was 'lost' at the Reformation. Apparently a loss of its 'essence' does not constitute a break in the identity of Christianity.

of something implicit in it to begin with, and the final result has been the enrichment of its life' (216). The 'something' with which Christianity began is, of course, the mind of Jesus. But mere action and reaction, always governed by and returning to the fixed content of a historical source, does not appear to warrant the name of 'essential development'. And, though it is asserted that the end is richer than the beginning, it is difficult to see how this could be so, even if it were possible to agree upon some point as 'the end'.

(iii) At other times the whole of the development of the Christian mind is viewed as the 'substitution' (e.g. of 'a mind about Christ for the mind of Christ', 45) of something foreign in place of the mind of Jesus : or as a 'departure' (140) from that mind. Indeed, Professor Atkins goes so far as to say that 'it would be possible to maintain that the mind of Jesus, as revealed in the Gospels, has had, in great ranges of historic Christianity, less influence upon the conduct of life than the mind of Mohammed upon Mohammedanism' (297). Or again, the mind of Christ has never wholly been lost, or else Christianity would long ago have itself been lost, but it has been much *overlaid*' (315). Indeed, in this mood, *every* phase which he distinguishes in the history of Christianity he regards as simply the 'overlaying' of the mind of Christ by something foreign to it; and progress lies in 'some lightening of its baggage-train' (317). Similarly, the so-called development of which he is writing appears as nothing more than 'interplay' between 'the essential and timeless contribution of Jesus with the whole content of Western civilization' (51); interplay, that is, between two elements the first of which shows no change at all and never coalesces with the second. But in what sense is all this a development of the Christian mind?

(iv) In another mood Professor Atkins uses the word 'modification' (248) to represent the character of the development he is considering. Or, meaning the same thing I think, he speaks of it as consisting of a series of 'adaptations' to meet new conditions. Thus, the first stage is the 'shading and colour' (34) which the mind of Jesus suffered at the hands of His first disciples. What Jesus bequeathed was not a 'Programme' but a 'spirit' which could be adapted to meet all circumstances. And this adaptation, though it may depart from the original in some respects, does not thereby cause a break in the identity of the religion (88). Here we seem to catch sight of something which might be called development. But what is given with one hand is taken back with the other, for the 'contribution of Jesus', His mind, is 'essential, timeless, and changeless' (51, 316) and departure from it constitutes a real break of identity.

(v) In two passages (one of which, however, is ambiguous) a fifth view is suggested. The development of Christianity is in the nature of an 'interpretation' of the mind of Jesus (88, 319). This is a common conception. But, since it also implies the existence of a historical 'source which is prior to the interpretation both chronologically and logically, and, at the same time, draws a distinction between 'what has come to us' and 'our interpretation of it', it seems to me indefensible. It has, however, an advantage over the other views, in that it may plausibly be made to seem consistent with real development and change.

(vi) Professor Atkins, however, has yet another mood. 'Jesus' contribution' was the historical beginning of an 'essential development' which he calls the making of the Christian mind; but Christianity is not mere adherence to this source, nor the mere amplification of a fixed and original datum, it is 'the deposit of its constituent centuries' (324). And in this mood he sees that it is contradictory to look for Christianity in a 'back to Jesus' movement—'the issues of Christianity have never been backward' (334). I cannot say more about this view than that it seems to me to contain the germ of a notion of Christianity more defensible than any other; and that Professor Atkins's book would have been better not only had he adopted one instead of six contradictory presuppositions, but if he had adopted this last rather than any of the others. Had he done so his book would have been very different from what it is.

Now, for the purposes of this review all I have attempted is to shew that Professor Atkins's book rests upon conflicting presuppositions. I have discussed these because they (or others to take their place) lie behind every history of Christianity, and the sooner they are thought out the better our histories will be. And I think it is important to see that they are not conclusions to be drawn from a study of history, but real presuppositions, and therefore necessary to be thought out *first*. It is for this reason, I suppose, that historians frequently treat them as matter of mere opinion, or as an opportunity for free speculation. There is, however, a further and wider question which I have not more than touched upon: Which presupposition about the nature of the development of the Christian mind is the most coherent? And all I can contribute towards the answer is the following elementary suggestions. (i) The notion that there has been no development or change is indefensible both historically and logically. (ii) The identity of a historical phenomenon cannot be preserved by mere adherence to a fixed original datum, because (*a*) there can be no identity without a real change of some sort, and (*b*) there is no fixed original datum for us to adhere to. (iii) If there has been change and development there must also be an identity, for without an identity there can be no change. Christianity is neither a bottle filled once and for all time, nor one into which anything may be poured so long as the label is retained. (iv) All these phrases—adaptation, interpretation, substitution, etc.—are misleading, remarks Professor Atkins (323). They certainly are; and that is the best reason for not using them. What we must keep hold of is the fact that we are discussing the development of a world of ideas, and consequently any 'physical' analogy is bound to be misleading. Ideas are not like bricks to be added one above another, nor are they like the pieces of a jig-saw puzzle merely to be replaced by one another. The first idea we have is in no sense the 'foundation' of all that grows from it; nor may a later stage be tested by comparing it with a former. In the development of a world of ideas a former stage, as such, is always lost in a later, and there can be no returning. (v) We must give up speaking of the 'essence of Christianity' if that means merely 'the most important part of Christianity'. Whatever Christianity is, it is not its 'essence' unless that be taken to mean the whole of it.

Nineteen

Experience of God

This book is what it claims to be—'A brief enquiry into the grounds of Christian conviction'. And I may say at once that it appears to me admirable both in plan and execution. It is divided into three parts. In the first it is suggested that religion claims that the objects with which it is concerned are real and that they are spiritual. And Mr Farmer distinguishes three elements in religion in virtue of which this claim is made: the coercive, the pragmatic, and the reflective. The coercive force in a religion belongs to what is sacred or seen to be of absolute worth; the pragmatic justification of a religion is its power to make a man at home in his world; and the reflective element in a religion is its theoretical coherence. The reflective element, however, is not a separate element but a combination of the other two. In discussing the coercive element Mr Farmer's argument appears to take the form, 'Religions in history all show a coercive element, and (when this has been analysed) we must attribute it to religion in general'; but he omits to show us how he first identifies the religions in history. And if this coercive character is one of the means by which a religion (and 'the touch of God') is distinguished from something else, then it were better not to confuse the issue by appealing to history, or by speaking of 'the coercive touch of God'; for, according to this argument, whatever is (in this sense) coercive, is of God.

The argument next turns to meet certain challenges to religion,—the challenges of bias, of theory, and of fact. And an exceptionally good account is given of the bias 'arising from the modern comparative study of religions'. Perhaps 'bias' does not quite express the meaning of the charge against this study from the point of view of religion. What Mr Farmer is really (and rightly) saying is that this challenge to religion rests upon either the fallacious idea that the psychological or historical origins of a belief are relevant to its force or justification as a religious belief, or the absurd notion that because beliefs have changed and are various they are

---

Review of Herbert Henry Farmer, *Experience of God: a Brief Enquiry into the Grounds of Christian Conviction* (London: Student Christian Movement Press, 1929). First published in *Journal of Theological Studies*, 31 (1930), 302–3.

all equally valueless. The chapter on the challenge of theory, however, appears to me irrelevant. For, if 'theology is a consequence of religion, not a cause of it' (and even then not a necessary consequence), any challenge which a theology as such seems to offer a religion as such is beside the mark and is no challenge at all, because it is based upon an *ignoratio elenchi*: and this is equally true of any other genuinely theoretical argument—e.g. a scientific argument. Under the head of the challenge of fact the questions of pain and evil are discussed.

The last part of the book consists of a rather formal application of these ideas to Christianity. This part is less satisfying than the rest, but that is probably on account of its brevity. Though, at moments, there is a suspicion that the more general argument of the earlier parts of the book is being used to justify existing theological conceptions rather than as a basis from which to criticize and reform them. However, here as elsewhere, Mr Farmer succeeds mostly in asking the right questions, even if he does not always provide satisfactory answers, and his argument rarely falls below a very high standard of relevance and consistency.

Twenty

Afterthoughts and *Aphorisms*

The reader who has long ago abandoned the hope of discovering wisdom in the pages of those slim volumes of *Great Thoughts* and *Golden Words* may yet, I think, find something worth his while in a book of aphorisms which springs from the experiences of a single mind. For what is tiresome in those collections of miscellaneous thoughts is the lack of any sense of unity, any sense that here are developed, with more or less consistency, the reactions of a single mind to its various experiences. Each thought, however great or golden, is solitary and consequently lifeless and unavailing. But, in a book of aphorisms which proceed from a single mind, he may expect to find some unity and consequently some enlightenment. And these expectations are, I think, fulfilled in both these books before me. They will not, of course, be interesting to everybody. Like most collections of *pensées,* they will not be of much interest to anyone not interested in himself, or not interested in what are, perhaps, the only two topics worth discussing—love and death. But to the right kind of reader they will afford, not a feast, but an exquisitely cooked cold luncheon. For there is nothing slipshod about the style of these aphorists; and, as Mr Smith says, aphorisms are salted not sugared almonds, and a mind without some element of frigidity, even of cynicism, is not likely to produce any worth our tasting.

The world which, ten years ago, burst upon us in *Trivia* was fascinating indeed. And what was intriguing was not merely the perfection of these 'pieces of moral prose,' but the revelation in them of a mind at once whimsical and profound, and one almost wholly disabused of what is commonplace. Here was a mind aware of the problems of life and metaphysics but temperamentally relieved of the necessity of finding any save a whimsical answer to them; aware, also, that local gossip is always more interesting

---

Review of Logan Pearsall Smith, *Afterthoughts* (London: Constable and Co., 1931); and Francis Herbert Bradley, *Aphorisms* (Oxford: Oxford University Press, 1930). First published in *Cambridge Review*, 52 (1931), 287.

than international politics, that men's weaknesses are more interesting than their virtues, and not ashamed to admit it. Here was supreme confidence, a Montaigne-like confidence, in personal appreciations; a man satisfied with the delights of conversation without requiring indisputable conclusions; a man reconciled to existence only on account of its extreme oddness; and a man without reticence. And here was a world in which asparagus and mislaid umbrellas jostled with the European situation for attention, and always won; a world in which men and women were continually meditating upon the universe at tea-time, and reflecting upon the odd contrasts of human existence—that minds which contemplate the universe should also catch buses, lose their luggage and buy shoe laces. And to this world, also, belong these *Afterthoughts*. Here the same oddities are remarked and the same difficulties propounded. Personal identity: 'How my reason totters in her contemplative tower, when people say they have seen me in the street.' The contrast between dreams and achievements: 'How many of our day dreams would darken into nightmares if there seemed any danger of their coming true'; and between achievement and enjoyment: 'There are two things to aim at in life: first, to get what you want; and, after that, to enjoy it. Only the wisest of mankind achieve the second.' The same enthusiasms: 'When elderly invalids meet with fellow-victims of their own ailments, then at last real conversation begins, and life is delicious.' The same detachment: 'People say life's the thing, but I prefer reading.' 'I like to walk down Bond Street, thinking of all the things I don't desire.' The same limits of endurance: 'I might give my life for my friend, but he had better not ask me to do up a parcel.' The same sensitiveness: 'How amazing are those moments when we really possess our possessions.' And the same ironical inconsequence; 'The world, as I know from books, is full of abominable evil; indeed, I myself, not many years ago, had some collars stolen in the wash.' But these *Afterthoughts* are not all whimsies: there is acid here, as well. 'Most people sell their souls and live with a good conscience on the proceeds.' 'When people come and talk to you of their aspirations, before they leave you had better count your spoons.' 'If with an excess of interest you peer into the lives of others, what you will probably find is that you will have to pay their debts.' And there is one topic on which Mr Smith is never inconsequent and rarely lighthearted—literature. A man may if he will, be a dilettante, but let such a one keep off literature. And here, as in his pamphlet, *The Prospects of Literature*, there is a note of disappointment when he touches the subject of contemporary literary achievement. In everything he is fastidious, and most of all in literature.

To turn from *Afterthoughts* to *Aphorisms* is to find oneself in a far less personal, less whimsical and less artificial world; there is nothing here which could be mistaken for a pose. For at once it is clear that to Bradley life, and not reading, is the thing. There is the same subtlety, the same absence of prejudice, the same acid tang, but there is also an added note of seriousness. Professional philosophers have not earned much of a reputation for themselves as sages where ordinary life is concerned: who does not prefer the *Maximes* of la Rochefoucauld to the arid verbosity of Schopenhauer's *Aphorismen*? But Bradley here is among the exceptions; this posthumous volume of thoughts has little in it to connect it with the life of a professional philosopher. And yet, readers of Bradley's philosophical works will not be surprised to find that the larger part of these aphorisms is concerned with love, nor to find that what he has to say is always fresh and often profound. 'If a woman loves you, you are seeking you know not what when you desire that she should also understand you.' 'Love in its essence tends to be immoral, for it is the instinctive reference of all to the pleasure of one being.' 'With two, love may be platonic, but with three this is harder.' There reappears here, also, the insistent problem of personal identity; and here too is the recognition of the radical disharmony of human existence. 'The secret of happiness is to admire without desiring. And that is not happiness.' 'Love is the passionate attempt to find oneself in another. And oneself is unique.' 'To love unsatisfied the world is a mystery, a mystery which love satisfied seems to comprehend. The latter is wrong only because it cannot be content without thinking itself right.'

But I have said enough to show the reader that he will find in these books many delightful, and some hard, sayings. And he need not be fearful of stumbling upon platitudes. By this I do not mean he will find nothing he has not experienced or thought of for himself, I mean he will find little insignificant or merely tiresome, and nothing vulgar, mawkish, or sentimental.

Twenty-one

Hunger and Love

This book of over 700 pages contains the story, told in the form of a kind of back-handed soliloquy in the second person plural, of the early years and struggles of a shop-assistant named Arthur Phelps, who suffers from a kind of intellectual and moral claustrophobia. 'The call of the belly and the search for a mate', together with his passion for 'culture' are the triple themes of the book. The dishonesty of his employers, the inaccessibility of knowledge and beauty, the prurience of bishops and mayors and the general obtuseness of mankind—these and other things beat upon his mind until 'you begin to get a sense of the Sinister overshadowing civilization, overspreading the life of mankind'.

Mr Bertrand Russell in his introduction says that Arthur Phelps, the hero of the book, is a man 'with a first-rate mind'. But it is a mind with peculiar obsessions,—a passion for amassing a vast quantity of knowledge and a feeling that 'it is degrading to a man to live without producing an effect.' Phelps feels that if he does not succeed, he must fail; and he lacks any real enjoyment of his own appreciations. In fact, what we are given is not the portrait of a 'first-rate mind,' but the portrait of another pathetic Kipps or Lewisham with his 'schema' and his 'certificates.' And the world in which he lives is not the universal world of love and hunger, but pre-war England. It is true that the author has tried by means of astronomical references, to create a kind of solar, firmamental environment, but it remains superficial; what is insistent is the atmosphere of England before the war. And Arthur Phelps, in spite of his rebellious mind, is a child of his age. And what, I think, is most impressive in the book is not the attempt 'to get over a new conception of the human,' but the way in which the ideas and sentiments of pre-war England have been caught, and the sense of 'growing barbarousness,' 'the smell of blood in the air' which belonged to that time. The ferocious irony with which the England of mid-1914 is attacked in the last three or four chapters is, I think, the best part of the book.

Review of Lionel Britton, *Hunger and Love, etc.* (London and New York: Putnam, 1931). First published in *Cambridge Review*, 52 (1931), 351.

Twenty-two

Adventures in Philosophy and Religion

This book consists of four dialogues and a fantasy, of which the most considerable is the first, entitled *Socrates's Adventures in Wonderland: or the Dawning of Dualism*. Socrates, returning to earth, meets with representatives of the more important modern philosophies, and one by one he exposes their shortcomings. These philosophies are considered mainly as so many attempts to overcome dualism, the dualism of mind and body; and each of them fails. And Socrates, while he is undergoing a kind of sentimental apotheosis at the end of the dialogue, asserts his belief in the reality of the physical and the psychical. This is followed by Mr Layman's somewhat tedious *Adventures in the New Theology*. The rest seems to me nonsense. The author appears to regard his book as a paragon, a piece of 'good-humoured fun'. Philosophical fun is a specialized taste; and when it is devoid of wit there are few who do not find it tiresome.

Review of James Bissett Pratt, *Adventures in Philosophy and Religion* (London: Macmillan and Co, 1931). First published in *Cambridge Review*, 52 (1931), 511.

Ethical Principles in Theory and Practice

The larger part of this volume is taken up with a discussion of the duties of man. There is a metaphysical introduction to this discussion, and a conclusion in which 'enlightenment' or culture, and religion are considered. The major premiss of the argument is that man has been given certain faculties, the development of which is part of the world-plan. And the professor believes that once this is granted man 'must follow the moral theory which has been developed in this book'. But when the phrase 'moral theory' is used it should be understood to mean, not what it usually means, but simply the fruit of Professor Driesch's reflections upon such topics as sex, marriage, war, education, property, patriotism, birth control, etc. If we accept the premiss, then, we cannot avoid agreeing with the professor's views on these subjects. The topics are arranged in a kind of system, but that does not, I think, make the discussion of them more valuable or less random. The reasons we are given for the performance of these duties are often original. For example, all the usual reasons why I should not kill another man are rejected in favour of this — because I 'do not know what death is'. And an interesting distinction is made between what is absolutely wrong, and what is wrong but admits of certain 'apologies'. For example, capital punishment is absolutely wrong: but the intentional killing of a man in self-defence admits of apology 'when the worth of the person attacked is clearly higher than the attacker'.

In this country we are not accustomed to go to our professors of philosophy for moral guidance. The reason for this is not, perhaps, because we have any very precise idea of the difference between philosophy and moral teaching, but because we see no reason to suppose that a good philosopher is necessarily either a wise (in the practical sense) or a good man.

Review of Hans Driesch, *Ethical Principles in Theory and Practice*, tr. W.H. Johnston (London: George Allen and Unwin, 1930). First published in *Journal of Theological Studies*, 32 (1931), 326–7.

And this book is not, I think, likely seriously to shake our faith. Professor Driesch's general position may be said to be benevolent rather than liberal, cautious rather than revolutionary, puritan rather than pagan, and Eastern rather than Western. But, as Schopenhauer remarked, *Moral-Predigen ist leicht, Moral-Begründen ist schwer*; and Professor Driesch has certainly chosen the easier task.

Twenty-four

Religion without God,
The New Divine Order,
and *Philosophy without Metaphysics*

The reader will, I think, find Dr Sheen's book not so radical as his title might suggest. In the first place, it is a study of modern theology rather than of modern religion. And secondly, the characteristic of modern theology which is discussed is its determination to dispense with *theism*. 'Without God' means, without 'God as traditionally understood'. The author, indeed, complains that, in spite of the fact theism is rejected, the word 'God' still appears in the writings of the philosophers and theologians which he is discussing: the word God, he concludes, has taken on 'an entirely new meaning'. But the argument which would persuade us that no conception of God is intelligible which falls outside traditional theism is verbal rather than instructive. And that modern theology cleaves to the word God, yet gives it a new meaning, seems to me neither surprising nor alarming.

The main position of the book is the thesis that modern religion replaces the belief in God by 'a faith in the conservation of human values'; it replaces theism by a form of humanism. After tracing this rejection of theism through the writings of Alexander, Whitehead, Otto, Russell, Croce, etc. (and this he calls the negative aspect of modern religion), Dr Sheen discusses the modern philosophies of Value, for value, he says, 'has become the primary object of religion'. And he then proceeds to 'pass a reasoned judgement on them in the light of history and the philosophy of "the most learned of the saintly and the most saintly of the learned", St Thomas'. The discussion of the ancestry and history of 'the contemporary idea of reli-

---

Review of Fulton John Sheen, *Religion without God* (London: Longmans, Green and Co., 1928); Karl Heim, *The New Divine Order*, tr. E. P. Dickie (London: Student Christian Movement, 1930); and Edmund Holmes, *Philosophy without Metaphysics* (London: George Allen and Unwin, 1930). First published in *Journal of Theological Studies*, 32 (1931), 434–5.

gion' is skilful and informing. And it is followed by an exposition of the shortcomings of this idea when compared with the Thomist position. In the hands of a writer less alive to the necessities of argument, this concluding section might easily have been no more than a continuation of the merely historical theme; but that is not here the case. And the result is an instructive, if tantalizing, book. The author is more than merely a learned Thomist, but I believe his argument would have been more cogent had he been content to leave behind the guide-book (which he knows so well) at the outset of the journey.

The main idea which lies behind Prof. Heim's book — which consists of three essays on Spiritual healing, Time and Eternity, and the message of the New Testament — is an attempt to work out some of the implications of the belief that religion is not a function among functions, a mere 'faculty', but an essential element of all human activity. Old dualisms — such as Nature and Spirit, Time and Eternity — must be reconsidered: and with them go also into the melting-pot of criticism notions such as that of miracle. The book represents, not (like Barth's work) a return to Kant, but a return to Goethe and Schiller, the champions of an undivided and indivisible life.

The theme of Mr Holmes's book is not, so far as he is concerned, novel. Philosophy is the 'love of wisdom', an intimate knowledge of reality which can be achieved only if we abandon ourselves to intuition and feeling. Metaphysics, on the other hand, is radically intellectual, the product of a vicious specialization; and in its hands philosophy becomes a mere game to be played according to the 'laws of thought'. Not only must philosophy and metaphysics be distinguished, but 'there is no place for metaphysics in philosophy'. The dispute is not, of course, merely verbal. Mr Holmes's metaphysical position is certainly uncompromising and is superficially unambiguous, but scarcely an appropriate subject for argument.

Twenty-five

John Locke

In spite of his other titles to fame, John Locke must, I think, be remembered and considered first as a philosopher. For, although the philosophical work for which he is justly famous was the product of the leisure hours of a life spent for the most part in political activity, and was neither published nor completed until he had turned fifty-eight, Locke's philosophy is so characteristic of the man and has exercised so great an influence upon subsequent thought that it must take a place in history which it never took in his life. The *Essay Concerning Human Understanding* is a work hindered by many weaknesses both of conception and composition. It springs, in the first place, not from any radical doubt, any purging scepticism, but from curiosity and a mild perplexity. Locke's insatiable curiosity is written all over his *Journals*, and his biographer says that he 'knew something of almost everything that can be useful to mankind.' Indeed, the view that it is equally unwarrantable either to doubt everything or to make extravagant claims on behalf of the human mind, which may be said to be the message of Locke's philosophy, was as much a prejudice and a compromise with which he began as the conclusion with which he finished. Locke is a cautious, patient thinker, not given to paradox and as little controversial as may be: there is nothing audacious about his speculations, and nothing dazzling or even brilliant about his writing. The *Essay* has perhaps less of the character of a *tour de force* than any other philosophical work ever published. And these, it seems to me, are in the nature of defects in a philosophical writer. Mere 'soundness' is a vulnerable quality in a philosophy; it is more at the mercy of time than audacity and brilliance. For in philosophy what is daring is provocative and will always retain its power to awaken, while what is cautious and sound is after a while forgotten, having about it a soporific effect. And it is always more difficult to doubt radically and intelligently than to believe. And again, it was not for the man who refused the opportunity of a career and preferment in the church for fear he might fail to make his mark there, when he turned to philosophy, to

First published in *Cambridge Review*, 54 (1932), 72–3.

set before himself any but a modest task. For the *Essay* is no system of philosophy, but a cautious attempt to determine the limits of our knowledge by enquiring into the character of the mind. It is a view of the limits of human understanding. And this attitude, also, more sensible to divisions, distinctions and separations than to agreements and unities, is responsible for many of the defects of Locke's philosophy. From its very plan his work was destined to be inconclusive and to result in a compromise. And it is the quality of compromise which is at once the distinction and the weakness of this philosophy. In virtue of this quality Locke was said (by Horace Walpole) to be the first philosopher who introduced common-sense into his writings. But it is a dangerous mixture. Common-sense and philosophy are not apt to agree; and when common-sense is represented as the criterion of philosophic truth the result can be nothing but error.

But what is characteristic and important in a philosophical thinker is not so much the conclusions he reaches as the way he sets about it. And it is here that Locke shows himself to be a genuine, perhaps great philosopher. Apart from 'a mind covetous of truth,' which is of course elementary, Locke stands out by reason of the independence of his thought. His thinking is his own; he does not make the foolish attempt to be a scholar and a philosopher at the same time. He was not ill-read in philosophy; but he knew that the philosopher's business is to think rather than to read, to know his own mind rather than that of others. 'This,' he says, 'I am certain, I have not made it my business either to quit or follow any authority in the ensuing discourse: truth has been my only aim, and wherever that has appeared to lead, my thoughts have impartially followed, without minding whether the footsteps of any other lay that way or not. Not that I want a due respect to other men's opinions; but after all, the greatest reverence is due to truth: and I hope it will not be thought arrogance to say, that perhaps we should make greater progress in the discovery of rational and contemplative knowledge, if we sought it in the fountain, in the consideration of things themselves and made use rather of our own thoughts than other men's to find it. The floating of other men's opinions in our brains makes us not one jot the more knowing, though they happen to be true.' Locke's independence and his modesty are remarkable in that they are, perhaps, the only uncompromising traits in a character otherwise given over to moderation. And further, Locke was not only an independent thinker and a candid thinker, but he chose a style of writing in agreement with his cast of mind — a colloquial style. He was as unwilling to use the language of the schools as merely to rehash the ideas of his predecessors. But in this matter of style he cannot be said to have been altogether successful. For, whatever the merits of saying what you mean in the language of social intercourse, it leads sometimes to misunderstanding which might otherwise have been avoided. And, for example, Locke's colloquial use of the word 'experience' resulted in an ambiguity which rends his philosophy from end to end. He was not a great enough writer to follow the track which avoids at once jargon and ambiguity — that is *nur für die Schwindelfreie*. Nevertheless, Locke's instincts were those of a philosopher; and his great achievement is to have thought systematically and to have escaped making a system.

A philosophy of this kind, something constructed to satisfy the thinker's own mind, without the attraction of brilliance or the provocation of audacity, is not one for which we should predict a long and influential career in the world. And the fact that for a century Locke's *Essay* was a centre of philosophical interest, not only in England (where commonplace philosophy has more chance than elsewhere) but also and particularly in France (where compromise is viewed with suspicion and modesty mistaken for weakness) seems to call for explanation. The fact of Locke's influence upon eighteenth century French thought is undeniable. The *Essay* was translated in 1700, and it was adopted as the official philosophy of the Encyclopedists until they could provide one of their own; and even then, what they provided was very much after Locke. Voltaire leads the chorus of acclamation in the *Lettres Anglaises*. A multitude of writers, he says, have written the romance of the soul; Locke has written its history. D'Alembert says in the *Encyclopédie*: 'ce que Newton n'avait ose ou n'aurait peut-être pu faire, Locke l'entreprit et l'exécuta avec succès.' Diderot admits himself a disciple. And Helvétius and Condillac recommend Locke by appropriating the greater part of his philosophy. Nevertheless, it was not, I think, merely on account of its merits that Locke's philosophy exercised so great an influence. What was influential was not so much Locke as a perversion of Locke; for the French thinkers saw in this Christian, English, Puritan, cautious thinker the founder of Deism and the apostle of Materialism. They made a system of what was never, in Locke's view, more than a methodical attempt to think clearly about the limits of knowledge, and in the name of that system they upset the world, for a little while. It was, however, in England itself that Locke's influence was most direct and genuine. Hobbes was infected with materialism, Berkeley and Hume (both of whom owed much to Locke) with paradox, and Locke, in spite of criticism and opposition, took, and for a while held, the supreme place in English philosophy.

But, for the Englishman, what is interesting and memorable is not so much the author of the *Essay*, the father of the so-called 'philosophy of experience' or the foundation member of the Royal Society, but rather the Locke who was in at the birth of the Whig party and who provided liberalism with its gospel and creed. It is the 'friends of freedom' who Locke's earliest biographer thinks will welcome his biography. Liberalism was not, of course, the invention of Locke; but, standing between two ages, he served as the filter by means of which Puritanism was drained of its immoderation and its 'enthusiasm' and was converted into what the eighteenth century knew as Whiggism and the nineteenth as Liberalism. Liberalism is Puritanism made respectable, and nobody contributed more than Locke to this piece of 'rescue-work.' Locke's doctrines of toleration (a limited toleration), of liberty (a reasonable liberty), of individualism (not a fanatical individualism), of the sovereignty of the people (to be exercised sometimes) and of property, are the seeds from which modern liberalism sprang. And perhaps 'the rights of nationality' and 'the perfectability of the human race' are the only ideas of importance which have since been added to liberalism. Locke believed in science, in freedom, in progress, in property and the pride of ownership, in stability, in moderation, in compromise, and he believed that truth (liberal truth) is great and will prevail; and it is because of his formulation of a view of life no less than of politics governed by these beliefs that he is counted the father of liberalism. Others, no doubt, before him had been liberals, others have done more than he in the practical application of these ideas, but no one has possessed a more comprehensive grasp of this least comprehensive of views. Locke was the apostle of the liberalism which is more conservative than conservatism itself, the liberalism characterised, not by insensitiveness, but by a sinister and destructive sensitiveness to the influx of the new, the liberalism which is sure of its limits, which has a horror of extremes, which lays its paralysing hand of respectability upon whatever is dangerous or revolutionary. And liberalism was for Locke as much a part of his temperament—Locke 'who never said anything which could shock or injure anybody'—as a thought-out view of life and politics.

Now, whether or not we should remember this side of Locke's character and work with gratitude must, I suppose, be a matter of opinion. But it is at least remarkable that at the present time the gospel of Locke is less able to secure adherents than any other whatever. At one time it seemed that liberalism, under the stimulus of the romantic movement, might be transformed into something less boring and upholstered; but the spirit of Locke prevailed. And it appears likely that the fate now of this liberalism is to die of neglect. The moderate individualism of Locke has no attraction for those who have embraced a radical, an Epicurean individualism. Locke's 'steady love of liberty' appears worse than slavery to anyone who, like Montaigne, is 'besotted with liberty.' Democracy, parliamentary government, progress, discussion, and 'the plausible ethics of productivity' are notions—all of them inseparable from the Lockian liberalism—which fail now to arouse even opposition; they are not merely absurd and exploded, they are uninteresting. Not a little, indeed, of the revolt against so-called Victorianism is in fact a revolt rather against Locke and his legacy of liberalism. This liberalism may have given us our liberties (though that is doubtful), it may be a view of things which will come again, but just now it is not one which commands attention or indeed respect. I am not, of course, referring merely to liberalism in politics and liberalism as a social gospel. The liberalism of Locke has invaded other interests than these; but everywhere it is equally dead. The liberalism, for example, which made a revolution in theology respectable and determined its limits is no less dead than that which sponsored the respectability of democracy. And everywhere what has been fatal to liberalism is its boundless but capricious moderation.

Locke's life and character, like his philosophy and like his liberalism, are full of instructive contrasts. His influence upon the politics of his time was immense, but always indirect; he could never be persuaded to take the stage. He was a successful politician, but a man without guile or ambition. He was a bachelor who kept accounts; a *bourgeois* who never had a home of his own; a man of property without any property. His life was spent in a great variety of places, in England and on the Continent, and in a great variety of occupations; but there is nothing of the cosmopolitan in his character. He was a busy man of affairs who appeared always to be at leisure. It was, however, fitting that he should live the full span of a man's life and should die, in the eighteenth century, without an epigram on his lips. He was moderate in everything except his love of moderation. There is nothing at all of pretension in his character; he was meek, and until recently he inherited the earth.

Twenty-six

The Social and Political Ideas of Some Representative Thinkers of the Age of Reaction and Reconstruction

This book, which is the seventh and last but one of the King's College series of lectures on social and political ideas, consists of eight lectures on as many social and political thinkers of the period 1815–1865, prefaced by a general survey of the period. The Age of Reaction (1815–1830) is represented by Chateaubriand, Hegel, and Coleridge; the Age of Reconstruction (1830–1865), by Owen, Mill, Comte, Austin, and Hodgkin. The reader will not, of course, expect to find here anything new; but among the essays are some which perform a useful service by giving a brief and lucid account of the ideas of one of these writers. From this standpoint, the best essays are the editor's on Austin, Theodora Bosanquet's on Comte, and Dr F. M. Page's on Owen. On the other hand, the essay on Mill is untroubled by an idea and is a mere compendium of common-place biography and still more common-place criticism; and the essay on Coleridge (by Keith Feiling) is disappointingly short and inconclusive The Master of Balliol's essay on Hegel is a courageous attempt to distil the *Philosophie des Rechts* into fifteen pages, but Hegel's book belongs so obviously to the Age of Reason (the subject of a previous course of lectures) and not to the age of Reaction, that its inclusion here is almost absurd.

Review of *The Social and Political Ideas of Some Representative Thinkers of the Age of Reaction and Reconstruction*, ed. F.J.C. Hearnshaw (London: Harrap, 1932). First published in *Cambridge Review*, 53 (1932), 332.

Twenty-seven

The Making of the State

This book appears to me to contain a great deal of sound sense put down without pretension and in a very readable manner. The author says that the special claim of the book to attention rests on the fact that in it the making of the State is studied from the standpoint of India. But he is too modest: the book is much more than that. It is a very sensible account of the different forces and elements which go to make a state; an account illustrated not only from the history of Indian institutions, but also from those of contemporary Europe, and Greece and Rome. Nevertheless, the final chapter, called 'The Making of India', is one of the most interesting [and] lucid chapters in the book.

There is perhaps one general difficulty which might be pointed out. The first chapter is called 'An Outline History of the State', and the whole book is cast in the form of an historical survey of the making of the State. But in what sense has this useful abstraction 'the State' a history? A history must surely be concerned with this or that State, and must depend for its value upon the degree in which it succeeds in elucidating the actual and particular course of events. There are, no doubt, common forces to be found in the making of every state, — religion, custom, law, etc. But if one is writing a history, what is important is to shew, not merely how a particular state conforms to some general rule or other, but exactly how, for example, religion has contributed to its development. This book, then, like so many others, suffers from the fact that it is not a genuine history — for 'the State' has no history — but an analysis cast into a misleading historical and chronological form, and therefore not a genuine analysis.

Review of Mariadas Ruthnaswamy, *The Making of the State* (London: Williams and Norgate, 1932). First published in *Cambridge Review*, 54 (1933), 359.

Twenty-eight

Interpreting the Universe

Every student knows that to popularise is to abridge, and that abridgment involves (if nothing worse) false simplicity. Popular history and popular science are alike in this respect. And it is impossible to suppose that popular philosophy can escape this fatal defect. These difficulties, however, have not deterred Professor Macmurray from setting down in a popular form what may be called a theory of knowledge. We begin with 'immediate experience.' This is the given material; thought is reflection upon 'immediate experience,' and philosophy is 'one of the more elaborate and systematic forms of our reflection upon experience.' Thought, however, is merely 'symbolic'; it substitutes ideas for immediate experiences. It is, in fact, a 'substitute activity' which aims always at overcoming some practical difficulty. All thought is for the sake of action. This general view, which is developed in the first three chapters, is, of course, grotesquely simple. But, what is worse, we are left with the impression that there is nothing deceptive in this simplicity. If there is anything a writer of popular philosophy should give, surely it is a sense of the difficulty of the problems involved; but here everything is so easy, obvious and unquestionable.

The rest of the book is taken up with an examination of three 'interpretations' of the universe – the mathematical, the biological or organic, and the psychological – the last being the most comprehensive and at the same time the least developed of the three. What is wanted now is a 'scientific psychology.' The mathematical interpretation held the field between Descartes and Kant, the organic between Kant and the present day, the interpretation of the future is to be psychological. The book is easily and interestingly written; but it is difficult to decide whether after all this attempt to popularise philosophy is not more foolhardy than courageous.

Review of John Macmurray, *Interpreting the Universe* (London: Faber and Faber, 1933). First published in *Cambridge Review*, 54 (1933), 395.

Twenty-nine

Idealistic Logic

This book is properly described as a study of the 'aims, method and achievement' of Idealistic Logic. It is at once expository and critical, and is the work of an adherent to the main doctrine. After some general introductory chapters, there is a good account of the 'traditional logic' and its downfall, from which we are led through the revolution for which Hume and Kant are held jointly responsible. The account of Kant's logical theories is specially full and interesting; and the more or less historical chapters are excellently conceived and carried out. The modern statement of the Idealist logical doctrine is next examined in four chapters. And these are followed by a full consideration of Cook Wilson's view, which is recognised as containing the most sympathetic and one of the most important criticisms of the Idealist position. The book, it is stated, has been developed out of a course of lectures. It is written with great candour and lucidity, and the reader is presented with no unnecessary difficulties. There is, perhaps, little new in this account of Idealistic logic, but the whole position is freshly and attractively discussed. I think that chapters eight and nine might be improved if the references to Bradley's works were made explicit in a few footnotes.

Review of Charles Richard Morris, *Idealistic Logic: A Study of Its Aim, Method, and Achievement* (London: Macmillan, 1933). First published in *Cambridge Review*, 55 (1933), 152.

Thirty

In Job's Balances

Chestov is a writer who has already made something of a stir on the continent; but this is a disconcerting book, for it is difficult to know how to take it. It is disconcerting on two accounts. First, to the English reader it is odd to find a professional philosopher pressing a philosophical doctrine—in this case a theory of knowledge—neither by means of an independent analysis of experience, nor (in the main) with reference to the writings of other professional philosophers, but with reference to writers such as Dostoyevsky and Tolstoy. I do not, of course, mean that it is to be expected that those who make a profession of philosophy have the monopoly of philosophic acumen; I mean that it is surprising to learn that writers like Dostoyevsky and Tolstoy have a theory of knowledge at all. And secondly, it is disconcerting to meet a writer who makes a philosophy out of misology. There have been, of course, many who have doubted the competence of reason to give reality (whatever that may mean); but rarely has a writer like Chestov come forward who makes a philosophy out of this doubt. And I think if we consider these two points we shall learn something of what Chestov has to teach us.

Let us take Chestov's misology first. His doctrine (which is stated most clearly in the first and last chapters, and illustrated in the six intervening chapters) is that, since Thales, almost the whole of European philosophical thinking has been on the wrong track. Philosophical writers, with few exceptions, have believed in reason and have sought for a truth which is universally valid. They have accepted unquestioned the principle of 'the autonomy of reason'; they have succumbed to an unexamined prejudice in favour of what is reasonable. And the result has been that philosophical thought, while boasting that it is 'free thought' (thought, that is, without reservation or presupposition), has been anything but free. Now, in spite

---

Review of Leo Chestov [pseud. of Lev Isaakovich Shvartsman], *In Job's Balances: On the Sources of the Eternal Truths*, tr. C. Coventry and C. A. Macartney (London: J.M. Dent and Sons, 1932). First published in *Scrutiny*, 2 (1933), 101–4.

of what Chestov says, there can be no real disadvantage in disentangling our thoughts, and I find a certain confusion in this charge which he brings against almost all philosophers and specially against Aristotle, Spinoza, and Hegel. Philosophical thought would be open to the charge that it is 'unfree', the charge of prejudice, if it never doubted reason; but this is an hypothesis which cannot be asserted. And if and where it has doubted this 'autonomy of reason,' but has found it impossible to maintain the doubt, then surely it is 'free' on account of its belief in reason. Of course, if we say that philosophical thought is 'unfree' whenever it reaches a decision, then a belief in reason is certainly slavery; but so also is a disbelief in reason. In short, it is not (as Chestov suggests) the failure to *reject* reason which necessarily leaves thought 'unfree,' but the failure to *doubt* it: and while it is true that few philosophers have rejected it, the impression Chestov gives that few also have had the courage or the candour to doubt it, is certainly false. But there is another and more serious difficulty in Chestov's doctrine. He writes all through as if 'the autonomy of reason' and the autonomy of scientific explanation were the same thing. Reason, 'rationalism,' science, and common sense are lumped together; and philosophy, because it believes in reason, is said to be committed to a view which sees the universe as a single, uniform, mechanical whole, a whole in which nothing is disconnected, in which everything is necessary. But this confusion of reason and science, which (in spite of what Hegel taught us) was almost a commonplace fifty years ago, is now a little out of date. There may be a 'case against reason,' but it should not be confused with the cases against 'rationalism,' science, or common sense. And again, this identification of reason and 'rationalism' leads Chestov to confuse 'what is universally valid' with 'what is universally believed.' He has little difficulty in showing that if we stick to what is universally believed we shall confine ourselves to merely 'normal experiences,' and that both science and common-sense have a horror of what appears to be abnormal. But the possibility of judgments which are universally valid in no sense depends upon there being anything whatever universally believed. The valid should be distinguished from the merely ecumenical. What is reasonable and mere normality (what is satisfactory to common sense) are not the same thing.

Chestov's philosophy, then, is a philosophy of misology. If thinkers, instead of reading Kant's *Critique of Pure Reason,* had read Dostoyevsky's *The Voice from Underground* or Tolstoy's *The Diary of a Madman,* they would have discovered that the universe is not an 'organic' whole, a whole of related parts, but a whole in which things 'exist freely,' a whole in which there are no necessary connections, in which one thing does not 'follow' from another. This 'vision' of the universe is what we get when we have conquered the prejudice in favour of reason, this is the revelation of the world which came to Plotinus and Pascal; and it is true. And why is it true? Because, it seems, suddenness, disconnectedness, spontaneousness, unexpectedness are the unmistakable signs of truth. But the strength (or weakness) of a misological philosophy is that it is barred from giving reasons for its conclusions; and this brings me to the first point I put down for consideration. Since argument involves self-contradiction, the misologist must retreat on to the ground of 'assertion' and 'evidence.' Everywhere in this book there is assertion; the belief in reason is said to be the 'lie' at the heart of philosophy. And to support this assertion we are given, not argument, but 'evidence', 'example', and 'illustration.'

The evidence Chestov calls to support his doctrine is, in some ways, the best part of the book. His chapters on Dostoyevsky and Tolstoy are certainly interesting. But I find it difficult to believe that either of these writers was conscious of the theory of knowledge attributed to him here. The great truth to be got from Dostoyevsky is, it seems, 'the conquest of the self-evident'; he teaches us to reject what is merely to be expected, what is normal, ordinary or (in Chestov's language) reasonable. Everything for Dostoyevsky is abnormal, fresh, *sui generis*. But surely this is true of every artist; it is just what art means. And I cannot see that it involves a theory of knowledge or a philosophy at all. It is not philosophy; it is instinct. For the artist, this is not a 'valid' way of looking at the world; it is the only way. More profound, I think, is Chestov's study of Pascal. There he is dealing with a writer perplexed with the problem of knowledge, if not as a philosophical problem, at least as a theological problem; and a writer whose conclusion is almost misological. And naturally enough, such a doctrine as Chestov's will find (or at least look for and appear to find) support also from Plotinus.

Philosophy, then, is free thought ; and because it is free it is misological. Philosophy is 'what matters most,' it is the attempt to find the meaning of life, to fix *le prix des choses;* and because it is these it is misological. *La raison a beau crier, elle ne peut mettre le prix aux choses.* And again, philosophy rejects the merely scientific, the merely mechanical explanation of the Universe, and therefore it must be misological. And on each of these points there is, I think, a certain amount of confusion and misconception. Chestov says: 'my task has consisted in showing that reason has not the power which it claims.' Certainly he asserts it, certainly he illustrates it. But it is difficult to determine in what sense he 'shows' it; for how can it be shown, explained? And this book, in spite of its eloquence, has not succeeded in convincing me that a misological *philosophy* is not a self-contradiction; indeed, this difficulty presents itself so constantly that as one reads one's first instinct is often to suspect an underlying irony.

Thirty-one

A New Argument for God and Survival

The project of constructing a new proof of the existence of God is one which must have kindled the ambition of many thinkers. The very improbability of the success of such a project must, for the ambitious thinker, increase its attractiveness. And a book which purports to offer a new proof of this sort is certain to win attention; the believer will open it with confidence, the atheist with apprehension. But it must be said at once that this book affords no ground for either the hopes of the one or the fears of the other. Its purpose is to construct a 'scientific' argument for the existence of a personal God and for a belief in human survival — 'an argument for religion which would be acceptable to scientific criticism.' And, briefly, the argument is this. Science has discovered 'that there are laws of nature to which phenomena conform,' and for the scientist natural laws seem 'to hold uninterrupted sway over the course of events.' But the honest scientist is obliged to admit the possibility that events may happen (indeed, may actually have happened) which violate the known laws of nature. And if such events can be found they afford all the evidence necessary for a firm belief in the existence of a Supreme Being. For some cause must be assigned for these violations of natural law, and that cause is God. The question to be settled, then (and the only question) is, Is there sufficient evidence for a belief in miracles — miracles being defined as 'events which violate natural law'? And the question is answered in the affirmative; the greater part of the book being taken up with an attempt to prove (*a*) that 'psychical phenomena' have been studied by scientists, and (*b*) that they are miraculous, they violate natural law. God, therefore, exists: and further, there are adequate grounds for believing in human survival in 'a world essentially like our own.'

Review of Malcolm Grant, *A New Argument for God and Survival and a Solution to the Problem of Supernatural Events* (London: Faber and Faber, 1934). First published in *Cambridge Review*, 55 (1934), 332.

Now, for me at least, the most disappointing feature of the book is that the proof adduced of the existence of God is not new: it is, probably, the oldest and most naive of all the many arguments.

The only novelty here is the attempt to demonstrate the miraculous character of all psychical or occult phenomena; and this, besides being novel, appears to me misconceived. Miracles are defined as events which violate natural law; but, since Mr Grant's conception of 'natural laws' is somewhat vague and certainly antiquated, his proof of the existence of miracles will lack cogency for the modern scientist. It is impossible to attach any relevant meaning to the notion of an event which 'violates natural laws' when these laws are conceived as statistical generalizations. And further, a theological argument, conceived with the express intention of influencing religious belief, of helping men who 'look round in despair for some remedy to cure the age of its evils,' but which is confined to proving merely *that* a God exists, without worrying about what sort of a God he is, must surely be considered to be barking up the wrong tree.

Thirty-two

Civitas Dei

In this book Mr Lionel Curtis, like a modern Augustine, reviews the history of the world from 'the dawn of civilization' to the present day in search of a 'guiding principle in politics.' And the principle he enunciates is that the only stable and progressive form of community is a 'commonwealth,' the essence of a commonwealth being the acceptance of the decisions of the majority as binding and the willingness of each member to put the interests of others on a level with his own. 'A commonwealth is simply the sermon on the mount translated into political terms.' Hellas provides an example of this commonwealth 'in its miniature form,' Jesus expounded its principles, and 'the statesman who made self-government possible for areas wider than city-States was Edward I,' for he added 'the principle that electors can be bound by those they elect,' to 'the principle that majorities can bind minorities.' It remains now for 'national commonwealths' to learn to 'function as organs of one international commonwealth.' It would, of course, be foolish to expect anything critical or profound from such a review of the history of the world, and it must be said that the history here is chiefly of the most generalised and superficial kind. Many no doubt will find Mr Curtis' thesis attractive; few, if any, will find it novel. And, personally, I admire the courage displayed in this undertaking more than the judgment.

Review of Lionel Curtis, *Civitas Dei*, 3 vols. (London: Macmillan and Co., 1934; second revised edition 1950). First published in *Cambridge Review*, 55 (1934), 450.

Thirty-three

Natural Law and the Theory of Society

These two volumes contain a translation of that part of Gierke's great work, *Das Deutsche Genossenschaftsrecht*, which covers the period 1500 to 1800 and which deals, in the main, with the exponents of political and legal theories based upon an idea of Natural Law. They contain also a translation of a lecture by Troeltsch on *The Ideas of Natural Law and Humanity* and of three or four valuable pages from Gierke's work on Johannes Althasius, and a long Introduction to the whole by Professor Barker. And we must be grateful that the translator has given us not only Gierke's text, but his notes and bibliographies also, which take up the whole of the second volume.

Gierke as an historian of political and legal theories is an impressive writer. He is impressive first on account of his profound acquaintance with the vast mass of political writings which belong to this period between the Reformation and the French Revolution; and secondly, because of his lucid judgment, his power of classification and his ability to generalise felicitously about these writings.

He is a genuinely critical historian; and the period he deals with in this part of his work is one which must have intense interest for those whose business or pleasure it is to consider the history of political and legal ideas. The difficulty and the danger in composing a history of political ideas lies in the fact that it is almost impossible not to de-individualise the various writers who come under review. Each tends to be represented as an example (with, of course, certain peculiar traits) of a general idea or theory. It is all very well to say that Hobbes or Rousseau cannot be understood apart from the background of Natural Law theorists in which they appear to take their place; but it is no less important to hold on to the fact that, while

---

Review of Otto von Gierke, *Natural Law and the Theory of Society 1500 to 1800. Five subsections from Das deutsche Genossenschaftsrecht, vol. 4. With a lecture on 'The Ideas of Natural Law and Humanity'*, by Ernst Troeltsch, tr. and intro. Ernest Barker, 2 vols. (Cambridge: Cambridge University Press, 1934). First published in *Cambridge Review*, 56 (1934), 11–12.

a writer like Hobbes may reach conclusions which place him along with others in a 'school,' his reasons and arguments may be so unlike those of writers who appear to be of a similar persuasion that to think of him as a member of this 'school' may be seriously misleading. For what is significant is not so much a writer's conclusions and dicta as his reasons and arguments. 'Schools' of thought are classifications of beliefs, and these, where they cut across a classification of reasons for belief, must present us with an imperfect view. Gierke, so far as is possible, avoids the more pressing dangers which beset an historian of ideas: but it is not possible to avoid them altogether in a work of this kind. He has a deep understanding of the writers with whom he deals — with the possible exception of Rousseau — and it is only to be regretted that his history stops short at Kant; but for that he was not responsible.

But Gierke as a thinker is, I think, less impressive. Clear and vigorous in his historical writing, when he comes to expound his own theory of the reality of group personality he becomes vague and inconclusive. His writing is excellent when he is pointing out and analysing the individualistic foundation upon which the whole Natural Law theory of Society was constructed. But when he comes to put something better in its place his views do not impress us with the force of necessity, they lack the power of a fully thought out theory.

Professor Barker's Introduction (which may be read in conjunction with Maitland's well known introduction to his translation, published in 1900, of an earlier section of Gierke's work) is an excellent piece of work, which greatly adds to the value of these volumes.

His faculty of lucid and orderly exposition is seen here at its best; and the sections on the Law of Nature and the School of Historical Law, apart from their intrinsic value, are a great assistance to understanding what Gierke is writing about and its importance. In other parts of this Introduction Professor Barker considers and gives us his views upon two much-discussed topics — the relation of Society and the State, and the nature of group personality. It is impossible here to consider these views with the seriousness they deserve. But it may be remarked that in dealing with society and the state we are presented with a relationship between two separate entities, the one lying 'behind' or 'stretching outside' the other. 'Though the state ... has supervened, as it were, upon Society, Society still remains. If Society has turned itself into a legal association, it has not turned the whole of itself into that form.' There is a 'voluntary life' and 'voluntary activity,' and this is the 'material on which there is stamped the form of the state.' Now, these categories of matter and form, outside and inside, behind and before, prior and subsequent — which are not, perhaps, consistent with one another — are, I think, scarcely satisfactory: and they are relics of that 'individualism' in political theory which while it is explicitly fled from is often implicitly succumbed to. And the notion of the State taking up and directing a separable part of the life of Society corresponds closely to the seventeenth century notion that when man entered political society he surrendered, not the whole, but a part of his natural rights — and it is a notion from which Hobbes might have rescued us if we had listened to him. Our political theory, it seems, is still under the domination of the categories of these seventeenth century thinkers, categories which we all recognize to be unsatisfactory but which nobody has yet shown us how to replace. The theory of group personality which, after an extremely lucid exposition of the views of others, Professor Barker propounds, is not at first sight attractive. At least, it is not so to me. It is an attempt to appropriate what appears to him the best elements of other well-known theories, it is in the nature of a compromise. And it is to be doubted whether any theory can be satisfactory which is a compromise. The theory is too complicated to be dealt with here, but it turns upon the notion that the 'inner core of the legal personality of groups' is their 'purpose,' for this purpose is the one permanent element. But whether we are right to look for the essence of personality, in any sense, in some permanent core, seems to be doubtful. Professor Barker suggests, further, that legal personality, unlike psychological or moral personality, is a construction, not a datum; but that it is not on that account less real. But he would appear to be on dangerous ground when he says that psychological and moral personality are 'an immediate datum of perception and consciousness.' A better line of attack would, perhaps, be to take personality in all its forms as a 'mental construction', one form being not less 'artificial' than another.

The volumes are excellently produced and exceedingly free from typographical errors. Page 198 is numbered 189; and the page heading of pp. 177–197 differs for no apparent reason from that of pp. 163–175. But these are negligible imperfections in a notable and very successful production.

Thirty-four

Aspects of Dialectical Materialism

Dialectical Materialism is described by those who profess it as the official philosophy of modern Communism; and this at once indicates its unique character, and makes any fresh exposition of its principles a matter of some general interest. Professor Macmurray, in one of the essays which compose this attempt to expound once more the notions of Dialetical Materialism, says that 'there is something fundamental in the philosophy of Dialectical Materialism which distinguishes it from all other philosophical systems which I know, and which establishes a gulf between it and them.' But he understates the case: Dialectical Materialism has more than one characteristic peculiar to itself, and the idiosyncrasy of being an official philosophy is the most peculiar of them all. To anyone who has attended to the history of philosophy this claim to an official character must appear a little naïve; even an indiscretion, when we consider how often the 'reception' of a philosophy has been a symptom of its decay. An official religion, or an official art, perhaps; these are not absurd ideas: but a received and an official philosophy, surely this is a little too heroic. Yet Dialectical Materialism boasts an imprimatur: and its defenders will not hear of it being anything but a philosophy, *the* philosophy; they will not tolerate the suggestion that perhaps it would be better to describe it as a religious creed.

And this characteristic is not without implications. The reckless courage with which this philosophy is defended, the jealousy with which the teaching of its inspired Early Fathers, Marx and Engels, is guarded against change and contamination, the violence with which all competing prophets are hustled out, like profane hecklers at a political meeting, must make

---

Review of Hermann Levy, John Macmurray, Ralph Fox, Robert Page Arnot, John Desmond Bernal, and Edgar Frederick Carritt, *Aspects of Dialectical Materialism* (London: Watts and Co., 1934). First published in *Cambridge Review*, 56 (1934), 108–9. Reprinted in *The Cambridge Mind: Ninety Years of the Cambridge Review 1879–1969*, ed. E. Homberger and others (London: Jonathan Cape, 1970), 134–9, as 'Dialectical Materialism: An "Official Philosophy"'.

a mere thinker wonder whether his life is not after all too insipid, and a religious fanatic whether he can really be sincere, such is his moderation. It is remarkable how often in these essays a writer will turn aside from argument with the incantation, 'Let us quote the *Communist Manifesto* again' or, 'As Marx himself says.' Mr Bernal's essays might have been written by Engels himself; his exposition is not even fresh in parts, it is uniformly stale. Indeed, the reader is left with the impression that Marx is the only *thinker* who has ever handled this philosophy of Dialectical Materialism; the rest are humble servants of the message of this often ambiguous oracle. In the hands of its expositors Dialectical Materialism is like a theology turned into a gospel, and a gospel turned into a dogma.

It appears to be more necessary that we should believe than that we should understand, and more necessary that we should accept than that we should believe. And this, perhaps, is comprehensible; if one really believed that one was in possession of the truth, it might be difficult to avoid fanaticism. But a philosophy, at once official and fanatical! Is there no refuge from the preacher?

Besides these, Dialectical Materialism, has, I think, three other remarkable characteristics which, if they are not unique, are at least noticeably peculiar. First, it is a philosophy constructed, with the aid of certain borrowed philosophical ideas, by men who were as nearly devoid of the *anima naturaliter philosophica* as otherwise thoughtful and intelligent men could be. Mr Page Arnot, it is true, tells us that 'Marx was the greatest thinker of all time,' and Mr Bernal, that Marx 'was not, in contrast to the founders of most philosophical systems, an ignorant man'; but whatever his greatness and however profound his information, there is nothing in his writings to suggest that he possessed that peculiar, and in some ways lamentable, turn of mind which makes a philosopher.

And he certainly never inspired genuine philosophical thought in anyone else. Some of the authors of this book are, indeed, professional philosophers, but even these (with the exception of Mr Carritt) appear anxious to discard some of the most elementary principles of rational argument. In the main, however, these expositors are amateurs in this difficult and dangerous enterprise of managing philosophical ideas. Secondly, Dialectical Materialism is an esoteric philosophy. I suppose the tendency to make the rules of the game in the course of play is not uncommon in philosophy, and in so far as it prevails in any philosophy that philosophy becomes esoteric. And this tendency is present to a remarkable extent in Dialectical Materialism. It is difficult, moreover, for the detached reader of this, or any exposition of the principles of Dialectical Materialism not to become conscious of the existence of some hidden source of knowledge or inspiration which, if only he were privileged to share it, might make plain much that must otherwise remain obscure. He is, in fact, told that unless he is 'actively participating in the class struggle to-day,' he will certainly fail to understand. This philosophy is one for initiates only. And further, in the actual doctrine of Dialectical Materialism there is a remarkable esoteric flavour; like the 'philosophical' theologians of the seventeenth century, the expositors of this philosophy seem to move in a world composed of an unbroken system of subtle correspondences. The same rhythmic motion or 'dialectic' governs the history of man, the chemical composition and changes of the world, the properties of numbers and everything else. These writers pass from one region of existence to another to find everywhere the transition of Quantity into Quality, Opposites Interpenetrating, and the Negative being Negated. What happens in one place has its analogue in another; in Dialectical Materialism the primitive passion for analogy is almost unchecked, and the result is a mystical and esoteric philosophy which can be paralleled perhaps only in the writings of the alchemists.

And thirdly, what must already be apparent, Dialectical Materialism is a philosophy more hindered and obscured by jargon than any other in the whole history of misplaced human ingenuity. One of the more critical writers in this book, Mr Levy, remarks upon the 'almost mediaeval language' in which the laws of the Dialectic are described. And it is difficult to avoid the feeling, as one reads these expositions, that, whatever there is to be said for this philosophy, the language in which it is described and defended is hopelessly stilted and archaic. The quaint jargon of Dialectical Materialism is, of all the defects of this philosophy, the one which might most easily be remedied, and is the defect from the remedy of which it would, at the present time, derive the greatest possible benefit. But to relieve a philosophy of the incubus of a jargon and to make it live requires a thinker, and such is nowhere to be seen.

Unlike many expositions of Dialectical Materialism, this book contains two essays in which this philosophy is subjected to something like a critical examination; both Mr Levy and Mr Carritt possess something of the detachment of mind necessary in philosophical argument. But Mr Carritt, at least, does not remain unanswered; for the volume ends with some Notes in Reply to Mr Carritt's Paper, in which Mr Bernal reasserts the pure Marxian principles in the old, decayed jargon and with the old, heroic violence. It seems that it is impossible for an intelligent man to take exception to any of the principles of Dialectical Materialism, because, unavoidably, he will find that what he has been objecting to is not the true doctrine, but merely one of the numerous 'distortions' which the authentic philosophy has suffered at the hands of bourgeois writers who have strayed into the Communist camp. The Marxian principle appears to be not merely that he who is not for us is against us, but also that most of the writers who think they are orthodox have, through malice, inadvertence or ignorance, promulgated a false (that is heterodox) doctrine. *Intelligent* objection is impossible. It is not difficult to understand that a critical attitude to a religion or a political creed is something which may have to be discouraged or even forbidden, but that this attitude towards what represents itself as a philosophy should be discouraged is at once ridiculous and pathetic. And a philosophy, the followers of which spend most of their time and energy merely quarrelling about the meaning of what Marx wrote and said, is one which is difficult to take seriously. For Heaven's sake, the reader gasps, let us have a little more argument and a little less oracular assertion.

Dialectical Materialism is already notorious for the generalisations about the course of history which are imbedded in its doctrines. And more than one of these essays illustrates both the importance of these generalisations to his philosophy and the extreme danger of such an alliance between philosophy and history. The doctrine that every philosophy is conditioned by the general social and economic circumstances in which it is conceived and elaborated, and the doctrine that a 'true' philosophy is that which is most closely tied and tied most consciously to the circumstances of its generation, and consequently that Dialectical Materialism is the only 'true' philosophy to-day, naturally lead those who hold them to issue statements about the course of history. And indeed, this philosophy may be said to be actually based upon certain historical judgments and to stand or fall with this truth or falsehood of these judgments. We are told, for example, that 'the modern European problem is a material problem. At least from the time of the Renaissance, European humanity, as distinct from most other societies at other times in history and in other parts of the world, has had forced upon it for its special task for humanity the solution of the problem of economic production'; and that consequently 'materialism' is the 'proper starting place for philosophy under modern conditions'.

And yet, setting aside the confusion of thought which stands behind this notion of philosophy *conditioned* by economic and social circumstances, how vague and flimsy is this sort of historical judgment. Certainly some of Marx's most profound ideas are concerned with history, but none of these writers show either any considerable knowledge of the history of Western Europe or any grasp of how an historical problem should be tackled. A statement such as, 'if we consider the development of science we shall find that it falls into three successive stages,' if it is intended for an historical judgment, shows all the ineptitude and misconception which might be expected from a philosophaster when he turns to history. The analysis of an idea is substituted for a patient and detailed exploration of a period, and history in any true sense disappears. It is *possible*, of course, to analyse any considerable historical change into the three steps which the Dialectic presupposes, and perhaps it is possible also to find Quantity turning into

Quality, and the Negative being Negated, but if you think that in such an analysis you are providing a history, or a substitute for a history, of this change, you must be more than ordinarily foolish. The dialectical materialist would appear to know so much about history and the world in general without recourse to any real study of the facts of the case that it is not, perhaps, surprising that he should treat these facts with some contempt. After all, his business is merely to illustrate his general theory by finding it everywhere exemplified in the world, and in that he can scarcely fail.

This reiteration of the principles of dialectical materialism, then, leaves us with the impression that it is impossible to say anything about them which is at once new and true; it is neither possible nor necessary to do anything but repeat what Marx and Engels wrote. The philosophy is full of ingenious ideas, and imbedded in it are some profound and illuminating *aperçus*; but the whole temper and attitude of its followers is so unphilosophical, so rigid, certain, and insensitive, and its doctrines are so full of half-considered information and so devoid of thought, that it must be supposed that the best there is to be said for it remains yet unsaid. Unless it can escape from this temper, from the tendency to descend from argument to authority, from the antiquated jargon in which it is expressed, from the inclination to indulge in the wildest exaggerations, and from certain obvious but disabling errors in its most flourished doctrines, it will never become a philosophical system worth considering. It will remain the creed of a body of men who, not content with doing what they believe will bring the greatest possible benefit to mankind, and regardless of their incapacity, are moved by a fatal urge to construct a theory to explain and justify their activities.

Thirty-five

Adventures of Ideas

This book may be regarded as a fresh attempt to restate the main outlines of Prof. Whitehead's position. It is a companion to *Science and the Modern World* and *Process and Reality*. Besides some new ideas and some fresh approaches, it contains an amplification and extension of much to be found in the earlier of these books, and a *résumé* of the doctrine expounded in the later. It is divided into four parts—Sociological, Cosmological, Philosophical, and Civilization: and, in general, it is 'a study of the concept of civilization, and an endeavour to understand how it is that civilized beings arise'. It is impossible to describe the contents in detail, partly on account of what appears to me the obscurity of many of the ideas themselves, and partly because of the obscurity of the connexions between the ideas; the reader is hurried from one idea to another, dazzled by flashes of brilliance, distracted by obscurity, or put out of patience by verbiage, and the connexions are left to look after themselves. But I propose to make a few remarks upon each of these sections.

(i) *Sociological*. This seems to be included as a kind of sketch of history of the 'European races' from the standpoint of the concept of civilization. But Prof. Whitehead's method of writing history is peculiar. He begins by selecting some general characteristic of Western European civilization, and he proceeds to trace back the evolution of this characteristic. History consists in the realization of ideas, the translation of ideas into customs, the issuing of 'general ideas into practical consequences'. One such idea is that of freedom: the 'abolition of Slavery' in 1833 is seen as the 'practical consequence' of Socrates's discovery of the human soul. 'Two thousand years had elapsed since the foundation of Plato's academy, since the reforms of the Stoic lawyers, since the composition of the Gospels. The great programme of reform bequeathed by the classical civilization was achieving another triumph.' And this general view of history is consis-

---

Review of Alfred North Whitehead, *Adventures of Ideas* (Cambridge: Cambridge University Press, 1933). First published in *Journal of Theological Studies*, 35 (1934), 73–5.

tently adhered to: history consists of the 'adventures' of abstract general ideas. But it is one thing to analyse an epoch, or a civilization such as ours into general ideas and to analyse the ideas themselves, and it is another to present these abstract ideas as if they were separate and operative (implicitly or explicitly) in the epoch itself or in the growth of the civilization. And the second of these projects is certainly misconceived. If we are to have a history of the growth of freedom, we shall want something more than the mere reference of each positive achievement of freedom to the working of an abstract and general idea. We shall want a detailed account of the course of events. And this is what we are never given. And in spite of much brilliant analysis, Prof. Whitehead's history (if that is what it is intended to be) appears to me to be unsound in conception. To the ordinary historian, the exploits and adventures of these ideas will appear little more than fabulous.

(ii) *Cosmological*. In this section the ideas whose adventures are described are of a different character; they are not sociological, but scientific ideas. The subject here is 'the influence of scientific ideas upon European culture'. It opens with a brilliant chapter called 'Laws of Nature'. But readers of Prof. Whitehead must be prepared not only for these flashes of brilliance, but also for what is obscure and even for what is commonplace. And the chapters on 'Science and Philosophy' and on the 'New Reformation' which follow, do not sustain the brilliant opening. It is, I think, impossible to discover what he thinks about the relation of science to philosophy; and in spite of some good remarks on the importance of theology, his reflexions on Christianity are not very striking. But what is more disappointing is that the main subject of the section—the influence of scientific ideas upon European civilization—seems to have been conceived with peculiar narrowness. The final question—what is the relevance of a scientific view of the world to practical living?—not only is not answered, but is not even considered. The influence of various scientific ideas is discussed but never the influence of the idea of science itself.

(iii) *Philosophical*. This section is, in the main, a *résumé* of Prof. Whitehead's philosophical doctrine. It is brief and concise; but since I do not understand it, there is nothing I can usefully say about it. It appears, however, to contain little that is not more fully discussed in *Process and Reality*: and it is relevant in this place mainly because this book is intended to be equally a record of the author's own adventures in ideas and of the adventures of ideas in the history of European civilization.

(iv) *Civilization*. The main ideas which here come in for analysis—qualities which go to form civilization—are Truth, Beauty, Art, Adventure, and Peace. The chapters on Truth and Beauty are to me obscure and I cannot be certain of their meaning. They are 'philosophical' chapters. But the chapter on Adventure, while it is devoted to an exposition of the rather commonplace theme that 'no static maintenance of perfection is possible ... Advance or Decadence are the only choices offered to mankind', contains, as usual, some penetrating observations. In the last chapter, however, entitled 'Peace,' Prof. Whitehead discusses the quality which, above all others, he takes to be characteristic of civilization. And here, in spite of obscurity, there is what appears to be a profound idea. Peace 'is not the negative conception of anaesthesia. It is a positive feeling which crowns the life and motion of the soul ... It is not a hope for the future, nor is it an interest in present details'. So far as I understand it, it is a kind of reconciliation to mortality, a feeling of permanence in transience, either reached after frustration and pain or seized intuitively in youth. Such a notion is not, of course, new; something corresponding to it is to be found in the doctrine of every profound moralist. But certainly there is here a brilliant analysis of the idea.

What may be said of most of Prof. Whitehead's books may, I think, be said of this one. It is an attempt to work out something in the way of a world-view; it is marred by much obscurity, vagueness, and disconnectedness, sometimes quite simple and commonplace ideas are put into rather pretentious language and (in the language at least) there is a tendency to a kind of American (or Anglo-Saxon) sentimentality; but it contains some profoundly thought-out ideas and many brilliant *aperçus*.

Thirty-six

The Horizon of Experience

The venturesome project of this book is a study of the 'modern mind'. The idea is that 'the "modern" attitude towards the world is mainly a sense that on the horizon of our present experience are new forms of truth and beauty'; and in this respect the twentieth century is said to resemble the sixth and the sixteenth. 'We stand between a traditional formulation which is inadequate to express our new experience and the possibility of some other formulation whose character is unknown to us ... The modern mind is fundamentally an impulse towards new values.' With this general (and perhaps a little worn) thesis in view, Mr Delisle Burns proceeds to an account of modern tendencies in science, art, literature, morality, religion, and philosophy. His reflections are, however, often tiresome and never profound. We are told that there is 'a deep sense of unrest, dissatisfaction' in modern literature; that the new experiments in music 'may have come too soon'; and that the poetry of T.S. Eliot 'is certainly not like Tennyson's'. But what I think is a more serious defect is that, while professing to be genuinely up to date, Mr Burns seems to be thirty (or more) years behind the times. This faith in progress, the belief that we are at the fresh dawn of a new era, this sense of horizon, and these philosophies of process and evolution, which are here taken to represent the 'modern' attitude, are not in fact modern at all. They may be better than anything we have today, but they belong, nevertheless, to the last century. What has taken their place is difficult to say, and it is unfortunate that there is nothing in this book to help us to identify it.

Review of Cecil Delisle Burns, *The Horizon of Experience. A Study of the Modern Mind* (London: Allen and Unwin, 1933). First published in *Journal of Theological Studies*, 35 (1934), 75–6.

Thirty-seven

Richard Hooker als politischer Denker

This short but thorough study of Hooker's political thought is an attempt to answer two questions. First, what is the character of Hooker's political theory, and how far was it original? And secondly, what influence had Hooker, as a political thinker, upon seventeenth-century English writers? About two-thirds of the book is devoted to the first question. A full and excellent account is given of Hooker's general conception of Law, his theory of society and of Church and State; and his relationship with earlier writers, especially Machiavelli and Bodin, is discussed. In the second part Hooker's influence upon Milton, Hobbes, Sidney, Locke, and various less well-known writers is examined and found to be considerable, even where (as in the case of Hobbes) there is little in common between the conclusions of the two thinkers. Altogether it is an admirable piece of work. The author keeps severely to the matter in hand, he is not concerned with Hooker's theology, and writes with brevity, precision, and lucidity.

Review of Gottfried Michaelis, *Richard Hooker als politischer Denker. Ein Beitrag zur Geschichte der naturrechtlichen Staatstheorien in England im 16. und 17. Jahrhundert* (Berlin: Verlag Dr Emil Ebering, 1933). First published in *Journal of Theological Studies*, 35 (1934), 76.

Thirty-eight

Thomas Hobbes

The story of the fortunes of Hobbes and his writings is not remarkable. He was attacked by his contemporaries with a ferocity which reflects not only their sense of outrage but also their sense of danger; his writings were rejected, not because they were bad philosophy, but because they were thought to have dangerous tendencies; his doctrines, or many of them, were then appropriated by other writers, their authorship first unacknowledged and then forgotten; his name began to appear in the works which passed for histories of philosophy, but only his name; towards the end of the nineteenth century there was a revival of interest in the man and his philosophy, a scholar's revival and part of a general revival of interest in the past of English philosophy, bringing with it, not only some of the best studies of Hobbes's writings (e.g. those of Tönnies and Robertson), discoveries of unpublished MSS, and a collected edition of his works, but also the beginning of what is called 'Hobbes research'; and then, quite recently, there was the discovery that Hobbes had a message for to-day, and with this discovery came a flood of fresh literature and the foundation, in 1929 after an international congress in Oxford, of a Hobbes Society. It is a common, if slightly sordid, history; and perhaps it is difficult to determine which part of it is the more sordid, the death or the exhumation. Side by side with the story, however, must be put another, not so long, but less inglorious: the story of his actual influence upon philosophical speculation, for it would be safe to say that he was never without readers. Leibniz admired his profundity; in spite of the dominating figure of Locke, Diderot, at least among the *Encylopédistes*, recognized his master, and Rousseau his creditor; Hegel, in a few brilliant pages in his *Geschichte der Philosophie*, appreciated his genius: he was the acknowledged father, in modern times, of English and German materialism; and his place in the Saints' Calendar of Rationalism was never disputed, though there is little or no evidence to support the view that Hobbes was a pioneer of Natural Religion and Rational Theology. As is so often the case, Hobbes was more

First published in *Scrutiny*, 4 (1935), 263–77.

profoundly appreciated by those who were content to read his writings than by those whose attention was directed to raising a public memorial to him.

The purpose of this article, however, is not to review the fortunes of Hobbes's philosophy, but to consider this contemporary interest in Hobbes and to consider the quality and effect of some of the more recent studies of his work. And in what I have to say I shall confine myself to the publications of the last ten years.[1] The questions I want to ask are, What have we learnt? and, What have we still to learn?

There are certain elements in the contemporary interest in Hobbes's writings which, since Hobbes is a philosopher, I should regard as unhealthy. In the first place, we are met with the suggestion that Hobbes is a writer whose work is peculiarly apposite to the post-war world. 'Hobbes's philosophy,' we are told, 'possessed precisely that character of balance and common sense that made him foresee the Great War, and, furthermore, the subsequent striving for peace resulting from a comprehension of the disastrous consequences of hate and murder. A number of scholars emphasized the fact that the present pacifist movement fulfils the dreams of this great enemy of war.' Now, this attitude towards the writings of such a man as Hobbes is, to say the least, both dangerous and unprofitable, because it directs our attention towards all that is most superficial and least significant in those writings. Every man, I suppose, has his political opinions, and sometimes they are opinions which will interest and inspire ages other than his own. But a political philosopher has something more, and more significant, than political opinions: he has an analysis of political activity, a comprehensive view of the nature of political life, and it is this, and not his political opinions, which it is profitable for a later and different age to study. And if it is contended that these political opinions belong themselves to that analysis, it must, nevertheless, remain a mistake to lift a few of them out of the system of his thought and give them an independent existence just because when regarded in this way they seem to meet present needs. And were we content to go back to Hobbes's writings and enquire what he means by 'war' (for example), we

---

[1] I have selected the following books, pamphlets, and articles: Ferdinand Tönnies, *Thomas Hobbes, Leben und Lehre*, 3rd edition (Stuttgart: Frommann, 1925); Frithiof Brandt, *Thomas Hobbes' Mechanical Conception of Nature* (Copenhagen: Levin and Munksgaard, 1928); Adolfo Levi, *La Filosofia di Tommaso Hobbes* (Milan: Società editirice Dante Alighieri, 1929); Zbigniew Lubienski, *Die Grundlagen des ethisch-politischen Systems von Hobbes* (Munich: Ernst Reinhardt, 1932); Heinrich Schreihager, *Thomas Hobbes' Sozialtheorie* (Leipzig: Institut für Politik, auständisches öffentliches Recht und Völkerrecht, 1933); John Laird, *Hobbes* (London: Benn, 1934); Karl Schmitt, *Politische Theologie* (Munich and Berlin: Duncker and Humblot, 1934); Otto von Gierke, *Natural Law and the Theory of Society*, tr. Barker (Cambridge: Cambridge University Press, 1934); Basil Willey, *The Seventeenth Century Background* (London: Chatto and Windus, 1934); Edgar Frederick Carritt, *Morals and Politics* (Oxford: Clarendon Press, 1935); Phyllis Doyle, 'The Contemporary Background of Hobbes' State of Nature', *Economica*, 21 (1927), 336-55; Zbigniew Lubienski, 'Hobbes' Philosophy and its Historical Background', *Journal of Philosophical Studies*, 5 (1930), 175-90; Leo Strauss, 'Quelques Remarques sur la Science Politique de Hobbes', *Recherches Philosophique*, 2 (1932), 609-22.

could scarcely avoid the conclusion that from this (in any case superficial) standpoint his views are no more significant at the present time than at any other moment in the history of mankind. I mean, briefly, that, in general, the only healthy attitude towards the writings of a philosopher is a philosophical attitude. Of course it is possible to take snippets from the writings of any man and use them as texts for a sermon; but do not let us confuse this with a study of his works or even with a genuine attempt to discover the present significance of those works.

But this attitude towards philosophical writing is to be found in a more radical form in some of the recent treatments of Hobbes's philosophy. There is not merely the suggestion that the significant meaning of his work lies in a few of his less impressive remarks, but the suggestion that, in the ordinary sense, his writing has no meaning at all. 'Metaphysical utterances which appear to be statements of "fact" are disguised imperatives, or at least disguised optatives; our studies of the philosophers would be more remunerative if we went to them, not for "truth", but in order to discern what particular *fiat* or *utinam* their teaching implies', writes Mr Basil Willey. And he follows it up with the remark that 'very nearly every statement of Hobbes can be reduced either to hatred and contempt of schoolmen and clerics, or to fear of civil war and love of ordered living in a stable commonwealth.' Now, that words have an emotive as well as a referential use has, of course, been known long enough; it was recognized by Hobbes himself, for example (*Leviathan*, p. 525). But it appears to have been reserved for more modern times to resolve all language into emotive symbols; and this resolution, involving a self-contradiction and carrying with it a philosophy of misology (if the phrase may pass), makes, I think, an unsatisfactory foundation upon which to base our study of a philosophic writer. And when we pass from the general view to the particular illustration, the unprofitableness of this view no longer remains in any doubt: it is difficult to understand how anyone who had considered Hobbes's writings could consent to (much less suggest) this absurd 'reduction'; it is not even plausible. All the complexity of Hobbes's thought is swept aside as irrelevant; what cannot be reduced to hate or fear is not Hobbes. I suppose it is impossible to prevent a misological critic from exercising his wits upon the writings of Hobbes, and something interesting may come of it in the end; but what comes of it will never be a satisfactory interpretation of Hobbes's meaning. And from anyone who undertakes a *tour de force* of this kind we may perhaps ask for something more brilliant. Certainly 'it is salutary to remind ourselves that in the *Leviathan* Hobbes has a "suasive" purpose', but to find nothing but this in the *Leviathan*, and to conclude from our reading that 'almost in Chinese fashion, he is bringing doctrines to a pragmatic test. Do they or do they not make for the maintenance of lawful authority? he is asking,' suggests that a closer attention might be given to the text. That philosophers often entertain ambitions extraneous to philosophy is known well enough, and that some of them appear to be unable to prevent these ambitions from contaminating their writings is a sad fact; but to select one of these extraneous purposes — that of the preacher — as the significant characteristic of a piece of philosophic writing appears to me to indicate a misconceived approach to the study of philosophy, and the result is likely to be anything but remunerative.

Now, if the philosophical study of a philosophy excludes this kind of attitude, it does not exclude what may be called a genuinely historical attitude. The detailed consideration of the actual meaning of a philosophical text, regardless of its present significance or of any view we may hold about the truth or error it contains, is certainly valuable; and, as we shall see, some of the best recent work on Hobbes is of this character. Hobbes, in the past, has suffered from a deficiency rather than an excess of this kind of study. There are now plenty of excellent biographies, not a few good expositions of the general outline of his system, and some interesting studies of his connexion with earlier and later thought; what we need is more of those detailed, and at least partly historical, studies and interpretations of his work. But the philosophical study of philosophy does, I think, exclude what may be called a *merely* historical study. There is, probably, less place for a merely antiquarian interest in philosophy than elsewhere; for what elsewhere is merely harmless and at worst an eccentricity, in philosophy becomes dangerous and positively misleading. There will always be new philosophy, and what is new may be valuable even if it is inferior to what we have already. It is the business of philosophy continuously to renew itself. And such new philosophy may arise from the study of what belongs to an earlier time; and the study of what belongs to an earlier time is profitable, in the end, only when it is related to a genuine renaissance. But the study, if it is to result in anything valuable, must be close: it is only by this detailed study of a philosophical text that it can become, not merely an inheritance, but an inspiration for fresh thought. Whether Hobbes's writings, when studied in this way, can ever yield the philosophical inspiration which has come from (for example) either Plato or Spinoza, is a question which admits of considerable doubt; but, in any case, it cannot be answered in advance, and the attempt (if it attracts us) is worth making.[2]

Setting on one side, then, these wilder and more wilful treatments of the philosophy of Hobbes, let us consider what we have got from our less speculative investments. Perhaps the most remarkable of our acquisi-

---

[2] In at least one respect Professor Laird appears to incline to the opinion that Hobbes can never be a source of philosophical inspiration of this kind. He writes, 'we should probably be wiser if we regarded him, not as a living influence, but as voice from the past whose clarity and incisiveness in a host of particular questions is a perpetual refreshment and a persistent incitement to the unthinking of many prejudices and to the rethinking of moral theory.' (op. cit. p. 289.)

tions – remarkable because it now appears odd that we should have had to wait so long for it – is a surer grasp of the connexion between Hobbes and the philosophy, particularly the political philosophy, of the Middle Ages. And perhaps this may be regarded as just one more detail in the mass of evidence that has now been accumulated to support the view that the revolution in politics, religion, and philosophy which was believed to have taken place during the seventeenth century has (at any rate as regards its speed and comprehensiveness) been grossly exaggerated. It is surprising now to turn back to those older studies of Hobbes and find him coupled with Bacon; and to have got rid of this misunderstanding puts us on the high road to a truer interpretation of his system as a whole. Perhaps we were misled by Hobbes's polemics against the schoolmen and by his personal connexion with Bacon into this belief that he was a writer who owed little or nothing to the Middle Ages and that he might be placed among the forerunners of modern science. But, whatever the cause of the error, it may now be said to have perished finally. And Professor Laird's recent book does more than record the death of this misconception; it has the great merit of providing an interpretation of Hobbes's work which recognizes the implications of this change of view. In an age when philosophy was giving way at every point to science, Hobbes stood firm: he had probably less patience or sympathy for experimental science than for anything else in the world – not excluding the Pope. In detail he rejected the whole of the scholastic view, and he was among the first to subject that view to a thorough-going criticism. And of all his contemporaries Galileo seems to have had greatest influence upon him. But his conception of the nature of philosophy and of philosophical argument was much more nearly related to that of Scholasticism than to the view of Bacon and his successors. Indeed, Hobbes was much too shrewd a thinker to reject as completely as he pretended to reject, without discrimination or consideration, the whole legacy of the scholastic philosophy. He was acutely aware of its weakness, but he knew it to be, in part at least, a genuine philosophy; and the expressions of hostility towards it which he allows himself arise, mainly, from an extraneous, non-philosophical interest and, if anything is to be neglected, must be neglected by a true interpretation of his work. Writing of Hobbes's immediate predecessors, Professor Laird remarks that 'every one of these authors would have admitted that Hobbes had played his hand without revoking. And the game that they all played had also been played by Hildebrand, Aquinas, Gerson, Occam and Calvin – old-fashioned players, no doubt, but players who always knew how many trumps were out.' And he concludes that however startling Hobbian novelties may be, they are nevertheless 'the moves of a master player who knew and kept to the medieval rules.' And how great a revolution this view constitutes in an interpretation of Hobbes's philosophy is known to those who have been brought up on earlier expositions.

Something of the same kind of revolution has taken place, also, in our ideas about the relation of Hobbes and Aristotle. Like Bacon, Hobbes regarded Aristotle as a dead hand in philosophy, paralysing thought and inhibiting further advance; and nobody was more fierce than Hobbes in his belief that, wherever else authority had place, mere authority had no place at all in philosophy. But here, again, we may easily be misled by Hobbes's truculence; the 'Vain Philosophy of Aristotle' taught him more than he ever admitted. The doctrines of the *Metaphysics*, the *Ethics* and the *Politics*, it is true, influenced him little; but I think a closer study would show that he took more than he ever cared to acknowledge from the Rhetoric. Of all the writings of Aristotle, the *Rhetoric* was the one which Hobbes had studied most profoundly, and many of its doctrines entered deeply into his philosophy.

The recent studies of Hobbes's writings, then, return a more discriminating answer than hitherto to the question, What is new in Hobbes? Our knowledge is greater, and our prejudice is less than that which earlier writers enjoyed and suffered from. We are no longer pledged to find in these writings nothing but the gospel of modern materialism; and we know that even if that is still to be found, the philosophy of Hobbes is in the nature of a palimpsest. And, if there is danger ahead, it lies in the exaggeration of the, at least, semi-medieval portrait with which this recent work presents us. For there can be no doubt that Hobbes's writings do represent a profound revolution in European thought, there can be no doubt that he was one of the most original of philosophers; and our task now is to determine the relevance of the new setting into which his writings have been put.

When we turn to consider, not merely what we have learnt during the last ten years from these general treatments of Hobbes's philosophy, but whether these years have produced any significant addition to our detailed knowledge of his writings, we have to record Professor Brandt's *Thomas Hobbes' Mechanical Conception of Nature*, perhaps the most important study of these writings which has yet appeared. Originally published in Danish in 1921, and translated into English in 1928, this volume is one of those detailed examinations of philosophical texts which are more valuable than all the handbooks and general expositions of Hobbes's philosophy that have ever been written. The programme of the work is set in its preface: 'This book proposes to show how the mechanical view of nature shaped itself to Thomas Hobbes. Strange as it may appear, this problem has never been treated in detail. As soon as we leave the province of more general considerations and seek detailed information, we are as a rule left in the lurch by the Hobbes literature which, as it is, is not very abundant. It is not only that a really critical account of Hobbes's natural philosophical main work *De Corpore* is still lacking, though some few points have been elucidated, but Hobbes's natural philosophical process of development is as yet nebulous. Enquirers have chiefly studied the main work which Hobbes published in his sixty-seventh year, but have almost entirely ignored the long process of development that must have preceded it.' We have here, then, an elaborate and detailed study of the development of a man's ideas. The questions asked are, 'What did Hobbes actually mean when he said that everything must be explained mechanically? Why did he think so? And, How did he arrive at this mechanical point of view?' And in answering them many subsidiary points have to be decided. The chronology of Hobbes's early writings presents difficulties; and in a writer apparently so independent as Hobbes, his relation to, and obligation to, Descartes, Mersenne, and Galileo is not easy to determine. Having settled these and other preliminary questions, Professor Brandt goes on to distinguish two periods in the development of Hobbes's natural philosophy; the earlier, 1630 to 1641, in which doctrines (many of them recognizably Aristotelian) were propounded which were later to be rejected; and the later, 1641 to 1655, in which the view of the *De Corpore* (published in 1655) was matured. And the work concludes with an elaborate examination of the *De Corpore* itself.

It will be thought, perhaps, that an enquiry of this sort into the minutiae of a dead philosophy is a profitless undertaking, or that it must compare unfavourably with more imaginative and less meticulous experiments in philosophical interpretation. Indeed, this may be expected to be the view of those intent upon the construction of a philosophy for themselves. But even they, if such were their view, would be wrong. If we are to read philosophy at all, we must read it with care and take the pains necessary for its understanding; and the exceptional value of Professor Brandt's work lies in the thoroughness with which it covers his subject. It may be remarked also that his formulation of the questions to be answered, and his whole conception of the business in hand, give a very fair guarantee of the usefulness of his conclusions. For what we must know about a philosopher, if we are to understand his philosophy, is not merely *what* he thought, but also *why* he thought it. Indeed, in philosophy, this *what* and this *why* are inseparable; taken apart each loses its meaning. In politics, in religion, in practical life it is not always necessary to enquire into a man's reasons for thinking as he does; but in philosophy these reasons are what give meaning to his conclusions; and it is, perhaps, on account of this that mankind in general must be so little interested in philosophy, and so little understand it, as always to wish to assimilate it to what can more easily be appreciated by neglecting this characteristic. Agreement between two men, in some fields, may be significant even if it be merely agreement about what is to be done, agreement about a conclusion; but in philosophy such agreement has no significance whatever; no two philosophers can be said to agree unless their conclusions and their reasons for those conclusions alike coincide. And it is particularly necessary in the case of Hobbes to enquire into the reasons he gives for his views, because he has, in the past, suffered greatly at the hands of expositors who are content to press the similarity of some of his views with those (for example) of Bodin, or even Machiavelli, and neglect altogether the dissimilarity of reason which lies behind it. And even the much advertised similarity between Hobbes and Spinoza almost disappears when their doctrines are closely examined. Hobbes's originality consists almost wholly in the reasons he gives for his conclusions, and a true interpretation of his work is impossible unless these are considered with the greatest care.

Now, if these are the most outstanding results of the study to which, during the last ten years, the writings of Hobbes have been subjected, there are also some important acquisitions of a more detailed character. Ten years ago it was possible for Vaughan[3] to write as if Hobbes was something other than the most profoundly philosophical individualist in the history of political theory, to write as if he were to be classed among those whose views must be rejected by the liberal tradition, as if his philosophy were a reaction against the individualism of his time, to assert even that Hobbes is 'the deadliest enemy of individualism.' And this false interpretation is no longer possible: Hobbes, we can now see, had more of the ground of liberalism in him than even Locke. I think that the true nature of Hobbes's individualism has yet to find its expositor, we have still to wait for the interpreter who will show us that this individualism is based, not upon any foundation in moral opinion at all, but upon a theory of knowledge, upon a thorough-going nominalism and an almost as extreme solipsism. But the progress which has been made in this direction is already enough to indicate the extent of the error involved in these earlier views. And again, it was long customary to expound Hobbes's political philosophy as a philosophy of Fear; this for example is what it is represented to be by Vaughan. But a closer study of the writings has shown that Pride, and not Fear, is the master-conception of this political philosophy. But here, also, we have still to ascertain the full implication of this revised view. And lastly, although it is (unfortunately) still possible for writers to simulate the grotesque moral indignation to which both Vaughan and Figgis are apt to abandon themselves, we may fairly be said, during the past ten years, to have outgrown this kind of absurdity. Hobbes, it has been said, 'put truth under the heel of policy' and 'dragged religion under the Juggernaut car of reason of state'; and his theory has been described as 'one of unadulterated despotism or nothing.' But these misconceptions, arising from a failure to

---

[3]   In *Studies in the History of Political Philosophy*, 1 (1925).

make elementary distinctions and from a fatal ignorance with regard to the foundations upon which Hobbes's views are based, are fast becoming errors of the past. And we may now find even an otherwise not profoundly instructed writer willing to distinguish between absolutism and sovereignty, and thus remove from the exposition of Hobbes's political philosophy a longstanding misrepresentation paralleled only in its foolishness by the confusion of absolutism and the Absolute which used to disfigure the interpretations of Hegel.

The misunderstandings of the philosophy of Hobbes which the work of the last ten years has removed are, in the main, misunderstandings due to ignorance. And if we turn to inquire, What remains to be done? the answer must be that we have yet to remove many misunderstandings due to lack of insight. 'Research' will never take the place of thought; and what Hobbes's philosophy stands in need of is a more profound consideration.

The student of Hobbes's philosophy is faced with an initial difficulty which requires to be met, not merely with patience, but with faith — I mean the difficulty of believing that Hobbes really means what he appears to say. For what he says is so unlike what is commonly said, and appears at first sight to be so extravagant, that the reader is inclined to exclaim, what Hobbes himself is said to have exclaimed on being presented with the proof of the forty-seventh theorem in Euclid's *Elements* — 'By God, this is impossible.' And some readers, so impressed with the impossibility of what Hobbes says, conclude that he meant something other than what he appears to mean, and make of his philosophy something more commonplace than it in fact is. Hobbes, we have to remember, is, of English philosophers, the one possessed of the greatest measure of philosophical imagination; and so comparatively rare is this in English philosophical writing, that we may almost be forgiven for failing to appreciate it in Hobbes. English philosophical writers are not, generally speaking, given to the construction of systems; and this abstinence is both the strength and the weakness of English philosophy. But Hobbes did construct a system, a complete and comprehensive view of the universe; and he conceived this system with such imaginative power that, in spite of its relatively simple character, it stands comparison with even the grand and imposing creation of Hegel.

And further, he had the capacity, the patience, and the opportunity to elaborate the details of this system so thoroughly that, whatever its imperfections, it cannot be said to have been imperfectly imagined or imperfectly elaborated. But if the power of philosophical imagination, a power possessed by only the greatest philosophers, is one Hobbes's most remarkable qualities, it is also the source of some of the more obvious defects of his philosophical writing. For his imaginative propensities are not confined to the conception of a comprehensive theory, they penetrate also the form of his exposition and his diction. To think in metaphors and not to restrain one's fancy must always be defects in a philosopher; and Hobbes, while complaining of these faults in others, suffered from them himself. In Hobbes's writing is exemplified both the virtue and the danger of philosophical imagination; he is an imaginative thinker, but also an imaginative writer. And it is not only the imaginative grasp of Hobbes's philosophical thinking which make it remarkable in the history of English philosophy: it has another equally unexpected quality. Radicalism, extravagance, the intrepid following out of a theory conceived in the grand manner and the absence of any sign of alarm, dismay, or compromise, are not qualities often to be found in English thinkers; but they flourish in Hobbes almost unchecked. As a nation we are more easily alarmed at the creations of our intellectual than at those of our practical activity; and we do not require to be persuaded that truth and moderation live in the same street, we believe it on instinct. But Hobbes appears never to have been even tempted to make his conclusions more moderate than he found them; and compromise and fear had no place in his intellectual character. And on account of this, also, Hobbes's writings are sometimes as difficult to credit as they are to believe. But it is as foolish to doubt that a writer means what he writes as it is insulting to doubt that a companion means what he says. And if we are to interpret Hobbes correctly, we must avoid this mistake. There are, of course, writers who do not know what they mean, but Hobbes certainly is not among these.

Now, if our insight into the meaning of Hobbes's philosophy is hindered by this initial difficulty of crediting its doctrines, it is apt to be restricted by a failure to appreciate the fact that this system is a philosophy. We are content to take its doctrines separately and are reluctant to follow Hobbes back to the foundation of his thought: we find embedded in its superstructure ideas with which we think ourselves familiar and, ignorant of what lies underneath, we do not question that familiarity. And bringing with us a somewhat different notion of what philosophy is from that which Hobbes himself entertained, we fail to adjust our expectations to what is offered us and consequently end by misinterpreting it. Let us consider briefly three examples of the restricted insight into Hobbes's philosophy which arises from this failure to appreciate its philosophical character.

It is often said that in Hobbes's view human nature is essentially selfish; and this doctrine of the selfishness of man is represented as the foundation upon which he builds his social and political philosophy, as the premiss of his reasoning. And it is suggested also that it is in his premisses, and not in his reasoning, that his error lies. But when we turn to what Hobbes actually wrote, and treat it as a systematic whole, we find that the essential selfishness of man is not, in Hobbes, a premiss, but (if the doctrine is to be found anywhere) is a conclusion, the result of a long and complicated argument. His premiss is a doctrine of solipsism, a belief in the essential isolation of men from one another, and expounded as a theory of knowledge. This isolation, it is true, is modified by 'the most noble and profitable invention of all other', speech; but it remains a merely artificial modification. And when this genuine premiss of Hobbes's argument is appreciated, the attribution to him of the doctrine of the essential selfishness of man is seen at once to be mistaken. Others have held an egoistic view of human nature, and have based that view upon their observation of human behaviour; but no such argument is to be found in Hobbes. His doctrine is that each man is unavoidably shut up within the world of his own sensations; and there is no more meaning in speaking of him as 'selfish' than there is in speaking of anything else that is monadically conceived as selfish — the universe as a whole, or an electron. Here also the reason for belief conditions the character of what is believed.

Again, Hobbes's doctrine of authority has suffered from its being isolated from the system of his thought. But here also Hobbes's argument begins not from a view of the *moral* character of man as so many theories of authority begin, or from insight into contemporary political needs, but from a view of the nature of man merely as an experiencing being. Hobbes's theory of law and government has, indeed, no ethical foundation, in the ordinary sense; but it is conceived throughout in purely naturalistic terms, and begins in the theory of language. The creation of language and the establishment of the state are, for Hobbes, inventions of the same character and serve the same end. The necessity of an absolute sovereign in the community arises not from any such subsidiary observation as the misery of mankind without it, but is a necessity exactly paralleled by the necessity of fixing the meanings of names if language is to serve any useful purpose at all. Hobbes's belief in the necessity of a single decisive authority does not arise from his political fears, and he does not think of this authority as a practical expedient; it is conceived and presented by Hobbes as a logical necessity. Pascal said, '*Lorsqu'on ne sait pas la vérité d'une chose, il est bon qu'il y ait une erreur commune qui fixe l'esprit des hommes*'; Hobbes asserts that there is never anything but a common error, that truth itself is a common error, and that since what is important is that it should be genuinely common, it must be fixed by authority. A language which is understood by only a single person and a way of behaviour which is pursued by one man independently of all other men are, for Hobbes, examples of the same kind of anarchy. And as authority alone can put an end to anarchy in the one case, authority alone can put an end to it in the other. For what is remarkable in Hobbes's doctrine of authority, and what on any other interpretation appears as a mere contradiction, is that it finds no place whatever for authority except in the control of men's actions. Both the intellect and the conscience are excluded from its control, and they are excluded because when a man is by himself, when he is speaking to himself, it is not necessary that the language he uses should be understood by others. Nobody was a more determined opponent than Hobbes of anything like authority in philosophy, in belief, in opinion; and his stand against the authority of Aristotle in philosophy is not merely not inconsistent with his view of the necessity of an absolute authority in matters of social conduct, but, when we consider upon what that view is based, is seen to be involved in it.

And thirdly, Hobbes's so-called Erastianism is different from the Erastianism of Erastus and different from the Erastianism of any other writer whatever, because it is based upon different reasons. His view of the place of religion and a Church in a community is a philosophical view; that of Erastus and of those who follow him is not more than an opinion about what is most convenient. Hobbes's view is based upon, not moral principles, but the principles of his theory of knowledge, upon his doctrines of nominalism and solipsism; theirs is based upon expediency and an observation of the world. And consequently they have, at bottom, little or nothing in common. Hobbes, it has been said, 'was an Erastian without limitations,' and it is this absence of limitations which makes it misleading to speak of him as an Erastian at all.

It appears, then, that Hobbes has come again; surprisingly, there seems even to be a prejudice in his favour at the present time. But our business must be to see that in this appearance he is neither applauded nor abused for views he never held. In point of knowledge we are in a better position with regard to Hobbes than our predecessors; our business is to improve our insight. And I think our insight will become deeper when we are more prepared to credit what he says, when we are more firmly persuaded of the error of taking his doctrines separately, and when we have grasped more surely that what we are offered by Hobbes is a philosophical system and not a mere collection of opinions. And someday, perhaps, Hobbes's writings will suffer the fate which has already overtaken the works of some of the more notable philosophers — they will be understood by others better than by the man who composed them.

Thirty-nine

Christianity and the Nature of History and *Religion and History*

These two books, concerned to a large extent with the same subject, are as different as they could well be in style and treatment. Mr Wood is a systematic, lucid, precise, and acute thinker, whose argument is easy to follow and whose conclusions are mainly orthodox; Mr McKerrow is often obscure, his writing lacks coherence, his thesis is never very clearly laid before the reader, and his conclusions, though to some extent familiar, are not recognizably orthodox.

Christianity and The Nature of History is the Hulsean Lectures for 1933–1934, and its subject is the connexion of Christianity and history, a theme which is interpreted in a somewhat disconcertingly heterogeneous manner; the fundamental question of Christianity and the nature of history being disposed of in the first lecture. Christianity is a 'historic faith'; what is the significance, and what are the implications of this 'fact'? We are given, first, an interpretation of the nature of history, which follows to a large extent the views of Troeltsch and Croce. The historian 'is concerned with those elements of individuality, uniqueness, once-for-all-ness, the irreversible and the non-repeatable, which escape the net of scientific generalization and make the central interest of the human story'. But in history there are certain events which change the human situation in such a way that it can truly be said that 'things can never be the same again'. These are the historically important events; the rest is relatively insignificant. And the business of the historian is to distinguish these events and to indicate their eternal significance. This view of history and the business of the historian is familiar enough, and it is represented here as the view of

---

Review of Herbert George Wood, *Christianity and the Nature of History* (Cambridge: Cambridge University Press, 1934); and James Clark McKerrow, *Religion and History* (London: Longmans, Green, and Co., 1934). First published in *Journal of Theological Studies*, 36 (1935), 323–4. Oakeshott also reviewed *Christianity and the Nature of History* in *Cambridge Review*, 56 (1935), 248.

the 'modern historian'. Mr Wood makes it the foundation of his argument, for he moves on, easily and appropriately, to shew how it supports the Christian view of the significance of the life of Jesus. But I do not think he has considered sufficiently its defects; and what he claims for it — the concurrence of the 'modern historian' — is certainly doubtful. However, it is a brilliantly argued lecture, and contains probably the best short statement of the view it recommends. The rest of the book is taken up with other, but not less interesting, matter. We are given in Lecture III an excellent account of what may be called the Christian interpretation of the course of events; in Lecture II, an acute examination of the Marxist interpretation of history as it appears in Kautsky's *Foundations of Christianity*: and finally, a discussion of the contribution of Christianity to the civilization of Western Europe. This variety, perhaps, makes the book less coherent than it might have been, but it enables Mr Wood to make many acute and enlightening observations and to indulge (moderately) his lively and brilliant powers as a controversialist.

Religion and History consists of two essays, not very closely connected in subject. The first, on the Principles of Sociology, is a thoroughgoing application of the concept of evolution to human society. The analogy between biology and human history appears sometimes a little forced — social organization before the Greek city-state is said 'to correspond to invertebrate forms, while polities correspond to vertebrate' — but the main thesis, that the process of human development is towards democracy, peace, and a world economy, is fairly clearly presented. The second essay, however, entitled 'Evolution in the light of Religion' is devoted to a consideration of the connexion between Christianity and history, between religious belief and historical event. Here the thesis is by no means clear, but I understand Mr McKerrow's suggestion to be that pre-Christian religions were naturally 'historical' (the gods were thought of as historical personages), that in Christian Gnosticism this historical element in religious belief was regarded as relatively insignificant, and that 'Catholic Christianity' reintroduced (for obvious and unexceptionable reasons) this historical element. Genuine Christianity, the Christianity of 'full-grown men', is Gnostic Christianity with its relative disregard of historical event; but such a religion could not, in the first years of our era, be widely appreciated, and 'Catholic Christianity' is a compromise for the benefit of 'babes'. This thesis is expounded in a detailed history of the early centuries of Christianity, but it becomes clear to the reader only in the final chapter.

Forty

Morals and Politics

Books which deal in a fundamental way with the theoretical problems of the rights and obligations implied in civil society are rare in these days when interest is concentrated upon practical questions, and *Morals and Politics* will be welcomed by those whose business or pleasure it is to think about the philosophical problems presented in political life. But it is certainly not a book for beginners. About two-thirds of it consists of brief summaries of theories of political obligation from Plato to Bosanquet, summaries which would be misleading or even meaningless to those not already acquainted with the writers discussed; and the remaining third is devoted to a brief exposition of Mr Carritt's own views. His main thesis is that obligation is not another and less exact way of expressing something else, e.g., interest; and he separates the writers with whom he deals into two main classes, those who, in different ways, wish to reduce obligation to something else, and those who, holding something like his own view, deny the possibility of such a reduction; and he reaches the remarkable conclusion that in all the long line of political philosophers, Locke alone (and possibly Kant) is on his side in holding that obligation is not a less exact way of thinking about some other fact, such as interest. This classification of theories is not, of course, novel; but it is carried out here better than elsewhere, and is certainly illuminating. Another of Mr Carritt's beliefs, which he elaborates here, is that political obligation is not a special kind of obligation, but merely a form of our general obligation to other individuals, and he ends the book with a sentence from Kant: 'A true theory of politics must begin by doing homage to moral obligation'. It would appear, however, that moral obligation, in whatever way it is conceived, is rather a datum of a theory of politics, and the attitude of a theorist towards his data should be critical and not one of merely reverential acceptance. Mr Carritt, like some other writers, appears to me to accept too easily the

---

Review of Edgar Frederick Carritt, *Morals and Politics: Theories of their Relation from Hobbes and Spinoza to Marx and Bosanquet* (Oxford: Clarendon Press, 1935). First published in *Cambridge Review*, 56 (1935), 449.

principle that obligation is *sui generis,* that an imperative can never be reduced to an indicative. But his remarks, brief as they are, on Rights, the General Will, and the Contract, are acute and interesting, displaying a critical faculty from the lack of which political philosophy has suffered much in recent years. With regard to his summaries of the views of other writers, I find them uneven. On Kant and T.H. Green he is excellent; but some other chapters suffer from the extreme compression of their theme, and that on Hegel, with all its emphasis upon Hegel's philosophy of history and its neglect of Hegel's fundamental concepts of consciousness, will, right, and moral personality is seriously inadequate. However, Mr Carritt has tried to do for political philosophy what other writers, like Moore, Broad, Prichard, and Ross, have been doing in a more elaborate way for ethics in general, and the result must be of the greatest interest to those who think about these matters.

Forty-one

The Political Philosophies of Plato and Hegel

It is impossible in a short review to do full justice to this book, which I take to be one of the most profound and illuminating contributions to the literature of political philosophy which has appeared in recent years. It is admirable, in the first place, because it is a scholarly and inspired analysis of two great documents in the history of political philosophy — Plato's *Republic,* and Hegel's *Philosophie des Rechts.* It is refreshing to find an author determined to keep close to his texts and to enquire into their exact meaning; and it is impossible here not to admire both this strict adherence to the matter in hand — the interpretation of two documents — and the subtlety of the interpretations. But the book is more than a mere exposition of two texts; it is a critical analysis. And if the criticism is primarily internal, concerned with the self-consistency of the main ideas of the *Republic* and the *Philosophie des Rechts,* it is also based upon a profound appreciation both of the idea and of the history of political philosophy. This is apparent, first, in the choice of texts, at once so similar and so different in their handling of the problems of political philosophy; and secondly, in the way in which Mr Foster expounds these similarities and differences, making them (among much else) an illustration of the fundamental similarities and differences which join and divide the ancient and the modern way of thinking about political problems. It is the differences, of course, which are more important and more difficult to apprehend than the similarities; and here the resources of a subtle and original mind are concentrated upon the interpretation, not of vague outlines, but of all that is most intricate and most characteristic in the texts concerned. There are, no doubt, readers who will find it difficult to agree with, perhaps, even the main thesis which informs the book — that 'to philosophize is to study the history of philosophy philosophically'. But none can fail to admire the accomplished

Review of Michael Beresford Foster, *The Political Philosophies of Plato and Hegel* (Oxford: Oxford University Press, 1935). First published in *Cambridge Review*, 57 (1935), 74.

way in which Mr Foster has said so much and said it so clearly and unpretentiously, in 200 pages, to illuminate the writings of Plato and Hegel, and the whole history of political philosophy.

Forty-two

Right: a Study in Physical and Moral Order

The author of this book admits that it has no real unity of design, but must be regarded as a series of loosely connected essays. And its title certainly gives a very imperfect notion of its contents. The first subject discussed is the origin of Right, which is entertainingly treated as a piece of natural history, moral right being connected (though it is difficult to see upon what grounds) with physical right-handedness in men and in animals, with the right-handed twist of many of the shells of fish and with other manifestations of right-handedness in nature. Mr Tilby then goes on to consider, in his rather sketchy and haphazard manner, the relation of rightness and goodness, which leads him on to a discussion of the nature of beauty and truth. The conclusion reached is that goodness, beauty, and truth are a trinity of ascending, not co-equal, values: goodness is loyalty to the permanent interests of the clan; beauty carries us beyond these local conditions, being an idea of perfect harmony and unity of form, design, and purpose, but it is still exclusive—excluding ugliness; and truth, unlike goodness and beauty, is genuinely universal, it includes everything and excludes nothing. The last essay deals with the concept of the Will of God, and is represented as an attempt to supply, what Christian theology has hitherto lacked, 'a consistent scheme which could be regarded as a definite or formulated doctrine' with regard to the Will of God. The book is breezily and boldly written; but the argument is often too slight to be convincing and the author's wandering style too frequently leads him away from the point.

Review of Alexander Wyatt Tilby, *Right: a Study in Physical and Moral Order* (London: Williams and Norgate Ltd, 1933). First published in *Journal of Theological Studies*, 36 (1935), 322–3.

Forty-three

History and the Social Sciences

When I was asked to take a part in this discussion it was suggested to me that, since it was improbable that I could make any serious contribution to the debate, I might as well provide the comic relief: I might, for example, consider my predecessor as an opponent and knock him down. But, having heard what he has to say, I fear the fun won't be so fast and furious as I had hoped. It is always more amusing (and also it is less trouble) to give the lie direct to an opponent than to fiddle about with fine distinctions and partial agreements; but it is rare to find two views so genuinely antithetical that they can be set at one another without more ado. And, since I cannot merely and altogether oppose what has already been said, I find myself in the invidious position of having to choose the less amusing part. I have no knock-out blow to deliver. The best I can manage is a feint with the right followed by a glancing left. It is difficult to forecast the effect of this somewhat oblique onslaught, but I can scarcely expect it to bring my opponent to the floor.

I want first to understand what we are to mean when we speak of history. I think some confusion exists in the minds of many who use this word; and I believe that we shall not achieve a satisfactory view of the relationship of history and the social sciences until that confusion is dispelled. My feint, you see, consists in suggesting to my opponent that there is something important which he has not yet thought about; and just as he is beginning to give us his opinion, I shall jump in and tell him what his conclusions ought to be. It is so familiar a subterfuge that perhaps it will fail altogether to deceive.

History, as I understand it, is a certain way of thinking and of writing about the past. There are many ways of thinking and writing about the past, but history is separated from all others by certain distinguishing

---

First published in J.E. Dugdale (ed.), *The Social Sciences: Their Relations in Theory and Teaching; Being a Report of a Conference Held Under the Joint Auspices of the Institute of Sociology and the International Student Service (British Committee), London, 1935* (London: Le Play House Press, 1936), 71–81.

characteristics. This, I know, is a clumsy and inaccurate way of speaking. The past is not 'there,' formless, meaningless material, waiting to be given shape and significance, if not by the historian, then by the philosopher or the sociologist. There is a past for every way of thinking: there is neither one pre-eminent past, nor is there any past at all except for some way of thinking. That, of course, is philosophy, and therefore introduces unnecessary complications; it is better, perhaps, to keep to the falsity of common sense and say that history is a certain way of thinking about the past. Yet, the word history is frequently used indifferently to mean a certain way of thinking about the past, to mean any and every way of thinking and writing about the past, and to mean what those who believe in its existence would call the past course of events itself, what actually happened, what was. And sometimes, even, the word is made to bear more than one of these meanings in a single sentence. But I think we must decide which of these meanings the word is to have, for otherwise we shall not escape ambiguity and confusion. For myself I should like to dismiss at once the notion that history is the past course of events itself separated from every and anybody's ideas about it, that history is what actually happened. I should like to dismiss this notion because I find it altogether meaningless. It depends upon the separation of 'what has come to us' and 'our interpretation of it,' and it introduces nothing but chaos into our intellectual world. History is not made by statesmen, by soldiers, or by men in the street, any more than entomology is made by insects; the one is made by historians, the other by entomologists. Of 'what actually happened' we know and can know nothing at all; if history were that it would be at once nothing and unknowable. No event, no past is historical unless it has survived in record; and further, not even all recorded events are historical events. History is not 'what actually happened'; it is 'what the evidence obliges us to believe.' And if history is 'what the evidence obliges us to believe,' then it is a way of thinking about the past, governed and controlled by rules of evidence, and is not the past itself separated from our knowledge of it. And further, I should like also to dismiss the notion of history as any and every way of thinking about the past; to dismiss the notion that every past is an historical past. There are, obviously, some pasts, or some ways of thinking about the past, which are distinct from the past in history. The remembered past, for example, is not, as such, an historical past; for memory is essentially personal. And again, the imagined or fancied past is a past different from the past in history. An imagined past, a past of myth or tradition, may, for some purposes, be valuable and significant; it may, for example, have an immense and beneficial control over belief and activity; but it is a past alien from that of history. And once more, there is what may be called a practical past, which, though it may not be a merely mythical or traditional past, must nevertheless be distinguished from the historical past. Here the past is thought of as merely that which preceded the present, that from which the present has grown or developed, and the significance of the past is taken to lie in the fact that it has been influential in deciding the present or future fortunes of men. The past, that is to say, is thought of in terms of the present and as explanatory of the present: it becomes a store-house of political wisdom, an authority for religious belief, the raw material for literature, or even a way of expressing a philosophical system. But this way of thinking of the past is, also, a distinct and different way of thinking of it from that which belongs to history. There are, then, ways of thinking and writing about the past which differ from the way in which the historian thinks and writes of it, there are pasts other than the past for history, and consequently history must be taken to mean something more definite and confined than merely any and every way of thinking about the past.

History is a certain, specific way of thinking about the past; and we are left with the question, what distinguishes the historian's way of thinking about the past? a question calling for a careful and detailed answer, in place of which, however, I can offer here only two observations.

First, the past in history is a dead past, and it is a past essentially unlike the present. The historian is interested in the deadness of the past, and in its dissimilarity from the present. What attracts his eye and fires his enthusiasm is diversity. He has a preternatural sensibility for the minute and detailed differences which distinguish one situation from another, one plan from another, one age from another. The modern instance does not attract him, for he knows that similarities appear only when details are neglected. The historical past is, thus, the product of the imagination; history is the perpetual recreation of lost worlds. No doubt there have been writers about the past so preoccupied with the condition and the problems of their present world that they were unable to distinguish past from present, but this failure of imagination is a measure of their failure to write history.

Now, the engagement of the historian with diversity and with dissimilarity does not imply that for him the past is merely a succession of unique events and situations; it does not imply that, in any philosophical sense, events for the historian are singular. An historical event is never a mere point-instant; it is something with a meaning, something that can maintain itself relatively intact and self-complete. Things in history are not bare particulars, they are changing identities; but the point at which change creates a new identity is, for history, determined, without entering into any ultimate question, by an imaginative judgment based in each case upon the available evidence. In short, there may be similarities (and certainly because the historian chooses to neglect them does not mean that they do not exist and cannot be elucidated), but the historical past is essentially a world of relative dissimilarities and diversities. Nor does this neglect of similarities imply (as is sometimes supposed) that the historical past is not a generalised past, that generalisation is foreign to historical thinking, or that the historian is merely an archivist or a collector of information which he is powerless to coordinate. That, though a common, is an absurd notion. An historical person, situation or event is itself unavoidably a generalisation; and history, no less than every other form of knowledge, consists of nothing but generalisations. But it implies that generalisation in history is limited, limited by the presuppositions in terms of which the historical past is constructed. And it implies that generalisation which conflicts with the historical concepts of person, situation, event, etc., is and must always remain, foreign to history.

My second observation is that history is thinking about the past for the sake of the past; it is a way of thinking about the past free from all extraneous interests. For many people the past has interest only in so far as the knowledge of it can be used for some ulterior purpose, just as there are people whose interest in horse-racing is confined to the money they can make by it. But of the one class it must be said that those who compose it are without the genuine historical sense, and of the other that they are not true racing enthusiasts but merely business men. For the historian the enjoyment of his pursuit depends upon no extraneous purpose or result; the attempt to imagine and elucidate a past, lost and different world from that in which he lives is, taken by itself, completely satisfying. And the introduction of an extraneous purpose, because it involves a totally different way of thinking about the past, is not merely the perversion of history, but its destruction. This, again, does not mean that the study of the past can yield nothing over and above all historical knowledge of the past; it means that the *historical* study of the past can yield nothing more.

Now, what I have attempted is to suggest a definite meaning for the word history, because I believe that until we know exactly what we mean by it we cannot determine its relations with the social sciences or with anything else. My view is that history is this particular (and no other) way of thinking about the past. And if it be this, then the absolute impossibility of deriving from history any generalisations of the kind which belong to a social science will, I think, follow. And I believe that only those who attach no particular meaning to the word history (taking it to be any and every way of thinking about the past), or those who think that history is 'what actually happened,' a course of events altogether independent of experience, can reasonably hold that history itself can supply either material or evidence for a social science. I believe, in short, that history and social science can be brought together only by those who are ignorant of the nature of either and careless of the interests of both - the professional matchmakers of the intellectual world.

This view of the matter depends, of course, as much upon a conception of science and social science as upon a conception of history; and consequently I must at least indicate what I take to be the nature of scientific knowledge. But here again a few observations only can be made. Science is the attempt to conceive the world in what may perhaps be called the most abstractly universal manner possible; it is the attempt to conceive and to generalise the world under the category of quantity, the type of generalisation aimed at being a statistical generalisation in some form or other. And a social science which conforms to this general character may, at least, be imagined. And if it is objected that there are at present few sciences which closely approximate to this character, we may somewhat reduce our requirements without surrendering our principle, and say that scientific knowledge is always in the form of universal generalisations. And again, a social science of this character may easily be imagined. It would be an attempt to discover and establish generalisations about the life and conduct, or some particular aspects of the life and conduct, of societies; and the observations with which such a science or sciences would be concerned would, no doubt, be taken partly from the present and partly from the records of the past. With the observations which might be made in the contemporary world we are not here concerned: what we have to consider are those derived from the past, for it is at this point that social science and history are said to come together in a common undertaking, it is at this point that history is said to contribute to, or even to be transformed into, a science of society.

Now, in order to make scientific use of the records of the past each event or situation must be transformed into an instance of a general rule; facts of the past must be regarded as ephemeral instances of the stable generalisations which a science of society seeks to propound. At first sight it would appear to be difficult to discover a means by which this can be achieved. If the facts of the past could somehow be reduced to figures, the difficulty would disappear; stable statistical generalisations would at once become possible. But to reduce the life and conduct of social life to the category of quantity, except in the case of such things as population and wealth, has been found so difficult an undertaking that sociologists have had to resort to less scientific methods. Recorded facts, they say, even when they cannot be reduced to figures, may be related and compared with one another in such a way as to give generalisations of value and significance. With the serious logical defects of the comparative method we are not concerned; all we need observe is that directly the facts of the past become instances of a general rule they cease to be historical facts. The scientific way of thinking about the past at this point, as at some others, begins where the historical way ends: where comparison begins, as a method of generalisation, history ends.

But there is another obvious way in which the scientific use of the records of the past is different from the historical use — a difference which, I believe, establishes a genuine cleavage. For the historical way of thinking, the position of an event or situation in the past, and its pastness, are both essential aspects: whereas the scientific use of the facts of the past is based upon a neglect of these aspects. The world of scientific generalisations is a world ignorant alike of past and future as such; it knows nothing of historical time, and recognises time only within its own world as a method of relating its concepts. To regard a fact as an instance of a general rule lifts it at once out of the domain of history by depriving it of its pastness.

My conclusion, then, which I have been able to support only with a few random observations, is that in spite of the use a social science may be able to make of the facts of the recorded past, it can make no use whatever of historical facts. Social science and history must think about the past in different ways and with different presuppositions. What history says is not denied by science, it is simply irrelevant to science. And only when history is misconceived and science is misunderstood is it possible to think of them concerned in a common undertaking.

Forty-four

An Introduction to Contemporary German Philosophy

'The general reader' in philosophy — if such a person can be imagined in England — must be supposed to tire easily of the works which are turned out for his benefit; they are for the most part tedious and uninspired; at best they are dully informative, at worst merely confusing and misleading. But if he were to turn to some of the great classics of philosophy he would find himself in another and brighter world in which it is a pleasure even to be bewildered. In this world of philosophical thought he may require some direction; and the sort of guide he looks for is one who speaks from an abundance of well-considered knowledge, one who is himself a philosopher, and one whose attention is not to be diverted from what is central to what is merely quaint and amusing. Dr Werner Brock is a guide of this kind to the world of contemporary German philosophy; and his book has just that proportion of information to suggestion which distinguishes a good from a useless introduction to a subject. The topic he has set himself to discuss is the position of philosophy in Germany since the reaction set in, soon after the middle of the last century, against the last great orthodoxy — Hegelianism. The central problem presented to philosophy during this period he takes to be the question 'What, in this age of science, is the task of philosophy, if any task still remains for it beyond the preservation and development of logic and the study of its own history?' And he considers the work of the seven most influential German philosophers of the last fifty years in relation to this question, thus giving the period and the book a significant unity. Husserl, Dilthey, and Max Weber are selected from the older writers who, inspired by 'the collapse of Hegel's philosophy and the emergence of the separate sciences,' gave philosophy in Germany a new life. In the second chapter the work and influ-

---

Review of Werner Brock, *An Introduction to Contemporary German Philosophy* (Cambridge: Cambridge University Press, 1935). First published in *Cambridge Review*, 57 (1936), 195.

ence of Nietzsche and Kierkegaard is discussed with great insight. And the third and last chapter is devoted to the work of Jaspers and Heidegger, with briefer remarks about some of the less-known contemporary writers.

The book as a whole is admirably conceived, so far as is possible it avoids technicalities, and it is written in a clear and agreeable style. And the bibliography with which it concludes adds considerably to its value. As an introduction to this period of German philosophy it is difficult to see where it could be improved; and as an interpretation it must be of great interest to English readers. For the road which German philosophy has taken during these years is, in many respects, different from that of English philosophy. But there are striking similarities. The question, 'What, in this age of science, is the real task of philosophy?' has been presented to the philosophical thinkers of both traditions, but more explicitly and expressly to those of the German tradition. The two traditions have reacted to the question in similar ways; the philosophical thought of both traditions has turned its attention to devising new methods: in both, philosophy has maintained itself, in an unusually hostile and preoccupied world, by renewing itself. But the German tradition is distinguished by the presence of two writers—Nietzsche and Kierkegaard—who have no counterpart in English thought; profound philosophical thinkers, yet writers whose influence springs from the force of their personality and whose natural voice is that of the prophet rather than that of the philosopher.

Forty-five

The Meaning of History

History here is the course of events; and this book is an interpretation of the course of events which we speak of roughly as the history of Europe. That history is divided into three main epochs: the first, 'the pre-Christian pagan period, whose feature is the immersion of the human spirit in nature and its direct organic blending with it'; the second, 'the Christian stage comprising the whole of the Middle Ages and marked by the heroic struggle of the human spirit against the natural elements and forces'; the third, the period of the Renaissance (now coming to an end), the period of 'man's self-affirmation,' marked by his control over nature. These three epochs are to be followed by a fourth, the character of which is yet unknown but which will be conditioned by the fact that 'European man to-day is emerging from modern history exhausted and with all his creative forces spent' — whereas he had 'emerged from the Middle Ages with accumulated and virgin forces, disciplined in the school of asceticism.' This schematic view of the history of Europe has as a background a set of moral judgments which determine the relative value of human ideals and activities, moral judgments which conflict directly with the secularism (intellectual and material) of the modern age.

There is, I think, among English readers an understandable prejudice against these attempts (which are associated particularly with Teutonic writers) to interpret in general terms the history of the world or of Europe; and those in whom this prejudice is strong will find little to attract them here. And even among those who are, in general, sympathetically disposed to these attempts to rationalise the total course of events, there will be many who find this scheme of epochs unconvincing, who will wonder (in particular) where Professor Berdyaev learnt his mediaeval history, and who will be dismayed by his extraordinarily restricted view of the nature of Christianity. But setting aside these difficulties, there remains for those who are interested a diagnosis of the present condition of European civilization and an assertion of a scale of values; the one intelligent and original, and the other eloquent and profoundly religious.

Review of Nicholas Berdyaev, *The Meaning of History*, tr. G. Reavey (London: Geoffrey Bles, 1935). First published in *Cambridge Review*, 57 (1936), 195.

Forty-six

The Historical Element in Religion

Professor Webb has chosen for the subject of the four lectures he delivered in Bristol last year on the Lewis Fry foundation, which appear here together with an epilogue, a topic of the greatest interest. His treatment of it is, I think, more profound and illuminating and more strictly relevant than any of the more recently published discussions; and though with greater space at his command he might have developed more fully some aspects of his argument, what he has given us is an admirably concise and lucid statement, which could not easily be improved upon, of the conclusions he has reached. The first lecture is devoted to the definition of the nature of the historical element in religion, and this definition determines (as it should) the view presented in subsequent lectures of the place and significance of this element. Religion is 'a mode of behaviour and activity carried on by men as members of a community' (p. 20), and it is unavoidably connected with the history and traditions of a community. In all religions whatever, there is a sense of 'oneself as belonging to a past'. The historical element in religion is, then, not 'the past as such', the past of the historian (p. 75); but neither is it a merely mythological past, 'tales told in explanation of a traditional ritual' (p. 34): it is the actual past life of the community felt and thought of by the individual as his own past. This may appear to be reducing the historical element in religion to smaller proportions and a less significance than it has often been credited with; and certainly, I think, there must be a grave doubt whether it should not rather be called the element of past in religion than the historical element. But there can be little doubt that, by starting from this position, Professor Webb is on firm ground. And his conclusion that the historical element in religion is 'closely bound up with the nature of religion as a form of experience' (p. 94), that all religions are unavoidably and essentially, in one degree or another, historical religions, is a reasonable conclusion.

Review of Clement Charles Julian Webb, *The Historical Element in Religion* (London: George Allen and Unwin, 1935). First published in *Journal of Theological Studies*, 37 (1936), 96–8.

In a lecture devoted to the 'Depreciation of the Historical Element in Religion', the writers discussed are, with one exception, those who hold, in one form or another, the view that all historical religions are, at best, only the one, true, natural religion in disguise, and that in so far as they are connected with a specific past they are certainly limited and possibly false. And Professor Webb shews that those who hold such a view as this — e.g. Spinoza and Lessing — are, in fact, misinterpreting the unavoidable character of religion itself. But he believes too readily that if this particular and extreme form of depreciation is disposed of, all others go with it. It would, for example, be interesting to know what he would say to the view which, not denying the unavoidable presence of this past element in all religion, asserted nevertheless that religion is essentially a matter of present and actual belief about the world — the view that although there is certainly a past which influences, and perhaps controls, present belief, it cannot itself be made a foundation or a ground of present belief.

The epilogue to these lectures is an attempt to indicate the kind of attitude which the previously explained view of the nature and significance of the historical element in religion implies towards some of the historical beliefs belonging to Christianity. And here the treatment is less adequate. The question which inevitably occurs to the reader of the earlier part of the book is, how on this slender but firm foundation can a defence be built of the importance which traditional Christianity has attributed to past events? And his conclusion at the end must, I think, be that the disconcerting thing about Christianity is that the historical element which (rightly or wrongly) belongs to it is something very much more than 'a consciousness of personal continuity with an actual life reaching back into the past, and shared with other members of a community' (p. 93). It may be that what Christianity asserts in excess of this is indefensible: certainly the only adequate defence of it would be in terms of a philosophical view of the nature of time and its relation with eternity, and a philosophical theory of belief, and these unhappily lie beyond the scope of this course of lectures.

Forty-seven

Collected Essays

The appearance of these two volumes, which complete the publication in book form of Bradley's writings, is a welcome occasion; for, although they contain little that has not before been printed, they make accessible for the first time some of his most characteristic essays. Here are reprinted, first, Bradley's two early pamphlets (now long out of print), *The Presuppositions of Critical History* (1874), and *Mr Sidgwick's Hedonism* (1877); secondly, twenty-seven essays from *Mind*, the *International Journal of Ethics*, and the *Fortnightly Review*; and thirdly, six short 'Replies to Criticisms and Notes' which (with one exception) appeared originally in the pages of *Mind*. To these are added two hitherto unpublished essays, *On the Treatment of Sexual Detail in Literature*, and on *Relations*; and a complete bibliography of his work.

The editors, who appear under the initials M. de G. and H. H. J., have performed their work admirably. The decision to arrange the essays in mainly chronological order was a wise choice; and the reader will be grateful for the care they have taken to provide all the necessary references and bibliographical details. The editing of the essay on *Relations*, which, left unfinished by Bradley, had to be pieced together from various MSS and notebooks, called particularly for care and patience, and has been performed with the greatest skill. Everything, in short, that the reader could look for from the editors has been supplied.

Considered from the standpoint of subject, these essays fall into four main classes. There are, first, two essays, appealing to a more general and less technical interest than the rest — *The Evidences of Spiritualism* (1885), reprinted from the *Fortnightly Review*; and *On the Treatment of Sexual Detail in Literature* (1912), hitherto unpublished — which are admirable examples of the handling of important and interesting questions by an acute and liberal intelligence. Secondly, there are the writings which deal with (in a general sense) logical questions — the pamphlet on *The Presuppositions of Critical History*, and the unfinished essay on *Relations*, on which Bradley was working at the time of his death in 1924. The pamphlet is interesting as

---

Review of Francis Herbert Bradley, *Collected Essays*, 2 vols. (Oxford: Clarendon Press, 1935). First published in *Philosophy*, 11 (1936), 114–16.

the earliest of Bradley's published work and because it is one of the earliest discussions in English of the logical and epistemological connections connected with history. He was right, I think, when in later years he became dissatisfied with its conclusions, but it remains for us one of the most original and acute discussions of these questions. The essay on *Relations* was intended to be a rehandling of a subject on which Bradley had already written much; and as it appears here it is more like elaborate notes for a treatise than an essay.

No fresh doctrine, so far as I can see, is propounded, but the discussion is fuller than any to be found in the *Principles of Logic* or elsewhere in Bradley's writings. He was right in believing that 'the question of relations, their ultimate nature and place in the world of reality and knowledge' is 'central'; and this treatment of it shows undimmed Bradley's intellectual vitality, his characteristic appreciation of difficulties, and his candid consideration of views which, in the end, he felt obliged to reject. What he has to say here and elsewhere on the problem of relations has yet, I think, to receive the critical consideration it deserves. Thirdly, there are the seven essays which deal with ethical subjects, ranging from the elaborate criticism of the *Methods of Ethics* contained in *Mr Sidgwick's Hedonism*, to the brilliant four pages which consider the question, *Is Self-sacrifice An Enigma?* And there are, fourthly, the twenty essays which comprise the main bulk of Bradley's writing on psychology.

It will be seen, then, that these volumes are valuable chiefly (though not exclusively) for collecting together Bradley's contribution to psychology. Bradley had a clear notion of what he thought ought to be the subject-matter of psychology and of the general character of psychological, as distinct from logical or metaphysical, questions. A sterile purism in thought is, of course, the last thing of which he may justly be accused; but he knew that there is a difference between theory and practice, between psychology and metaphysics, between ethics and moral sensibility, between religion and philosophy, and he knew that distinctions of this kind are essential to clear thinking. In one section of *Mr Sidgwick's Hedonism* he gives us again (he had already given them in *Ethical Studies*) his views about the general character of ethical thought, and in more than one of those psychological essays he indicates his notion of the general character of psychology. *A Defence of Phenomenalism in Psychology*, originally published in 1900 in *Mind*, states his view most comprehensively; and, while it is a view which, I think, must come to be accepted more and more as psychology assumes a genuinely scientific character, it is one of which we require still to be reminded. Bradley began the publication of these essays on psychological subjects after the appearance of the *Principles of Logic* in 1883, and they continued to appear at intervals in *Mind* until 1904; but they came mostly from the period subsequent to the publication of *Appearance and Reality* in 1893.

His writing on psychology is characteristic of Bradley in two respects. It is concerned entirely 'with the analysis of the main constitutive concepts — e.g., sensation, thought, association, attention, memory, will — which form the framework within which 'experimental psychology' (with which he confesses himself 'scarcely at all acquainted') works. His task, he conceived, was to make some contribution towards the further determination of this framework of concepts, and so towards the creation of a more settled terminology in psychology (ii. 377). And he was certainly right in believing that 'in analysis there is still much to be done' (i. 180). In this respect he takes his place within the general purpose of the traditional 'English analytical school.'

But further, besides the superior subtlety and acuteness of Bradley's analysis when compared with such earlier representatives of this school as Bentham or James Mill, his writings on psychology are characteristic in respect of the attention they pay to, and the inspiration they draw from, the great mass of Continental work on the subject which belongs to the second half of the nineteenth century. Bradley's independence of judgment, in metaphysics no less than in psychology, is, perhaps, apt to obscure the remarkably wide acquaintance he had with the work of others, both in England and on the Continent. To the end of his life he remained, not only an independent thinker, but also a reader (cf. ii. 653), and a reader always more interested in the work of his contemporaries than in that of earlier writers.

Nevertheless, in spite of this foreign strain in his reading, Bradley takes his stand, as a psychologist, among his contemporary English writers — Bain, Sully, James, Ward, and Stout — and differs from them, not so much in outlook as in opinion, and because he never produced a systematic treatise on the subject. It may be remarked also that Bradley was a man admirably equipped for making a notable contribution in the analysis of psychological concepts. Added to a clear perception of the general character of psychology and the nature of its problems and presuppositions, he had a remarkable power of self-analysis, an acute and imaginative appreciation of difficulties, and great common sense.

His contribution is, of course, fragmentary in that his writings do not contain a discussion of all even of the most important problems of psychology; but whenever he takes up a topic his treatment of it is thorough and masterly. The essays on *Association and Thought*, on *What do We Mean by the Intensity of Psychical States*?, and on *Active Attention*, perhaps stand out from the others by reason of their comprehensiveness. And the three elaborate essays on *The Definition of Will* remain his most notable single treatment of a psychological problem. The contents of the volumes are, I think, unlikely ever to turn out to be Bradley's most important work; but it does not require any perspective of time to make these writings on psychology appear, within their limits, some of the best in the English language.

Forty-eight

Bernard Bosanquet's Philosophy of the State

This is a sympathetic exposition and defence of Bosanquet's philosophy of the State. It is a useful piece of work, competently and thoroughly carried out. Its usefulness lies, I think, in the fact that this so-called Idealist theory of the State is the only theory which has paid thoroughgoing attention to all the problems which must be considered by a theory of the State, and at the same time is a theory which has yet to receive a satisfactory statement. And any attempt to understand *The Philosophical Theory of the State*, which still remains (with all its defects) the most comprehensive account of this theory, is a useful preliminary to restatement. Preachers, journalists, politicians, and moralists have all had their whack at this theory, and they are satisfied that they have discredited it. But it still retains some vitality, and when, if ever, a philosopher turns his attention to it again, he will find what this book has to say both relevant and valuable.

It consists of 300 pages, and is divided into four chapters; and it is only in the last chapter, the last hundred pages, that the author comes to grips with Bosanquet's philosophy of the State itself. The earlier chapters are devoted to discussions of the object and method of political philosophy, the historical basis of Bosanquet's theory, and Bosanquet's general philosophical position. And this proportion seems to me, on the whole, to be right. It is impossible to understand this theory of the State apart from the general philosophy to which it belongs, and when that is understood the obscurities of the political philosophy are few and relatively unimportant.

Mr Pfannenstill takes Bosanquet's theory to be an example of what he calls a 'universalistic' theory, and contrasts it with what he calls an 'individualistic' theory. These theories are alike in being 'ethico-normative' theories; but the main difference between them lies in their different con-

---

Review of Bertil Pfannenstill, *Bernard Bosanquet's Philosophy of the State. A Historical and Systematical Study* (Lund: C.W.K. Gleerup, 1936). First published in *Philosophy*, 11 (1936), 482–3.

cepts of freedom. There is, however, a point of importance which he does not consider. What he speaks of as the 'individualistic' theory, in all the examples of it that we have, has always been distinguished by a hedonistic ethical foundation; and the 'universalistic' theories differ from it in their rejection of hedonism. And again, while Bosanquet's philosophy of the will is thoroughly and intelligently discussed, not much is said expressly about his philosophy of the self. Yet it is its thorough consideration of the self which distinguishes this theory from the so-called 'individualistic' theories, which are inclined to treat the self as something too important to be examined.

Throughout the book, Bosanquet's theory of the State is taken together with that of Hegel, Green, and Bradley, and the criticisms of Hobhouse and others are considered with care. The author never attempts to go beyond Bosanquet, or to point out how the defects of Bosanquet's exposition might be remedied; indeed, he recognizes few defects. He is concerned almost entirely with removing the more obvious misunderstandings of that theory, which (though some of them are obvious enough) are sufficiently widespread to be worth while considering, and with giving a systematic exposition of Bosanquet's thought. And, within these limits, and in spite of its rather uncritical attitude, it is as complete a guide to Bosanquet's theory of the State as one could wish.

Forty-nine

The Political Philosophy of Hobbes

This is an excellent and timely piece of work. It has the great merit of not wasting time by going over all the old ground; it is a work of genuine scholarship based upon a thorough reconsideration of all the relevant writings of Hobbes; and its interpretation of Hobbes is subtle and original. And further, it comes at a time when what is required in the study of Hobbes is just the fresh insight into Hobbes's writings which it provides. Mr Strauss has a number of new or hitherto incompletely emphasised views with regard to the basis and genesis of Hobbes's political philosophy to defend and explain. Hobbes is presented, first, as an opponent of the natural law theory of society; his theory of the State is shown to be based upon, neither the moral principles of the traditional natural law theory, nor (like Spinoza's) upon purely naturalistic principles, but stands midway between the two. In one of the most original chapters in the book Mr Strauss distinguishes three main periods in the history of Hobbes's thought; first, the period when he was under the influence of the traditional theory, secondly, the period in which he turned away from philosophy to history and particularly to a study of Thucydides, and thirdly, when he returned to the study of philosophy and constructed his own theory of the State, based upon a new moral outlook. And the distinctive innovation of Hobbes is taken to be his rejection of *law* and his substitution of *right* or *claim* as the principle from which the State is to be deduced, a substitution which has since dominated political theory in Western Europe.

Many and powerful arguments are produced in defence of these and the other theses maintained in this book; and Mr Strauss is very rarely guilty of exaggeration, trying to make the evidence prove more than it does. But I think he exaggerates slightly Hobbes's originality. Certainly Hobbes broke away from one tradition, the tradition which had for many centuries

---

Review of Leo Strauss, *The Political Philosophy of Hobbes; its basis and genesis*, tr. E. M. Sinclair (Oxford: Clarendon Press, 1936). First published in *Cambridge Review*, 58 (1937), 150.

dominated political theory, but he did not free himself from it entirely, and he did not found an entirely fresh tradition. His theory, particularly in its substitution of *will* for *law* as the basis of the State, belongs to a tradition already established long before the sixteenth century; though it is true that never before had that tradition found so masterly an exponent.

It is impossible here to deal fully with the whole of the extraordinarily subtle and suggestive interpretation of Hobbes which this book contains; it must suffice to recommend it to all who are interested in the history of political theory as a first-class piece of work.

Fifty

Ideology and Utopia

It would be a pity if the somewhat turgid and involved style in which this book is written, its at first sight alarming terminology, and its rather miscellaneous character which it derives from its origin in three different German publications, should stand in the way of its being widely read. For it is an acute and valuable contribution to its subject, and is inspired at once by a genuinely scientific spirit and a desire to give some practical help towards understanding and coping with the present situation – political and social – in Western Europe. What Dr Mannheim calls the sociology of knowledge is an examination of the political and social ideas of an epoch or a community from the standpoint of their genesis and context in the culture of the community in which they find place.

In his discussion of the history of the sociology of knowledge it is stated that the point of view which made such a study possible 'actually emerged with Marx, whose profoundly suggestive *aperçus* went to the heart of the matter.' But Dr Mannheim's view is at once wider and more accurate than anything to be found in Marx's writings, for he conceives the 'situation,' in terms of which the political and social ideas of an epoch are to be examined, not in terms of production or 'class,' but in terms of a more profound conception of the nature of a society. All thought is a social product, and we must go back to the social situation in order to understand the real meaning of the ideas of an age or a community. These ideas Dr Mannheim classifies into two groups – ideologies and Utopias. Ideologies are, roughly, mental fictions which are accepted by those who are anxious to stabilize the social order in which they find themselves and which are developed in order to explain and defend that order. Utopias are the ideas which are 'incongruous with the state of reality in which they occur' and which represent a desire to replace our existing social order by another. Ideology and Utopia, then, stand for two fundamental states of mind or

Review of Karl Mannheim, *Ideology and Utopia. An Introduction to the Sociology of Knowledge*, tr. L. Wirth and E. Shils (London: Routledge, 1936). First published in *Cambridge Review*, 58 (1937), 257.

kinds of thinking about social and political matters; and the intellectual history of a community can be seen always as a conflict between them. And Dr Mannheim goes on to illustrate this thesis from the history of modern Europe, and to show how a genuine science of politics might be built upon this analysis. The book belongs to what is now an established tradition of great vitality in the recent history of social investigation, a tradition which owes more to Marx and Nietzsche and Max Weber than to any other writers. Its strength and interest lies in the systematic and profound way in which the thesis is worked out and illustrated; its weakness lies, I think, in the rather unsatisfactory attempt, which goes along with the thesis, to prove the inadequacy of so-called 'classical logic' and all non-sociological approaches to human knowledge. Marx's theory of 'absolute relativism' obviously left something to be desired, and I cannot say that Dr Mannheim's observations on the subject leave me satisfied. But, whatever its defects in detail, it is an extremely suggestive work which deserves all the care that its reading demands.

Fifty-one

This Freedom of Ours

This volume of eleven brief lectures is an attempt to state what the freedom of an Englishman consists of, how it came to be, how it is protected, and how it should be further guarded and increased. It is a defence of British liberal democracy. It may be considered from two standpoints — as a book of talks written and delivered for the B.B.C., and as an account of the nature and genesis of the British Constitution. As a book of talks it is excellent; it has all the merits and avoids some of the defects of B.B.C. lectures. Its tone is critical without being revolutionary; its thought is clear and simple without being condescending; its style is breezy without being silly; its information is reasonably accurate without being pedantic. All this we should expect from Mr Frank Birch; his wit, learning, intelligence, and modesty are seen to excellent effect; he has succeeded in a difficult task. As an account of the nature and genesis of the British Constitution the defects of the book are, perhaps, only those inherent in its origin and purpose. It has behind it a considerable knowledge of English constitutional history, it is based to a fair extent on Dicey but goes beyond Dicey at the points where it is now generally admitted that Dicey was wrong, or is now out of date. But the necessity of brevity has made its history at many points very superficial; not only are we never taken behind the elaborately set scene in which appear successively the men who won us our freedom, but it is never suggested that there is anything behind it. And what, perhaps, is more serious, Mr Birch's thought tends to stop just where the ordinary man's thinking stops; he doesn't help us to overcome our intellectual limitations, he only states them clearly. He is content with a bald contrast between force and persuasion (the latter being the essence of liberal democracy); he is content to describe democracy as 'government by the people', he anchors himself to an undefined 'Equality of opportunity' as the principle of democratic society, he thinks that now we have got Adult

---

Review of Frank Birch, *This Freedom of Ours. The Book of the Broadcast Talks* (Cambridge: Cambridge University Press, 1937). First published in *Cambridge Review*, 59 (1937), 55.

Suffrage only our laziness or stupidity can stop us putting that principle into practice, and his account and criticism of Communism and Fascism is too brief and superficial to be worth while. In short, the talks no doubt served a useful purpose, of their kind they are first class, and no one could be better suited than Mr Birch to give them; but as a book it is less easy to see its value, and its price is certainly excessive.

Fifty-two

The Modern Mind

The first sentence of this book proposes an interesting thesis for examination. 'This is a study of some changes in the use of the English language; in particular, it traces the influence of material science on common speech, and it shows in turn the effects of these changes on our attitude to religion, poetry and science itself.' Our attention is attracted; for the difficulties and dangers are enough to inspire at least an ingenious argument, and the subject is connected with much that is in the minds of the not negligible body of people to whom the principles and products of science are by no means the last word in human wisdom. But, alas, the reader is quickly disappointed, for three good reasons. First, the 'changes in the use of the English language' are studied very sketchily; there is nothing profound in the treatment. Secondly, the diagnosis of those changes is far from convincing; their attribution to the influence of 'material science' is supported by nothing very compelling by way of argument or evidence. And thirdly, almost from the first page the author shows an alarming and disconcerting tendency to wander from his thesis; it is one of the most undisciplined philosophical books it has been my fortune to read. It may seem ungracious to consider first the disappointment that the book arouses, but since it is great and comes, not from expecting something which is not promised, but from the author's own treatment of his own subject, it tends to overshadow the incidental acuteness and interest of much of what he has to say.

'Between 1640 and 1680, the language became a more exact logical instrument, the change was the result of conscious and deliberate effort.' 'People became more literal-minded, seeing in words only one unique unemotive reference.' 'Our capacity to hear and understand the overtone of meaning has slowly but continuously declined.' 'That which cannot be said in the language of mechanics is thought to be false.' In short, during the last three centuries or so the English people (and perhaps others) have

---

Review of Michael Roberts, *The Modern Mind* (London: Faber and Faber, 1937). First published in *Scrutiny*, 6 (1937), 208–10.

suffered a loss of poetic sensibility similar to that described in the famous passage in Darwin's *Autobiography*—'an atrophy of that part of the brain alone, on which higher tastes depend'; poetry, and religion whose language is poetic, have lost at the expense of a logical and matter-of-fact attitude of mind and use of language. This is 'the modern mind' in Mr Roberts' diagnosis, and no doubt there is truth as well as exaggeration in the view; and only those who are intellectually callous or have to thank their education for a perverted sense of what is valuable can regard the situation as satisfactory. I think the case is overstated, but there is enough truth in it to make it worth while to examine.

But Mr Roberts goes further. He attributes this decline in sensibility to the fact that the English language as well as the English mind during those three centuries got into the hands of the scientists, who, for their own purposes, manufactured not only a kind of 'basic' language, but a language which, because it was merely basic, was debased. And this language, and the mentality which goes with it (defined here as 'materialistic'), has, by the operation of a kind of Gresham's law, driven out the genuine poetic language. Sense has destroyed sensibility, we are the inheritors of a bankrupt language, and it is science which is to blame. Here too, no doubt, there is truth, but also gross exaggeration. That the scientific writers alone are to blame is certainly doubtful, and the view would have to be supported by some much more profound analysis than is given us here if it were to be made convincing. On the face of it, it would appear difficult, if not impossible, to prove that this one element in the history of these three centuries is responsible for this alleged decline in language; and to set about such a proof argues a lack of historical sense. Unless we are to make 'science' responsible for all the anti-religious forces of modern civilization, the view cannot be maintained; and we can make it responsible only by an exaggerated view of its influence. No doubt science, and the kind of language it requires for its purposes, has influenced our use of and sensibility to language, but to ask us to believe that science alone is responsible for the alleged 'literal-mindedness' of the modern world is asking, not only too much, but also more than the evidence produced goes to show. Very little attempt is made to study systematically the result of scientific interests upon the English language and literature; and the historical examination of English style and diction, which a proper exposition of Mr Roberts' thesis would suggest, is altogether to seek.

The third ground of my disappointment in this book is that again and again, just when we seemed to be about to follow up some promising and relevant line of argument, we are headed off to pursue something, in itself often interesting, but only vaguely connected with the matter in hand. And this lack of discipline makes the book unsatisfactory both as history and as analysis; it detracts from the value of Mr Roberts' undoubted learning, and it has the effect of suggesting a much less acute mind than some of his observations show him to possess.

But if this book as a whole is disappointing, and if it shows a certain amateurishness in its treatment of philosophical ideas, some of its chapters, and many incidental passages, contain matter for thought, admirably presented. Chapter V, for example, on Reason and Imagination in the Eighteenth Century, traces the history of the 'gradual restriction of the concept of reason' during the century. A large part of the book is taken up with scattered discussions of the relations of science and religion, and many of the views seem to me worth stating—indeed, some of them are worth more attention than they get, for Mr Roberts sees clearly enough that the relationship of science and religion is not one of direct antagonism (the one never denies what the other asserts), but he never gets as far as a comprehensive view of the relationship. What he gives us tends always to degenerate from an analysis of a relation to a defence of one side against the other. And his view that the peculiar danger of the modern mind is to conceive religion in terms of science, to 'turn a personal God into a celestial mechanic' is somewhat one-sided; the danger from political and business analogies I should have thought was just as great. The 'tricks of language and unconscious analogies' by which, for example, the Book of Common Prayer often makes out the universe to be a political arena and God a political figure, may have been replaced in the modern mind by scientific analogies, but this is not the only malady which that mind suffers, nor, I think, is it now the malady most pressing for a cure.

Fifty-three

The Concept of a Philosophical Jurisprudence

The object of this essay is to consider the meaning and possibility of a philosophy of law and civil society. The present position of enquiry in this subject is characterised by confusion and ambiguity, and it must be supposed that a critical discussion which did no more than make clearer the nature and causes of the chaos would be valuable. I hope to do more than this, to reach some positive conclusions and to suggest the direction which enquiry must take if it is to throw off its inheritance of confusion. But my first business must be to examine the present position of enquiry and to consider the character of its defects.

I

There are certain elementary ambiguities, promoted by the current use of the word 'jurisprudence', which we shall do well to avoid. This word I shall take to denote the 'theory of law'; and by the 'theory of law' I mean the rational explanation or interpretation of the nature of law. We shall have to return to these expressions in a moment; but for the present they serve to make clear that what I want to discuss is not 'case-law' or 'judge-made law', or the practice of a court, or judicial explanation or interpretation, or any of the other subjects which are or have been designated by the word 'jurisprudence', or its equivalent in other European languages, except the 'theory of law'. Jurisprudence, for me, stands for a theory and not the materials out of which a theory springs, for an explanation itself and not for what is given and requires explanation, for an interpretation of the nature of law and not an interpretation (such as a judge may give) of a law or a body of laws. And precaution is necessary in this matter of initial designation not only on account of the number of essentially different subjects which the word 'jurisprudence' is now used to

First published in *Politica*, 3 (1938), 203–22, 345–60.

indicate, but also because the expression 'philosophical jurisprudence' can have a *prima facie* meaning only when 'jurisprudence' stands for an explanation or a theory of the nature of law. I propose, then, to use the word 'jurisprudence' in the only way which does not make the expression 'philosophical jurisprudence' immediately nonsensical. And this is not a new or exotic use of the word; it is one of its current meanings, and I wish to do no more than, for the present enquiry, confine it to this meaning.

Now, the expressions 'theory', 'explanation' and 'interpretation', even when it is clear that they are to be applied to 'the nature of law 'and not to any particular law, body of laws, or system of laws, are liable to be misleading. They are apt to suggest, as my use of them in the preceding paragraph shows, that we have two things to deal with, (i) law, and (ii) the theory, explanation or interpretation of law; whereas, in truth, there is only one thing: law. The 'nature of law', and a theory, explanation or interpretation of the nature of law are the same thing. Any reading of law is an explanation of law; the difference between explanations is one of degree and relative comprehensiveness. What is true of the interpretation of a text is true universally of interpretation; the text and interpretation are one and inseparable. It is true that we appear to begin with one thing, the text, and proceed to a second thing, the interpretation; but what we call 'the text' is itself an interpretation, a meaning, for which (in interpretation) we substitute another, different or more extended, interpretation or meaning. Theory, explanation, interpretation are attempts to find and expound the meaning *in* what is given, and what is given and its meaning are not two things (as they appear to be when we use the misleading expression, 'the meaning of …'), but one. To state, then, more accurately, the position I wish to maintain: anything we may say about the nature of law is, within its limits, a theory, explanation or interpretation of the nature of law; and we can say nothing about the nature of law which does not imply and involve a theory of law. No absolute division can be maintained between statements about the nature of law by which some may be considered to be 'theories of law' and others something less; but jurisprudence appears when our statements about the nature of law reach the degree of comprehensiveness that permits them to present themselves as, at least *prima facie*, satisfactory and complete explanations of the nature of law. Jurisprudence is the exposition, in more or less detail, of the nature of law; it is the attempt to reduce the phenomena of legally organised society as such to order and coherence; and it is a theory, explanation or interpretation of law in this sense only.

When we turn to our writers on jurisprudence, that is to writers who undertake not merely to comment on the nature of law, but to give us more or less extended and thought-out explanation of law, we find (as is not surprising) not only a number of different explanations, but also a variety of kinds of explanation. And it is these different kinds of explanation that I wish to consider, for among them is to be found (variously defined) what is called a 'philosophical' explanation or interpretation. I do not propose to consider all of them or any of them in great detail; what I am primarily concerned with is philosophical jurisprudence, and these other kinds of explanation are merely the setting in which writers on the general nature of jurisprudence are accustomed to place it.

It is convenient, first, to notice what may be called *analytical* jurisprudence. Various attempts have been made to define the character of the explanation of law which goes under this name, but I have seen none that is altogether satisfactory. It is admitted that the adjective is unfortunate and even misleading; but it is admitted, also, that the expression 'analytical jurisprudence' may stand for an explanation or interpretation of law which does not defy definition and which can be seen to be distinct from other kinds of explanation. It is not necessary for us to enquire whether any writer is to be found who has adhered strictly to this conception of jurisprudence, much less to enquire whether there is or has been a school of writers which has professed an exclusively analytical jurisprudence. We are concerned solely with the essential character of a certain kind of theory of the nature of law. How are we to think of it? 'The purpose of analytical jurisprudence,' writes Salmond, 'is to analyse, without reference either to their historical origin or to their ethical significance or validity, the first principles of law'.[1] And Allen suggests that what is being insisted upon by the 'equivocal epithet' 'analytical' is 'the examination of legal rules "without reference to their goodness or badness"'.[2] Now, I take it that negative accounts of this kind cannot be regarded as satisfactory; if we are to have a coherent view of the character of this kind of jurisprudence we shall require something more than a list (which could, of course, be extended indefinitely) of the views of the nature of law which it neglects to pursue or rejects. We must look further; and when we do so we are met, by Allen, with the view that what is really meant by 'analytical jurisprudence' is the science of law, and that its character is determined by its method of enquiry which is 'inductive and not deductive'. But when we have considered what this can mean we shall not, I think, find ourselves much better off. The expression 'the science of law' belongs to an age which used the word 'science' less precisely than we have come to use it; and if (which is

---

[1] *Jurisprudence*, p. 5. [Presumably John William Salmond, Jurisprudence, which had reached a ninth edition by 1937.]

[2] Carleton Kemp Allen, *Legal Duties and Other Essays in Jurisprudence* (Oxford: Clarendon Press, 1931), p. 15. The expression, of course, comes from Austin. But neither author makes clear whether by 'without reference to their goodness or badness' he means, 'without making a judgment about their goodness or badness' (i.e. a moral judgment), or, 'without relating them to ethical conceptions' (i.e. considering them in relation to the ideas of good and bad). And to exclude the one is not to exclude the other.

doubtful) the expression was once illuminating, it is certainly not so now. And when it is coupled with a theory of knowledge which makes an absolute distinction between an inductive and a deductive enquiry, the obscurity is only increased. There is, of course, no such thing as a 'purely inductive enquiry'; and least of all is such an enquiry characteristic of 'science'. Induction, I suppose, means keeping your eye on the facts; but it does not tell you what facts, and until we have some means of identifying our facts there is no such thing as an enquiry: 'pure induction' is pure nonsense. Once more we are baulked. What we are looking for, and what we are not given, by this (or so far as I know any other) writer is a positive and coherent view of the character and presuppositions of analytical jurisprudence.

There are, I think, two fundamental presuppositions which lie at the root of an explanation of law which may be called analytical, and which determine its character. First, there is the belief that there are certain basic elements in law *qua* law, that law as such has a skeleton of principles. And secondly, there is the belief that these are the essential principles of law, that in them lies the nature of law and that an exposition or interpretation of the nature of law is the exposition or synthesis of these principles. And it appears to me that what is required for a definition of analytical jurisprudence is nothing more than the recognition of these presuppositions. Its character does not lie in what it excludes, but in what it asserts; not in what it denies, but in what it affirms and presupposes. It, like every other intellectual enquiry, begins with certain presuppositions. And these which I have suggested are genuine presuppositions. The second is obviously so; and it implies a philosophy of identity which the analytical jurist, as a rule, does not examine but merely assumes. And if the first appears to be the product of an inductive examination of legal systems, the appearance is misleading; for any such inductive examination depends itself upon a definition of law, depends, that is, upon a presupposition, and 'induction and not deduction' is nowhere even in sight.[3] Here, then, is a precise and self-contained kind of theory or explanation of the nature of law, based upon its own presuppositions and different from every other kind of explanation; here is a genuine attempt, working with a recognisable hypothesis, to reduce legal phenomena to order and coherence. It is, of course, to be pursued in detail; and it remains for its professors to show us where it will lead. But what distinguishes it from all other explanations is not the exclusion of both ethical and historical considerations (indeed, it does not belong to its character to exclude these altogether and absolutely), but its presupposition that law is a body of interrelated principles. It is distinguished, that is, by the philosophy of identity which it assumes.

---

[3] The obvious defects of Salmond's definition quoted above are (i) it does not tell us what sort of analysis it is to be, it merely tells us some of the things it is not to be; and (ii) it assumes the existence of 'first principles of law' without recognizing that this is an assumption.

Now, it must be supposed that Allen, for example, sees, though darkly, that this type of jurisprudence depends upon the presuppositions I have stated. He admits, in the essay from which I have already quoted, that the belief that there are certain 'basic elements on which law *qua* law is built', that there are 'certain elements which are inherent in the very conception of law, considered as a phenomenon of social life, whatever the disparities may be in detail' in different legal systems, belongs to this kind of theory of law. And he writes of these basic elements as the 'essential principles of law'; and of jurisprudence as 'the systematic synthesis of them'. But he fails to recognise that these beliefs are presuppositions and that it is these presuppositions which define this type of jurisprudence. The first belief he attempts to justify by an argument from the inductive examination of legal systems, and the second he takes as a matter of course, assuming no possible alternative. And for his definition he falls back upon what this kind of explanation appears to exclude and upon the blessed word 'science'.

I will consider next the character of *historical* jurisprudence.[4] There are writers who, misled by the fact that the professor of an analytical jurisprudence may, without deserting the principles of explanation which govern his activity, have recourse to history, have reached the conclusion that there is no such thing as historical jurisprudence. There is legal history, and there is the use made of legal history by those who desire to reduce legal phenomena to order and coherence; but 'historical jurisprudence' is an expression with no distinctive meaning. I think, however, that this scepticism is misplaced. 'Historical' may not be the most appropriate adjective by which to distinguish a certain kind of explanation of the nature of law, but there is, nevertheless, a kind of explanation, different from all others, which the use of this adjective is intended to distinguish. An analytical jurisprudence may *make use* of history; but what, at least, we shall expect from an historical jurisprudence is that it will itself be conceived in the terms of history. And these terms are precisely what the analytical explanation is not conceived in. The fundamental principle and presupposition of an historical jurisprudence is the belief that the meaning of law lies not in certain abstract and abstracted 'essential principles of law', but in the history of the society or civilisation which is governed by and lives under a system of law. The essential character of law lies in its being a product of time. That is, historical jurisprudence is based upon a specific rejection of the philosophy of identity which leads to the view that law is a body of interrelated principles. Analytical jurisprudence may, perhaps must, go to the history of law in order to find and distinguish the 'es-

---

[4] It should be understood throughout that I am not considering schools of thought in jurisprudence, but types of explanation of the nature of law. That is, 'historical jurisprudence' does not stand for the jurisprudence of the 'historical' school of jurists, but for a theory of law which this school only partially apprehended and developed.

sential principles' which it conceives it to be its business to expound; but its aim is always to extract and abstract principles from that history. Historical jurisprudence, on the other hand, rejects the entire notion of essential principles, for historical explanation is, necessarily, not in terms of essences but in terms of historical individuals. It goes not only to legal history, but also to the history of a civilisation; and its results are not the abstract generalisations of analytical jurisprudence, but historical generalisations presented as such. Not only is its method historical, but its conclusions also are historical. There is, then, no difficulty in distinguishing historical from analytical jurisprudence; they are explanations of the nature of law based upon different and opposed presuppositions; they are distinct from one another not merely incidentally and in a matter of emphasis, but in principle. The expression 'historical jurisprudence' does not, like the expression 'comparative jurisprudence',[5] represent merely a method of research available to any jurisprudential enquiry; it represents a specific kind of theory or interpretation of the nature of law.

To distinguish historical jurisprudence from legal history is, however, a matter of greater difficulty, and, in the end, it is, I think, a matter of degree. It is possible to conceive the history of law so widely that it includes the history of the civilisation expressed (in part) in a system of law; and when legal history is conceived in this way it may not differ greatly from what I should call historical jurisprudence. Nevertheless, differences remain, and they are important to the understanding of the character of the attempt to explain the nature of law which is denoted by the expression 'historical jurisprudence'. First, legal history must always be the history of a specific body of legal rules and legal ideas; a history, perhaps, that relates them to their context of social and political ideas and institutions, but nevertheless a history of a particular society and its self-expression in law. Whereas historical jurisprudence involves an attempt to go beyond this and achieve, if possible, generalisations about the relation of law and civilisation of a wider character. And secondly, while legal history does not involve the presupposition that in writing the history of a body of legal rules and ideas we are presenting the fullest possible explanation of the nature of law (that is, legal history pretends to be nothing more than a history of law), histori-

---

[5] Comparative jurisprudence, when it means something to do with theory of law and not merely the laudable (but for our purpose irrelevant) attempt to consider the differences in national laws with a view to abolishing some of them, is a method of enquiry and not a type of explanation. Nevertheless, it is possible to see how it might be interpreted to represent a type of explanation. The principle, the presupposition which would determine its character would be the belief that the nature of law lies in what is *common* to all developed systems of law, that the essential principles of law are essential merely in virtue of their appearance in all systems of law. This presupposition, it should be observed, is different from the presupposition I have attributed to analytical jurisprudence, though it is one often to be found in the writings of those who profess an analytical enquiry. However, the view that what is common is, as such, what is essential invokes so indefensible a philosophy that it is a matter of congratulation that comparative jurisprudence has never been developed as a distinctive type of theory of law.

cal jurisprudence is expressly an explanation, an interpretation, a theory of law based upon the presupposition that law is its history, that the nature of law itself lies not in certain abstract essential principles of law, but in the history of law. Historical jurisprudence is not an attempt to unearth and exhibit what are (equivocally) called the 'origins' of legal rules and ideas, but to explain the nature of law in terms of the history of law. It involves not only an historical study of law, but a presupposition about the ultimate value of such a study.

Within this broad but definite conception of historical jurisprudence a variety of treatments are possible. But it is a limited variety, the differences depending always upon the conception of the historical context to which law is related in order to be explained and interpreted. And, in the end, the variety is, I think, arbitrary and logically unjustifiable. If we begin with the presupposition that the nature of law lies in the history of law, if we begin (for example) by referring law to the *Rechtsbewusstsein* of a society, there is no point in the exploration of the historical context at which we can justifiably stop. We may begin with a strictly conceived juridical historical context, but the logic of our presupposition will drive us to the political, institutional, economic, religious and social history which lies behind a body of legal rules, doctrines and ideas; we cannot stop short of the history of a civilisation.

Nothing like a thoroughgoing *psychological* interpretation of the nature of law is, I think, to be found in the literature of jurisprudence, but it is obviously a possible kind of interpretation and one which must be considered. And even if its value turned out to be small, it is not difficult to determine the general principles of its character. Law would be referred to the context of the 'psychology' of the makers of law, of the individual members of a community living under a system of law, or of the community as a group; and the explanation of the character of law would consist in this reference to this context. Law, perhaps, would be seen as the outcome of the activity of the human will; but the 'will', for this kind of explanation, would be a psychological, not a metaphysical entity. This type of explanation would, no doubt, explore the emotional context of law, and take note of the so-called irrational sources and tendencies of human desire and human action. And again, it might find in law the expression of moral ideas, but these moral ideas would themselves be explained in psychological terms. But whatever the actual contents might be of a psychological jurisprudence, the general character of this type of explanation would be determined by the presupposition that law is the expression of human personality, and that only an examination of the working and mechanism of human personality can afford an adequate explanation of the nature of law.

Having discussed analytical, historical, and psychological jurisprudence I have considered the three most clearly defined types of legal theory; but there are others, less precisely defined, which ought to be noticed. In particular there is what may be called the *economic* interpretation of the nature of law, and there is the *sociological* interpretation of the nature of law. Both these interpretations share, in part, the presuppositions which determine the character of historical jurisprudence, and therefore cannot be distinguished from it absolutely. But the one is an attempt to limit the historical context of law to what is believed to be the essential character (as distinct from its total character) of a civilisation and its history; and the other is an attempt to extend the context of law beyond a specifically historical context to what is spoken of as a sociological context.

It is not necessary to consider the details of the economic interpretation of law as they appear in the work of those who profess it. Many of these details are extraneous to the principle of explanation which belongs to and distinguishes this theory of law; and in the hands of some of these interpreters this economic jurisprudence degenerates into a theory, not of law but of legislation, a series of (mostly) historical generalisations about the making of law. But, in spite of much errant speculation, the principle which informs this kind of interpretation remains secure and distinct: it is the belief that the essential character of a civilisation lies in the prevailing conditions of the production of the material means of subsistence and in the economic organisation which springs immediately from these conditions,[6] the belief that law is part of a social superstructure which is built upon and determined by this foundation of economic organisation, and the belief that, in the last analysis, the final explanation of the nature of law (as of any specific system of laws) can consist solely in the reference of law to the foundation from which it springs. The nature of law lies neither in certain essential principles of law, nor in the history of law, nor in the comprehensive history of a civilisation, but in the essential foundation of a civilisation; and a theory of law is the relation of law to this, and not to any other, context. That an interpretation of the nature of law based upon these presuppositions will be distinct from all other kinds of interpretation (that is, from interpretations based upon other presuppositions) is, I think, clear enough; necessarily it presents itself as the only true and comprehensive interpretation, and since it is not either inherently absurd or so ambiguous as to be indistinguishable from other kinds of interpretation, it may take its place in the variety of kinds of theory of law which compose what is called jurisprudence.

---

[6] Cp. 'The first presupposition of all human history is naturally the existence of living human individuals, the first historical act of these individuals whereby they distinguish themselves from animals is not that they think but that they begin to produce the means of living.' Otto Neurath, *Empirische Soziologie: der wissenschaftliche gehalt der geschichte und nationalökonomie* (Vienna: J. Springer, 1931), p. 41.

Sociological jurisprudence[7] I have said is distinguished by its conception of the context to which law must be related in order to be explained fully. It is not a purely historical context; that is, a sociological jurisprudence will look not only to the past. It is not a purely material or economic context; that is, it will not attempt to reduce the social context of law to the conditions of production characteristic of a civilisation. What distinguishes it is its refusal to treat as irrelevant any element in the physical and social context of law; in the last analysis the meaning of law lies in the total physical and social environment of law. Law is the product of a civilisation, it is a means of maintaining a civilisation; it is a means of furthering a civilisation: and jurisprudence, the theory of law, is the exposition in detail of this general conception of the nature of law. Here again, is, I think, a kind of interpretation of the nature of law distinguishable from all others in virtue of its presuppositions. Certainly it has elements in common with the historical and with the economic interpretation of the nature of law, but its specific rejection of the essential presuppositions of both these interpretations constitutes it an independent theory. It has its place in the chaos of modern jurisprudence.

The purpose of this brief sketch of the world of jurisprudence is to indicate the world in which philosophical jurisprudence finds itself. No doubt there are other interpretations of the nature of law than these; and certainly we are offered a variety of conceptions of philosophical jurisprudence, which we shall have to examine later. But, whether or not a comprehensive survey of the world of jurisprudence would increase the variety of interpretations competing for recognition, and whichever of the various conceptions of philosophical jurisprudence we prefer, it remains true that the outstanding characteristic of this world of jurisprudence is its chaos. Jurisprudence is the name given to an unresolved variety of explanations of the nature of law; and an unresolved variety is a chaos. The first, and I believe greatest, defect common to all the current conceptions of philosophical jurisprudence is that it is conceived as one kind of explanation of the nature of law among others in a variety which it is not even considered necessary to attempt to resolve. By a wide tolerance it is allowed to exist; but such tolerance is only an excuse for a failure to recognise that unresolved variety is the same thing as confusion and that until a relationship, or a series of relationships, have been established between these different kinds of interpretation the confusion will remain.

Now, it is true that certain attempts have been made to relieve this situation in the world of jurisprudence, but since all of them are based upon a neglect of the fundamental character of the variety to be resolved they cannot be regarded as satisfactory. Two, perhaps, deserve notice. First, there

---

[7] As an example of this type of jurisprudence I have in mind Eugen Ehrlich, *Grundlegung der Soziologie des Rechts* (Munich and Leipzig: Duncker and Humblot, 1913).

The Concept of a Philosophical Jurisprudence 163

is the view that each of these kinds of interpretation is true and valuable for particular aspects of law. No one of them can be said to supersede any other, to be more comprehensive than any other or to offer a relevant criticism of any other: the variety of kinds of explanation merely reflects the irreducible variety of aspects of law. 'We cannot examine nineteenth century legislation,' writes Pound, 'without perceiving that organised pressure from groups having a common economic interest is *the sole explanation* of many things upon the statute book'.[8] That is to say, the economic interpretation of the nature of law is, at some points, though not at all, the only true and relevant interpretation; at other points, and for other elements in law, we may have recourse to other kinds of interpretation. And secondly there is the view for which jurisprudence is confined to one type of explanation of law and the others are regarded not as competing kinds of explanation, not, indeed, as kinds of explanation at all, but as methods of enquiry to be made use of when necessary in the pursuit of a theory of law. Thus, for example, there is no such thing as an historical jurisprudence, or a sociological jurisprudence; history and sociology are merely enquiries which provide some of the material for the construction of an analytical jurisprudence, and philosophical jurisprudence is dismissed as a work of supererogation—the philosophical contemplation (whatever that may mean) of the conclusions of analytical jurisprudence. But the radical defect of these and all similar attempts to relieve the chaos of an unrelated variety of kinds of explanation is that they neglect the actual character of the variety to be resolved. What we are faced with is a variety of kinds of explanation each of which, necessarily, asserts itself to be, in principle, final and complete. These are not differences of emphasis; they are differences of principle. What we have to do with is not a set of complementary methods of enquiry, but a set of mutually exclusive types of explanation. If, for example, the economic interpretation of law is the true interpretation, if, that is, it is true that the nature of law is to be satisfactorily explained only by relating law to the context of the conditions of production in a civilisation and that this is all that is necessary for its satisfactory explanation, then analytical jurisprudence (the explanation of the nature of law in terms of the essential principles of law) must be inadequate, at best a partial explanation and as false as it is partial.[9] And further, the conception of explanation implied in the sentence I have quoted from

---

[8] Roscoe Pound, *Interpretations of Legal History* (Cambridge: Cambridge University Press, 1923), p. 113 (my italics). Similarly, James Bryce, *Studies in History of Jurisprudence*, 2 vols. (Oxford: Clafendon Press, 1901), ii. 184, writes of the historical explanation of law: 'It explains many conceptions, doctrines and rules which no abstract theory can explain, because they issue not from general human reason and the nature of things, but from special conditions in the country or people when the law in question arose.'

[9] 'The jurist imagines that he operates with *a priori* propositions, but they are only economic reflexions.' Engels.

Pound is one which altogether destroys the basis of jurisprudence as the attempt to reduce legal phenomena to order and coherence. If we are allowed to improvise a fresh principle of explanation for each observed phenomenon our last state will not fail to be worse than our first.

The first conclusion, then, that I have to offer with regard to the world of jurisprudence as it is commonly presented to us is that it is distinguished by confusion and ambiguity. What is lacking is a coherent philosophy of explanation, and until this is supplied the confusion will continue. Philosophical jurisprudence is merely one among a variety of unrelated kinds of interpretation of the nature of law, and while it is merely this, it is necessarily impossible to determine its validity, or, indeed, to determine its character. If philosophical jurisprudence were presented to us as a member of a scale or hierarchy of explanations of the nature of law, a scale which exhibited all kinds of explanation in terms of a single standard of validity, or if it appeared as an explanation related in some other way to other explanations, then there would be less reason for us to be ashamed of the present position of enquiry in jurisprudence. But, in fact, it is either rejected altogether, or invited to join a chaos of unrelated types of explanation. 'Englishmen seem to have assumed as a fact a philosophy of law, but they have not been at pains to indicate its nature', wrote Professor Buckland nearly fifty years ago; and the only difference in the present situation is that the rot has spread to the continent.

It is time now to consider more closely the conceptions of a philosophy of law which the present position of enquiry offers us. There are, I think, five different conceptions to be found in the modern literature of the subject. Each of them assumes that a philosophical interpretation of law is merely one interpretation among others, to be pursued if we feel inclined, to be tolerated or to be dismissed as ineffectual. But apart from agreement to regard a philosophy of law as one of an unrelated variety of explanations of the nature of law, these five conceptions of its character are sufficiently distinct to merit separate consideration.

In the first place, a philosophy of law is conceived as the application of certain previously thought-out philosophical ideas, or some previously thought-out general philosophical doctrine, to law and the legal organisation of civil society. The business of a philosophy of law, it is assumed, is to conceive of law in such a way as to make it appear to *illustrate* some philosophical doctrine. The philosophy of law is itself nothing more than a special instance or application of a general philosophical theory; it merely exemplifies or illustrates. This, of all the conceptions of a philosophical jurisprudence that we are offered, is the least adequate; it displays in an extreme form what I believe the other four conceptions we are to examine display in one degree or another, an ignorance of the nature of philosophy, and it carries us directly to the contradictory conclusion that a philosophy of law is not itself philosophical. According to this view the only genuinely philosophical part of a philosophy of law is something prior to and independent of the consideration of legal concepts which the philosophy of law itself comprises. Philosophy is related to a philosophy of law merely as a presupposition, and the consideration of legal concepts, which is taken to be the actual business of a philosophical jurisprudence, is never itself a philosophical consideration, it is merely a consideration which presupposes some philosophical doctrine or other. In short, philosophical jurisprudence is philosophical in only a derivative sense, and if it became itself genuinely philosophical it would defeat its own ends, it would return into the general philosophical theory of which it was an illustration and cease to have any evident connection with law. And as an explanation of the nature of law it would clearly leave much to be desired.

The second view of the nature of philosophical jurisprudence which calls for notice is that for which the philosophy of law is what results from the employment of 'the metaphysical or *a priori* method' of enquiry. I cannot say that I fully understand what is intended by this description, but I take my account of this view from Bryce's essay on 'The Methods of Legal Science'.[10] Bryce claims to be describing the method which such writers as Kant and Hegel use in investigating the nature of law. The philosophy of law, it appears, consists in the examination of certain abstract ideas such as Right, Duty, Obligation 'in relation to Morality, Freedom and the human Will generally', and the construction, by way of deduction from these ideas, of a coherent system of law and legal relations. In virtue of this it is called an *a priori* investigation, and what distinguishes it from all other kinds of enquiry is its *a priori* method. Now, it is not clear to me why, or in what sense, a metaphysical enquiry is thought to be necessarily *a priori* in method, nor why an attempt to devise a perfect system of law and legal relationships should be thought to have anything at all to do with a philosophy of law. Let us consider these difficulties in turn. What, I take it, is suggested here by calling this method of enquiry an *a priori* method is that it begins from general principles and not from observed facts; the general principles being these abstract ideas of Right, Duty etc., and the facts being actual legal rules and doctrines. And if any enquiry into the nature of law is to be called *a priori* which refuses to accept as complete and not to be questioned or revised the interpretations of the nature of legal entities as they appear in a text book of law, then, I suppose, this enquiry is *a priori*. But then so are all other enquiries which are in the least degree illuminating. Neither analytical nor historical jurisprudence accept law in the character in which it first appears to them; both are attempts to expound the nature of law by relating law as it first appears to some general principle and in this way transforming and making fuller our view of the nature of

---

[10] *Studies in History and Jurisprudence*, ii, 172.

law.[11] In short, this attempt to define philosophical jurisprudence as an enquiry into the nature of law which is 'deductive and not inductive' is as misconceived as the attempt we noticed earlier to define analytical jurisprudence as an enquiry which is 'inductive and not deductive'. If a priori here means 'not from experience', then, since no knowledge is or could be *a priori*, the term is a piece of meaningless jargon; in this sense an *a priori* method is not a possible method of enquiry. The absolutely *a priori* is the nearest thing to the absolutely absurd. And if it means, 'from some experience, but not merely from what is given directly in a first and superficial knowledge of law', then the expression *a priori* applies equally to all thorough-going attempts to explain the nature of law, and affords no means of differentiating a philosophical explanation from an explanation of another kind: in this sense both analytical and historical jurisprudence are *a priori*. The second difficulty raises questions which will appear again in connection with the third of the conceptions of the nature of philosophical jurisprudence which I have chosen to consider, and I will postpone what I have to say about it. But even if it could be met satisfactorily, this view of the nature of a philosophy of law would remain ambiguous and ill-defined, and it does not appear to me to be a recognisable description of the work, for example, of Hegel.

I pass now to the third, and perhaps most common, conception of the nature of a philosophy of law. According to this, philosophical jurisprudence is the consideration of the rules and doctrines of law from the standpoint of their goodness and badness, and the determination of the end that ought to be pursued in making and administering the law.[12] Such a consideration may, of course, take a variety of forms ; the goodness and badness of a law may be taken to mean its fitness or unfitness to meet what are conceived as the needs of the society or they may be taken to mean the agreement or disagreement of a law with some ideal and absolute standard of justice. Such differences are, however, secondary; what all such explanations have in common is their attempt to judge law itself from the standpoint of its goodness and badness and their attempt to determine the general nature of the end which the law itself should be designed to produce. And this is called an ethical or philosophical interpretation of the nature of law. Questions of fact are separated from questions of right, and a philosophical jurisprudence is taken to be concerned with questions of right, not to define the nature of 'right', but to determine the rightness or wrongness of the legal arrangements of a society; not to define a criterion,

---

[11] Cp. Allen, op cit., p. 16. '[T]he essential principles of law do not lie on the surface; they can be discovered only by penetrating through a multitude of distracting appearances.'

[12] Cp. 'The task of the theory of law is not definition. It is to find out the means by which certain specified rules of law operate; and if one believes that there is no distinction between the theory and the philosophy of law, this means to discuss the end which a system of rules ought to serve.' Ivor Jennings (ed.), in *Modern Theories of Law* (Oxford: Oxford University Press, 1933), p. 83.

but to deliver precepts, and to construct an ideal system of legal relationships. Now, in the view of many writers this conception of the philosophy of law will not brand it at once as essentially non-philosophical. But in my view it does so. The notion that the business of a philosophy of any sort is actually to determine ends is, I think, false. The philosophy of law may plausibly be supposed to undertake the task of representing the legal arrangements of a society as means to the achievement of some end, and even the task of analysing the general concepts of means and end (though this should be regarded as a particular philosophical doctrine requiring substantiation, rather than as the universal form of philosophical theories of law); but this is something quite different from the determination of which among many suggested ends the legislator and the law ought to pursue. Even so muddled a philosopher as Bentham recognised, in his lucid moments, that 'happiness' in his theory of legislation stood, not for an end which ought to be preferred to any other that might suggest itself as an alternative, but for a brief analysis of the nature of what alone is an end in itself, of what alone is desirable for its own sake. To investigate the nature of a moral criterion is an ethical and a philosophical enquiry; but to determine the goodness and badness of a law involves a moral judgment which the philosopher as such is in no better position to give than any other member of society. In short, this view of the nature of philosophical jurisprudence is less than satisfactory because it attributes to the theory of law a character which really belongs to a theory of legislation, and to the philosophy of law a character which is essentially non-philosophical.

An attempt to interpret sociologically theories of the nature of law which are presented as philosophies of law provides a fourth view of their character. Such an attempt is to be found in the writings of Dean Pound[13] and elsewhere. A philosophy of law is conceived as an explanation or interpretation of the nature of law in terms of what is sociologically useful at a particular stage in the life of a civilisation or a society. The function of philosophical jurisprudence is to provide a view of the nature of law appropriate to the needs of a society. Thus the Natural Law theory is regarded as 'a philosophical theory for a period of growth'; it was elaborated in order to retain stability in a time of rapid change. And the Natural Right theory is a philosophy of law appropriate to 'an era of discovery and colonisation and trade'. If this view were presented to us as merely a description of a function which what might for other reasons be called philosophical theories of law have performed or may be expected to perform, there would be no reason to quarrel with it. No doubt a period of rapid growth in the legal organisation of a society would find useful a Natural Law philosophy and would give its adherence and blessing to such a

---

[13] Roscoe Pound, *Introduction to the Philosophy of Law* (New Have; London: Yale University Press; Humphrey Milford, 1922), pp. 15–83. *Interpretations of Legal History*, pp. 30–32.

philosophy. But it is presented as something more; it appears as a conception of the nature of the philosophy of law. And considered in this character it leaves much to be desired. Merely to relate a philosophical doctrine to some social purpose which it might conceivably be made to subserve is to do something much less than to define the nature of philosophical enquiry. If no more than this could be said of a philosophical doctrine, then the only relevant criterion for judging its adequacy as an interpretation of the nature of law would be the efficiency with which it performed what was assumed to be a useful social purpose, and the only relevant criticism would be the demonstration of its failure to serve such a purpose. Each philosophy would be true in its own place—if 'true' could still be said to have any meaning. But the adjective 'philosophical', to have any significance worth considering, must mean the same thing whether it is attached to a theory of law or (for example) to a theory of belief. It must not be made to mean, 'subserving some temporary social need by providing a useful myth' when it is attached to a theory of law unless we are prepared to accept this meaning universally. And to accept this meaning universally implies (among much else that is disconcerting) a theory of knowledge which refuses to be judged by its own standards. And this contradiction appears wherever (as here) a sociology of knowledge is substituted for a philosophy of knowledge. And further, in order to establish this view it would be necessary to show that the different 'philosophies' of law appeared in different and only in appropriate circumstances ; and this, I believe, is impossible. Both the Natural Law theory and the Natural Right theory of the nature of law come to us from the ancient world and flourish together in the modern world, and as philosophies of law are entirely independent of any use that may have been made of them by judges, legislators or statesmen.

Lastly we come to the view that philosophical jurisprudence consists of relating what are conceived as 'the conclusions of jurisprudence' to general philosophical principles. It accepts the results of, say, an analytical jurisprudence and considers them in conjunction with some philosophical doctrine. This, we are told, 'is really what the great works of "philosophy of law", such as Kant's and Hegel's, seek to do.'[14] And it is suggested that philosophical jurisprudence is really the 'philosophy of jurisprudence'. I do not propose to examine this conception of philosophical jurisprudence in detail; its ambiguities and errors are on the surface and themselves cry out for its rejection. As a description of the work of Kant and Hegel it is difficult to recognise, and different from the description we have noticed in Bryce, which is itself equally difficult to recognise. But further, the notion that it is the business of philosophy to accept the conclusions of special enquiries—history, jurisprudence, physics, etc.—and relate them,

---

[14] Allen, op. cit., p. 17.

unchanged, to 'general philosophical principles', though once popular, is now on all hands seen to be the nonsense that it always was. For philosophy these 'conclusions' are never, and never could be, mere data to be accepted; to consider them as such involves a misconception of the nature of knowledge, of philosophical enquiry and of the character of the so-called 'conclusions'. Any genuine synthesis of 'results' must be a reinterpretation; and in interpretation what is given is accepted, not categorically as something already established, but hypothetically as a useful starting-place for thought. If 'general philosophical principles' come in anywhere it is at the beginning and not at the end, in an examination of the presuppositions upon which these 'conclusions' rest and not in a kind of harmless and ineffectual synthesis of the 'conclusions' themselves. The best, perhaps, that can be said of this view of the character of philosophical jurisprudence is that no more ingenious way could be found for at once extending to it an apparent tolerance and depriving it of any coherent meaning whatever.

So far I have been considering the ideas about the character of philosophical jurisprudence that the modern literature of the subject offers us. And the general concept of a philosophy of law which they appear to imply seems to me exceedingly incoherent and unconvincing. A philosophy of law, according to these views, is really nothing better than a contradiction; it is a philosophy which, for one reason or another, is not philosophical and one which if it became genuinely philosophical would cease to have any close connection with law. It is said to be built upon a philosophy but when it is examined there is nothing at all philosophical about the superstructure itself. It is said to imply a philosophy; but the philosophical doctrine is never taken to imply the theory of law. It appeals to criteria which are anything but philosophical. It is tolerated in the world of jurisprudence mainly because it has been deprived of any recognisable philosophical character. And the world of jurisprudence into which it is patronisingly admitted is itself nothing better than a chaos of unrelated kinds of explanation of the nature of law.

Now, I do not suggest that the views I have considered are the only views which a wider study of the literature of the theory of law would supply. What I have been considering is the views which seem to satisfy writers at the present time, and to have satisfied them for some considerable time past. But I believe that the confusion and ambiguity which distinguishes these views would to a large extent be resolved if we returned, without our prejudices, to a study of some of the great philosophical theories of law which our civilisation has produced. Neither Aquinas, nor Hobbes, nor Hegel, nor even Green was guilty of these follies. Whatever lack of success may have attended their attempts to construct a philosophical theory of law, they knew quite well what a philosophy of law is and they knew that it could not be any of the things which we are now told that it is. Anyone, then, who attempts to think out afresh a conception of philosophical jurisprudence, while he will find little help in the present position of enquiry, is certainly not without guidance. And with the help that there is to be had from the great traditions of philosophical thinking about law, I propose now to attempt the construction of a view of the character of philosophical jurisprudence which shall, at least, avoid the errors and difficulties which discredit the current views.

II

I take it that, whatever else is required of a philosophical jurisprudence, it must at least be philosophical: the main defect of the concepts I have examined is that they attribute to philosophical jurisprudence a character which is non-philosophical. And in order to avoid the confusion which has resulted from this error we must, in the first place, be clear about the character and attributes of a philosophical enquiry.

A philosophical enquiry, as I understand it, is not a kind of enquiry different from all others, and philosophical knowledge is not a special kind of knowledge derived from some special source of information. It has its *differentia*; but what is primarily important is to see it in its place in the common world of intellectual enquiry. Philosophical thought and knowledge is simply thought and knowledge without reservation or presupposition. The aim in philosophy is to arrive at concepts which, because they presuppose nothing, are complete in themselves; the aim is to define and establish concepts so fully and so completely that nothing remains to be added. Definition is a matter of degree. All thinking is the attempt to define concepts, and philosophy is merely what occurs when thought is allowed to follow its own bent with unqualified freedom. Thought, the character of which is exemplified in every attempt at intellectual comprehension, is perfectly exemplified in philosophical comprehension. A philosophical doctrine, therefore, should not be understood as a kind of solid basis upon which things like science and the conduct of practical life ultimately rest; science and practical life, as such, have no philosophical foundations. It should be thought of as something which happens at the end, when the concepts of science, or common-sense, or practical life are subjected to the revolutionary and dissolving criticism of being related to a universal context. Thus, any complete following out of the demands of thought has a constant tendency to *overbalance* into philosophical thought; for until it has become philosophical it must remain relatively unstable.

Now, all this requires fuller explanation; each of the statements in the preceding paragraph must be examined, extended, made clear if we are to have a philosophical definition of the concept of philosophy.

The Concept of a Philosophical Jurisprudence

The starting place in philosophy is not some remote region of experience known only to the philosopher, it is not with self-evident ideas or axioms, it is not with the conclusions as such of special enquiries. Philosophy begins with the concepts of ordinary, every-day knowledge; and it consists in an extended, detailed and complete exposition of those concepts, an exposition which is itself a definition. A philosophy of law, for example, does not begin with already defined and accepted abstract ideas such as the ideas of Right, Duty, Obligation; it begins with the ideas about law which anyone who has not considered the question may be supposed to have; it begins with any concept of law a man, however uninstructed, may happen to find in his head. In philosophy, therefore, there is no such thing as a transition from mere ignorance to complete knowledge; the process is always one of coming to know more fully and more clearly what is in some sense already known. And there is no such thing as a mere addition to philosophical knowledge; the process is always one of radical reformulation of the whole of what is already known. It is not the extension and elaboration of the meaning of a concept, but the establishment of a new and more comprehensive meaning. The philosophical concept, that is, at once comprehends and supersedes the concept given to philosophical enquiry.

The process in philosophical enquiry may be regarded, from one point of view, as a process of getting rid of, or of resolving, the presuppositions and reservations contained in whatever concepts are presented for examination. This is sometimes thought of as a process of laying, or discovering, *foundations*; but it is misleading to think of it in this way. For when these presuppositions have been revealed, and *a fortiori* when they have been resolved, the originally presented concept has been entirely transformed and superseded. And, moreover, the aim in philosophical enquiry is not merely to achieve concepts with no unexamined or unjustified presuppositions, but to achieve concrete concepts from which the division between presupposition and conclusion has vanished. Presuppositions and conclusions are alike abstractions to be got rid of; and the only way of getting rid of them (without merely denying them) is by establishing concepts in which the two elements are, not equally well-known, not merely held together in agreement, but actually unified. The philosophical concept is not a collection of abstracts, it is not, for example, a scientific or a common-sense concept plus the presuppositions which lie behind it, but is itself a concrete unity. And it is this because this is what a fully defined concept must be.

In philosophical enquiry, then, the task is one of definition, not the definition of words, but of concepts. And definition is the making clearer of something which is already to some extent apprehended and therefore to some extent clear; it is essentially the removal of ambiguities in a concept which is presented and is, therefore, not merely ambiguous; it is making more definite what is already to some extent defined. Philosophical definition is, in this sense, a matter of degree: we never move from what we are entirely ignorant of to complete knowledge, but from what we know to what we know more fully and more clearly apprehend: we never move from an accepted axiom (a fixed and finished definition) to the theorems implied in the axiom, but from an imperfectly defined concept to that concept more perfectly defined. That is, at each step we redefine what is already in some degree defined, and our aim is the establishment of a concrete concept, devoid of ambiguity and partiality.

Now, that this is the starting place and this is the process in philosophical enquiry will be clear, I think, to anyone who has studied the history of philosophical thought. The so-called Socratic method is an example, though an imperfect example, of the process I have been trying to describe; so also is the method of enquiry pursued by Kant and Hegel; so also, though more obscurely, is the method characteristic of Scholastic philosophy. In what I have said, and in what I shall say about the nature of a philosophical enquiry I have not been drawing upon merely my own personal convictions; I have been describing what I have learnt from the history of philosophy. But the truth of this view of the nature of philosophical enquiry does not rest merely upon the fact that it is the view implied in the work of celebrated philosophers, but upon the fact that no other starting point and no other process are available. Of everything that philosophical enquiry discusses we have learnt something in the nursery; even the most unreflective of mankind will find in his head concepts of truth and error, right or wrong, reality and appearance, and the philosopher must begin with these if he is to begin at all. The one thing there is no difficulty about in philosophy is knowing where to begin. And the process of redefinition is the process involved in all intellectual enquiry whatever. Knowledge is always the getting to know more fully something that is already known. Philosophical enquiry is peculiar merely because, in the pursuit of this process it is governed by a radical scepticism with regard to every stopping place that is suggested; it is suspicious of every attempt to limit the enquiry.

This, then, is the starting point, and this is the process in philosophical enquiry; but a word must be said of the conclusion. So far I have said that the aim in philosophical thought is the achievement, by means of a continuous process of redefinition, of concrete concepts; and this requires to be amplified. There are four characteristics or attributes of the philosophical concept to which I wish to draw attention. It is (i) New, (ii) Categorical, (iii) Affirmative, and (iv) Indicative. These characteristics do not, of course, exhaust its character.

(i) New. A philosophical concept is essentially the redefinition of an already formulated concept. Philosophy is the attempt to redefine its given concepts concretely, that is in relation to a universal context, the context of the totality of experience. And, consequently, a philosophical concept (e.g. of law) *must* be different from the given concept with which philosophical enquiry starts. There *must* be disagreement between a concept as it is for, say, common-sense, and as it is for philosophy. Now this, for many people, is a stumbling-block; for them it is proof, or at least a symptom, of the unreality and falsehood inseparable from philosophy. But the principle involved seems to me clear and simple. If what is undertaken is a transformation, you must not reject the result because it is different from what you began with. And, of course, the important implication in this principle is that 'verification' in philosophy cannot be by mere 'reference to the facts'. 'The facts' are merely 'our ordinary way of regarding the facts', or, 'the concept as it is for common-sense', and these, though they are the starting place of a philosophical enquiry, are necessarily irrelevant as a criterion for the result of philosophical enquiry. It is *ex hypothesi* impossible for the philosophical concept of, say, justice, to agree with (in the sense of being the same as) the concept as it is for common-sense; and consequently it must be false to suppose that agreement with the common-sense concept is the criterion by which the philosophical concept is to be judged. 'Verification' in philosophical enquiry lies always ahead in what the concept is to become, and never behind in what it was when we first began work upon it. Nevertheless, although it is an error to suppose that a philosophical definition can be verified by referring it to these so-called 'facts', it is incumbent upon the philosopher to show as fully as he can how his redefinition is connected with and arises out of the less comprehensive definition with which he began. That is, his definition must be presented as a conclusion from a continuous argument. A philosopher can establish his definition only by showing in detail the process of definition and by showing that his conclusion is itself concrete.

(ii) Categorical. A philosophical concept must always be in the form of a categorical judgment. By this, I do not, of course, mean that it may not be tentative; I mean that it may not be hypothetical. Hypotheses are reservations, presuppositions; and the whole business of philosophy is to get rid of reservations and presuppositions. But to say that a philosophical concept must be categorical means more than this; it means that definition in philosophical enquiry aims at comprehending the whole character of its subject and its character as a single whole. Of course it is not possible or desirable that every aspect of a concept should be indicated explicitly in a philosophical definition; but if the definition is to be philosophically satisfactory it must be possible to show how it has implicitly included or superseded all other views. A philosophical concept is categorical because it is complete. And compromise, concepts defined in the form of 'a little of this and a little of that', is always unsatisfactory in philosophical enquiry; for compromise is the sign of lack of completeness in definition, the sign of makeshift.

(iii) *Affirmative.* A philosophical concept must always be an affirmative or positive concept, never merely a negative concept. Negativity is merely a sign of an imperfect definition. And where the given concept is negative, one part at least of the business of a philosophical enquiry is to transform this negative into a positive. This, perhaps, is only another way of saying that a philosophical concept must be categorical; hypotheses are always a negative element. And this transformation of a negative into a positive is a typical example of the process in philosophical enquiry — a process which involves the examination of the implications *in* what is given. A negative always and unavoidably implies a positive, and until this positive is brought to the surface what we have must remain only partly coherent. Salmond's definition of analytical jurisprudence quoted above is an example of a negative concept calling out to be transformed into something positive.[15]

(iv) *Indicative.* This again is not a separate characteristic of the philosophical concept, but one implied in its categorical and affirmative character. And it means that wherever an imperative is presented, philosophy must transform it into an indicative; wherever 'ought' presents itself the business of philosophy is to uncover the implied 'is'. A mere imperative is an abstraction, a conclusion based upon a presupposition but which has become separated from its presupposition; and philosophical enquiry exists to create concrete concepts in which neither the separation nor the distinction between presupposition and conclusion any longer exist.

Let us bring together what we have learned about philosophical enquiry by considering briefly its nature from a fresh standpoint. All explanation, all interpretation may be seen as a matter of deciding upon and examining the appropriate setting for what is to be explained and of exhibiting it in its place in that setting. Given a 'text', something partially disconnected, obscure, imperfectly conceived, explanation is the attempt to find the 'context' and to relate text and context so that they become a single whole. But each context which presents itself as *prima facie* appropriate is seen itself to require explanation, to belong to a setting and to lack significance so long as it is not seen in that setting. Consequently, the process becomes the search for a context which does not require a further setting in order to be understood, a universal, self-complete context. And the task in philosophical enquiry is, precisely, to find and elucidate such a context and the special subject of its enquiry in that context. For what the text is depends upon the context; it has a fresh meaning for each context to which it is related; and it has its full and comprehensive meaning only in a universal, self-complete context. There are, then, two main stages in the process of

---

[15] See Part I of this article, p. 156.

The Concept of a Philosophical Jurisprudence

philosophical enquiry; distinguishable, but inseparable. First, there is the identification, the mere designation of the subject of enquiry. If we are to determine the meaning of the concept 'law', we must first know how to apply the word 'law'. And this is to be learnt only by a critical examination of the ways in which the word is ordinarily used. But such an examination leaves us with merely the definition of a word, leaves us with merely the identification of a thing. We have that one thing clearly before us, but we have nothing else; we have the text, but its full meaning is still to seek. We must, then, proceed, secondly, to the definition of the concept. And this involves not merely having the one thing (in this case of a philosophical jurisprudence the one thing is 'law') clearly before us, and being able to recognise it every time it appears, but also knowing its relationship to other things, knowing it in a world of related things, knowing it in its context. And our task becomes a double task — discovery of a context which is self-complete and the elucidation of the subject of our enquiry in the terms of this context. Many contexts will present themselves, and each, in so far as it is *prima facie* separable and significant, will claim to be the universal context we are looking for. But in so far as it is unable to maintain such a claim, it will suffer rejection in favour of a more complete context. Thus, every explanation whatever is, from one point of view, the relation of a text to a context; and a philosophical explanation is one which, in principle, is the relation of its subject to what I have called the totality of experience because this alone is a self-complete context, a context which criticism cannot turn into a text itself requiring a context.

Nobody, I hope, will mistake these remarks about the nature of philosophical enquiry for an exhaustive treatment of the subject; but that, when related to the matter in hand (the concept of a philosophical jurisprudence), they introduce us to a view somewhat different from the current views is, I think, obvious. They attribute to philosophical jurisprudence a character at once less ambiguous and less pretentious than it is accustomed to bear. And when the implications of this view of philosophy are examined it will be found to give us a principle by means of which the prevailing chaos in the world of jurisprudence may be resolved; instead of a chaos of unrelated kinds of explanation of law, jurisprudence becomes, what it must be if it is to be anything at all, a world of related explanations. Let us consider the matter more fully. If philosophical enquiry is what I have suggested it is, what will be the character of a philosophical jurisprudence?

It is unnecessary for me to apply in detail my view of the nature of philosophy to the study of the nature of law; I have given the principle, and the reader, if he cares, can easily apply it for himself. It is clear where a philosophical jurisprudence will begin; it is clear what course a philosophical enquiry into the nature of law will pursue, and it is clear also what, in general, may be expected by way of result from such an enquiry. But, in case they may be overlooked, I will point out what I take to be the two most important characteristics of a philosophical jurisprudence. First, it will cease to be merely one among a number of unrelated explanations of law; it will be one explanation of the nature of law in a hierarchy of explanations. It has the authority to create this hierarchy by supplying a universal criterion by which the adequacy, the relative completeness of all explanations may be determined; and the exercise of this authority transforms the chaos of jurisprudence into a world. And secondly, it will have a definite place in this hierarchy of explanations — at the end. And it is by virtue of this place in the hierarchy that it possesses the authority I have attributed to it. Philosophical jurisprudence, in short, has a two-sided character: it is one explanation of the nature of law among others, and it has the authority inherent in its character to judge the relative completeness of all explanations and so make of all explanations a related whole or world. How can this be?

A philosophical enquiry, I have suggested, has for its purpose the concrete definition of its subject, it aims at relating its subject to a context which is universal, a context which I have called the totality of experience. And a philosophical enquiry into the nature of law is the attempt to reduce the phenomena of legally organised society to order and coherence by relating them to the totality of experience. But philosophical thought, we have seen, is not a peculiar kind of thought with special sources of information at its disposal; it is simply thought which has been allowed to follow its own bent with unqualified freedom — freedom from reservation and presupposition. And it follows from this that a philosophical jurisprudence, in so far as it achieves what it is its purpose to achieve, is at once the most complete kind of explanation of the nature of law (for *ex hypothesi* the context to which it relates law is complete) and the criterion by means of which the relative incompleteness of other explanations can be determined and established. Consider how a philosophical enquiry into the nature of law would proceed. It might, perhaps, begin with the definition of the concept of law supplied by what we have called an analytical jurisprudence, an analytical jurisprudence which attempted to explain the nature of law not by relating law to something outside itself but by deducing its nature from a study of what were presupposed to be legal systems. This concept of law, under the pressure of criticism, would prove itself to be abstract, for the context it appealed to and relied upon would quickly reveal itself to be narrow and incomplete. A wider, less inadequate context would be sought, and found, perhaps, in the politics of the community which lived under a system of law. But, again, the political context would be seen to have a setting to which it must be related if it is to make itself immune from supersession. And from politics the enquiry might turn to history, to economic organisation, to social structure, to individual and social psychology, to moral ideas, each suggested stopping place proving itself in turn insecure. But at some point the pursuit would stop, not in an artificial arrest, not in a state of disequilibrium, but because a point had been reached beyond which it was not possible to go because there was no beyond. And the detailed elaboration of that point would be a philosophy of law. There would be no necessity in this pursuit for the enquiry to pass through every one of these stages, and there are others which I have not mentioned;[16] it might take a different course, and reach its end not by a process of allowing each of these stages to prove its inadequacy, but by a critical examination of more elementary concepts of law than were to be found in these suggested explanations. But whatever course it took it would retain its double character; it would be, in so far as it was successful, a complete explanation and in virtue of this it would supply the criterion by means of which the relative completeness of all other explanations could be determined and by means of which a world of explanations could be created.

But one thing further must be noticed. It is clear, I think, that a philosophical enquiry into the nature of law would very soon apprehend the incompleteness of the explanation of the nature of law offered in an analytical jurisprudence and would make the best of its way to something less abstract. And so with other relatively incomplete explanations, other relatively incoherent concepts of law. But its judgment would not be, 'Analytical or historical or sociological jurisprudence has proved itself an incomplete explanation of the nature of law; henceforth let no one pursue such an explanation,' but, 'These explanations are incomplete, some more so than others; henceforth let no one who pursues them believe that they are other than what they are.' Its principle, in short, is, 'Everything is true so long as you do not take it for more than it is'. And its business would not be to meet each kind of explanation upon its own ground and do for each what each is attempting to do for itself, but to examine the ground of each kind of explanation, and to examine it from the standpoint of its ability to provide the principle of a complete explanation.

The situation, then, which a philosophical enquiry into the nature of law has to meet is, in effect, the claim on the part of a variety of different and mutually exclusive explanations of the nature of law to be *the* explanation, to provide, that is, a complete explanation which comprehends and supersedes all others. For what is asserted implicitly in every explanation is that it explains; and to explain must mean to explain fully. And the first task of a philosophical enquiry is to examine these claims. 'A legal system,' we are told, 'can best be understood in the light of the conditions under which it

---

[16] E.g. the context of law which is implied in the so-called 'institutional' theory of law.

has grown up'.[17] And again, 'Dean Pound in his book *Interpretations of Legal History* has shown in his analysis of the legal philosophies of the past that each of them is primarily an attempt to formulate in general terms the ideals and purposes of law at a particular period'.[18] What is asserted here if it is not the 'primacy' of what may be called sociological interpretation of the nature of law? It is suggested that this is the 'best' or most complete kind of explanation. But what are the grounds of this assertion? To substantiate it would mean, among other things, the conviction of analytical or psychological jurisprudence of radical defect, of partiality. The explicit suggestion is that this sociological context is at once an appropriate and a self-complete context by reference to which the nature of law is fully revealed; and the implicit suggestion is that all other contexts will reveal in law a nature that is less than its full nature. And so on, with each of these kinds of explanation; each makes a similar claim. And the first business of a philosophical enquiry is to adjudicate these claims. And it can do this only by a critical examination of their grounds. In short, the unavoidable situation is one in which every kind of explanation of the nature of law claims to be what I have called a philosophical explanation; and until this situation is cleared up jurisprudence remains a chaos of conflicting claims. And it can be cleared up only by the establishment of a hierarchy of explanations the principle of which is, 'one explanation is better than another if the context to which it refers law for explanation is a more complete context'. And if, for example, the sociological explanation of law is to maintain the primacy claimed for it, what must be shown is that the sociological context is a context which criticism cannot turn into a text itself requiring a context. And it is just this which Dean Pound and the other champions of this type of explanation have never attempted.[19]

Now, it is not difficult to imagine a reader who will say to himself — 'I can understand that jurisprudence must remain a chaos of unrelated kinds of explanation of the nature of law until some connection has been established between them. And I can understand that nothing short of a universal criterion of adequacy will turn this chaos into a world. Briefly, I can understand that a great service to jurisprudence would be performed if a kind of explanation of law could be found which had, inherent in its nature, the authority to be the operative criticism of all explanations; and a

---

[17] Wortley, in *Modern Theories of Law*, p. 141.
[18] Goodhart, in *Modern Theories of Law*, p. 1.
[19] The representative set of writers who examined, in the volume *Modern Theories of Law* (1933), some contemporary theories of law did not, so far as I can see, produce between them a single radical criticism of the types of theory involved in the theories they discussed. No better indication could be found of what I have called the chaos of modern jurisprudence than this volume. It should be remembered that the chaos I have remarked upon is not the result of the existence of a number of different theories (these there will always be, and since they are critical of one another they are not unrelated to one another), but of a number of different, mutually exclusive and unrelated types of theory.

philosophical explanation is not a bad name for this kind of explanation. But, beyond this service of criticism, what would be the actual contents of a philosophical jurisprudence?' And scepticism of this kind is certainly in place. It can be met, however, by the following considerations. First, no kind of explanation of the nature of law could have, inherent in its character, this critical authority unless it were a complete explanation. If in this sense there is no such thing as a philosophical jurisprudence, then there is no such thing as a world or whole of jurisprudence; all we would have, and all we could have, is this chaos of unrelated kinds of explanation. But we cannot have this, because it conflicts with the very nature of explanation. A kind of explanation which is abstract and incomplete is only another name for a kind of explanation that does not explain, a kind of theory which does not reduce to order and coherence the phenomena of legally organised society, a kind of interpretation which fails to interpret. And if two or more conflicting kinds of explanation offer themselves (as we have seen in the current view of the matter they do) the one supposition that is intolerable is that they are all equally adequate. Some or all must be abstract and incomplete and consequently must fail to explain. They may each serve a special purpose, and the pursuit of each may always retain its usefulness, but judged as explanations of the nature of law they cannot be all equally complete. And if they are not equally complete, then there is, hidden in this chaos, the principle of a world; and the principle of a world is a kind of explanation which comprehends and supersedes all others. In short, if a philosophical jurisprudence had no actual contents it could not perform the service of criticism which jurisprudence cannot do without. And secondly, a philosophical jurisprudence of the kind I have suggested is not something which exists merely in my imagination, it is not something I have invented because it is intolerable that it should not exist; it is to be found, living and active, in the work, for example, of Aquinas, of Hobbes and of Hegel. The Natural Law theory of civil society, in any of its forms, is, for example, precisely a philosophical jurisprudence of this character, and nothing but an ignorant scepticism could doubt that this theory has a positive content. I am not suggesting that this particular philosophical theory of law has the monopoly of the truth; I am suggesting merely that it has a positive content which enables it, for better or for worse, to exercise the kind of critical authority which belongs to a philosophical theory.

We have come, it seems, a long way from anything that what I have called the present position of enquiry has to offer. To the best of my ability I have done what I made it my first business to do, to make clearer the nature and causes of the chaos which prevails in what goes by the name of jurisprudence. And I have tried to show also how, in principle, a philosophical jurisprudence might be conceived; I have tried to show the kind of service that such a jurisprudence could perform in the study of the nature of law. This is a positive conclusion, and the concept of a philosophical jurisprudence I have suggested, whether or not it is entirely satisfactory, is certainly free from the main contradictions and ambiguities which make nonsense of the current views of the matter. And further, it is the concept which an examination of the great texts in the history of the philosophical enquiry into the nature of law suggests. But the second part of my undertaking remains to be considered; if this concept of a philosophical jurisprudence enables us to make a fresh start, unencumbered with the absurdities of the present position, we need to know the direction which enquiry may most profitably take, we need a programme of study, we need (what is singularly lacking to-day in philosophical jurisprudence) an agenda. And I will conclude this essay by offering some brief remarks on this topic.

III

The greatest hindrances which stand in the way of a fresh and profitable start with the philosophical enquiry into the nature of law are the prevailing ignorance about what has already been accomplished in this enquiry, and the prejudice, that springs from this ignorance, that little or nothing has been accomplished. But we have seen that philosophical jurisprudence need not be of the confused and anomalous character which is at present attributed to it. And I have suggested that a consideration of the history of philosophical enquiry into the nature of law confirms us in this conclusion. The first item on our agenda, then, is a thorough reconsideration of the history of the philosophy of law, and in particular of the great texts which belong to that history. And the reason for this is not obscure. The philosophical enquiry into the nature of law is not something that we can begin to-day *de novo*, and spin out of our heads and out of our present experience, without reference to what has gone before. It is true that if we construct a philosophical theory of law it must stand absolutely on its own feet, it must not be based upon some authority outside itself. But that does not mean that it must be, or can be, without relation to what has gone before. A poem must carry with it the immediate conviction that it is the expression of emotion, but that does not mean that it must, or indeed can, put itself outside the poetic tradition of the language in which it is written. If, then, a fresh start is to be made, it must be made with as profound a knowledge as we can acquire of what I shall call the tradition of Western European philosophical jurisprudence. And a brief consideration of the general character of this tradition will not be out of place.

Every philosophical doctrine, and consequently every philosophy of law, may conveniently be seen to consist of three main elements. First, it is the attempt to answer a certain kind of question with regard to the nature of law, it is the attempt to relate law to what I have called the totality of experience. That is to say, a man is properly called a philosopher not primarily in virtue of holding a particular doctrine, but in virtue of having submitted himself to a particular kind of curiosity. Secondly, a philosophical doctrine is an ordered system of answers to the questions which a philosophical curiosity brings to the surface; it is a body of opinions, of conclusions reached. And thirdly, it is a system of reasons given for conclusions reached; it provides a *ratio decidendi* for every *obiter dictum*. But it is important to observe that, although for certain purposes, such an analysis may be legitimate and useful, the elements into which it breaks up a philosophical doctrine are in fact quite inseparable from one another and must be held together firmly if the philosophy is to be understood. We need to know, if we are to understand a philosophical doctrine, not only the questions considered and the answers given, but also the reasons provided for the answers. And we need to know the reasons not merely in order to be able to judge whether the conclusions are well-founded, but in order to know what the conclusions themselves are. In a philosophical doctrine the *what* and the *why* are genuinely inseparable, and this is one of the peculiarities of philosophy.

Now, the character of a philosophical doctrine is important because it determines the character of what I have called the tradition of philosophical jurisprudence. And I have preferred to speak of the tradition, rather than the history of philosophical jurisprudence because (besides its natural preoccupation with questions of *who* and *where* and *when*, and with the attribution of ideas and doctrines) this history has, generally speaking, concerned itself not so much with concrete philosophical doctrines, as with the conclusions or opinions separated from the questions and the reasons, and with the supposed effects or influence of those conclusions. Of course there are histories not altogether vitiated by this defect, but they are rare; and the general disrepute into which the history of philosophy (and the history of philosophical jurisprudence) has fallen may be attributed to this concern with dead and meaningless abstractions instead of with actual and concrete doctrines. The common classification of philosophical doctrines is a classification which recognises only the *obiter dicta* of the philosophical tradition and ignores the *rationes decidendi*. By the tradition of philosophical jurisprudence I mean, then, the history of philosophical jurisprudence philosophically conceived, seen as a living, extemporary whole in which past and present are comparatively insignificant. The pursuit of this tradition will not be concerned with the discovery of the source or origin of the doctrines, or with the attempt to separate the old from the new, but with the understanding of the entire world of philosophical ideas which belongs to the great texts of philosophical jurisprudence, to understand these texts in terms of their total philosophical content, and that total content in its place in a tradition of enquiry. Our apparent satisfaction with the examination and juxtaposition of the conclusions of philosophical jurisprudence has perverted our sensibility to this tradition and has deprived it of its power to inspire fresh thought.

But, it will be said, the history of Western European philosophical jurisprudence shows us not a single tradition, but a number of traditions; and this is certainly true if our attention is concentrated upon doctrines, and even more true if our attention is directed solely to conclusions. But the tradition I am concerned with is, primarily, a tradition of philosophical enquiry; and this, I believe, is a single tradition in the sense that it is the universal context of every text in the history of philosophical jurisprudence. It is true, of course, that many philosophical writers are unconscious of their place in this tradition, unconscious even of the existence of this tradition, but none are outside it. Just as there are English poets (Blake, perhaps) who appear to stand on the edge of the English poetic tradition, so there are philosophers (Hobbes, for example) who appear anxious to detach themselves from the philosophic tradition; but Blake is as impossible without Shakespeare and Milton and much that he himself had never read, as Hobbes without Aristotle, Epicurus and Aquinas. However novel the views of a philosophical writer, whatever fresh turn he may give to the study of these questions, to the pursuit of the satisfaction of this curiosity, anyone acquainted with the philosophical tradition will at once recognise something familiar in his work. This unity survives whatever disrupting force there may be contained in the variety of doctrines which find place in the tradition. And just as it would require a social revolution more radical than any we have evidence of if the poetic tradition of a society and a language is to be destroyed, so Western European philosophical jurisprudence would have to find something other than merely new doctrines if its tradition is to come to an end. And part at least of the chaos of modern jurisprudence arises from the fact that we have lost the sense of this tradition.

Our first business, then, if we are to make the fresh beginning which the present position of enquiry calls for is to regain a sense of this tradition of enquiry. But we need to know what we are to look for in it, what we are going to do with it, how we are to use this sensibility when we have reacquired it. And the answers to these questions are given in the nature of the tradition itself. A tradition is not something which is merely conformed to, nor is it anything fixed and finished. Nevertheless it is something which has stability and continuity even in those elements which change and vary. It is not something to which we must adhere; it is something which provides the starting point and the initiative for fresh enquiry. It is no use looking to it for finished conclusions, for settled answers to fixed questions, because it is not a tradition of conclusions or even of questions, but of enquiry. It can give us nothing finished. What it gives us, and it is something that we cannot do without, is a firmer consciousness of what we are trying to do. Not only does it give us a sense of the unity of past enquiry, the sense that A's questions and A's answers cannot be understood without understanding the, perhaps, quite different questions and answers of B, but it gives us the knowledge that we cannot understand our own questions and answers without understanding the questions and answers of others. It may suggest to us the direction which enquiry must take by bringing to light the questions which have never been fully considered: for long enough, for example, philosophical jurisprudence has played with ideas which involve a far more radical consideration of the nature of knowledge and the nature of will than these problems have ever received at the hands of, at least English, writers on the philosophy of law. But even if a fuller knowledge, a philosophical knowledge, of the tradition of philosophical jurisprudence, provided us with no such specific suggestions for lines of enquiry, it would, I think, give us the consciousness of what we are trying to do which, at the moment, is our chief lack. And it is for this reason that I put a renewed study of this tradition in the front of the programme of enquiry which is to lead us out of the confusions and ambiguities of the present position.

Fifty-four

The Principles of Art

Since I doubt my capacity to give in this review any adequate and convincing impression of the value and importance of this book, I can do no better than state at once that it is the most profound and stimulating discussion I have ever read of the question, What is art? The field of aesthetic enquiry has not, indeed, been barren up till now, but this book gives us so much that it is difficult for us to persuade ourselves of the value of what we had before. It is the work of an artist and a philosopher; it is written with a charm and a vigour which matches the subtlety and sanity of its doctrine; and it leaves the reader with the impression that he has been in touch with a mind of altogether exceptional learning, tact, and penetration. All these are qualities that we have learned to expect from the work of Professor Collingwood; anyone who had read *Speculum Mentis* or *An Essay on Philosophical Method* would open this book anticipating a brilliant performance, but here is something even better than he could have expected. It is a delight to witness the masterly unfolding of its argument; it is equally a delight to follow the author when he steps aside from the exposition of his main thesis to reinterpret Plato's remarks on art, to expose the 'quibbles and sophistries' of Freud's views on magic, or to give us his reflections on the condition of art yesterday and to-day.

'The business of this book is to answer the question: What is art?' It is not, however, an attempt 'to investigate and expound eternal verities concerning the nature of an eternal object called Art,' but an attempt to deal with the problems which force themselves upon anyone 'who looks round at the present condition of the arts in our own civilization.' It is the attempt of an artist and an historian, fortified by the critical mind of a philosopher, to make clear to himself the nature of art and the conditions of its life in the

---

Review of Robin George Collingwood, *The Principles of Art* (Oxford: Clarendon Press, 1938). First published in *Cambridge Review*, 59 (1938), 487. Reprinted in *The Cambridge Mind: Ninety Years of the Cambridge Review 1879–1969*, ed. E. Homberger and others (London: Jonathan Cape, 1970), 139–41, as 'Collingwood's Philosophy of Art'.

world to-day. Anyone who begins to cultivate this field will find in it a luxuriant growth of weeds, and there is plenty of hard hitting in this book; but of carping criticism the reader will find nothing.

The method of exposition, which is also a method of thought, which Professor Collingwood pursues, may be called a Socratic method. First, without any suggestion of a theory, he tries to disentangle what, as a matter of fact, we all know about art, in the belief that the truth is to be found *in* what we all know about it, though often that truth is not exactly what we at first take it to be. This leaves us with a number of philosophical questions to be investigated, because in stating what we all know about art we make use of words and expressions — sensation, thought, emotion, language — which call for analysis. Lastly, there comes the construction of a Theory of Art, a synthesis of the truths which have emerged and established themselves in the earlier discussions. And it may be said that not the least of the delights of this book is its masterly handling of this method.

The argument begins, then, with an attempt to distinguish Art from not Art, to make certain that we know how to apply the word 'art' where it ought to be applied and refuse it where it ought to be refused. And it leads to the rejection of certain things which, though they are often confused with art, have a character different from that of art. These are craft or skill, magic, and amusement. The confusion of these things with art is dangerous because it has led, in each case, to a false aesthetic theory and to the perversion of art itself. These opening chapters admirably display Professor Collingwood's acute critical mind and are among the best in the book. But destruction is followed by construction, and art proper is shown to have two characteristics: expression of emotion and imagination. And the conclusion of this first inspection of the subject is that 'by creating for ourselves an imaginary experience or activity we express our emotions; and this is what we call art.'

But 'what this formula means, we do not yet know.' And in order to find out we must penetrate a world of philosophical analysis, consider the nature of sensation, feeling, thought, and emotion, and the nature of language. This, for the ordinary reader, will be the most difficult part of the book; but he need not be afraid of it, for the doctrines are expounded so lucidly that all but the absolutely unavoidable difficulties are absent.

The last part of the book, consisting of three chapters — Art as Language, Art and Truth, and The Artist and the Community — contains the final expression of his theory of art. It would be stupid here to attempt any exposition of the doctrine, and worse to offer any criticism of matters of detail. The value of the book does not depend upon our being convinced by the doctrine (though I myself find it singularly convincing); it lies in the experience it offers of following a masterly discussion of all the fundamental questions which any doctrine must consider. And Professor

Collingwood's concluding reflections on the condition and future of art in England are of exceptional interest.

This is not the sort of book that has to be recommended with the qualification that the hard labour entailed in reading it will be rewarded in the end; the reader is rewarded on every page. If there is anyone who, because of the nonsense he has been obliged to read, doubts whether a philosopher can talk sense about art, let him read this book. It has something to offer anyone interested in literature or art; it is a book in which, for example, anyone engaged in the study of literature in a University will find illumination. And it is a book which anyone who can take pleasure in a profound and critical piece of philosophical thinking will find a delight.

Fifty-five

Swords and Symbols

Attractively written, in a terse and lucid style, this book is an acute analysis of what the author (an American lawyer) calls the 'technique of sovereignty.' The history of all political units, cities, states, nations, alliances, and federations has been, in his view, the story of the battle for the achievement and retention of sovereign power. But this sovereign power is essentially a limited, local, and unstable *superiority*, never an absolute supremacy. And the reason for this is that the weapons by which sovereign power can be achieved and maintained are never exclusively in the hands of the sovereign power itself. 'Governments are limited by their impotence to absorb all interests in the community, and, therefore, to control all political weapons.' These weapons are law (which is essentially based upon force and is of value to the sovereign 'because it serves notice on the subjects upon what occasions and in what circumstance the sovereign will use force'), economic power, propaganda, and education. None of these weapons is exclusively in the hands of the sovereign power, and the very use of power by the sovereign is apt to create opposing forces which must be satisfied or destroyed if the sovereign is to survive. The political process, consequently, is this complex and uncertain business of maintaining power, and the 'art of sovereignty' lies in the satisfaction of adverse interests without surrendering superiority. Mr Marshall expounds this thesis with a wealth of varied and apt historical examples, and his publishers without undue exaggeration compare the book to *The Prince* of Machiavelli. But the philosopher will not find in it much to interest him. The analysis is carried out consistently and acutely at a level of thought which precludes any philosophical consideration of the subjects touched upon. Sovereignty is considered solely in terms of power, law is mere force, liberty, popular sovereignty, right and wrong are mere symbols, propaganda weapons in the struggle for sovereignty. It would be absurd to quarrel with so vigorous and acute a book for being what it is

Review of James Marshall, *Swords and Symbols* (Oxford: Oxford University Press, 1939). First published in *Philosophy*, 14 (1939), 493–4.

and not something else, but it is unavoidable that so narrowly limited an analysis of the political process should, in the end, be unsatisfactory because of its abstractness.

Fifty-six

Reason in Politics

Mr Smellie has a most attractive way of writing which makes his book a pleasure to read: to a lucid style he adds an easy turn of phrase and an excellent judgment in what he quotes from other writers. It is a style, too, which accords with the character of the book—a character which is, at first, a little difficult to assess. Essentially, I think, it is a book of acute reflections upon the history and present condition of thought about the first principles of politics. I say 'a book of reflections' in order to indicate its somewhat miscellaneous character; the reflections are by no means random, but their unity lies rather in the fact that they spring from a single, well-ordered mind ranging over the problems of political theory rather than from any more superficial orderliness. It is a bold thing for a young man to write in this way, because it is a way of writing that more quickly reveals the quality of his mind than any other—just as the quality of a man's mind is unmistakably revealed in an attempt to write fiction, where all the concealments at the disposal of the historian, the scientist or the essay-writer are discarded and the mind is thrown back upon its essential self and stands or falls by what it can create. And it may be said at once that Mr Smellie comes out of this self-imposed ordeal a clear winner. He does not, like so many others, scrape home on a store of acquired information; he rides easily and has plenty in hand at the finish.

One does not know quite what to expect in a book called *Reason in Politics*; it is an excellent title, but it opens up a very wide range of expectation. But the relevance of the title to the contents of this book is, I think, that it is a book about man's reasoning about political activity and political arrangements; a book which considers what men have thought about these things and then applies itself to a fresh and reasoned consideration of political activity today. It is divided into three parts, the first of which consists of five chapters on the history of political thought. The earlier history is treated in two excellent reviews, one covering the period to 1600

Review of Kingsley Bryce Smellie, *Reason in Politics* (London: Duckworth, 1939). First published in *Politica*, 4 (1939), 167–8.

AD and the other the period from 1600 to about 1800. To sketch the history of two thousand years of Western European political thought in eighty pages is a hazardous undertaking, but Mr Smellie has succeeded in saying something worthwhile because he has been content to select boldly and give us his own reflections on that history. He does not attempt to establish any main lines of thought or traditions in Western European political thought, and this, perhaps, is a disappointment; but it is amply made up for by the quality of what he does give us. The later history is treated in three chapters of a more analytical kind, on Utilitarianism, Hegel, and Marx. I miss from the chapter on Utilitarianism any mention of Paley, who is a writer who does not deserve the neglect into which he has fallen and whose work affords the clearest example of the way in which the hedonistic foundation of Utilitarianism was developed from the Natural Law theory by positing the happiness of mankind as the evident will of God. Chapters on Hegel are apt to be maddeningly disappointing, for they are usually written by those who have never closely studied the *Philosophie des Rechts*, but Mr Smellie's chapter is an exception, partly because he is too wise to reject the best English guides—Bradley and McTaggart.

The second part of the book consists of four chapters, Metaphysics and Politics, History and Politics, Economics and Politics, and Ethics and Politics. These discussions never lack interest, and Mr Smellie is always well on top of the point which he is considering, but I think they reveal what I feel to be the main disappointment of the book. Each of them lacks a certain conclusiveness. I do not mean that they fail to provide a comprehensive treatment of their subjects (that, obviously, is not part of their intention); but each of them begins so well, with so much vitality and insight, that to find them in turn tailing off and stopping short of any definite conclusion rather from a sort of tiredness than because the writer has come to an end of his reflections, is unavoidably disappointing. In each of them the thread of argument is easily lost, and they seem to lack an argument to knit them together. Nevertheless, they succeed in being what, perhaps, they were intended to be—reflections on a theme rather than passages in an argument.

The third part, two chapters on the Nature of the State and the Future of the State, concludes this book of reflections. The author ranges over a great many of the problems presented by the contemporary condition of Western European civilization, making his acute observations and leading the reader to consider again the foundations of civil society. Mr Smellie has read widely and deeply, and writes out of a full and cultivated mind. And he has succeeded in imparting to his writing a tone of genuine reflectiveness which is as attractive and stimulating as it is rare. Thank God for someone who still believes in reason and is content to be intelligent.

Fifty-seven

The Politics of Democratic Socialism

This book is the work of one who calls himself a Social Democrat, and its theme is 'the theory and practice of democratic socialism.' Mr Durbin's position, therefore, involves a rejection of the views both of those who seek social and political salvation in a return to a more fully operative 'capitalist' system, and of those who, embracing the creed of Marx, propose a revolutionary method (involving the so-called dictatorship of the proletariat) of achieving a socialist society. The first set of views he rejects because it is non-socialist and incidentally (he thinks) undemocratic; the second because it is based upon a false view of history and because it is destructive of democracy. Sorel said that what he wanted to do was to moralise Marxism a little: Mr Durbin wants to democratise socialism and socialize democracy.

There can be little doubt that anyone prepared to argue the social democratic position rationally is assured in advance of a sympathetic hearing: the position has not always been fortunate in its defenders, but it is one which must have great inherent attraction for many people (at least in England) at the present time.

Briefly, the line of Mr Durbin's argument is as follows. Capitalism (which means a rational technique in industry, unlimited acquisitiveness as a motive in individual life, and a steady expansion of output) is at the present time in a period of transition: 'a sub-type of capitalism is coming into existence under our eyes. We live in a period in which the basic institutions of the recent past have been so greatly modified that a new system is emerging.' These changes are, for example, the destruction of the mobility of labour by organisations such as Trade Unions designed to remove the insecurity belonging to a genuinely *laisser-faire* economy, the growth of social services financed out of taxation which has 'struck heavily at the funds available for capital accumulation' and has consequently reduced

---

Review of Evan Frank Mottram Durbin, *The Politics of Democratic Socialism* (London: Routledge, 1940). First published in *Cambridge Review*, 61 (1940), 347–8, 350.

the power of industry to expand, and the immense extension of the central control of industry by means of public boards, corporations, authorities, marketing schemes, etc., which amounts to a 'frontal attack upon the institution of *laisser-faire* itself.' This emergent type of capitalism (which is here called 'State organised private monopoly capitalism') is not yet in a state of collapse; it is far from unstable, it still possesses powers of expansion, and it has 'much to recommend it to a short-sighted democracy.' Nevertheless, it is ossified, restrictionist and unjust, and the contemporary problem is how to combine 'the virtues of capitalism—rationalism and mobility—with democratic needs— security and equality—by the extension of the activity of the State upon an ever-widening and consistent basis'.

The contemporary world has before it a detailed suggestion—that of Communism—about how this is to be achieved, and Mr Durbin turns to examine this suggestion. For a variety of reasons (some of them sound) he rejects it, and the way is open to consider, first the nature of democracy and secondly the 'strategy of democratic socialism.' His conclusions, briefly, are those which the British Labour Party has sponsored in its publications (though Mr Durbin tells us he reached them by an independent consideration of the situation), and which Dr Dalton has expounded in *Practical Socialism for Britain* (1935). And the principle that underlies all his thought is that democracy and socialism are parts of a single whole; either without the other is impossible.

This brief summary does less than justice to the detail and comprehensiveness of Mr Durbin's argument. The conception of the book is, in most respects, admirable; and a glance at the list of contents is likely to make more than one reader think that here at last is what he has been looking for—a work which, holding together economics and politics, provides a thorough consideration of the whole complex problem. Surmounting with courage the difficulty that he is dealing with a variety of subjects each of which is a specialised field of study, Mr Durbin aims at considering the whole 'complex reality of human society.' And though, as he admits, he has often nothing novel to say, the reader will go far before he finds, for example, a more lucid and intelligent analysis of the present position and tendencies of capitalism. Moderate without abating any of his desire for a radical reform of the present social and economic system, full of common-sense without being commonplace, acute without degenerating into mere cleverness, there is much to admire in Mr Durbin's presentation of his case. It is a book which one does not regret having read with care.

Nevertheless, the book in many respects (and not all of them mere matters of detail) fails to fulfil its promise; social democracy to-day still awaits a really coherent exposition. We ask for bread and we are given, not indeed a stone, but a lump of imperfectly mixed and a trifle underdone dough. The style of the book, though vigorous and sometimes eloquent, and its construction, with its constant cross-references and references to Mr Durbin's projected *Economics of Democratic Socialism*, is frequently a source of annoyance to the reader; and repetition too often takes the place of a more careful formulation of the argument. But it is Mr Durbin's blind spots, rather than any actual defect in knowledge, which hinder him as an expositor of social democracy. Nobody can write on this subject without involving himself in a few philosophical statements; and philosophy, unfortunately, is one of Mr Durbin's blind spots. If one thing is certain it is that the main doctrinal weakness of the social democratic creed is its inability to divest itself of the philosophical enormities of nineteenth-century individualism, and no exposition of social democracy can be considered successful which does not attack this problem. And yet the reader will find Mr Durbin accepting all these enormities as a matter of course without even indicating any sense of their unsatisfactoriness. He writes as if his philosophical education had been confined to a superficial study of Bentham and J. S. Mill — admirable writers (or at least one of them), but, taken alone, unsafe guides. And the result is that the most rickety part of the social democratic creed is left as ramshackle as it was before: a philosophy of crude and uncritical individualism is in fact inconsistent with social democracy. Beside this major fault, Mr Durbin's other philosophical ineptitudes — e.g., the equation of judgments of value to 'feelings,' of 'irrational' and 'subjective,' and his half-hearted and imperfectly defended excursions into what he calls 'analytical psychology' — are scarcely worth mentioning.

And it is this philosophical blind spot which leads him astray in his criticism of the Marxist doctrine of the so-called economic interpretation of history. There is often excuse enough for misunderstanding the cloudy and dogmatic teaching of Karl Marx, but there is little excuse for believing that the economic interpretation of history is a theory about the motives of human action, and none at all for taking it to mean that the sole human motive is rational acquisitiveness. But this is Mr Durbin's view. And his main argument against the doctrine — that it must be wrong because men act from a variety of motives — implies not only a misunderstanding of the doctrine itself, but also a bold rejection of the possibility of ethics and indeed of the whole of philosophy which, no doubt, he would have defended in detail if he had appreciated it. Moreover, it is disappointing to find so determined an opponent of Marx infected with the Marxist disease of quibbling about inconclusive historical examples. There is some sound argument in Mr Durbin's rejection of the Communist strategy, but it is hopelessly obscured by irrelevance and error — which is a pity because the Marxist is apt to take any misunderstanding of his doctrine as a confirmation of its truth.

The analysis of democracy which forms a necessary part of the thesis of this book is conducted under the inspiration of Reginald Bassett's *Essentials of Parliamentary Democracy*, and reproduces both the merits and the defects of that work. Democracy, it is asserted, is not a particular kind of civilisation, but a method of taking political decisions. But when this method is examined it turns out to imply a certain scale of values, in short, a certain kind of civilisation, yet its characteristics cannot be considered because of the original assumption that democracy is merely a political method. Mr Durbin makes all the mistakes of those who insist upon identifying democracy with what is peculiar to it and consequently turning it into an abstraction. It may pass the time agreeably to consider democracy as the expression of 'a certain type of emotional character' and to talk about frustration and 'the animism of the primitive mind,' but no degree of psychological insight will make up for a failure to consider the historical mediations which have given us, both in fact and in idea, all we have and all we know of democracy. And once again the reader, looking for a sound analysis of democracy, will be disappointed by having all the old clap-trap about government by consent and the greatest happiness of the greatest number, thrown at him.

In dealing with the programme and strategy of reform it is not so much Mr Durbin's optimism which causes us to hesitate in our approval, but the failure to show unequivocally how these changes, brought about by this democratic method, will achieve the desired end. This most important point, the relationship between the analysis of the present predicament of capitalism and the programme of reform, is disposed of hastily in a single page. The defects of the present condition of capitalist economy may be all that they are said to be, but it does not follow at once that 'the case for a planned economy, centrally controlled, in order to pursue expansionist and equalitarian policies, is urgent and overwhelming'. The ignorant and the sceptical will be glad to be more fully instructed on the questions of how precisely this form of state socialism will, of itself, solve the problems which need solution and whether it will do so without any sacrifice of the values it is designed to conserve. It is not enough merely to meet some of the views (as Mr Durbin does in an Appendix) of those who are not overwhelmed by the case for 'the extension of the activity of the State upon an ever widening basis'; the case itself must be connected more closely with the analysis of present conditions. But perhaps the instruction we await is on the way in Mr Durbin's *Economics of Democratic Socialism*.

Fifty-eight

Men and Ideas

To those who never knew Graham Wallas it has sometimes been difficult to reconcile the great impression he seems to have made upon those with whom he was in immediate contact and the actual quality and content of his published work. His friends and his pupils appear to have been impressed primarily by the freshness and freedom of his thought; Gilbert Murray in the brief but interesting biographical introduction to this volume says, 'I never knew anyone so completely free from fixed orthodoxies, prejudices, and partisan feelings.' But in his published work this freedom and freshness appears often as a kind of erraticism and lack of centrality. It was almost as if what was a great moral virtue in him became an intellectual defect. His admirable readiness to learn from every occasion was reproduced in an unfortunate anecdotal method of argument; his constant alertness of mind seemed to impose upon his thought a miscellaneous character. Being without the temptation to over-organize his ideas and observations (a neat theory having no inherent attraction for him), he lacked at the same time the urge and the power to pass beyond a mere empiricism.

This is a collection of some of his essays and addresses, selected and edited by his daughter, and covering a period of about thirty years, 1901 to 1930. It includes biographical essays on Robert Owen, Ruskin, William Johnson Fox, and his favourite and greatly admired Bentham, essays on political and social subjects (Socialism and the Fabian Society, the British Civil Service, etc.), and essays on the theory and practice of secondary and higher education. These essays illustrate both the wide-ranging and the essentially suggestive character of his thought. His observation is always acute, his advice wise, and his inspiration clear. But this, like Graham Wallas's other books, leaves the impression that future generations will require not only his published work, but also a biography in order to appreciate the full quality of the man.

Review of Graham Wallas, *Men and Ideas: Essays etc.*, ed. M. Wallas (London: George Allen and Unwin, 1940). First published in *Philosophy*, 16 (1941), 95.

Fifty-nine

Politics and Morals

Nothing that Croce wrote can fail to give the reader an experience of intellectual refreshment; with age he has lost none of his remarkable vigour of mind, and his profound study of the modern Western world has given his thought something of the quality of a vision. It is not easy at this stage to say something fresh and revealing about the relation of politics and morals, but although the doctrine expounded in this book is not new, it is much more than a repetition of what others have tried to teach us. Starting from the view that political action is 'action guided by the sense of what is useful and directed towards a utilitarian goal' (a view such as is to be found in Machiavelli) and its corollary that 'political action *per se* cannot be qualified as either moral or immoral,' Croce goes on to show that political action is never self-sufficient but exists always in the wider world of the moral consciousness and consequently policy is always unavoidably related to some moral ideas — the 'cynical political man' is a mere abstraction. And 'in this continuous transformation of morals into politics, which still remain politics, lies the real ethic progress of mankind.' This theme is developed in what are, in effect, a number of essays rather than chapters in a continuous argument; and in the course of the exposition there are some brilliant pages on the modern history of the philosophy of politics.

The other great theme of the book is Liberalism. Anyone already familiar with Croce's writings will not find here much that is not more fully set out in larger works; but the discussion is always vigorous and profound. There are interesting chapters on the Contrasting Political Ideals since 1870 (in which the debt to Liberalism of all anti-Liberal thinking is shown), on the relation of Liberalism and free enterprise, and on The Bourgeoisie; an ill-defined historical concept, in which the ideas of Sombart and Groethuisen are examined.

Review of Benedetto Croce, *Politics and Morals*, tr. Salvatore J. Castiglione (New York: Philosophical Library Inc., 1945). First published in *Philosophy*, 21 (1946), 184.

Sixty

The Idea of History

No small part of the native genius of a philosopher lies in the perception of where in the world of contemporary speculation is the point from which advance may best be made; for such a perception (coming as it must early in life) springs less from a profound study of the history of philosophy than from an intuitive apprehension of what is opportune. Collingwood's genius led him to perceive that, while for three centuries philosophy had concerned itself primarily with the logical and epistemological problems thrown up by natural science, little discussion had been given to the no less difficult problem of the character and possibility of historical knowledge. And it may be said that, with the single exception of Croce, he is the only philosopher of first-class ability to give prolonged and concentrated attention to this problem. *The Idea of History* contains all that is recoverable of his achievement in this direction. But, unfinished and scrappy though it is, it is enough to show that if he had been unhindered by ill-health and early death he could have done for historical knowledge something like what Kant did for natural science.

Collingwood died before he was able to put into final form his reflections on historical knowledge. What we have here has been selected and edited by Professor T.M. Knox from the considerable body of manuscripts which Collingwood left behind. The only previously published writing reprinted here is his Inaugural Lecture as Waynflete Professor of Metaphysical Philosophy *On Human Nature and Human History* (1935) and the British Academy lecture on *The Historical Imagination* (1936). The editor's admirable preface explains the character of the manuscripts with which he has had to deal and the circumstances in which they were written, and contains besides an appreciation, at once moving and critical, of Collingwood as a man and as a philosopher, for which all friends and students of Collingwood will be grateful.

About two-thirds of the book is based upon lectures on the philosophy of history, originally composed in 1936, which trace the changing charac-

Review of Robin George Collingwood, *The Idea of History*, ed. T.M. Knox (Oxford: Clarendon Press, 1946). First published in *English Historical Review*, 62 (1947), 84–6.

ter of the conception of the historian's subject-matter, method, and aim from the emergence of historical thinking in Greco-Roman civilization to the present time. Much of this account, particularly the early part, is written with Collingwood's accustomed subtlety and brilliance; all of it exemplifies his remarkable powers of critical sympathy. As an historian of ideas his outstanding quality was imaginative appreciation of the mind and purposes of the writers whom he considers. The peculiar generosity of his appreciation sprang, not from any lack of ideas on his own account, but from an ability to detect the conditions and difficulties that produce the limitations of a writer's achievement; it sprang from the conviction that everything which comes to the historian has value and meaning if only the imagination can detect it and the intellect grasp it. The task of the historian of ideas, as he saw it, was precisely to understand a writer more profoundly than the writer understood himself, just as the task of the historian of feudal society (for example) is to understand that society more profoundly than anyone who merely enjoyed it could understand it. But I think the reader of this account of the history of historical thinking will suffer some disappointment as he proceeds. For, while the earlier part consists of an examination of how the historical writers of the ancient world went about their business and the presuppositions that lie behind their achievement, the later part comes to consist more and more of an examination of the ideas of philosophical writers about the nature of historical knowledge, and the historian himself is less and less called upon for evidence. And the final chapter on scientific history contains scarcely any examination of modern historical writing, though it does call upon the philosophical reflections of such historians as had any to offer. No doubt Collingwood saw that a study of the eighteenth and nineteenth centuries of the same kind as his study of Greek historiography was impossible, and indeed less necessary, on account of the growth of what may be called the self-consciousness of historical thought. There are, of course, gaps in this account of historical thinking, caused mainly by the scale on which it is conceived, and often the treatment of important periods is very slight, but the only serious gap is the absence of a discussion of the importance of the study of Christian origins in raising the problems of the nature and possibility of historical knowledge during the last two hundred years, an importance that makes, for example, Schweitzer's *Von Reimarus zu Wrede* a classic in the history of historiography.

The last hundred pages of *The Idea of History* is all that remains of Collingwood's projected work on the principles of historical knowledge, but it is enough to put him ahead of every other writer on the subject. He discerned that history had come to take its place beside natural science as a presumptive form of knowledge, and conceiving it one of the tasks of philosophy to reflect the dominant interest of a time, he concluded that the contemporary philosopher had a special obligation to examine the nature of historical knowledge. His first concern was to distinguish historical from scientific knowledge, and establishing its autonomy in its own field, he enquired into its character and possibility. History is knowledge of the actions of human beings that have been done in the past, acquired by the interpretation of evidence. Since it is concerned with human actions it is always a history of thoughts and ideas, and, in the end, it consists in an imaginative entry into the minds of people now dead. Its purpose is self-knowledge: historical knowledge is knowledge of what man has done and thus of what man is. It is impossible to follow Collingwood into all the subtle detail of his conception, but brief (and owing to the occasions of its exposition, somewhat disconnected and repetitive) though the argument is, it is profoundly thought out and brilliantly expounded. But it must be observed that, almost imperceptibly, Collingwood's philosophy of history turned into a philosophy in which all knowledge is assimilated to historical knowledge, and consequently into a radically skeptical philosophy. In which direction he would have gone from this position, for it is not likely that he could have stayed there, it is impossible to guess. The important thing is that he had made a notable contribution to the philosophy of history before he sheered off on this fresh tack.

The question that the historian as such no doubt will ask is, what is the bearing of this or any analysis of the epistemological problems involved in historical knowledge upon the task of writing history? At every point in his philosophy of history Collingwood drew upon his actual experience as an historian, and there is no doubt that he considered himself to be a better historian for having thought out an answer to the question: How is historical knowledge possible? But what he says of natural science he knew to be no less true of history: 'Long before Bacon and Descartes revolutionized natural science by expounding publicly the principles on which its method was based, people here and there had been using these same methods, some more often, some more rarely. As Bacon and Descartes so justly pointed out, the effect of their work was to put these same methods within the grasp of quite ordinary intellects.' The true historian is not necessarily a self-conscious historical thinker. Historical imagination belongs to his genius, and he uses it as a native faculty which is as much a natural gift as an aptitude for mathematics or music, escaping the errors of the positivists and others, not by a reflective knowledge of the philosophical principles of historical thought, but by means of his intuitive grasp of his own subject, and without knowing in detail what he is escaping. The problems of the philosopher, though real, are of his own making, arising from the questions he, but not the historian, must ask himself. Collingwood happened to possess in large measure the genius both of the historian and the philosopher.

Sixty-one

The Liberal Tradition

Professor William Aylott Orton's *The Liberal Tradition* is a restatement of the faith of liberalism, 'the oldest and richest tradition in political history', now in danger of being destroyed. Because liberalism is not an abstract idea or a rationalist plan for society, but an attitude to social and personal life, coeval with our civilization, this restatement takes the form of a history of the liberal tradition. The core of the tradition is taken to be Acton's—'liberty is not a means to a higher political end. It is itself the highest political end'. And, though he recognizes the place they occupy in the history of this tradition, Professor Orton will have nothing to do with a purely secularist or rationalist liberalism. The tradition is traced from ancient Athens, through the middle ages, to its modern avatars. About half the book deals with the last hundred and fifty years, and it ends with three chapters on the contemporary situation of the liberal ideal. He has too great a faith in liberalism to be merely nervous about its future, but he sees it [as] very much a stranger in the present world. This is a book for the 'general reader'. But not because its scholarship is hazy; quite the reverse, it is a book of sound scholarship, full of acute judgments and flashes of originality. Indeed, it may be said that it is one of those books the excellence of which springs from a half-concealed foundation of great and well-considered knowledge. But, covering the ground it does, there is no space to show at any point all the workings of criticism. It is written with great vitality and often brilliance, there is hard hitting at well-chosen enemies, and at the back of it all is an acute and cultured mind. It is a book for the general reader because it can be given to him with the certainty that he will be neither bored nor misled.

Review of William Aylott Orton, *The Liberal Tradition: a Study of the Social and Spiritual Conditions of Freedom* (London: Cumberlege for Yale University Press, 1945). First published in *English Historical Review*, 62 (1947), 262.

Sixty-two

Western Political Thought

The author of this book suggests that it should be regarded, not primarily as a work of scholarship, but as a guide-book through the history of Western European political thought for the uninitiated, and that his distinctive character as a guide is that he has his eye on 'the social background which conditions thought.' There is, of course, no one kind of guide whose merits are so great that he should be taken as the model of all guides. The instructive, the reflective, the imaginative, the formal and the chatty, the brisk and the unhurried—each of these types will acquire and hold his following. Mr Bowle is an informative guide, who goes for the big things first— for Plato, for Aristotle, Augustine, Aquinas, Hobbes—and he clearly has some appreciation of them. But often he is at a loss to express that appreciation effectively, and is capable of filling in time with the most commonplace observations. He is not the sort of guide who loses his own way (that requires genius), and he does not often allow himself to dart off down an obscure alley. He can instruct, but he does not infect either with enthusiasm or with doubt. He sometimes shocks his audience, but never surprises them. What he plants in the mind is too often something ready-made, not a seed capable of growth. Indeed, if the truth is told, he is not a guide likely to charm or inspire his following into forgetting that it is lunch-time, or even to prevent some of them slipping out of the party for a quick drink.

In his broad idea of the course of European political thought, Mr Bowle seems to give in without much of a struggle to all the old, crude periods and categories into which it has been cut up and parcelled out. No book which covers the ground from the Neolithic to the Industrial Revolution can be expected to give much of an impression of the subtle mediation of the changes which compose the story, but to have had a less naïve acceptance of the crudities of the outline of history would have been a refreshment, which indeed is rather more easily provided in a history of ideas than in a history of institutions. But while it is disappointing to find one-

---

Review of John Bowle, *Western Political Thought* (London: Jonathan Cape, 1947). First published in *Spectator*, 179 (1947), 626.

self back again with nothing more subtle than Antiquity, the Middle Ages, the Renaissance, the Age of Reason, etc., in a book on the history of ideas, it is also disconcerting to be offered, in detail, a history whose categories are so little touched with criticism and so little representative of the real quality of ideas. This history seems to be constructed round a sort of fixed skeleton of constants, themselves immune from change. The 'European mind' is something to which this history happens. 'Hellenic objectivity' makes its periodic appearances. Something called 'science' or 'the scientific attitude' emerges, disappears, and re-emerges at irregular intervals, but itself suffers no detectable change; the immense differences between Greek and modern science are passed on unrecognised.

These, however, are defects of detail, most of them merely missed opportunities; a more serious fault in the book is its curiously 'unhistorical' attitude. In a work of this sort it is, perhaps, permissible to write of 'the main stream of European civilization,' but not, I think, to write of it as being turned on and off as if by a celestial controller. And the point of view from which the Greek city and the Middle Ages appear as 'failures,' from which the seventeenth century may be seen as (in some respects) a 'retrogression', from which Montesquieu and Rousseau can be regarded as 'lucky to be born' at the time when they were born, is more of a political or a moral than an historical point of view. And it is unfortunate that so much of what Mr Bowle says of the writings of the political thinkers is overshadowed by this unhistorical attitude.

Sixty-Three

Contemporary British Politics

The appearance last year of two books, one on contemporary British Socialism and the other on contemporary British Conservatism, gives an opportunity to take stock of the politics of our time. The books are not equally helpful in this enterprise: Mr Hogg's, for all its brisk controversy, is a work of some profundity of thought and offers an interpretation of one of the great traditions of British politics, but Mr Parker, buoyed up with the sense of being on top of the world, provides only a complacent situation report of the achievements of the Labour Party. But one way or another, in what they say or in what they assume, the books at least offer a starting-place for reflection.

Each of these political parties, it appears, is inspired by what may perhaps be called a philosophy. That of Socialism is the philosophy of the Mandate; that of Conservatism is the philosophy of natural law. The philosophy of the Mandate is a philosophy of will. The will of the majority of the electorate at the time of a general election is the supreme authority; the actions of a government based upon this title are unquestionable. Periodic application must be made to the electorate to discern its desires, but the clearly expressed desire of a majority requires no other authority to establish its validity. As a constitutional doctrine this has no great antiquity in British parliamentary history, although it raised its ugly head in the seventeenth century and has from time to time been appealed to by those who should have known better. Indeed, the circumstances in which the practice of representation grew up in British government did not call for, or suggest, any particular theory; the constitutional doctrine of the Mandate made its appearance at a later stage, when a simplified explanation was being looked for. Its merit is its simplicity; its defect is its remoteness from political reality. It is conceivable as the basis of the government of a voluntary society which drew up its articles of association at its inception, and

---

Review of John Parker, *Labour Marches on* (London: Penguin Books, 1947); and Quintin Hogg, *The Case for Conservatism* (London: Penguin Books, 1947). First published in *Cambridge Journal*, 1 (1948), 474–90.

Mr Parker believes it to be the operative principle of the Labour Party. But does he really think that Socialism is merely what the majority of the Annual Conference of the Labour Party from time to time votes for? And if not, how can a Socialist Party base itself solely upon the will of that majority? And when the theory is offered as the ground of the authority of the government of a community that never had a beginning, a community whose arrangements are unavoidably a partnership between past and present, a community that has a long established way of living and of conducting its business, the difficulties are increased. 'Rank majorities may give a nation law', said Grattan in 1790, 'but rank majorities cannot give law authority.' The difficulties become insuperable when the Mandate is represented, not only as a constitutional doctrine, but as a philosophy of just government. This, however, is what Mr Parker seems to believe; and he is willing to go so far as to identify democracy with the unhindered operation of the mandating activity of the temporary majority of the electorate. But his confidence is not so great that he allows himself to leave the matter there: he wishes to make certain that the majority is on his side by arranging that its livelihood will depend upon the maintenance in power of his party.

One of the mistakes of the Conservative Party in the present parliament has been to repudiate some of the actions of the government on the ground that a mandate for them was lacking; Mr Hogg, however, does not fall into this error. Rightly, he will have nothing to do with so half-baked, so equivocal a theory, and puts in its place a doctrine of natural law. That there is a limit to what a temporary majority may do appears to him obvious, and 'the limit is set by a body of doctrine which we may call the natural law, which is the same for all sovereign bodies, and limits the number of claims upon the individual which the group may make'. 'The essence of democracy', he continues, 'is not bare majority rule; the right to reform the law may be legally and in certain directions morally and politically unlimited in scope, but here and there a wall is fixed beyond which it is not lawful to go. On the wall is inscribed the words 'Natural Law', and if rulers overleap it even majority rule becomes the tyranny of a mob, the more irresponsible because it is anonymous.' This is well said. At least it rescues us from the absurdity of attributing absolute authority to the will of a temporary majority. And if it were a limitation based upon constitutional custom there would not be much to criticize. But as a philosophy it leaves much to be desired. So simple a doctrine of natural law cannot be held to survive the criticism (not of Bentham, which is negligible) but of Burke and of Hegel. And not only is it too abstract to offer much practical guidance, but also the notion of a criterion which is merely an external *limit* is scarcely good enough. If he had followed the lead of Burke in this matter, Mr Hogg would have found himself upon firmer ground, and ground not less habitable by the Conservative.

The field of contemporary British politics seems, then, to be occupied by two parties, each inspired by a philosophy of some sort, but neither by a sound or even coherent philosophy. This is a misfortune, but not a crippling misfortune. Reputable political behaviour is not dependent upon sound philosophy, although error so profound and complicated as that which the Labour Party seems to have embraced is apt to be a hindrance. In general, constitutional tradition is a good substitute for philosophy (indeed, philosophy is of little practical value until it has found expression in a constitutional tradition), and British politics is, above all, rich in this respect.

Setting aside philosophy, the projects and methods of contemporary British politics seem to spring from two main sources: a legend of mass unemployment and a legend of war. I say 'a legend', because although mass unemployment and war are the two dominating experiences of our time, our politics spring not so much from the experiences themselves as from something that has been made of them.

'At the back of the minds of all those who have been through the twenty years between the two wars is the fear of a fresh slump and widespread unemployment', says Mr Parker. This is the experience. The legend begins when he asserts that 'in the past full employment has never been secured in a "free" economy', that a slump is inevitable in the United States of America, and that Keynes demonstrated that the only way to avoid mass unemployment was by the institution of a centrally planned economy. And, while the legend is the spring of Labour policy, a preoccupation with the problem is common to both parties. Obsession with a single problem, however important, is always dangerous in politics; except in time of war, no society has so simple a life that one element in it can, without loss, be made the centre and circumference of all political activity. There is, further, a widespread belief that the problem of mass unemployment is capable of solution. Some writers (Conservatives among them) appear to believe that the problem can readily be solved by a little trick of administrative technique which, if it is performed at the right moment, is without danger of miscarriage and will itself produce no other problem. Socialists, however, basing themselves on the legend rather than the experience, have come to believe that no price is too high to pay for a solution—indeed, the solution appears to them to be worthy of some great price: to achieve it without establishing a centrally planned economy; seems to them disrespectful to the exaggerated magnitude of the problem. Now, even if the experience upon which these politics are based were the most relevant experience at the present moment of our history, and even if the legend had much more truth in it than in fact it has, all this would be hampering. But the full defect of this inspiration of policy at the present time lies, of course, in the fact that the malady from which we are least likely to suffer (except as the result of some of the remedies put into operation to present it) is mass unemployment. Our first great misfortune, then, was that the mainspring of British politics in 1945 was an experience and a legend which were not immediately relevant to our situation.

The second spring of policy and method is a legend of war. And here, I think, the two parties divide more precisely. To the Conservative, war appeared to have produced a perversion of our society which it should be the aim of contemporary politics to cure: here was an identifiable mischief to be removed. Every change that had been brought about by the condition of war was suspect. The conversion of our society from a state of war to a state of peace might be slow and difficult, but it was a real and necessary conversion. The Socialist, on the other hand, took the opposite view. He embraced the legend of war without reserve. In its simple and emotional form this legend found expression in the view that 'the people wanted a purpose in peace as cogent as that given them in war'. And Karl Mannheim (among others) gave it a more intellectual expression: 'By making the necessary adaptations to the needs of war one does not always realize that very often they contain also the principles of adaptation to the needs of a New Age.' 'The war', says Mr Parker, 'led to a vast extension of State intervention in the economic field. Thinking elements within the Labour Party hoped that many of these wartime experiments would continue.' And 'the Labour Government was fortunate in taking office at the end of the war'. In short, the condition of a society at war seemed by no means a perversion, and consequently there was no intention whatever of changing that condition; propaganda demanded talk of a 'smooth change-over from a war economy to a peace one', but the real belief was in the positive value of the effect of war upon society. What is the ground of this belief? First, of course, it is based upon the perception that the politics of Socialism are the politics of crisis, a perception which leads Mr Parker to doubt the possibility of any large scale growth of Socialism in the United States without a catastrophic slump first taking place. Crisis must be preserved and promoted if Socialism is to have a chance. But secondly, and more immediately, it was based upon the naïve confidence that the planned economy of wartime was a huge success, that it eliminated waste and simplified production and consequently could be taken as the model of all business enterprise. And erroneous as this belief is, it is not half so damaging as the willingness to accept also the effect of war upon society as beneficial — the deprivation of liberty and the conversion of the consumer into someone who is not permitted to demand but who must take what he is given with a glad heart.

. But if the project of a centrally planned economy (and with it, unavoidably, a centrally planned society) owes much to the legend of war, it is a mistake to suppose that it is the project of only one party in contemporary British politics: one party may have gone further than another, but Mr Morrison's claim that 'the idea of planning is now over and above party politics' has some substance, and not only because the word is used in half a dozen different senses. Even Mr Hogg says that 'one of the biggest swindles ever put across the people by a political party is the Labour claim to be the only party which believes in planning'. It is a mistake also to think of it as a political novelty which will disappear with a decade of peace (if we are allowed it) and a decade of full employment (if the present planners permit it). This is a piece of shortsightedness which infects even Professor Jewkes's admirable *Ordeal by Planning*. For the truth is that central planning is the product of an academic ignorance of how the business world works, and a common ignorance of how society lives, which have been growing on us for many years. It may be true, as Professor Jewkes says, that central economic planning 'originated, as many evil ideas originated, in Germany in the war of 1914-18 when it was conceived as a technique for war administration'. But what has to be accounted for is the enthusiasm it generated, not only in Lenin, but also in less eccentric and less egoistic politicians. A centrally planned society is, of course, the simplest of all societies, and offers the greatest prizes of power to those who can get in on the ground floor. It appeals not only to the ambitious politician, but also to the ignorant politician. Economically it is based upon a simplified, mechanistic conception of production and distribution; quantitative, physical controls can be understood by those who could never reach a proper understanding of the kind of control the English common law and the law merchant for centuries exercised over some departments of activity, and for many years over all. Politically it is based upon the naïve idea that power can be controlled only by setting up some greater and uncontrolled power to do the controlling. And socially it is based upon a simplified view of human life, a mental horizon which includes 'the individual' and 'the government' of the day and nothing else. But the ignorance which makes central planning seem desirable may be either that of the politician or that of the electorate. The politician may know very well that a regime of this sort leads only to slavery and wretchedness, but pushed forward and supported by the mandate of an ignorant electorate bemused with the illusory promises of security and prosperity which it is believed central planning has to offer, his ambition will prompt him to say what is expected and to offer what is desired. A centrally planned society is the ideal of all rationalistic politics, and rationalistic politics have been with us long enough for them to be unlikely to disappear in a decade, even in the most promising circumstances: an excessive desire and hope of security is an emotion which has long since invaded and overrun European life and politics.[1] Conservatism, as Mr Hogg expounds it, is opposed to rationalistic politics, and its opposition is firmly based upon a belief in the virtues of a society which has not succumbed to the servility of central planning. But still, there is hesitation. Of course he has no use for a *laissez-faire* economy or society, but he writes often as if such a society and such an economy had existed at some time in the past. It is not firmly and clearly enough stated that a genuine *laissez-faire* society has *never* existed anywhere on earth at any time, and that what through all the centuries has prevented its existence is not central planning, but a rule of law which has emphasized duties at least as much as rights between private individuals, and that no conceivable extension of these rights and duties will ever produce a centrally planned society, which is something of an altogether different quality. (A writer like Mr Parker who sees in the Factory Acts the forecast of a centrally planned society is a trifle too muddled in the head to make a reliable secretary for a tennis club, much less a guide for a nation.) It is the great merit of Conservatism that it has resisted the pressure of circumstances and a misled electorate to embrace the project of a centrally planned society; its present weakness is that it has not resisted that pressure with the absolute conviction with which it should be resisted. If there ever comes a time when two parties compete for power on the basis of rival plans, an even larger lunacy than that from which we at present suffer will have established itself.

It might be expected that what may be called the traditions of British politics would retain some hold on the projects and methods of contemporary policy, and it is relevant to inquire how far this is so. The chief departures from these traditions appear to be three: the current idea of the categories of British politics, the appearance of not only a new party but of a new kind of party, and the current misconception of the nature and function of the Opposition.

The categories of British politics, according to both these writers, are Left and Right. If this were really so it would imply a closer approximation of British to Continental politics than I had supposed to be the case, and it would deprive British politics of much of their individuality. But, of course, it is not so; this is a piece, and perhaps the most corrupting piece, of current nonsense. There may be some faint approximation between the Labour Party and the continental parties of both the Left and the Right (in the politics of rationalism, that is in continental politics, extremes are apt to meet); its roots are not as firmly fixed in the traditions of British politics as one would like. But there is nothing whatever in common between British Conservatism and any of the categories of continental politics. Loose talk of this sort about British politics merely liberates a fog of unreality,

---

[1] Cf. Burckhardt, *Weltgeschichtliche Betrachtungen*, 1906.

and lost in this fog British politics may become detached from their real root in British society and its history; and it is to be regretted that the guilty men in this respect belong to all political parties. And when these categories of Left and Right are transplanted into the past, the writers who perform the operation merely make themselves ridiculous. 'From the time of the Civil War in the middle of the seventeenth century', says Mr Parker, 'political opinions in Britain have tended to divide between two main Parties, one of the Right and one of the Left.' And it is to be feared that he is only copying the fantasy of English history current in Socialist circles. But then, it is the sort of statement one expects from a man who believes that 'an adequate study of civics' is the best education for a politician. And when these writers go on to a cant identification of Conservatism with Fascism and both with reaction, the fantasy is complete. Fascism, at least, has nothing to do with reaction; it has both wind and tide in its favour. But if it is too much to expect the Socialist to awake from his dream and cease to think of himself as Left and his opponent as Right, it is not too much to ask the Conservative (who, if he follows Mr Hogg, does not think of himself as Right) not to encourage the Labour Party to dramatize itself as Left.

The novelty of the Labour Party has not, I think, been sufficiently explored, but it is a subject that can only be touched upon here. Two points are of note. The first is the relation of a Labour Administration to the Annual Conference of the Labour Party. As Mr Parker says, 'the supreme authority of the Labour Party is the Annual Party Conference ... It consists of delegates of all affiliated organizations with voting rights in accordance with the strength of affiliated membership'. The Conference is 'a remarkably democratic institution'. And the motion tabled by the Lewisham (East) Divisional Labour Party for the Conference this year, a motion which is commonly believed to be somewhat eccentric and since withdrawn, is only a precise elaboration of the prevailing doctrine with regard to the authority of the Conference: 'When the Labour Party is the governing party in the country, conference decisions shall be binding upon the Government and shall be acted upon within the programme of the Parliamentary Labour Party.' It means that, under a Labour Administration, Parliament is demoted to the position of an executive body for carrying out the items of a programme determined each year by an irresponsible body. Needless to say, the government of this country has not yet acquired this character without reservation, but it is the character of British government implicit in the structure of the Labour Party. And were it ever established without qualification a constitutional revolution would have taken place beside which the revolution invoked in central planning would be insignificant. We may perhaps remind ourselves that it was one of the requests of the Nineteen Propositions (1642) 'that the great affairs of the kingdom may not be concluded or transacted by the advice of private men, or by any unknown or unsworn councillors'.

But secondly, a Labour Administration owes another allegiance, springing from the sources of its power. The Trades Union Congress is a constitutionally irresponsible body which appears to exercise a powerful influence over the decisions of a Labour Administration. But more important, since the repeal of the Trade Disputes Act (1927), the political funds of the various trade unions have become the major source of the Labour Party's income, and through them the Trade Unions may gain a control over a larger number of parliamentary candidates and seats. But Mr Parker continues: 'the permission given, as a result of the repeal of the Trade Disputes Act, to the Civil Service Trade Unions to link up with the T.U.C. and to create political funds will almost certainly lead to more direct representation of the Civil Service Trade Unions in the House in future.' And he does not appear to recognize anything remarkable in writing like this. It used commonly to be supposed that a Member of Parliament represented his constituency, but the structure of the Labour Party evidently has a tendency, not only to make a Labour Administration subservient to irresponsible advisors, but also to turn the House of Commons, so far as Labour representatives are concerned, into a sort of syndicalist assembly.

Every schoolboy knows that the Opposition in the British parliamentary tradition has a positive function to perform: it is to be regretted that there are so many politicians who do not properly understand what that function is. And this is a matter of some importance, because as soon as real knowledge of the function of opposition disappears, the Opposition will come to be thought of as an expensive luxury, a piece of wastefulness, and therefore to be planned out of existence. The truth is that parliamentary government as we know it depends for its continued existence more upon the Opposition than upon the party in power. Mr Parker's ignorance is profound, and consequently dangerous. He patronizingly suggests that when the Conservative Party has been a little longer in opposition it may perhaps learn how to behave as an Opposition should—which, it appears, is to keep quiet in the face of the might of the majority. There is a vague suggestion—it is a cloud no bigger than a man's hand—that to oppose is to commit *lese majesté*. His chief specific criticisms of the present Opposition are, however, that it offers too few 'constructive suggestions', that it is without an alternative plan, and that it is disunited. Now, Mr Hogg (and anyone else who knows anything about British parliamentary government) knows very well how foolish these criticisms are. It is, and always has been, the business of the Opposition to oppose, to criticize, to expose foolishness, corruption and mismanagement wherever they lie hidden. It is required neither to make constructive suggestions (though the present Opposition has made many) nor to have an alternative plan. And, in general, it may be said that a disunited Opposition is as necessary as a united government. The present Opposition has not, perhaps, made the most of its opportunities, opportunities greater than have ever before been offered to an Opposition. It is true that the administration of departments and (it would appear) the instructions given to the drafters of Bills have often been so incompetent that it has been difficult for criticism to know where to begin; but the delay and folly of the government's foreign policy, and the grand stupidity of its finance, have been too easily passed over. A more resolute, relentless, tireless, extempore criticism of administrative blunders, a criticism that let nothing pass, that was constantly on the tail of ineptitude, would have served the country better than the careful construction of an alternative policy, though, of course, it is the business of an Opposition while pursuing the first to be thinking about the second. However, if it is less efficient than it might be, the present Opposition has at least kept alive the true principles of opposition and has resisted the temptation to abandon opposition for the plugging of an alternative plan.

Whatever the obscurity which surrounds the spring and circumstances of contemporary British politics, these writers leave us in little doubt about their aims. And the most probable method of discovering what the two great parties have to offer is to inquire into the sort of society each thinks desirable. Let us consider this question first in respect of the Labour Party. The purpose of its present activities, we are told, is to bring into being 'a really vital social democracy'. This, of course, is equivocal. What does it mean? And how is it to be achieved?

It means, first, the 'reconstruction of British economy on a planned basis'; a centrally planned economy operated by physical controls. Mr Parker, on an early page, allows himself the use of the expression, 'a planned economy on democratic lines', but later on, in one of his rare moments of ingenuousness, he admits to a doubt about the validity of 'the distinction between totalitarian and democratic planning'; a government committed to central planning must not hesitate to exert the necessary pressure on the economy to achieve its ends, a pressure which includes the direction of labour. But, of, course, like the abolition of the right to buy and sell a medical practice, this must be thought of as an acquisition of freedom rather than a deprivation. What, in practice, the reconstruction of British economy on a planned basis involves is known already to most people in England, and those few who are still without direct experience of it can learn from Professor Jewkes's *Ordeal by Planning*.

That a planned economy means, also, a planned society, Mr Parker is in no doubt. The 'very wide powers over the whole industrial life of the nation' which planning entails, are powers also over every individual in the society. Their exercise involves the destruction of the consumer, who is replaced by the mere recipient of what is given to him, consumer goods becoming allowances to keep the human machine efficient and to provide incentives to work. Individuality, however, is not totally destroyed; it is maintained by a minimum allowance of 'personal property', which is distinguished from non-permissible private property by the usual sophistical Socialist argument. The shining vision of the future (how unlike that of William Morris whom Mr Parker has the temerity to mention) is that of a society in which everyone is an employee of the government, a society upon which has been fixed and riveted the deadly grip of the corporation employee mentality, a society in which everyone has a 'post' given him by 'the community' (Edward VIII is described as having 'shown himself unsuitable for his post'), which will 'choose the best individuals to occupy all the most important posts whether in industry, the universities, the arts or government'. And Mr Parker estimates (by the perhaps injudicious inclusion of the employees of the Co-operative Movement) that by 1950, a trifle over six million persons will be employed in what he calls 'public concerns'. Socialism will have arrived when 'the majority of the working population are employed by public concerns of one kind or another'. This society will derive its peace and stability from its monopolistic structure, and the world (in its turn) will be at peace either when 'all the major powers have economies that are primarily socialistic in character' or (at least) when a 'power to plan world resources as a whole' has been set up. And further, the dominance of the Labour Party in England will at the same time, and by the same means, be assured. 'There is a widespread desire in the lower middle class and in the upper sections of the working class to secure posts in the Civil Service', says Mr Parker. And the Labour Government is desperately anxious to draw into its direct or indirect employment as many people as possible. For whoever owes his employment to the planners will keep the planners in power by his vote. Patronage is the basis of political power. So runs Mr Parker's surprising doctrine. It is a simple plot to establish, not by force but by subterfuge, a single-party system and the slavery from which it is inseparable.

The best that can be said for the method by which this 'really vital social democracy' is to be achieved is that it is appropriate to its purpose. It consists in the concentration in the hands of the Government of much of the power which is at present widely distributed throughout our society. The power that derives from monopoly is not to be wastefully dissipated, it is to be appropriated by the Government; and along with it, into the same maw, are to go many of the small powers (the rights) exercised by countless individual men and women. The public ownership—nationalization—of 'the main resources of the community' is merely a means to the end; it is necessary, not because private enterprise is inefficient or monopolistic, not for any of the reasons daily given in Parliament, but because 'the creation of a planned economy would be quite impossible without a substantial part of the industrial structure being in national hands'.

Now, the interesting question is, Why is not all this recognized by its promoters as despotism and by those who suffer under it as tyranny? There are, I think, three main reasons. First, it is not recognized as tyranny because of the vast emotional and intellectual confusion there is with regard to the nature and conditions of freedom. A man who, before the Truck Act, was defrauded of his wages, knew himself to be, to that extent, a slave. He might be well-fed, secure in his job and enjoying a rising standard of living; nevertheless, he was not to be gulled into thinking that he was as free as he would be if his wages were paid him in cash. The Truck Act set him free. It did not say to him, 'The price of this freedom is a bit off the other end of your freedom': it was a gratuitous addition to his freedom made by a civilized society, and if it had not been this it would not have been freedom at all. And this is the truth that has been lost in the confusion: if you are required to pay with freedom for an offered freedom, you can be certain that what you are offered is not freedom at all, but something else. It may be something you value, it may be something for which you are willing to pay freedom in order to acquire, but it is not itself freedom. Now, the situation under a centrally planned economy is that *everybody* (with the partial exception of the planners themselves) is deprived of so much freedom that the regime would at once be recognized as a tyranny were we not deluded into thinking that what we were being offered in place of the lost freedom was freedom of another sort or in another direction. A centrally planned society is not an example of one of those apparently simple situations (beloved of the Socialist) in which, by a sophistical argument, it can be pretended that freedom is taken from one but given to another: *everyone* is deprived. It offers us neither a gross nor a net addition to our freedom. And when it comes to be seen that what it offers (pretending that it is the same, or just as good, as freedom) — security, prosperity, etc. — it cannot in fact supply, the bargain will seem an ill bargain even to the man who values these things more than his freedom.

Secondly, the tyrannical character of our planned society is not recognized because the regime was not introduced by a *coup d'état* or its equivalent. Sensitiveness to tyranny is always apt to lag behind the inventiveness of tyrants, and our political perceptions, in the absence of a lively political imagination, are very much at the mercy of our political experience. Mr. Parker claims no more for his party than that the changes it has set on foot are 'on a par with the Reform Act of 1832 or the big social changes carried through by the Liberal Government of 1906'. It is a judicious understatement of the facts which by this time will delude no one. But the absence of a *coup d'état*, though important at first, must be counted among the wasting assets of the Labour Party. Established tyranny cannot for ever conceal its character except from willing slaves.

Thirdly, this is not recognized as a despotism because of the mediocrity of the planners. We have been taught to look for the spring of great achievements and great catastrophes in great and strong personalities. And we have learned to beware of extraordinary ambition. But the lesson is out of date. All our traditional resources of resistance have been trained upon outstanding genius or over-mighty power, but they have been turned in the wrong direction. Our political observation has been educated to detect only the despot who, in Lincoln's words, belongs to 'the family of the lion or the tribe of the eagle'. Suspecting a tyranny, we look for a Strafford and find only a Cripps, we look for a Cromwell and find only Clem Attlee—and we are reassured. But if the experience of our time has any unmistakable message for us, it is that tyranny can spring from mediocrity and despotism from inferiority. The ambition we should beware of is the petty ambition to keep on the crest of the wave, the ambition which is satisfied with the illusion of affairs. Gisevius has shown us that the real tyrant in Germany was not Hitler, but the German people. *Les esclaves volontaires font plus de tyrans que les tyrans ne font d'esclaves forcés*, and the tyrants they make are distinguished by their mediocrity.

The conclusion that the reader is encouraged to draw from Mr Parker's book (a conclusion reinforced by many of the actions of the present Administration) is that the Labour Party has an *incentive* to become despotic (it is moved by the 'pitiless fanaticism of an idea'), that it has the *means* to become despotic, and that it has the *intention* of becoming despotic. 'Democracy in this country', the Home Secretary has told us, 'is very much on trial.' The conclusion, on the other hand, from Mr Hogg's book is that Conservatism has no incentive to promote despotism and that the aim of Conservative politics is to guard society against all those concentrations of power which are liable to result in despotism.

The Conservative has no shining vision of a New Age—partly because he is sceptical about the value of such visions and partly because, whatever their value, he does not think they should be the stock-in-trade of the politician. 'While others extol the virtues of the particular brand of Utopia they propose to create, the Conservative disbelieves them all, and, despite all temptations, offers in their place no Utopia at all but something quite modestly better than the present. He may, and should, have a programme. He certainly has a policy. But of catchwords, slogans, visions, ideal states of society, classless societies, new orders, of all the tinsel and finery with which the modern political charlatans charm their jewels from the modern political savage, the Conservative has nothing to offer. He would rather die than sell such trash, and consequently it is said wrongly by those who have something of this sort on their trays that he has no policy, and still more wrongly by those who value success above honour that he ought to find one.' Politics are a limited activity, a necessary but second-rate affair. 'The Conservative contends that the most a politician can do is to ensure that some, and these by no means the most important, conditions in which the good life can exist are present, and, more important still, to prevent fools and knaves from setting up conditions which make any approach to the good life impossible except for solitaries and anchorites.' This has the merit of according with human experience. At least it is a form of politics which does not expect improbable changes in human nature, either for the worse or for the better, and which, further, does not assume that such changes have already taken place.

Within these limits, what is the business of the politician — whether he is in office or out of office? Of the two main functions he exists to perform, the first and most important is to prevent the concentration of power in a society and to break up all concentrations of power which have the appearance of becoming dangerous. The general name for all forms of political disease is the concentration of power in the hands of a part, whether that part is a private individual, a corporation, a union, a party, a majority, a minority or a government. And consequently those charged with the guardianship of a society (that is, the Adminstration and the Opposition) have a first duty to preserve a diffusion of power. As circumstances change power will tend to become concentrated in new centres, and the politician must be wary in discovery and courageous in action. To perform his beneficent function he does not require, when in office, to wield a supreme and crushing power; he requires only to wield a power greater than that which is concentrated in any one centre of power. Nor does he need to act arbitrarily or extravagantly, except to repair some dereliction of his own duty. Any experienced society, and above all our society with its long tradition of resistance to tyranny, has at its disposal an armoury of laws and methods amply sufficient to defend itself against the overmighty ruler or subject. Nor, on this view of his function, will a politician expect, or think it good, that he and his party should be permanently in office, much less will he think it good that the Opposition should be silenced or abolished. If the task of the Administration is to disperse dangerous concentrations of power in the society, the equally important task of the Opposition is to guard the society against a secret and insidious concentration of power in the Administration.

The reason for all this is not obscure. It is based first upon the observation (confirmed in the history of every society) of the corrupting tendency of the exercise of power. 'Power means the exercise of force; it corrupts by undermining a man's will and reducing him to the level of his own slaves. A slave-driver, getting out of the habit of explaining to his slaves what he means them to do, gets out of the habit of formulating his intentions even to himself ... The lack of free will, the inability to resist the pressure of emotional forces, which makes the slave a slave, is also what makes the tyrant a tyrant.'[2] But secondly, the politics of the diffusion of power are recommended because they are the only guarantee of the most valuable and substantial freedom known to human beings. This freedom is, in fact, the product of the exercise of the politician's function of preventing concentrations of power. Political freedom is inseparable from the diffusion, the sharing of political power. And economic freedom, Mr Hogg says, can spring only from 'the diffusion of economic power, that is property, as widely as possible throughout the community'.

The politician in office may be said to have a second function to perform. It is to take the initiative in seeking out the current mischiefs and maladjustments in a society and to set them right, not arbitrarily but by bringing to bear upon them the legal principles which constitute the recognized method of adjustment in any experienced and civilized society. And in order to perform this function he must have in his mind not only 'the individual' (who may be either the beneficiary or the sufferer of the mischief) and 'the government', but also the vast mass of healthy relations between the members of a society (some established by law and others by custom) which, from any point of view except that of revolutionary *jusqu'aboutisme*, are more important than the few which are morbid.

Now, how are these functions to be carried out? I think it is in answering this question that Mr Hogg is unhappily led to write in a manner inconsistent with the general view he is advocating. He sees clearly enough that the main integration of our society (or of any civilized society) lies in the fact that a man has the assurance that, if he takes a certain line of action, consequences will ensue which he can forsee with reasonable certainty. This certainty is the result of the predominance of the law—a law based originally on the common law, but in the past hundred years or so gradually developed by legislation so as to emphasize the element of obligation as well as that of right. Maladjustment appears when the enjoyment of these rights and duties leads to dangerous concentrations of power. He sees also that the necessary readjustments must be *in pari materia* with the integration itself—that is, an adjustment which, at any point, replaces rights and duties of individual men by an overhead plan, is destructive of an integration based upon rights and duties. But, as a relic of an old intellectual error, he thinks of these rights and duties as 'limitations' and of their adjustment as 'interference'. It is an unfortunate way of thinking which is inherent in the simpler forms of a natural law conception of society. The truth is, however, that we do not begin by being free; the structure of our freedom is the rights and duties which, by long and painful human, effort, have been established in our society. Individuality is not natural; it

---

[2] Collingwood, *The New Leviathan*, p. 156.

is a great human achievement. The conditions of individuality are not limitations; there is nothing to limit. And the adjustment of those conditions are not interference (unless they are overhead adjustments); they are the continuation of the achievement. But the intellectual error involved in Mr Hogg's way of thinking would not be so damaging were it not for the fact that the step from these ideas of limitation and interference to the idea of adjustment by means of overhead planning, with physical controls, is as short as it is disastrous. And it is a step which Mr Hogg, perhaps inadvertently, takes when he writes with approval of social adjustment by means of 'the rearrangement of incentives' in industry. The bug of rationalistic politics has bitten the Conservative. To have hoped that he might be immune from the universal infection was, perhaps, excessive optimism. But his powers of resistance are great, and when he has recovered from it, the policy he should pursue at home will be clear. It is a policy of diffusing all those morbid concentrations of power which have grown up in our society during the last fifty years, not by means of an overhead plan (which itself involves a morbid concentration of power), but by means of small adjustments in the rights and duties of individuals. Are industrial monopolies a danger to freedom? Is the exercise of certain rights restrictive upon production? Does the legal framework, within which the social and business activities of the society take place, encourage injustice, cruelty, fraud, frustration, bad workmanship, fear of unemployment, ignorance, apathy, disease? Do our present rights and duties check the springs of human enterprise, the exercise of which in all its forms is the only source of happiness? To answer these and similar questions as best we can, avoiding dangerous obsessions with any one problem, and to remove the mischiefs revealed, is the beginning and end of policy.

This, perhaps, is an exaggeration. The conduct of the foreign affairs of the society must be added to the duty of the politician in office. This, indeed, may at times appear his most important duty, and at such times the danger is that the methods employed in it may be reflected back upon the governance of the society itself. For the conduct of foreign affairs is recognized as the exercise of the Prerogative, and demands an extraordinary concentration of authority. Hegel was right when he identified the abstract individuality of the state with its conduct of foreign affairs. But, further, it is not to be supposed that politics at home can, any less than any other human activity, be conducted without love and hate, generosity and resentment. The contingencies of human life and the wilfulness of human character are reflected in politics as clearly as elsewhere. But the main points are, that politics are a limited activity, that they consist in the gradual readjustment of human relationships (and not in the administration of things) by fallible men, that there is no end to the process, and that their method should be one which does not neglect the fundamental structure of those relationships. No doubt politicians will always be gamblers, but they should back the field and leave private enterprise to bet on the favourite.

This is a difficult policy to pursue in an age which has so long preferred the reign of rationalist planners to the reign of freedom. It is unspectacular, and unimpressive to the mass of men and women brought up on melodramatic politics. Its positive demands are reasonableness, sincerity, patience, self-restraint, moderate foresight and a knowledge of the principles of integration and adjustment imbedded in the history of our society. But they are human qualities, qualities which a Member of Parliament might be expected to possess or to be capable of acquiring, common qualities in comparison with the godlike vision and superhuman mental grasp which the successful planner must have and which our planners certainly have not got. Such a policy is, indeed, a kind of perennial politics, the form of all politics which make use of the past achievements of our society in enterprise and organization and which endeavours to add to those achievements. But there is still room for differences of programme, for differences of opinion about what to do next and for differences of judgment about where the current dangers lie. And these will be the *differentiae* of political parties. What there is no room for is a party whose leaders seek to establish a despotism and to fix upon society an external order.

British democracy is not an abstract idea. It is a way of living and a manner of politics which first began to emerge in the Middle Ages. In those distant times almost the whole outline of this way of life and manner of politics was adumbrated, an outline which has since been enlarged by experience and invention and defended against attack from without and treason from within. So convincing was this subtle manner of integrating a society that it became the model for peoples whose powers of social and political invention were unequal to their needs. The common law rights and duties of Englishmen were transplanted throughout the civilized world, the pride of those who possessed them and the envy of those who did not; a gift far more important than our gift of parliamentary institutions. In this process some of their flexibility was lost; the rights and duties were exported, the genius that made them remained at home. Peoples, desirous of freedom, but dissatisfied with anything less than the imagination of an eternal and immutable law, gave to these rights and duties the false title of Nature. Because they were not the fruit of their own experience, it was forgotten that they were the fruit of the experience of the British people. For many years now, these children of our own flesh have been returning to us, disguised in a foreign dress, the outline blurred by false theory and the detail fixed with an uncharacteristic precision. What went abroad as the concrete rights of an Englishman have returned home as the abstract Rights of Man, and they have returned to confound our politics and corrupt our minds. Our need now is to recover the lost sense of a society whose freedom and organization spring, not from a superimposed plan, but from the integrating power of a vast and subtle body of rights and duties enjoyed between individuals (whose individuality, in fact, comes into being by their enjoyment), not the gift of nature but the product of our own experience and inventiveness; and to recover also the perception of our law, not merely as an achieved body of rights and duties, the body of a freedom in which mere political rights have a comparatively insignificant place, but as a living method of social integration, the most civilized and the most effective method ever invented by mankind.

Sixty-four

The Analysis of Political Behaviour

If you want to be frightened, read this book; as a portent of the end of civilised life it is far more unnerving than the atomic bomb. After forty, one naturally prefers a holocaust to the ignominy of being buried alive under the indiscriminating volcanic ash of 'social reconstruction'. Professor Lasswell, distinguished as a lawyer as well as a sociologist, is a 'friend of Democracy', but he is a friend from whose attentions ordinary democracies (with a small 'd') should pray to be delivered. He is the professor of an empirical 'science of democracy', which is the workshop where the implements necessary for the achievement of democratic ideals are forged and the arsenal where they are stored. It is a science which is to political science in general what medicine is to biology. 'People need to be equipped with knowledge of how democratic doctrines can be justified. They cannot be expected to remain loyal to democratic ideals through all the disappointments and disillusionments of life without a deep and enduring factual knowledge of the potentialities of human beings for congenial and productive interpersonal relations.' And the survival of democracy now depends upon 'the timing of special research' into the technique of democratic life. The truth is, of course, that what we need is not a technique of moral progress, but to be made aware of the values we are in danger of losing. And as we wade through his laboured analysis of childish examples of the problems of behaviour (the efforts of a short-tempered administrator to 'set a praiseworthy pattern of administrative conduct') and listen to his reiterated theme – 'The democratic ideal includes a decent regard for the opinions and sensibilities of our fellows. The moralists who have championed this ideal in the past have made no progress towards the discovery of methods appropriate to the understanding of the thoughts and feelings of others. The instrumentation of morals has had to await reliable methods of observation' – we wonder why he does not, just for a moment,

---

Review of Harold Dwight Lasswell, *The Analysis of Political Behaviour: an Empirical Approach* (London: Routledge and Kegan Paul, 1947). First published in *Cambridge Journal*, 1 (1948), 326, 328.

forget these obscuring abstractions and consider the realities of moral endeavour: why do I not get on with my neighbour? The conceptual difficulties which make hay of some of the more general essays in his book—difficulties about the meaning of 'Democracy' and a 'free society'—are not, of course, so evident in the essays which deal with narrower subjects, and whatever value this book may have lies in these. Lawyers, also, may be interested in the long essay on Legal Education and Public Policy.

Sixty-five

The English Festivals

Mr Whistler has written a charming and profound book on an important and fascinating subject. His theme is the festivals, the 'holidays', in which the English people have recognised and appreciated the rhythm of the natural and the civilised year, making of it a microcosm of the wheel of life: Christmas, New Year, Twelfth Night, Easter, May Day, Whitsun, Midsummer, Harvest, and sixteen other celebrations which fill out the spaces between. Few of these festivals have lost all trace of their spring in the pagan religion of our distant ancestors, but few also have held out against Christian conversion. They are the most ancient customs of our society, more ancient than any of our beliefs, and in their recovery from the Puritan attack in the seventeenth century (which was as much an attack upon leisure as upon the way in which it was used), they have shown their power to survive even the pitiless fanaticism of an idea. To the contemplation of these festivals Mr Whistler brings a fine perception of significance, an acute eye for detail, a strong sense of the enveloping emotional life which they focus and interpret, so that his insight does not dispel the inherent charm and mystery and his explanations do not cheapen. But his object is not merely antiquarian — to recover some of the lost lore of these festivals; it is to offer 'a guide to the festivals of England as they are and as they might be'. He knows well enough that deliberate 'revivals', with their ostentation and self-consciousness, have little power to prevail against time. But he knows, also, that each of these festivals has always been flexible and adaptable. He observes that within living memory the customs of Christmas have changed, the tree replacing the Kissing Bough; that festivals, such as Plough Monday and St George's Day, have been given a new life: and that such innovations as fireworks have made a place for themselves in the ritual of already established celebrations. He observes, also, that the genius of the English people created (not *ex nihilo*, but probably out of the dim reminiscence of the ritual of All Hallows) a new festival,

---

Review of Laurence Whistler, *The English Festivals* (London: Heinemann, 1947). First published in *Cambridge Journal*, 1 (1948), 382, 384.

Guy Fawkes Day, the one surviving Festival of Fire in our country. And he concludes that each of these traditional festivals is capable of improvement and adaptation by those who, aware of the range of human emotion which they focus, think they are worthwhile improving and adapting. But the question proposed by the circumstances of our time, when the enemy of these observances is lack of leisure and means to practice them rather than an opposing idea, is, How long can a custom starve and live? And if the answer which Mr Whistler gives is not very hopeful—'Ten years perhaps; hardly more. If in their *total* austerity modern wars were to last as long as ancient ones, memory would cease to inspire action; there would emerge a way of life stripped clean of gestures and unfurnished; hollow as an empty room'—his book is neither anxious nor apologetic.

Sixty-six

Nietzsche

The queue which, in the early years of this century, lined up in front of Nietzsche is now, fortunately, thinning out. And with this hindrance removed, we are beginning to have an opportunity to observe the man and his work unembarrassed by the exaggerated reverence of his injudicious admirers, the mistaken enthusiasm of the culture-philistines up from the suburbs, and the protests of the injured. The Nietzscheans and the anti-Nietzscheans, who made of him the purveyor of a doctrine to be embraced or rejected, a Master to be followed or foresworn (who made him, what he never was, a Nietzschean), have done their worst, and have left behind them a trail of misconceived expositions and commentaries—*De Kant à Nietzsche, Von Darwin bis Nietzsche*, and the rest. But now that the din is somewhat subsided, there is a chance that a more intelligent sort of interpreter will have a hearing—those who got what they could from Nietzsche, whose imagination he fired, and who were aware of him as an artist whom either to abridge or to systematize was to destroy.

The mistake of the Nietzscheans and their opponents was a preoccupation with what was least significant in Nietzsche's work, the remedies he proposed for the ills of European society. They saw in him the apostle of a New Aristocracy, the defender of the strong against the insidious mediocrity of the weak, the preacher of salvation through the pursuit of 'more robust ideals'. It was a quack Nietzsche (largely of their own making) whom they hailed as Master or Enemy: for anyone who proposes a cure for so radical a disease in mankind is pretty well self-convicted of quackery. But those who are now beginning to make themselves heard recognized in his writings, not remedies, but a profound and imaginative diagnosis of a crisis in European culture. He sounded an alarm: for the world in which Nietzsche detected the crisis was as insensible of its predicament as we are of the speed at which the earth is whirling through space. Nor did he merely reveal the crisis at the heart of the trance and diagnose its character

---

Review of Janko Lavrin, *Nietzsche: an Approach* (London: Methuen, 1948). First published in *Cambridge Journal*, 1 (1948), 450, 452.

in the general terms of 'nihilism', 'irreligion', and 'weakness'; he elaborated his diagnosis in detail with untiring insight in every field of human activity and in phrases which (when rescued from the interpretations of commonplace minds) have the power of opening up vistas of reflection and setting the imagination on fire. In art, insight (diagnosis) is an end in itself. The remedy is not something that *follows*: if it is anywhere it lies in the diagnosis itself, in the removal of the corrupt consciousness, and if we are to understand Nietzsche, we must understand him as, in this sense, an artist.

Professor Janko Lavrin calls his book 'an Approach'. His aim is 'to point out the bond between Nietzsche's personal fate on the one hand, and the trend of his thought on the other', to show the spring of Nietzsche's diagnosis of the crisis of European culture in the circumstances of his own life. In the hands of a less intelligent writer, his project might have degenerated into the application of a formula to Nietzsche's work. But if 'to approach Nietzsche the philosopher through Nietzsche the man' is a formula, it is one which is derived from Nietzsche's own writings; and, in any case, Professor Lavrin has a mastery over it which saves it from degeneration. Of the relation between Nietzsche and his time, he writes: 'the personal element in Nietzsche's philosophy may have at times deflected or even distorted the trend of his thought, yet it never undermined his interest in mankind and its future. Nor were the analogies he drew between his own dilemma and that of modern decadence entirely arbitrary, since in both cases the problem of averting the menace of disintegration was of primary importance. The vigilance with which he followed the various phases of his own ailments undoubtedly sharpened his eyes also with regard to the evils of his epoch, some of which he saw more clearly, one is tempted to say — more clairvoyantly — than any of his contemporaries'. On the character of Nietzsche's malady he accepts, with some reserve, the conclusion of Dr Vorberg that it was syphilis. But, instead of seeing in Nietzsche's writings merely the reflection of his disease (whatever it was), he explores the hypothesis that 'the scrutiny with which Nietzsche followed up the phases of his malady helped him to diagnose certain ailments of Europe probably better than a healthier individual could have done ... Whatever one may think of his remedies, we cannot deny that his sharp perception unerringly detected many a cause of these modern evils which were to be more fully tasted only by the generations which came after him'. In short, whatever may be said against Professor Lavrin's approach, it at least enables him to avoid the worst errors of the Nietzscheans and their opponents. And if it is true (as I believe it is) that the most valuable sort of book on Nietzsche is, not one about Nietzsche, but one which passes on what has been fired by Nietzsche in the writer's imagination, then this unpretentious book is certainly worth while. Indeed, I believe it to be the most enlightening brief treatment of its subject in English.

Sixty-seven

Masters of Political Thought

The *Masters of Political Thought* is a project to expound the history of political thought, for the benefit of university students, by means of substantial extracts from the writings of the better known political theorists interspersed with comment and interpretation. It aims to combine the merits of a text-book and a source book. This volume is the second of three, and the writers it represents are Machiavelli, Bodin, Hobbes, Locke, Montesquieu, Rousseau, Burke, and Bentham. One is left to guess why Spinoza has not been included.

Such a book is not, and does not pretend to be, a history of political thought. Not only does it move from peak to peak with little indication of the ground between, but also it gives little opportunity to explore a tradition of thought should one make its appearance. In order, however, to make up for these potential shortcomings, Professor Jones introduces his selections of masters with a short essay designed to indicate the general nature and importance of political thought and the 'defining characteristics' of the period he covers. It is a disappointing essay, vague and scrappy. It over-emphasises the 'breaks' (the Renaissance and the Industrial Revolution) with which he contends his period begins and ends, and it finds the unity of the period in its speculations about sovereignty and 'the conception of the State as a natural organism'. It is a difficult period to deal with, but a more convincing principle of unity might have been discovered.

The chief value of the book, however, must lie in the interpretation it offers of each of the writers represented. In general, these interpretations err on the side of the commonplace: they steam-roller all the subtleties and make everything a trifle easier than it really is. When all the simple errors of Hobbes and Locke and Burke have been pointed out to us, one begins to wonder why anyone should think of them as 'masters'. And were the *Contrat Social* nothing more than it is here made out to be, it would cer-

Review of *Masters of Political Thought, vol. 2: Machiavelli to Bentham*, ed. W.T. Jones (London: Harrap, 1947). First published in *Cambridge Journal*, 1 (1947–8), 636–7.

tainly not have kept Kant from his afternoon walk. If one follows Nietzsche's precept of interpretation—to understand an author better than he understood himself—one needs to be more rather than less subtle. But, though none of these chapters can be called a masterpiece of interpretation, three of them (on Hobbes, Locke, and Rousseau) are substantial and leave us in no doubt of Professor Jones's views. In respect of Hobbes, no defects are uncovered which have not already and often been remarked upon: though many of them are, I think, beside the mark. His ethics are taken to be a simple form of Naturalism, his work is distinguished as 'the first *scientific* social theory', and by a *tour de force* the *Leviathan* is fully explained as though it came to an end at chapter thirty. And there is a sort of misapplied ingenuity in finding difficulty where Hobbes found none—in sovereignty by institution—and in seeing no difficulty where Hobbes was clearly in a quandary—in sovereignty by acquisition. Locke's theory is removed almost entirely from its historical context and made to appear the simplest and least ambiguous of contract theories. How political obligation can rest both on consent and on the Law of Nature, is a question which any reader of Locke is bound to ask, but it is one which Professor Jones does not tackle. And there is no discussion of Locke's idea of trusteeship. In dealing with Rousseau, Professor Jones always is safe where he can detect a 'core of plain common sense', but at sea when paradox makes its appearance.

The passage of time is, perhaps, making some improvement in our interpretation of the writings of political theorists, and this book is certainly superior to the sort of thing that was being written fifty years ago. Nevertheless, it is disappointing; and one would doubt the value of the enterprise if the first volume of the series, by Michael Foster, were not greatly superior to the second.

Sixty-eight

Why We Read History

No publisher, it seems, is satisfied with his list unless he is running one of these horrifying series of little books designed to offer the sort of education which may be acquired standing on one leg, or, to translate the Roman poets' phrase, travelling on the top deck of a bus. There is, of course, nothing intrinsically harmful in the little book on the great subject. It is the series that is horrifying; it approximates beekeeping (a profound and subtle art) to shorthand, and science to technology, and does little but add to the illusions with which we are surrounded. However, a series is, now and again, redeemed by one of the individuals which comprise it, and it is a pleasure to come across a little book written, as this is, with such urbanity and sense of style (though 'old Vico' is difficult to swallow) and with so great a freedom from pretentious nonsense.

We live in an intellectually corrupt age, and the writing of history has not escaped the general corruption. The reading public, it is supposed, has a clear idea of the sort of illusion it desires; it wants something short, simplified, and informative. And the writer (with, of course, the great exceptions) either supplies it or shies off obliquely into the dim world of pseudo-research. The contemporary interest in history is centered upon the use to be made of it, upon the dogma it can be made to prove; concerned only with the future, we pervert history to our purposes. Ours is not the first generation to turn history into a formula for teaching the conduct of life, but knowing rather less than our ancestors about how to behave, we clutch at the project rather more crudely. There is room, then, for a fresh discussion of why we read history.

Mr Smellie has written an engaging essay on this subject. He discusses the meaning of history (on two different levels), the use of history, the history of history, and ends by giving some advice on what to read about history. He is clear-headed, wide-ranging, and informative. But the charm of the essay springs from the informal, reflective mood in which it is written;

Review of Kingsley Bryce Smellie, *Why We Read History* (London: Paul Elek, 1947). First published in *Cambridge Journal*, 1 (1948), 766–7.

its real theme is 'why I read history'. In general it may be said that what he has got out of it is pleasure and instruction, and he values both. He is precise and analytical about the instruction, and he manages to convey some sense of the pleasure without exactly examining its character. It is only in the last chapter that he shows some sign of degenerating into the true style of the 'little book'. He makes many excellent recommendations about what to read, but here and there his list contains some pretty boring and some pretty tendentious reading matter; the student perched on the top deck of the bus will take his Smith or his Jones from his pocket, but he will soon find himself looking out of the window, and he will be well advised to continue doing so. The conception of history which informs Mr Smellie's recommendations is that which earlier in his essay he points out as having emerged in the nineteenth century—'history as a continuous genetical causal process'. And in consequence his main emphasis is upon books which are informative about a great variety of aspects of the past and present of Western Europe. It would have been a welcome relief if he had slipped in the recommendation of some historical masterpiece—like Rosebery's *Napoleon: The Last Phase*—which arouses no extraneous passions and releases us from the burden of history as the intellectual and moral preface to the contemporary world, and if he had relented so far as to recognize the legitimacy of sitting up in bed on a Sunday morning to read the history of the Popes, not because it is important but because it is fascinating.

But there is one point of serious criticism which must be made. Mr Smellie quotes with approval Acton's 'shining precepts' for the student of history. Many of them are, no doubt, excellent; a critical study of them would, by itself, make an excellent essay on reading history. But the enormity hidden in the middle of them should not have been passed by without comment: 'Judge ... character at its worst.' Here is a precept so preposterous, so myopic, so sadly corrupting that without the aid of any other error it has the power of transforming history into a gallery, not of rogues, but of moral abstractions.

Sixty-nine

Father, a Portrait of G.G. Coulton at Home

This is a brilliant book. Like any other portrait, it is an artist's vision; it springs from the meeting of two personalities, both strong, aggressive, and uncompromising, and not from any enterprise of passive observation. His daughter's intention is to set down the plain truth of the domestic personality of her father. This, as she remarks, is a 'task not likely to please sentimentalists, friend and foe alike, who would prefer anything but the plain truth; but it will be great fun and Father would certainly have enjoyed seeing me at it. It would remind him of that grim little story he used to tell of the siege of Paris: two old hungry folk sitting down to eat the carcass of their little pet dog, and the old woman saying, as she swallowed a morsel: "How poor Fifi would have enjoyed these bones."' (This I am sure is true; at any rate it is ruled by that strangely positivist conception of historical truth that governed all Coulton's work; the belief that evidence consists of a number of independent 'facts' and that a proposition can be established by a *catena* of evidence.) To the generation to which Coulton belonged it might have seemed a little shocking that a daughter should write thus of her father, but it is all done with so much affection that we never for a moment doubt that, whatever the difficulties of living with him, the author of this book would not have had him any different. The reader, never involved in the difficulties, is altogether convinced that a difference would have been a change for the worse. This is not the work of an *enfant terrible* letting off steam, nor of a scientist botanizing on her parent's grave; it is a portrait done with great skill, sureness of touch and tenderness.

To the world Coulton was known as a distinguished medieval historian, as the author of books (such as *Christ, St Francis and To-day*) which discussed some of the questions of the time, and as a brilliant controversialist.

Review of Sarah Campion, *Father, a Portrait of G.G. Coulton at Home* (London: Michael Joseph, 1948). First published in *Cambridge Journal*, 2 (1948), 116, 118.

But the theme here is Life with Father — and it is a story which makes the best of Clarence Day seem forced and exaggerated. The book overflows with anecdotes, some of them set down with perhaps a tinge of bitterness, most (when recollected in tranquillity) with delight, all with affection. To live with so intractable a man as Father was no picnic, but it is clear that the family was never bored — except perhaps with the endless flow of advice and instruction which was poured out for the benefit of the children. Every side of his turbulent domestic life is illustrated in these pages — travelling abroad, the real and the imaginary financial crises, Father's oddities with regard to food and clothing, and what the author calls 'the family shindies' some of which must have been shattering. There are brilliant pages in which are described Coulson's rooms in St John's College, the 'carnival' of getting him off from home for a day in college in his old age, the special brew of cocoa he insisted upon having, his contraptions and inventions, his unpractical practicalness, the bath chair, and (perhaps best of all) the ceremony of gathering the harvest of the pear tree, which is better than any of the exploits of Uncle Podger. And if one asks oneself why it is better, I think the answer is that Father in this incident is not, like Uncle Podger, merely an impersonal epitome of endearing human folly, but an individual eccentric in the great academic tradition.

Mercifully in these pages we are spared psychological analysis. But the author finds in what she calls his 'Puritanism' her father's deepest obsession. It appears at many levels, some trivial, others important, and it was something that made the life of his family difficult. Speaking of travel abroad, she says: 'Looking back on it all later, I see that my memories of one of the loveliest tracts on earth are blistered and spotted by memories of Father's Puritan raising his ugly head from alp or meadow or stream, and forbidding us to enjoy without earning, and causing some family row or other to make sure we should have nothing so pagan and simple as an uncomplicated love of Switzerland.' It was something, also, which made his own life difficult: but while he could more easily throw it off in moments of enjoyment, it hung over the children as a cloud. Men who, replete with every sort of crotchet and obsession, make every day of domestic life potentially a stormy day and who are yet not intolerable husbands and fathers, will usually be found not only to possess some compensating charm or greatness which removes the sting, but also to have characters remarkably free from those major domestic vices — such as secretiveness or an unappeasable unhappiness or restlessness — which really do make life with them impossible. This is certainly true of Coulton. The picture we are given is of a warm, untidy life — the one obsession from which Father was wholly free was the commonplace obsession of tidiness — and it is pointless to speculate on how different it might all have been if it had revolved round a less self-willed man, or if instead of these two rebellious daughters he had had 'a gentle little girl in a white frock who came to him to be read to, and sweetly educated'. Everybody's life from the domestic point of view is something of a hash, and a man who can survive so severe an inquisition into his character and come out of it a most lovable man, in whom every oddity served only to endear, clearly has a touch of greatness. Those who knew him should be delighted with everything in this book (except the silly Introduction by Kingsley Martin), and those who never knew him will be delighted with his portrait as a work of art in which insight has made exaggeration unnecessary.

Seventy

Bulwer-Lytton

This little book seems to have sprung mainly from the natural interest that a grandson has in his grandfather: it does not succeed in persuading the reader that, apart from the tie of blood, the author would ever have been inspired to write on this subject. Its theme is Bulwer-Lytton as a novelist. It does not lack discrimination, the Earl of Lytton prefers some of his grandfather's books to others and can explain the grounds of his preferences; but it cannot be said to be a study of the novelist and his work. It is a plain, unpretentious, colourless, and severely external account of Bulwer-Lytton's literary activities, enlivened by a single shaft of wit—Constance Vernon (the heroine of *Godolphin*) being said to leave on the reader 'the impression of being a typical Bulwer-Lytton heroine in an inadequate disguise'. There is nothing reflective or analytical in the way it is written; it attempts nothing that can properly be called literary criticism. But the task of giving an account of the contents of the more important novels and plays and of the circumstances in which they were written, has been efficiently performed. We are given the impression of a serious, sincere, incredibly industrious writer of remarkable fluency, very considerable learning, and a highly developed visual imagination. But of the literary world which Bulwer-Lytton inhabited, and of his place in it, we are given no reliable impression at all: of the fever and the fret nothing remains. Biographical details, apart from those concerned with the literary career, are here necessarily reduced to a minimum, but it is regrettable that no room has been found for anything like a study of Bulwer-Lytton's exceedingly complex and elusive character. We are given scarcely a hint of the high spirits, the flamboyance, the shyness, the self-pity, the vanity, the kindness and generosity of his character, of which only the duller, more staid and balanced side is revealed. The dandy never appears. The chapter on Bulwer-Lytton's political activities is interesting, but unnecessarily defensive: there is nothing either discreditable or even remarkable in his change of party in 1850.

Review of Victor Alexander George Robert Bulwer, *Bulwer-Lytton* (London: Home and Van Thal Ltd, 1948). First published in *Cambridge Journal*, 2 (1948), 188.

Seventy-one

Man and Society

Miss Gladys Bryson's *Man and Society* is a useful and scholarly piece of work, in which enthusiasm makes up for a certain lack of inspiration in style and treatment. It modestly claims to be a summary of some of the ideas about man and society that belonged to the eighteenth-century school of Scottish philosophers, of whom the most important were Hume, Adam Smith, Ferguson, Hutcheson, Dugald Stewart, Reid, Kames, and Monboddo, and as such to be a chapter in the intellectual history of the century. But in fact it succeeds in being something more than a summary. The ambitious project that united these writers was the exploration of a science of man and society based upon the newly elaborated empirical methods of physical science; and such fascination as this study has, lies in the impression it gives of the genesis in British thought of a *science* of morals and politics, the rise of a new science out of modes of thought that were not scientific. Miss Bryson shows these writers to be dominated by the idea that society is natural, in a modern and not merely an Aristotelian sense, and that all social relations and institutions may be traced back to their spring in the nature of man. In this she sees them as the progenitors of modern sociology. But she is more successful in analyzing their ideas and in connecting them with the ideas of their contemporaries on the continent and with what was to come, than in depicting the slowly mediated changes which produced this remarkable school of Scottish thought.

Review of Gladys Bryson, *Man and Society: the Scottish Inquiry of the Eighteenth Century* (London: G. Cumberlege, for Princeton University Press, 1946). First published in *English Historical Review*, 63 (1948), 272–3.

Seventy-two

Reason and Unreason in Society

Professor Morris Ginsberg's *Reason and Unreason in Society* is a collection of essays and lectures each of which is a variation upon the theme of the part played by reason and unreason in human affairs. This general theme is elaborated philosophically, psychologically, historically, and sociologically; it is illustrated in studies of national character, the causes of war and anti-semitism; and it is pursued in sympathetic and critical reviews of the work of Hobhouse, Westermarck, and Pareto. Rational behaviour is, briefly, behaviour controlled by reflective thought and determined by the consciousness of its purpose. And in the history of morals the gradual rationalization of moral judgments is taken to be one of the surer signs of moral progress. Of course, any study of human behaviour reveals large tracts of unredeemed irrationality, the defects of which are the interest of the sociologist, the opportunity of the demagogue and the despair of the moralist; but the faith that inspires these essays is that reason cannot, in the end, be helpless in the face of problems of value. Both on this practical question, and in the scientific questions relating to sociology, the general impression left by this book is one of optimism with regard to method and of critical scepticism with regard to the results so far achieved. Again and again, in examining the work of sociologists, Professor Ginsberg recurs to the theme, 'more knowledge', 'more evidence', 'better technique'. There is an impressive quality of care and unhurried deliberateness about his arguments and of humility about his conclusions. Everywhere he sees difficulties, which make him readier to show how an enquiry should be conducted than to pursue it himself. But, though he is convinced that the enquiry is worthwhile and that the time has now passed for the sociologist to apologise for his presuppositions and method, there are many readers who will find this book richer in casual perceptions of a controlled and sceptical mind than in results assured by a method whose validity has been decisively demonstrated.

Review of Morris Ginsberg, *Reason and Unreason in Society* (London: Longmans, Green and Co., 1947). First published in *English Historical Review*, 63 (1948), 414.

Seventy-three

Puritanism and Democracy

The theme of this book is the religious and intellectual foundation of the civilization of the United States of America. It is, and is intended to be, a book for the times. It was written during the war; its background is the scepticism which since the beginning of this century has been corroding American ideals; and, in effect, it is a reasoned reassertion of the creed of America. But its genuine learning and the quality of its reflectiveness make it something more than a mere *livre de circonstance*. Indeed, there can have been few occasions when a philosopher of high repute has more profitably turned his mind to the needs of his generation and has produced a book so illuminating and so much to the point.

Puritanism and Democracy are, for Professor Perry, the two systems of ideas which united to determine, not the whole, but a large part of 'the distinctively American tradition, culture, institutions, and nationality.' The first is 'the creed of certain Englishmen in the sixteenth and seventeenth centuries;' the second is 'the creed of certain colonial Americans who waged a war of liberation, and created a new political constitution, at the close of the eighteenth century.' Both have their roots in European culture.

The plan of the book is straightforward. The first of the three parts into which it is divided is mainly historical. Puritanism and Democracy as historic systems of ideas are examined and their contribution towards the 'making of the American mind' traced in detail. The Puritanism with which Professor Perry is concerned is not merely the doctrines which are peculiar to the Puritans, it is the whole complex system of ideas which had its roots in mediaeval Christianity. And the Democracy with which he is concerned is 'the political and social creed which was the professed ground of the American Revolution of the eighteenth century,' a creed which derived from the philosophy of the Enlightenment. But the first part is only an introduction to the real theme of the book, which is a long and elaborate analysis and appraisal of both Puritanism and Democracy in the

Review of Ralph Barton Perry, *Puritanism and Democracy* (New York: The Vanguard Press, 1944). First published in *Philosophy*, 23 (1948), 86–7.

American tradition. The spirit in which this is undertaken is indicated in the following passage:

'Puritanism and Democracy, under these or other names, form a substantial part of the heritage of Americans. The chief source of spiritual nourishment for any nation must be its own past, perpetually rediscovered and renewed. A nation which negates its tradition loses its historical identity and wantonly destroys its chief source of spiritual vitality; a nation which merely reaffirms its tradition grows stagnant and corrupt. But it is not necessary to choose between revolution and reaction. There is a third way—the way, namely, of discriminating and forward-looking fidelity.'

Here Professor Perry appears not merely as the historian of a tradition, but as a critic with a keen eye for its shortcomings. Yet, as he expounds it, the tradition itself is seen to have a certain power of self-criticism; while Puritanism and Democracy often re-enforce one another's errors, they also correct and complement one another's limitations. There is in these pages, which compose the bulk of the book, much to admire and little to regret. Their outstanding merit is that, whatever one may think of the conclusions, one becomes certain as one reads that Professor Perry will waste no time before getting to the essential topics to be considered and will argue his point of view with lucidity and enthusiasm.

One matter of some importance may perhaps be remarked upon. In his analysis of what may be called the philosophy of American democracy (the central argument of which is contained in a chapter called 'The Supremacy of Reason and Conscience') the whole emphasis is placed upon its generation from the optimism of the philosophy of the Enlightenment—the confidence that from tolerant discussion 'the truth would emerge and prevail on its own merits', the confidence in human reason. Historically, no doubt, there is considerable evidence for this view of the generation of democratic theory. Nevertheless I think it is a mistake to identify democratic theory with optimism of this sort, and even historically it is a view that needs to be corrected by a recognition that much that is characteristic of democracy is a reflection of scepticism (doubt not only concerning the power of human intelligence to arrange a satisfactory state of society, but also concerning the whole idea of a permanently good society) rather than of intellectual optimism.

Seventy-four

Decadence

A reviewer of a book by Dr Joad is now in the position of a juryman at the Assizes who is already familiar with the defendant and thinks he knows the case from having read about it in the local paper when it came before the magistrates. There is no one so unfortunate as not to know something about this writer. So we open the book with the expectation of all we have been led to expect — a virgin clarity of mind, readiness of phrase, pert (possibly perverse) comment, wit, wisdom, intellectual entertainment. But as we read we perceive that this is not the man we thought we knew. It is not the work of the *enfant terrible* we had heard so much about; it is the work of an *enfant terrible* who has grown up (as, alas, so often happens) into sober and prosy maturity. The brisk attack has given place to long-winded exposition; the man who once waited to speak until he was certain that it was not his turn now loses his effect in a continuous monotone; where there was once sustained argument, there is now only the muddled and hasty glancing at ideas as they fly past.

It is a book about philosophy, and the first fifty pages are given to a defence of the philosophical populariser; but for a book about philosophy it is remarkably repetitious and disorderly. Subjects are begun, dropped, taken up again with a grand inconsequence, and the author is constantly waking up with a guilty start to direct the reader to the relevance of the last twenty pages. The innumerable cross-headings are a tribute to the inattention of the reader, and the extraordinary typography (in which sub-headings appear in type twice as large as the main headings) adds to the general confusion.

The ostensible theme is decadence. And Dr Joad suggests that decadence may be 'identified as the valuing of experience for its own sake, irrespective of the quality of the experience, the object of the experience, that upon which experience is, as it were, directed, being left out of account.

Review of Cyril Edwin Mitchison Joad, *Decadence: a Philosophical Enquiry* (London: Faber and Faber, 1948). First published in *Spectator*, 180 (1948), 290, 292.

Decadence, then, is defined as the "dropping of the object."' Now this is a bright idea, but how he arrives at it is difficult to discern. It appears that he knows already that vitality, vigour, exuberance, youthfulness, the Roman Republic, the Elizabethan Age, Chaucer, Rabelais, etc., are non-decadent, and that the eighteenth century, selfishness, the present day, Debussy ('because he produces on me a lowering effect') and Virginia Woolf are decadent. And what he pretends to offer in his definition is 'the common core of the notion of decadence in most of the many senses in which it is used.' But I believe the reader would be well advised not to pay too much attention to this; the state of mind Dr Joad is describing is never convincingly connected with decadence, and the real theme of the book is this state of mind and its consequences, and it is only at many removes related to so-called decadence.

Experience for its own sake: this, for Dr Joad, means activity not determined by an ulterior object to be achieved or realised, activity whose satisfaction is internal. It involves scepticism in belief, conduct divorced from values, thought immersed in subjectivism; it involves philosophical error, worthless art and moral distraction. It is a condition particularly at home in large urban centres of civilisation, it is encouraged by the natural sciences when they offer themselves as a guide to life, and it ends in *accidie*. It is illustrated in the conclusion of Pater's *Renaissance,* in the precept that 'to travel hopefully is better than to arrive,' in the craze for speed, in 'assaulting mountains by means of mountain railways' instead of on foot, in art as self-expression instead of the pursuit of beauty, but not, it appears, in rock-climbing, dancing, going for a walk, or knowledge for its own sake.

Having analysed and explored this state of mind, Dr Joad proceeds in the second part of the book to lay about him more in the manner we are accustomed to expect. His theme is the reflection of this state of mind in contemporary society, its art, literature, criticism, music, drama, politics, education, taste and general behaviour. He is a little nervous about committing himself on the subject of poetry, but on every other topic he has decided opinions. He has no very high opinion of the average human being or of the prospects of the race. The bomb, of course, is given its page. Taken altogether, I am more impressed by Dr Joad's emotions than by the powers of argument displayed in this book. He is a civilised man, with an unpretentious love of music. He thinks that the *douceur de vivre* disappeared in 1914 (I should have put it at 1906), and he is a passionate defender of the countryside against spoliation. But he appears in this book as a man of erratic and somewhat restricted sympathy: one of the things he doesn't understand is the charm of fashion, and any man who has no sympathy for this is likely to find the human race both puzzling and more stupid than it really is.

Seventy-five

Science and Society

These two essays on the pursuit of scientific knowledge in relation to the arrangements of society, one by a geneticist and the other by a philosopher, should be read by everyone interested in the subject. Both are brief: neither can be said to touch the bottom of the theme, but neither is merely superficial. The enterprise of Dr Darlington is to investigate the conflict between science and society, which he sees as 'the conflict between Discovery, which I take to be the active principle of science, and Continuity, which is in some measure the necessary condition of society'. This is not a necessary conflict, inherent in the nature of the opposing elements; rather, it is psychological, and consequently understood to be capable of resolution. At the present time, however, it is acute and a grave hindrance both to science and to society.

The conflict appears first within the world of scientific research and even within the mind of the scientist himself. Every notable discovery involves the destruction of hitherto accepted knowledge, and has to overcome the inertia of what is already established. This is the conflict in its purest form — the obstacle to the acceptance of new discovery being the continuity of scientific knowledge embodied in the doubts of the discoverer and the interests of institutions engaged in teaching science. But a more serious conflict appears when economic interest, official and professional laziness, or the general aversion from change common to all organized societies opposes the *application* of scientific discoveries which have won the acceptance of scientists. That the new knowledge should offend some interest, institution or individual is unavoidable. But the offence may be overcome (and the conflict resolved) by the maintenance of an absolute freedom of scientific inquiry and by the education of the society, and those who hold the initiative in making its arrangements, to a more

Review of Cyril Dean Darlington, *The Conflict of Science and Society*, Conway Memorial Lecture (London: Watts and Co., 1948); and Arthur David Ritchie, *Science and Politics*, Riddell Memorial Lecture (Oxford: Oxford University Press, 1947). First published in *Cambridge Journal*, 1 (1948), 689–97.

ready understanding and acceptance of what scientific research has from time to time to offer. Dr Darlington expounds this simple thesis lucidly and illustrates it with apt examples. Perhaps he makes the contrast too rigid; science appears as all discovery and society as concentrated resistance, whereas, of course, all sciences have sprung from practical social arts which continue to have sources of change and improvement independent of science. And many readers will find Dr Darlington's views on education a trifle crude. But, so far, few will disagree with the main thesis.

He has, however, a second theme, not so well considered. He is understandably convinced that science is good for men and that all good men will want to avoid the wastefulness of failing to apply scientific discoveries rapidly and effectively to human affairs. And he is convinced, also, that nothing but evil can come from the subordination of scientific research to political interest or doctrine — a subordination he observes not only in Russia. But these convictions lead him to some strange conclusions. Most of his readers will be moved by his indignation at the neglect of the Forestry Commission to make use of the accumulated results of plant genetics and its indifference to research in plant breeding; he convinces us at once that here is a shocking enormity. And the long reign of superstition in cattle breeding is made to appear, what no doubt it is, a major event in the modern history of human folly. But there is nothing in what Dr Darlington says to show that he would not expect to carry our sympathy with him if, instead of choosing these examples of the failure to apply scientific knowledge to human affairs, he had expressed his horror and contempt for the poisoner who, neglecting the latest knowledge which would have provided him with an undetectable poison, disposes of his victim so ham-handedly as to be discovered in his crime. Or rather, it appears that Dr Darlington might recognize the distinction, but would insist that it is a distinction which itself springs from scientific knowledge and can be reduced to the terms of genetics. How deep a confusion of mind is involved here is difficult to say; it is possible that Dr Darlington belongs to the strict sect which believes that the theory of evolution, besides putting 'man in his place in the universe', is also the only reliable source of moral judgments. At all events, it is in exploring some such line of thought that he reaches the conclusion that the political arrangements of a society, its policy, should be based wholly upon the discoveries of scientific research whenever discoveries relevant to the situation exist. He thinks that scientific discoveries may, and often do, oblige the acceptance of 'fundamental political doctrines', and that this is not recognized by the politician only on account of his 'genuine and habitual effortless ignorance', and by the scientist only because his mind is still conditioned by an out-of-date effort to shelter science from the corruption of politics. For example, he asserts that 'modern statistical methods ... have transformed our knowledge of how to extract information from numbers. They have become in recent years one of our most powerful and most general instruments of discovery. Our great Governmental departments are busy collecting numbers, so-called statistics, on a vast scale every day. On the understanding of these numbers policy should be based'. And that it is not so based is due only to the politicians' failure properly to appreciate the method. He appears to mean that the use of modern statistical methods itself, without any previous or intervening judgment about the ends believed to be desirable, is a sufficient guide to political enterprise. Again, he finds himself able to reject the whole 'notion of equality' as a worthless superstition on the ground that it conflicts with genetic truth. He does not say that what he really means is that a politics based on belief in genetic equality will come to no good because it is based upon an illusion—a conclusion consonant with his premises. He goes the whole hog. And the only indication that he does not intend to do so is the weight he gives to Acton's opinion that a belief in equality is the foundation of tyranny, though he does not reveal to us what genetic discoveries enable him to judge that tyranny is undesirable. And further, he ventures to assert that 'the fundamental problem of government is one that can be treated by exact biological methods. It is the problem of the character and causation of the differences that exist among men, among the races, classes, and individuals which compose mankind'.

In all this Dr Darlington might appear to be allying himself with the muddle-headed school of scientific politicians whose eccentricity has long been recognized. But I think, rather, that it springs in his mind from an unduly restricted view of the nature of politics than from a gross misconception of the value of scientific discovery. No doubt it is true that a society which 'had sound plant breeding would have more wheat', but this can scarcely be said to involve a 'fundamental political doctrine' or to be the model of all political problems and enterprises. No statistics, however well-handled, will by themselves tell a man what to do, much less what he ought to do. It is safe to say that politics which did not embody a genuine love for erring human beings and even a delight in their endearing stupidities (as well as a desire to relieve society, with the aid of scientific and other knowledge, from some of the consequences of error and stupidity) would be evil. And politics which considered only the results of scientific investigation would not be evil; they would merely be impossible.

Professor Ritchie is not so lively a writer as Dr Darlington, but he is a more careful thinker. He has also the advantage of more space in which to develop his argument and to observe the necessary distinctions. He investigates two important questions. (1) Whether the pursuit of scientific knowledge has social and political implications that justify its control in some manner by society, and (2) whether, if it is decided that the pursuit of scientific knowledge (or of activities closely connected with it) should be controlled, the method of control can itself be scientific — that is, whether there can, properly speaking, be a science of politics.

In discussing the first of these questions Professor Ritchie distinguishes at once between the pursuit of scientific knowledge (which he calls 'science in the strict sense') and the application of scientific (and other) discoveries to human affairs, which he calls 'technology'. Science in the strict sense differs from technology, not necessarily in inspiration, but in respect of its internal coherence. 'The theories of pure science form a systematic whole capable of indefinite expansion.' Whereas 'there is no system or internal coherence about technology; its development is determined by outside causes – by varying social needs, varying economic conditions, the state of scientific knowledge the idiosyncrasies of inventors, who hit on this dodge and not on that'.

Now, Professor Ritchie believes that the pursuit of scientific knowledge should be completely free from external control by society, that it should be autonomous. This is a view that many will share. But I do not think his supporting argument is altogether satisfactory. He asserts the fact that if the pursuit of scientific knowledge is externally controlled it will perish; 'if it is forbidden its independence it will not be deflected from its course; it will die out'. This is a view of the nature of scientific research with which I do not wish to disagree. I think it is exaggerated. Certainly some sorts of limitation on scientific research would be fatal to it; if, for example, the scientist were allowed to pursue only those lines of research and to publish only those results which seemed to agree with a prevailing political prejudice.[1] But it is not so certain that every kind of social control is destructive of scientific research. However, what is more important is that Professor Ritchie does not make it clear that this is not in itself a satisfactory *kind* of reason for insisting upon this independence. If the freedom of scientific research is to be properly grounded it must be on the basis of its value to society, and not merely upon the crude fact (if it is a fact) that its freedom and its existence are inseparable. The questions which have to be considered are, What is the precise value to society (apart from any technological applications) of the pursuit of scientific knowledge? And can this value be enjoyed only when scientific research is autonomous? Professor Ritchie, it is true, does consider these questions, but not in a way that convinces us that he knows them to be the heart of the argument. His answer appears to be that its value lies in the respect for truth that it engenders. This, at least, is the right *kind* of answer; a respect for truth can be imagined to be desirable for its own sake. But is it a convincing answer? There is no doubt that

---

[1] An interesting discussion of this topic will be found in Professor M. Polanyi's article on 'Freedom in Science' (*Nineteenth Century*, April 1947). Attention should also be called to his brilliant Riddell Memorial Lecture on *Science, Faith, and Society* (Oxford: Oxford University Press, 1946)

in the past respect for truth and the unimpeded pursuit of scientific knowledge were closely bound up with one another, but it is not so clear that this is now as true as it once was. And further, even if we accept this answer, it cannot be said to lead us unavoidably to the conclusion that the pursuit of scientific knowledge ought to be autonomous. The society is yet to exist which permitted genuine autonomy to *any* human activity whatsoever; to claim genuine autonomy is to claim to be free of all the framework of civil and criminal law which constitutes the shape of a society. And among the limitations our society puts upon the pursuit of scientific knowledge is that it should not involve unnecessary cruelty to animals. However, in general, it may be agreed that it is in the interests of society not to qualify the independence of the pursuit of scientific knowledge, though further consideration of the grounds of this conclusion is, I think, required.

'Technology', on the other hand, the application of scientific discoveries to human affairs, clearly requires social control of some sort, and in no hitherto existing society has it ever been suffered to operate uncontrolled. Its value to society depends not upon the state of mind it promotes but upon performing specific services in society which are judged to be individually beneficial. A society may be foolish and refuse to avail itself of a scientific discovery which would be beneficial to it, but this sort of foolishness is defective judgment about something concerning which society is obliged to make a judgment of some sort; it cannot be supposed that every application of scientific knowledge to human affairs is always good merely because it is what it is. So far, I think, Professor Ritchie's argument is unassailable. Its only defect is that he confines his notion of control in respect of technology to only one kind of control, to restriction. A well-ordered society may be supposed on occasion to use its customary or legal authority of control, not merely by way of limitation but also by way of the promotion of the application of scientific discovery to human affairs. This, however, is a small point. The more important question is, In what manner can and does society control technology? And in answering this question Professor Ritchie embarks upon an illuminating investigation of the way in which one of the most ancient branches of technology has been controlled in Western European societies — the branch of technology called Medicine. That medicine is a technology is clear; it is the application of scientific knowledge to human affairs. The knowledge itself is, of course, morally neutral; it is capable of being used for the benefit or to the detriment of mankind. By what means has society sought to ensure that its use shall be good? By the Hippocratic Oath. This oath constitutes the intervening judgment (which Dr Darlington believes to be either unnecessary or to be itself based upon scientific evidence) between science and society. No doubt the oath has been no more than a rough and ready control, and I think Professor Ritchie makes too much of it in isolation. It was never, in fact, the oath *alone* as a formula, which constituted the control, but always the oath in its place in the whole moral habit of the society, and the oath supported by certain legal obligations. However, although this is a relevant example of the kind of control society may exercise over technology, it does not, for Professor Ritchie, provide the model for all that is required on every occasion, and it certainly does not include all that has been projected in the way of social control.

'It will be granted', he continues, 'that where there is a contact between politics and science or technology, the problems that result are problems of morals. It may be said, however, that morality itself is properly a branch of science; that there is a science of society or of social conduct to provide a scientific basis for morals.' This is his second theme. And it is here that the argument is not as clear to me as I should like it to be. He appears to me to be attempting to establish two propositions, which are imperfectly distinguished, not equally profitable and perhaps even mutually exclusive. The first proposition is that no social or political science can ever be a science in the strict sense, and consequently no 'technology' springing from a social science can ever constitute a strictly speaking scientific means of controlling human activity in general, and in particular human activity when engaged upon exploiting genuine technologies derived from the physical sciences. The argument runs somewhat as follows. What is required is a social science and an appropriate technology which would do for this human activity what a physical science and its appropriate technology does for, say, plant breeding. But when we consider both the materials and the methods of physical sciences we discover at once that they are fundamentally different from those with which the projected social science would have to work. And if, further, we consider the manner of the application of discoveries of physical sciences, we find that this too is something that, *ex hypothesi*, a social technology cannot emulate. The sort of knowledge which constitutes discovery in a physical science is a knowledge either of abstractions or of simplified objects which can be observed experimentally and expressed mathematically, while the social science would require a knowledge of concrete human beings. And while the technology which springs from a physical science involves only the control of physical objects, the control which would be required of the social technology would be the control of human beings. In other words, the technology which is the fruit of a physical science is always the administration of things, an activity which involves only knowledge of things and the use of force, while the only technology which can be supposed to spring from the social science is the control of persons, an activity which involves knowledge of concrete human beings and the use of, not force, but persuasion; for to force individual behaviour is not to control it, but merely to disallow it. The conclusion of the argument is, of course that a social technology devised to control the use by man of technologies derived from the physical sciences is, in the strict sense, impossible; its defect in this respect is that it never achieves a fully scientific character. This is a familiar proposition and a familiar argument, though Professor Ritchie has made something of it for himself. It is often thought to be a sophistical argument, a mere quibble about the word 'science', but although it is certainly more substantial than that, I cannot say that I have ever been convinced by it. It appears to me to contain a truth which nevertheless lies hidden. However, Professor Ritchie's conclusion is that 'there is no science of statesmanship or politics or persuasion, if by science we mean the results of a systematic inquiry comparable to that of the physical sciences'.

The second, and more profitable, proposition is that, if a social or political science could be found which was a science in the full sense, then the very qualities in respect of which it was scientific would disable the technology which sprang from it from controlling human activity and especially from controlling human activity when engaged upon the exploitation of the technologies derived from the physical sciences. Or, in other words, the project of the technological control of technology is self-contradictory. Now, the advantage of this proposition is that in order to demonstrate its truth it is not necessary to show that a social or political science in the full sense either can or cannot exist. All that needs to be shown here, in order to show the impossibility of the strictly scientific control of human affairs, is that the more strictly scientific the means the less they are able by themselves to control human affairs. I do not think that Professor Ritchie ever exactly formulates or tries to demonstrate this proposition; it seems to be something he has at the back of his mind while he is arguing about the first proposition. And this is unfortunate, because, if this proposition could be established, it would establish conclusively what the demonstration of the first proposition could establish only inconclusively. The only positive notice Professor Ritchie takes of it is when he is dealing with the suggestion that Law is a social technology capable of controlling human activity. He thinks it profitable to pursue this suggestion because if a true social technology is to be found anywhere it is surely to be found in law. Now, law is concerned with certain limited human ends: the maintenance of peace and civil order, the just settlement of disputes, and the preservation of civil liberties'. But it is clear at once that it is a technology incapable, by itself, of controlling human affairs in general, and in particular of controlling human activity when it is engaged in exploiting the technologies derived from the physical sciences, because it is incapable of controlling itself. And, what is more important, the more closely it approaches to the condition of a genuine technology the more certainly it lacks control over itself, and lacks authority to control what lies beyond itself. Indeed, the defects of law as a scientific means of controlling human affairs are a function, not of its scientific imperfection, but of its scientific virtues. A rule of law as such is as unprotected against injustice as a scientific discovery as such is unprotected against evil results when applied to human affairs; they share the same defects, the lack of an inherent principle of self-control. A society always looks outside its positive law for a criterion of justice by means of which to control that law (precisely as it looks outside the technology of medicine to the Hippocratic Oath in order to control the practice of medicine); and normally, says Professor Ritchie, it has found that criterion of justice in an ideal or natural law. I doubt whether this is either a satisfactory account of the direction in which the criterion of justice has been sought or of the direction in which a genuine criterion is likely to be found; this notion of a natural law is perhaps the least convincing of the current formulae of moral criteria. But, whether or not this is so, the substance of the argument remains: law requires to look outside itself in some direction, and the more strictly scientific it became the more certainly would this be so.

Professor Ritchie does not investigate the claims of other so-called social sciences (economics, for example) to provide a technology capable of controlling human affairs. Nor does he consider the possibility of a science (and a technology) of justice itself. But, then, he does not require to do so. As I understand it, he has been trying to establish a proposition which, if established, would fix upon the character of any social science an inability to provide a technology to control human affairs proportionate to its scientific character. It is a bold attempt; I wish it had been undertaken more directly.

There is, however, another point which should be considered: the oblique effect of what we call 'science' in the minds of those who have been subject to its influence. It may be demonstrable that there cannot be a science, in the strict sense, of human affairs, and it may be demonstrable that if there were such a science and if a genuine technology followed, it would not itself provide the sort of control of human affairs which every society needs and has always practised; but it does not follow that the scientific enterprise and the approximation to a social science that has been achieved and may be extended are wholly without legitimate influence upon the way in which we think about the ends to be pursued in human affairs. The fact of the matter is, it is impossible to separate absolutely in the mind that sort of learning from experience we call 'science' and that sort of learning from experience which is involved in judgments of value. And one of the important oblique effects of the scientific enterprise has been to make necessary a reform in the way in which the ends pursued in society are stated, and consequently the way in which they are thought about. But to trace these positive, though indirect, relations between 'science' and society is a project for another occasion.

Seventy-six

The State and the Citizen

Since the publication in 1899 of Bosanquet's *The Philosophical Theory of the State* no general work on political philosophy by an English writer has impressed those interested in the subject as being of first-class importance. What has been written in the last fifty years is great in bulk, but small in philosophical content. This is remarkable because Bosanquet's work did not leave the subject in so firm a state of equilibrium that it was difficult to know in what direction advance could be made: the book was recognised to have grave defects, though its most important shortcomings were not those which its contemporary critics fastened upon. But from another point of view it is not so surprising. The febrile political activity of the period was not the most inspiring background for philosophical reflection; intense concern with the practical and the transitory, where it does not produce pseudo-philosophy, is apt to inhibit philosophy altogether. At any rate, for one reason or another, the vigour and originality which marked the ethical thought of the period found little reflection in political philosophy. The best work has been historical and interpretive; but even here — when one considers much of what has been written recently about Plato — the perverting tendency of current politics has had an unfortunate effect.

Mr Mabbott's book is perhaps too slight to be taken as convincing evidence that the tide, in this respect, has already turned; but it has qualities which raise it above anything else of its kind that has appeared during this period. It is described modestly as an *Introduction to Political Philosophy*, but the fact that it is designed for a popular audience appears only in the ease and lucidity with which it is written; there is no covering up of difficulties and no attempt to make things easier than they are. No doubt there are intricacies which, in the interests of balance and economy, are not pur-

---

Review of John David Mabbott, *The State and the Citizen* (London: Hutchinson's, 1948). First published in *Mind*, 58 (1949), 378–89. Oakeshott also reviewed Mabbott, *The State and the Citizen*, in *Cambridge Journal*, 2 (1949), 316, 318.

sued. Mr Mabbott makes allowances for the weakness of his readers, but he never condescends, and he wastes no time at all on what is attractive but irrelevant. In short, it is a book which deserves to be taken seriously.

In writing such a book the greatest difficulty to be overcome is the first—to know where or how to begin. Only the boldest will begin, like Hobbes, in the centre of the subject and without reference to predecessors in the enterprise; the less venturesome or those, like Mr Mabbott, whose audience requires to be led into the subject gradually, will look for some mediating device which nevertheless will not hamper or prejudice the subsequent argument. What is required is something imperfect but familiar, in the criticism of which the writer can make the advances he desires to make—not a foundation, but a mere beginning. Others have found such a device in an appeal to political experience, in the statement of a 'theory of the first look' or in the idea of a 'minimum city' such as Plato and Aristotle take as their starting place. Mr Mabbott finds what he needs in a consideration of some of the ideas of four writers—Hobbes, Locke, Rousseau and Hegel. The chapters in which he considers what these writers have to say are not intended as studies in the history of political philosophy, but as opportunities to harvest what is relevant in them for political philosophy to-day; hence the refusal to go behind Hobbes, the first great theorist of the political world in which we live. And from this point of view they are exceedingly skilful chapters. From Hobbes we learn the root principle that the *first* business of government is to provide security; from Locke, a confused doctrine of individualism, popular sovereignty and the common good; and from Rousseau, a similar, but more advanced, vindication of government in terms of the freedom it promotes, the will it expresses, and the good it establishes. By the end of the chapter on Hegel and the Hegelians (an excellent chapter) all the major *problems* of political philosophy have been elicited from the solutions which these writers have proposed, and on the way Green has been subjected to a sympathetic but relentless criticism. The position reached so far is that 'every act which is right and satisfying to a human agent is so because it serves to bring about a social or common good' (p. 48), that the obligation to obey law and government is part of 'a wider obligation which may constrain a citizen in his whole moral life as well as in his abstentions from crime or rebellion' (p. 49), but that the State is 'the real liberator of man's moral nature, ... the supreme and unique focus of his loyalty and affection' (p. 55). If, says Mr Mabbott, 'we were content to remain within the four corners of this vigorous creed, political authority would require no further defence. Any law which furthered the good of the State would be evidently right ... a citizen could never evade the claim of the State to his obedience, nor could he even rightly pursue any object other than the good of his community' (p. 55). Our starting place in short, is with what may be called a doctrine of the 'maximum' city. And the political philosophy which Mr Mabbott elaborates in the rest of the book is presented as what remains of this doctrine when it has been whittled down by criticism, when it has been purged of its exaggerations.

The first object of criticism is to determine the principle of the *limits* of State activity. The view that there are no such limits and therefore no such principle (this doctrine of the 'maximum city') is found to withstand without much difficulty two forms of attack. Neither the doctrine that 'there are certain sacrosanct departments of human life where the interference of the State is illegitimate' (the doctrine of Natural Rights), nor the doctrine that since compulsion is destructive of morality (the moral value of an action lying solely in the freedom of its motive), the activity of the State is limited (in Green's words) 'to those actions which are better done from a bad motive than not done at all', can survive serious consideration. A substantial and defensible limit is, however, to be found in the existence of 'non-social values in moral action'. The motives of an action and the amount of effort directed to doing right are morally valuable (though they are not the only things morally valuable), and they lie beyond the control of any association. And further, when action is aimed at consequences which are intrinsically good, these goods are sometimes 'non-social and therefore *a fortiori* non-political', and consequently are not controllable by the State. Truth, beauty, religious worship are examples of such non-social values; so also is freedom, which is defined as 'the ability to choose action A without pressure or threats by others aimed at preventing me from doing A or getting me to do B through fear of the consequences, which they will bring about if I do A or omit B' (p. 75). The common good then, which is not 'the good of a society' (a meaningless expression) but 'a state of affairs involving relations between individuals, a state of affairs intrinsically social' (p. 91), is not the only good. 'Productive of the common good' is not an exhaustive definition of right action. Moreover, there are duties, such as fidelity to promises, payment of debts and the saving of life, which are not the service of any association; they are owed to men as men. And these duties constitute a further limit to the claims of the 'maximum city'.

The State, then, is an association, and this (properly understood) provides the principle of the limit to its capacity to promote the moral ideal; there are goods beyond the reach of any association to procure. But further, the State is not the only association. It is 'distinguished by (a) territorial limits, (b) inclusiveness within these limits, (c) the power in its officers to exercise force and the fear of force as instruments of policy, and (d) the possession by its officers of ultimate legal authority'. And on account of its particular character it is limited in its capacity to procure even those goods which, in general, depend upon association for their achievement. Consequently, the second and final object of criticism is to determine which among the social goods the State, as this particular kind of association, is capable of procuring. This involves a consideration of the desirable ends for which political organisation is necessary or desirable, the relation of States to other associations, relation of States to other States.

'What ends require for their achievement the organisation of men by reason of their domicile rather than on any other basis? What ends are attainable only, or most effectively, by law supported ultimately, if need be by force?' (p. 101). These questions reveal at once one social good which cannot be effectively procured by the State. 'Sympathy and willing co-operation, wherever they are found, are intrinsically good' (p. 95). But a State is too large an association, and one too ready to resort to compulsion, for it to be a successful vehicle of solidarity of feeling of this kind. And further, a comprehensive unity of feeling in a State (though it is valuable when it appears as loyalty and is particularly valuable in war) demands the surrender of so many other goods that it must be regarded as 'too expensive to be justified.' Other associations, such as the family, are much more capable of promoting this good. There are, however, social goods — such as security, the maintenance of a certain standard of social conduct and the orderly settlement of disputes — which can only be enjoyed by means of the State. And there are other social goods which, though they may be obtained up to a certain level by means of a great variety of different forms of association, are now to be enjoyed most effectively when the form of association involved is the State. About these Mr Mabbott refuses to dogmatise, but he considers that health (because the establishment of the germ theory of disease involves a recognition that no man can maintain his health in an unhealthy community), communications, education and certain economic ends fall into this class. Nevertheless, the freedom of members of a State to enter into a great variety of associations, some of which extend beyond the borders of the State, is a *prima facie* good which should be interfered with only when it conflicts with those goods which it is the express purpose of the State to secure. No association may properly claim autonomy, but 'so far as the purposes of any association include any spiritual interest, its complete freedom from State interference is essential in respect of that interest' (p. 123). In Mr Mabbott's view a State is not a moral agent, and consequently, he is able to reduce the problem of the relations of States to one another to the question, What is the duty of the citizen of one State to the citizen of another? and the question, What are the duties of governments to one another? The first he answers without difficulty 'as between citizens of different States, in their direct relations with each other, there are no moral principles differing from those holding between citizens of the same state, save that membership of the same State (like common membership of any other association) gives priority to the claims of fellow members' (p. 139). The second raises some ticklish points, but is answered, in the main, on the lines laid down by current international law. But just as some associations are too large to be effective means for pursuing certain social goods, so the State may be considered too small for the achievement of some of our most sought-after ends, though there are substantial reasons for believing that the erection of a World-State at the present time would be undesirable.

In the last part of the book Mr Mabbott returns to reconsider the basis of State unity. He rejects the idea that this unity springs from a general will or a corporate self; this is dangerous mythology. The State is an association of individual men; it has no collective mind, and can have no interests beyond the interests of its members. In thought we shall avoid, wherever we can, all expressions which by hypostatising abstractions, encourage us to believe in the existence of a collectivity, for such expressions are merely misleading. And in practice we should avoid the identification of our State with any non-political purpose or ideal, because such an identification is destructive of internal peace and security and the heightened sense of unity it furnishes is merely an illusion. 'The State is no ultimate or genuine unit and has no ultimate or absolute value' (p. 161). In order to provide what is within its power to provide—a means of securing certain social goods—it must win loyalty as well as mere obedience: but it is only a corrupt loyalty which knows no service but the service of the State.

The major part of this book consists of a single, close-knit argument of which I have tried to give the gist. There are moments where I am unable to follow Mr Mabbott, and moments in the argument which I find unconvincing; but there is no great benefit to be had from an examination of them. Many are small; some are without consequence to the main doctrine. But there are two or three large questions which it may be profitable to consider.

The first of these is the question, What is political philosophy? Mr Mabbott devotes an appendix to it. His method is characteristic: the questions for him are, Has political philosophy (or political theory) a place of its own, a 'field' of which it is the exclusive occupant? And if so, what distinguishes it from all other intellectual enterprises? He admits to a difficulty in separating political philosophy from 'social psychology, from economic organisation and from the historical study of political institutions'. But he resolves it by means of a system of classification: 'social theory' is the general study of the whole field of social phenomena, a field which may be parcelled out into exclusive areas, many of which are now cultivated by means of 'empirical enquiry by scientific methods' — anthropology, social psychology, jurisprudence, economics, and political science. Political philosophy occupies an area of its own within the general field, the frontiers of which are determined by two considerations: first, the phenomena it contains are 'political' (*i.e.*, political philosophy is concerned with one particular form of human association), and secondly, the method of cultivation is 'philosophical' and not scientific (the discovery of 'new facts'), or practical (the establishment or approval of a particular kind of political organisation). The positive enterprise in political philosophy is to elicit certain 'general principles of politics'. These principles are 'permanent' and not merely the 'local prejudices' of a particular civilisation. Nevertheless, they are capable of 'application' of being 'followed'. The philosopher is pictured as ascending a cathedral tower. At each level the view changes, new things come into range and the old things (conscience, duty, law, liberty) change their appearance. He may tire and stop half way, he may suffer from vertigo, and he has no means of knowing when he has got to the top — but he does his best.

Now, I hope it will not be considered either disrespectful or pedantic to say that there is a certain amount of confusion here. It is remarkable how easily writers on the *genres* of knowledge gravitate towards some form of positivism. First, this notion of exclusive areas is unfortunate. The divisions it suggests are both arbitrary and of the wrong sort, and they presume similarities which cannot be defended: whatever is the relationship between anthropology and economics, it cannot (on Mr Mabbott's own showing elsewhere) be the same as the relationship of either to political philosophy. Whatever else it is, political philosophy cannot be what is left over when the social sciences have staked their claims. Secondly, general principles which can be 'followed' and whose value lies in their applicability must have practical consequences implicit in them, and yet we are warned against expecting any but the most abstract conclusions from a political philosophy. And thirdly, the distinction, explicit in the otherwise most attractive simile of the ascent of the tower, between what 'things' *are* and how they *look*, is, I think, wholly misleading: if they look different, they are different, and if one 'thing' looks different the entire scene is different. And when one reaches the ground again, in what sense can we 'apply' the view we had from the top of the tower?

However, Mr Mabbott offers another and better method of understanding what he means by political philosophy; he directs us to the chapters of his book, observing that 'whatever the merits of the arguments advanced in them, these arguments are no part of social psychology, anthropology, jurisprudence, or any other empirical science'. This I think is true. And if philosophy is (what I take it to be) saying something such that, if true, things would be as they are, much of the argument of these chapters is genuinely philosophical. But there are lapses which seriously disfigure it, lapses into an irrelevant practical attitude. What I have called the doctrine of the 'maximum city' (which Mr Mabbott attributes to Hegel) is designated as 'political absolutism' or 'totalitarianism', and its professors are said 'to *make* the State ... the supreme and unique focus of man's loyalty and affection' and to *advocate* complete government control of all activities. The theory of Natural Rights is discussed as if it were, not an attempt to say something such that, if true, things would be as they are, but an attempt to set a limit to the activity of the State. The 'problem of the relations between different associations' is presented as the problem of what relations *ought* to be made to prevail between them and the proper occasions of State intervention. The whole section on the place of the State is described as a discussion of 'what any government can do and ought to do'. Hobbes is said to have 'a low and cynical view of human nature' — epithets scarcely applicable to a philosophy of individualism. And Hegel is represented as preaching a doctrine about the 'proper powers of government'. In short, I think there is confusion between the point of view from which one might assert that 'the State is an association of a certain character, therefore its place in our lives is such and such, and if we observe it to be taking a place which *ex hypothesi* it cannot take, then there is something wrong with our observation', and the point of view from which one might assert that 'the State is an association of a certain character, but since the exercise of that character is not necessarily beneficial, we need to consider what it should be permitted to do and for this we require some information beyond our information about its character'. The first of these points of view I believe to be philosophical, and it is the point of view of Plato, of Hobbes, of Spinoza, and of Hegel. The second is merely a view of the proper functions of government, and if we adopt it we may hope to be able to say whether a law is good or bad but we cannot prevent ourselves being led into all sorts of circumstantial considerations, and our conclusions will depend upon the kind of relationships we desire to cultivate (or are in the habit of cultivating) with other men and will be far from permanent.

One further point may be mentioned here. Mr Mabbott conceives a political philosophy as, necessarily, a 'theory of political obligation'; political obligation is regarded as a datum which the philosopher must analyse and of which he may hope to find a ground and limits. Now, an obligation is something we owe; it is a practical relationship between two or more men. In the simile of the ascent of the tower, it is something visible at the ground level. No doubt it, or propositions in which it is expressed, stand in need of analysis; but we cannot be certain, until we have made the ascent, that it is not one of the 'things' which will be invisible from half way up let alone from the top. And if it is invisible, it can form no part of a political philosophy. Consequently, I think it is a mistake (unless we know in advance that it will appear, and appear unchanged at all levels) to assume that a political philosophy must be cast in the form of a theory of political obligation. Of course, every political philosophy must show what has become of political obligation — just as it must show what has become of everything else visible at ground level — but this is different from treating political obligation as an irreducible concept.

If one asks oneself what is the root presupposition which governs Mr Mabbott's manner of considering the problems of political philosophy and the conclusions he reaches, I think the answer will be — 'everything is what it is, and not another thing'. Everywhere there is the attempt, to circumscribe, to determine limits; and the relations between things are always taken to be external to the things themselves. This attitude certainly provides a great and valuable discipline to thought. It enables Mr Mabbott to write some excellent pages in criticism of the notion of a collectivity, and on the current jargon — 'society', 'community', 'group', 'State' — of contemporary political philosophy. But it does not always serve him so well. It gives to his world a strangely atomistic appearance: external and internal, self and others, social and non-social are assigned to separate compartments; no activity is permitted to have any relevant consequences beyond its intended consequences; what the State cannot 'directly produce or control' is outside the area of the State; we are urged 'to think concretely about the law', but the law is never allowed to be anything but a number of separate, independent laws, each made by a legislature and each prescribing and compelling a specific action; and human behaviour is never allowed to be anything but a number of separate and independent actions.

This attitude is, of course, a handicap when Mr Mabbott is making historical judgments or considering things from a practical standpoint. To say that 'the political and economic theory of *laissez faire*' was 'developed by Adam Smith from the individualism of Locke', and that 'the results of *laissez faire* in the industrial field are well-known and only a few instances need be cited' (the instances being confined to the conditions of child employment), is, surely, too gross an abridgment to be allowed to stand. And it is one thing to hold that there are 'no *a priori* grounds for State action' in many departments of industry, but it is an unfortunate abridgment to conclude that, on this account, a claim to interfere 'must be determined in each case by empirical enquiry' into the probable 'success' of State action, if 'success' means (as it appears to mean) 'economic success' in each case taken separately. But this atomistic presupposition comes most powerfully into play when Mr Mabbott is dealing philosophically with 'the individual' and with that association of individuals which he calls 'the State'.

'Individuals', 'private selves', are Mr Mabbott's starting place. Each self is what it is, and not another thing. Its relations with other selves may determine what it does, but not what it is. Now that this 'individual' is something observable at ground level no one will doubt. And we may be grateful for Mr Mabbott's vigorous and convincing disposal of the notion of a 'collective mind'. But that does not absolve us from considering who this 'private individual' is, where he came from and what are the necessary conditions of his existence. The 'private individual' as I understand him is an institution, a social, indeed for the most part a legal, creation, whose desires, emotions, ideas, intelligence, are social in their constitution. Nothing, I take it, is more certain than that this individual would collapse, like a body placed in a vacuum, if he were removed from the 'external' social world which is the condition of his existence. This does not mean that he is part of a collective mind; but it does mean that the last word has not been said by calling him 'private'. Perhaps the greatest disservice the whole enterprise of establishing a collective mind or a corporate personality as a respectable philosophical conception has done in political philosophy is to stand in the way of a proper consideration of the nature of the individual, of the citizen himself. And further, the 'individual' who is visible at ground level may have a different appearance when we have ascended the tower, and in Bosanquet's words, 'the whole notion of man as one among others' may dissolve. But even if this were to happen, it would be a disaster if on our return to ground level we should attempt to 'apply' what we had seen from the top; that leads only to the current confusion of 'social service' with activity the motive of which is self-abnegation. The 'private individual' is an institution of the greatest value; the philosopher's business is to discern the nature of his individuality.

A political philosophy, may, I think, spring either from reflection upon the individual or from reflection upon the State; both roads lead to the same destination. Much of what Mr Mabbott has to say about the State is the result of genuine philosophical reflection. But here again, the discussion is too often arrested just as it appeared to be coming to grips with the concrete situation. The chapter on the ends for which political organisation is necessary begins excellently, but ought not some consideration to have been given to all that unavoidably follows in the train of an organisation to procure security, a standard of public behaviour and the orderly settlement of disputes? Is it saying something such that, if true, things would be as they are, to recognise in the law of marriage or of property only what this law commands or expressly permits? Moreover, in spite of the admirably precise distinctions which abound in this discussion, I think we are given, in the main, a theory of legislation in place of a theory of law, and the consideration of the nature of the State is too often crowded out by a theory of the proper functions of government.

The heart of Mr Mabbott's political philosophy is his distinction between social and non-social goods, and his belief that there are duties which men owe to men as men and not as members of a common association, ideal or actual. But I do not think that all who share his conviction that the 'service of the common good' does not exhaust the moral ideal, will find these distinctions satisfactory. We are agreed that we are considering only the activities of men who are associated with other men, who are, in fact, citizens. And it would appear that for men in this condition there can be no such thing as a non-social action or activity in the sense of a concrete action performed or activity pursued which is devoid of social consequences and which owes nothing to society. So long as a man is a member of an association, his actions and pursuits cannot avoid having social repercussions, if only because they modify or confirm his character and consequently his relation with those who are associated with him and hence the rules and customs of the association. It is, for example, impossible to isolate (as Mr Mabbott tries to isolate) artistic activity (activity in pursuit of the beautiful) from social consequences merely on the ground that its social consequences depend upon 'publication or practical application' neither of which are 'essential conditions of the activity'. The fact that an activity has 'no practical end to serve' does not deprive it of social consequences. And further, the spring of the actions and pursuits of such men cannot be insulated from the conditions of living in association with other men; it will always be a misdirection of enterprise to attempt to separate what a man owes to himself, in this respect, and what he owes to himself as a member of an association. Neither the language of the poet nor the idiom of worship (even though it be private worship) is private, and both poetry and worship would, without them, be other than they are.

Nevertheless, it may be that, even if there can be no such thing as non-social *activity*, there is a non-social *good*. And Mr Mabbott suggests that actions performed solely because they are believed to be right (conscientious actions) and activity in pursuit of truth, beauty, holiness or freedom involve goods of this sort. By calling these goods 'non-social' he means that their goodness is independent of the good or bad social consequences which spring from these activities, and that these goods cannot be procured or controlled by social activity. In short, there is a value in the motive from which an activity springs, and where the motive is not procurable or controllable by society, a non-social good may be said to exist. Occasionally Mr Mabbott slips into a way of writing which looks as if he believed that there are concrete actions and activities which are non-social, but this, I think, is clearly impossible: 'acting from a certain motive' is not a concrete situation unless the action were devoid of consequences, which is inconceivable. He is on firmer ground when he insists that there may be a value in some actions, in respect of their motives, which is non-social because it is 'irrelevant' to, independent of the value that lies in their social consequences and because it is not procurable or controllable by society.

Now the questions to be considered are, (1) Is the value that belongs, for example, to the conscientiousness of an action independent of the value of the consequences of the action? and (2) Is it true that the conscientiousness of an action is, in its spring, insulated from society? I cannot see that either of these questions can be answered in the affirmative. In the first place, no association and certainly not the State, is indifferent to the motives of its members. The State to which we happen to belong is one which on many occasions approves of conscientious actions as such, which considers conscientiousness itself to be a social good and is prepared to protect it and to forgo certain other goods (or conveniences) in favour of the good which belongs to conscientiousness. Conscientiousness here belongs to the common good. And where it does so it must be considered good on account of its place in the common good and it cannot, without further qualification, be a means of escape from the common good. The good that arises from conscientiousness or disinterestedness is not convincingly separated from the good which belongs to the consequences of actions. And in a society which gives no recognition whatever to conscientiousness as part of its common good, conscientiousness itself will have no significant value. I cannot follow the view which finds an 'absolute value' in conscientiousness: indeed, this talk of 'absolute values' and 'intrinsic goods' seems to me defenceless against the sort of criticism which Mr Mabbott brings to bear upon the idea of 'natural rights'. In the second place, though it is true that *ex hypothesi* the State cannot compel the disinterestedness of disinterested activity, it would be a mistake to think that, on this account, the motives of actions are insulated from the State. Indeed, living as a member of an association is always an education in motive, and what cannot be compelled may yet be procured and can certainly be controlled. In the end, it is impossible to insulate actions themselves or even the motives of actions from their 'external conditions'. Of course, a government which sets about the direct legal control of artistic, scientific or religious activity (beyond the control, often very material and going very deep, inherent in the civil and criminal law) would find that it had destroyed these activities; but it should be recognised that wherever these activities are 'free', their freedom is the gift of the State: they are not 'naturally' free in Mr Mabbott's sense of freedom.

The last point to be noticed concerns the duties said to be owed to men as men. And here again, I am not convinced that Mr Mabbott has found an escape from the 'service of the common good'. Why do I 'believe that I ought to pay my German bookseller'? If we say, 'Because I am a man and he is a man', are we saying something such that, if true, things would be as they are? I think not. This is a duty put upon me by the service of the common good, not of an ideal society, but of my own State. And when, as in time of war, this ceases to be my duty as an Englishman and it becomes wrong even to attempt to pay him, it ceases, for the time being, to be a duty at all. There was a time when throughout the civilised world the 'word of an Englishman' was the common expression for a promise which would certainly be honoured — not because Englishmen had a high sense of duty towards men as men, but because they were educated in a high sense of duty, in this matter, to one another. To break one's word to a Chinese was to let down, not the Chinese, but 'the old school'. My view is, then, that I believe that the 'service to the common good' is an inadequate expression for the whole of a man's duty, but that, in spite of a vigorous and illuminating attempt, I do not think Mr Mabbott has succeeded in detecting the principle of its inadequacy.

Seventy-seven

The Triple Challenge

The sub-title of this book is 'The Future of Socialist Britain'. It is written in a kind of 'politics told to the children' style—patronizing, enthusiastic, and complacent—with a liberal use of the device of stating a problem (in oversimplified terms) and letting the statement stand for the solution. Politics, it appears, consist in having a theory, putting it to a practical test, and hoping for the best; the politician is the administrator of political ideas. British Socialist politics are represented as putting to a practical test 'two vast and so far unproved assumptions'—'that a planned socialist system is economically more efficient than a private-enterprise capitalist system', and 'that within democratic socialist planning the individual can be given a larger social justice, a greater security and a more complete freedom than under capitalism'. The hero of the adventure is Mr Attlee, 'one of the most considerable and formidable figures in British political history'. The test, on the whole, is going well; at least, when the larger miscalculations are attributed to circumstances, the minor miscarriages can be admitted with unctuous humility. But what makes one blush is not the complacency about achievement (even in respect of Burma): it is the more radical complacency which is prepared to risk the happiness and liberty of fifty millions on a single experiment. Socialism in Australia or Scandinavia is small beer for Mr Williams: 'the stakes are not high enough. But in Britain they are as high as they could conceivably be. If the experiment succeeds the rewards will be enormous in terms of human wellbeing and national power. If it fails the consequences may be measureless.' And he calls this politics.

The triple challenge is the project of changing (in response to an assumed necessity) the social and economic face of England, of transforming British Imperial policy and of finding a foreign policy appropriate to the new Britain. The doctrine propounded in these pages is that of a Social-

---

Review of Edward Francis Williams, *The Triple Challenge. The Future of Socialist Britain* (London: Heinemann, 1948). First published in *Cambridge Journal*, 2 (1949), 313–14.

ism which is a *via media* between 'capitalism' and the totalitarian planning which belongs to communism, and that of a Socialist Britain as the *tertium quid* between the U.S.A. and Russia. Socialism—this 'challenge to the assumptions of capitalism and communism alike'—consists in 'democratic planning', 'securing an integrated pattern of development' and at the same time leaving a 'maximum possible freedom of choice to the individual'. This sort of thing will do very well as a party gag on an election platform. That is its proper place; its ambiguity is attractive if not convincing. But we may not unreasonably ask for something more from a serious political writer. However, Mr Williams's case is that planning is inevitable in our present circumstances. The impoverishment of Britain after the war has produced a 'revolutionary situation', and this, coming on top of the inherent inefficiency of capitalism, brought to power the only party which properly appreciated the necessity of planning. It is not to be expected that Mr Williams should consider the defects of a planned society from the point of view of efficiency; his uncritical eye sees what he calls the 'new pattern of government', the pyramidal structure of the Labour Administration (with the Prime Minister sitting at the apex), as something merely to be admired. The only danger he recognizes is that which a planned society offers to freedom as we know it. But he reassures himself with the thought that after all Socialism belongs to the age-old attempt to tame power and that the monopolies it creates are 'public' and not 'private' and are controlled by the 'community'. Mr Williams will not, I think, succeed (where others have already failed) in convincing his readers that 'democratic planning' is anything better than a verbal reassurance acceptable only to those who really care about planning more than anything else; the doctrine is collectivist, the rhetoric only is liberal. And now that the politicians are beginning to take some note of the criticism which facts offer of their theories, it is time political writers began to show signs of having considered the large body of serious criticism to which this idea of central planning has been subjected since the Fabian Society first formulated it for the English people.

The faithful, no doubt, will be edified by the contribution to socialist hagiography which Mr Williams offers in his character studies of Attlee, Bevin, Cripps, and Morrison. It cannot, however, be commended for its insight. He has taken most trouble with Mr Attlee, but here as elsewhere he is carried away with his own nice-sounding phrases and the portrait is at once vague and wooden; and the line between appreciation and sycophancy is not always securely observed. A socialist desiring to know something of his leaders will find more insight in Mr Colm Brogan's *Our New Masters*, in spite of its lack of sympathy, than in these pages of Mr Williams.

Seventy-eight

How to Stop the Russians without War

Without some degree of simple-mindedness I suppose one would never get as far as opening a book with this title—not because the project is inherently impossible, but because it is too much to expect that it might be simple enough to go into a hundred and fifty pages. But when one is in a proper fix (as I suppose we are) one is apt to be credulous: nobody who really cared about the salvation of the world could suppress an itch to open Joanna Southcott's box: and there comes a point when one is prepared to pay money for a recipe for making omelettes without eggs or for a painless means of mastering the tobacco habit. Of course, there is a snag somewhere; but only the strong-minded can refuse the offer without a feeling that he might be missing something. And, indeed, you will be missing something if you do not open this book. For under its Hyde Park orator title there is some sense mixed in with the usual nonsense. Mr Sternberg gained fame in 1938 as the author of *Germany and a Lightning War*; he began what the wrapper of this work calls his 'unbroken record of accurate prediction of great events and world trends'. As a prophet he may have enjoyed remarkable success, and the prophetic parts of this book are pretty convincing and not unnecessarily ambiguous. But unfortunately one has to be more than a prophet to write a successful book on this subject.

Mr Sternberg writes for an American public: he is anxious to instruct the government of the U.S.A. in the matter of its foreign policy. Beyond doubt an intelligent man of European experience might have something to say which it would be worth the while of the U.S.A. to listen to, and it is disappointing that Mr Sternberg never gets beyond the generalities which now pass for political wisdom. However, he is a man of considerable information, his words are often precise and always forceful, and his attitude is agreeably matter-of-fact. But he reveals a sadly muddled mind at the critical point.

Review of Fritz Sternberg, *How to Stop the Russians without War*, tr. R. Mannheim (London: Boardman and Co., 1948). First published in *Cambridge Journal*, 2 (1949), 425–7.

He assumes that neither the U.S.A. nor Russia wishes seriously to interfere with the affairs or the territory of the other — at present a fairly safe assumption. He is concerned with the policy of each of these great powers with respect to Asia and to Western Europe. It is agreed that the policy of Russia, both in Asia and in Europe, is a policy designed to extend its control if not its frontiers. And it is agreed that both Asia (or at least China) and Europe are pretty well helpless, if left to themselves, to prevent this extension. If the Russians are to be stopped, it is the Americans who must do it: how?

Mr Sternberg considers the obvious solution that they should be stopped by force, by a 'shooting war'. And it is here that his reputation as a prophet adds weight to his words. On the assumption that, at the outbreak of such a war, the Russians were not in possession of an efficient atomic bomb, he is prepared to forecast that the U.S.A. would win, and would win without suffering any damage. But on the outbreak of such a war the Russian armies would rapidly occupy the whole of Europe and much of Asia, and 'a war against the Soviet Union would have to be won not only in Soviet territory but in Europe and Asia as well'. It would not be a 'lightning war': and in order to win it, not only Russia, but large parts of Europe and Asia would have to suffer atomic bombardment. And in victory 'the United States would no longer be a great State among other States. *The United States would then be an island in a sea of barbarism*'. 'A war with the Soviet Union, though bound to end in a victory for the United States, would be fraught with the most terrible consequences not only for the Soviet Union, whose cities and industrial centres would be pulverized by atomic warfare, but also for Europe and Asia, which would be turned into deserts. In a United States surrounded by a world of barbarism, all democratic and progressive institutions would be destroyed.'

So far (for about a hundred pages) the information has been convincing and the argument cogent. No doubt there are persons in the U.S.A. who need to be told these things. And even when the conclusion — that a shooting war is no solution — began to be obvious, the argument held our attention, and the desire to turn at once to the end of the book (the answers section) could be suppressed. As in the old-time serial, at the end of chapter four the hero is left hanging over the precipice by his bootlace: 'if war against the Soviet Union is no way out, if it offers no solution, what then is the solution? ... *There is a way*'. The rescuers are audible; will they be in time and have the proper tackle? We turn the page to find a chapter headed: WE HAVE TO BE MORE PROGRESSIVE THAN THE RUSSIANS. Can it be true that when the box is opened there is nothing inside but this mouldy recipe for salvation? Such is the darkness, it is difficult to say. There may be something else that I have mislaid. But the confusion of thought in this last chapter would be hard to beat.

Its first line of argument seems to run like this. A helpless Europe and Asia are ready to accept help from either Russia or the U.S.A., and will choose for their helper whichever of these powers 'they feel to be the more progressive'. In this respect Russia has stolen a march on the U.S.A.; it stands out as a great 'progressive' power, which has captured the hearts of Asiatics and Europeans alike with the offer of 'a higher standard of living'. Meanwhile the U.S.A. has pursued a policy — e.g. in China, Germany, and Greece — of alliance with the 'strong reactionary, more or less anti-democratic, Fascist or semi-Fascist groups'. The influence of the great progressive power, Russia, will go on increasing, at the expense of the U.S.A., until there is 'a basic change in American foreign policy', and the U.S.A. comes forward with encouragement and assistance for 'democratic socialist planning' (that is, a higher standard of living and personal and political liberty) in Europe and in Asia. But just as we are getting used to this simple view, in which the world is divided between progressives and reactionaries, with Russia as a 'progressive power', winning allegiance to itself by the offer and even the gift of a higher standard of living, and the U.S.A. as a reactionary power which has lost its way in China, Germany, Greece and elsewhere, the scene changes. Indeed, it must change because, on this reading, the enterprise of 'stopping Russia' is itself 'reactionary' and pointless. A new Russia makes its appearance. 'Because with present emphasis on military production a significant improvement in the living standards of the masses is impossible; because millions of Russians have seen that not only the middle classes, but also the workers and peasants in central and eastern Europe live much better than they do — for all these reasons the Soviet regime is very eager to produce new successes, new conquests, in order to show its superiority over *all* other systems.' 'The goal of Russian policy', we are told, 'is clear and unmistakable: to dominate all Europe in the same way that Russia already dominates the countries between Russia and Germany'. In short, Russia appears (e.g. in China), not as the enemy of 'parasitic landlords', but as the enemy of the Chinese. And it would appear that to be 'more progressive' than the already progressive Russians would involve the U.S.A. merely in the expense of giving two stones instead of one to Asiatics and Europeans who asked for bread. The net result of the whole argument is to deprive the word 'progressive' of any meaning at all, and to make it appear that in order to stop the Russians the Americans must become so like the Russians that the bewildered Pole or Malayan could scarcely be expected to detect the difference. If Russia is 'progressive', God help us all if the U.S.A. were to become 'more progressive'. The picture of Russia as a kind of benevolent commercial traveller who knocks at the door and offers the housewife a good line in genuine prosperity at the absurdly small price of loss of personal and political liberty is, of course, an agreeable fantasy when compared with the real position—a Russia who acquires a skeleton key to the back-door and is found in the morning with his feet on the mantelpiece ordering breakfast. And it is not surprising that the pious talk, with which the book ends, about a united, democratic, prosperous, progressive, socialized, socialist Europe and Asia, falls a trifle flat. Indeed, the whole chapter—the answer to the question—is a peculiarly muddled and unconvincing form of the utterly unconvincing thesis that if you want to stop a Russian you must become a Socialist.

Principles and Ideals in Politics

The opportunity offered by a single lecture is unavoidably restricted, and if it is to be seized, a boldness in assumption and a sparingness of qualification (neither very congenial to the philosopher) are necessary. But when these limitations are accepted by the author without complaint, the audience is not likely to grumble, and something good may come of it. In addition, perhaps, especially when the subject is philosophical and the audience not one of professional philosophers, success will depend upon the choice of a not too recondite topic, upon the avoidance of excessive subtlety, and upon the generation of a feeling of intellectual excitement: the lecture must have the character of an intellectual entertainment.

Judged by these standards, Professor Field's lecture is a great success. His subject is the moral assumptions which can be detected at the back of political conduct, his thoughts are subtle without being excessively so and he manages to impart an atmosphere of intellectual excitement. 'The special function of the philosopher', he suggests, 'is to try to extract from the way in which people talk and act the assumptions that in fact they are working on. He has then to develop them, to show their implications, their relations of compatibility and incompatibility with other views, their consequences, and so on. Then the philosopher can help to make clear the nature of the possible alternatives'. But it is beyond his modest purpose to suggest to people what is right or wrong in motive or conduct.

Political conduct is apt to spring from one or other of two general motives. These are not always exclusive of one another, and on occasion they may desiderate the same line of conduct. Nevertheless they are distinct and can be opposed. The first is the belief that there are certain principles, laws or rules of behaviour, compliance with which is the form of all laudable conduct. This assumption may appear in a narrowly legalistic form, or, if the principles are of a more general character, it may give great

---

Review of Guy Cromwell Field, *Principles and Ideals in Politics*, L.T. Hobhouse Memorial Trust Lecture No. 18 (Oxford: Oxford University Press, 1948). First published in *Cambridge Journal*, 2 (1949), 444, 446.

freedom as well as guidance to conduct. But, one way or another, the view is that there are certain sacrosanct principles. On the whole, Professor Field thinks, 'the tendency in modern times is to approve of this point of view', though frequently with some reservation: *fiat justitia ruat caelum* as a general point of view, but we hope not to suffer the final consequence. But even with this reservation, it is a point of view not without its dangers to society. The second, and alternative belief, is that laudable political conduct is conduct springing from the pursuit of an ideal, conduct which is judged not by its conformity to a principle, but in respect of its achievement of an end. A common form of political conduct springing from this motive is devotion to a cause. And perhaps the best of Professor Field's pages are given to reflection upon the nature and characteristic excesses and defects of this sort of political conduct.

Professor Field finds neither of these points of view entirely satisfactory; both are capable of supporting conduct which no one would hold to be laudable, and neither is easy to establish to the exclusion of the other. 'We seem to need', he says, 'some general scheme or point of view which will recognize, on the one hand, that at any rate some actions have a positive or negative moral quality of their own, and cannot be judged entirely by their relations to an end or result beyond themselves. And, on the other, it must be recognized that no action can ever be judged entirely in isolation apart from its accompaniments or results or relations to anything outside itself.' Such a point of view, he suggests, is to be found in the claim 'that the only things morally good in themselves, and therefore properly to be regarded as ends in themselves, are certain states of mind of individual human beings'. But time did not permit the exploration of this theme.

Eighty

The Modern Approach to Descartes' Problem
Notes on Descartes' Règles
and Descartes

None of these is a great work, but each in its own way is interesting and all are lively and vigorous. The project of Sir Edmund Whittaker is to consider how far the intervening centuries have brought nearer the achievement of a philosophy (such as Descartes sought at the beginning of the seventeenth century) reformed 'by a new method framed in the likeness of mathematics'. In some respects, he regrets, the enterprise is no nearer to fulfilment. Descartes' hope 'was to create a universal science or general philosophy which, like mathematics, should be accepted by everyone without question; in this he failed. His successors to the present time have to their credit a long tradition of brilliant work in philosophical criticism, but common consent has not been secured for any one definite constructive system; and the situation today is not dissimilar from that which confronted Descartes'. But 'since the sixteenth century the initiative in intellectual progress has lain pre-eminently with the men of science; and the intervention of philosophers has been in general unfortunate.' And it is to the natural scientists and mathematicians that we owe whatever success we have achieved in the direction in which Descartes pointed. For not only have these enlarged the boundaries of our knowledge and transformed the science of logic, but they have kept alive what Sir Edmund takes to be

---

Review of Sir Edmund Whittaker, *The Modern Approach to Descartes' Problem. The Relation of the Mathematical and Physical Sciences to Philosophy*, Herbert Spencer Lecture (London: Thomas Nelson and Sons, 1948); Sydney Montague Jacob, *Notes on Descartes' Règles pour la direction de l'esprit* (London: International Book Club, 1948); and Paul Valéry, *The Living Thoughts of Descartes* (London: Cassell, 1948). First published in *Cambridge Journal*, 2 (1949), 629-30.

the central principle of Cartesianism—the notion that 'the true aim of metaphysics is to complete the direct scrutiny of nature by reflecting on, and laying bare, its presuppositions, concepts and principles; so that philosophy *follows* mathematical and physical science, and does not *precede* it', a principle which 'entails the consequence that philosophy, like physics, must be a progressive subject, the conceptions of one generation being transcended by those of the next'. From this has sprung up in our own day the beginnings, and more than the beginnings, of a philosophy 'based upon physicomathematical science' which is able to provide not only a rational account of 'reality' but also to 'incorporate the notion of value' and hence to set both ethics and aesthetics on a more profitable road. The result is that the 'promised land' which 'Descartes saw from afar is now open to be entered'.

How far all this has survived the criticism to which it has been subjected (how far, indeed, a metaphysics which 'laid bare the presuppositions' of natural science can be expected also to accept them as unquestionably valid) Sir Edmund does not inquire. But if this picture of Descartes as the father of positivism is not executed without doing some violence to history, and if his estimate of the achievements of positivism errs on the side of optimism, they have at least been accomplished with the skill and lucidity we should expect from such a writer.

Mr Jacob is a mathematician—he describes himself, modestly, as, not a high priest, but a lay-brother of the Order—interested and learned in mathematical logic, but concerned here principally with the method of education implied in Descartes' *Règles*. And he has written an exceedingly interesting set of notes on the subject, which deserves a place in the literature of Cartesianism. The revolution in education which was implicit in Descartes is, in his view, not yet fully accomplished. Descartes pleaded for 'our recognition of the unity of all knowledge, a recognition which present-day educational authority might be disposed to grant, as a pure formality; but which, in practice, seems to be totally denied. For is not the multitude of subjects taught in the schools and universities by a system of water-tight compartments, without any attempt to weld them into a philosophical whole, a virtual denial of that unity? And if the philosophical unity is lost sight of, so also is the moral unity which should underlie every step in the pursuit of learning'. Descartes wanted 'learning to be acquired by direct personal thinking', and we have still far to go on this road, particularly (in Mr Jacob's opinion) in the teaching of mathematics. But he is aware of the elements in Descartes' thought which point in the other direction, and can appreciate why it was that Pascal found himself unable to 'forgive' Descartes.

M. Valéry has written a brief and brilliant introduction to the latest volume of Cassell's *Living Thoughts Library*. He describes it as a sketch of Descartes' 'intellectual personality', and in effect it is a masterly account of the mind and method of this great philosopher. M. Valéry disclaims the ability to discuss the technicalities of Descartes' philosophy, and writes instead 'in terms of altogether elementary impressions'. But they are the impressions of an exceedingly acute and lively mind, and the result could hardly be bettered for its purpose. Perhaps the two great moments in Descartes' intellectual life are a trifle over-dramatized, but he gives a truer picture of his subject than that which Pascal conveys in his unfortunate description of Descartes as 'a geometer who is only a geometer'. The volume which M. Valéry introduces contains, in translation, the whole of the *Discours de la Méthode*, some brief passages from the *Meditations Métaphysiques* and half a dozen of Descartes' letters.

Eighty-one

Socialism and Ethics

The writings of true believers normally make sad reading, not merely because they are disfigured by arrogance, but because for many years now they have degenerated into the repetition of a formula: no other religion ever became so intellectually stagnant in so short a time. But what makes this book worth while, in spite of its troubled verbiage, its ignorance of history and its naïve faith, is the absence from it of the usual sanctimonious arrogance: Professor Selsam (an American) is a quiet, reasonable writer, who propounds his doctrine in a civilized manner. His object is 'to show that socialism represents a fusion of objective social science and the highest ethical ideals of the ages'.

The good, he maintains, is what we need and desire; 'the needs and desires of men alone make a thing good'. This is a view which he attributes not only to Marx but also to Spinoza. He offers no analysis of this definition, and if we follow his argument I think we shall find ourselves encouraged to put 'desire' on one side and concentrate on 'need'. We begin, then, with a naturalistic ethical doctrine, not (unfortunately) convincingly argued, but stated on the authority of Marx and common sense. Every society sets up an ideal which incorporates its interpretation of human need, and the activities of a society, as approximations to this ideal, reveal this interpretation. We are concerned with two different sorts of society, the first of which is called 'Capitalist Society'. This is a society based upon the ownership of property by individuals, a society in which the means of production are owned privately and consequently one in which 'a factory is not built to make shoes because people want and need shoes. It is built because, people needing shoes, a profit can be made by producing them.' The master in this society is, alternatively, the owner of the means of production or 'the market' — it is not quite clear which. Now, what are the moral values of this society, what is its interpretation of human need? They will, of course, be the moral values of the 'masters', the dominant

---

Review of Howard Selsam, *Socialism and Ethics* (London: Lawrence and Wishart, 1947). First published in *Cambridge Journal*, 2 (1949), 692–4.

class. But if we consider the activities of this sort of society we find that its interpretation of human need has had the following remarkable results:

> The death-rate drops steadily and the life span increases. Great plagues are as extinct as the dodo and the dinosaur. Many of the physical ills that have cursed humanity have been conquered, while others, such as blindness, deafness and bodily deformity have been alleviated. The majority of the population in capitalist countries are not only literate but also have a technical competence and at least a speaking acquaintance with some of the culture of the ages. In recent years the moving picture and the radio, in spite of their shortcomings, have brought not only recreation but the materials of culture to the great masses of people and even to the most outlying regions. Parks, playgrounds, beaches, camps and automobile travel have made healthful recreation possible for millions who knew no such thing only a generation ago, etc. etc.

This seems to Professor Selsam not at all a bad interpretation of human need; he finds these things good. Capitalist society, following its interpretation of human need, has, indeed, acquired 'the facilities for producing sufficient material goods for a decent life for all'. But there is a debit side to the account. These goods are not enjoyed by *all*, and they are uncertain: capitalism, so far from overcoming poverty, unemployment and war, actually causes and supports characteristically virulent forms of these evils. With all this tremendous advance, with almost unlimited productive forces at our disposal, there is a growing gap between productive capacity and actual production, there is poverty in the midst of potential plenty. Indeed, so impressive are the evils of a capitalist society that it may be said to 'operate totally irrespective of human values' [real needs?]. This is not due to the malice of individual capitalists, it is the fault of the system. Marx predicted this crisis, and it has now appeared. Every man asks of the economy under which he lives that it shall satisfy his needs; the capitalist economy fails to do this for the vast majority with the certainty and the fullness that they demand.

This situation has inspired a new sort of society — that is, a new interpretation of human need, a new moral ideal and a new structure of society to bring about and to embody the satisfaction of this need. This new sort of society is a Socialist Society, and we are lucky in having an example of it before our eyes in Russia. If a society could be established in which production were for need and not for profit, and if the need were that of 'the working class', then all the great but unfulfilled promise of capitalist society could be harvested. The operative 'need', the moral ideal, in this society is that of the 'organized workers', 'the vast majority', 'the people'. This, to the uninitiated, might appear to be a merely class interpretation of need and neither better nor worse than any other. But Professor Selsam has an answer to the difficulty:

> Here [he says] we have an apparent anomaly that causes mechanical-minded intellectuals no end of difficulty but that class-conscious workers and all who have learned to think dialectically can easily understand. The attempt to solve current problems by appealing to so-called universal moral truths, to the 'common good', to humanity in the abstract is in danger of being an idle gesture and even of beclouding the real issues. On the other hand, appeals to and actions in behalf of the working class, while giving superficially the appearance of being concerned with the good of only a part of humanity, turn out to be in fact the only true humanism ... The working class carries with it in its own class morality, the only true human ethics.

The moral ideal, then, is the need of the majority, 'not because the goals of the working class are good in and of themselves, but rather because they are the sole means to general human progress and the widest human good'. And there is a further reason why the needs and desires of the 'working class' should be the operative needs and desires. Where 'need' is the need of a small class (as it is assumed to be in a capitalist society), there is no opportunity of determining and satisfying that need *scientifically*; need and desire fall apart and men desire what they do not need. But when the 'need' becomes the need of the masses (and no other need is recognized), this can be determined scientifically, satisfied economically by a standardized product, compulsorily supplied. It can be *proved* 'that such and such a dietary deficiency causes rickets'. 'Science can tell us what our people need and want and what would be good for them', and 'it is not too fantastic to suggest that there are cultural needs' which can be similarly determined and supplied in the same manner. In short, 'the use of science in determining values implies and requires a community of interest' such as exists only in the masses of a society. But we are warned that it would be a great mistake to suppose that socialism is an attempt 'to bring civilization down to the level of the barracks'.

Now, how far all this is orthodox doctrine is difficult to determine. It rests upon the absolute acceptance of some of the orthodox dogmas, such, for example, as the inevitable decline in the standard of living in a 'capitalist' society. But without inquiring into the inconsistencies of the argument, two observations may be made. First, the good life here is nothing other than the enjoyment by more and more people of more and more of everything: 'the ever-increasing development of all the productive forces of human society and the resultant improved living standards of all people are at one and the same time the index of social evolution and the rational goal of mankind.' In short, this is the plausible ethics of productivity, distinguished from 'capitalism' only by being alleged to be more successful. So far as I am concerned it involves a revolting nothingness, which has only to be successful to reduce human life to absolute insignificance. Secondly, the 'socialist' society is presented here as a society in which only those desires are approved which all can satisfy at the same time: none shall have what all cannot enjoy. The desires of the masses (in so far as desire is allowed to appear at all) are to be the standard for everyone, and the result is a tyranny of the majority. Or, when 'need' is substituted for 'desire', the result is the tyranny of those who determine the need, the 'scientists'. Of the two, any sane man would no doubt choose the former; but it is a desperate alternative.

Eighty-two

The Tree of Commonwealth

Every schoolboy used to know Edmund Dudley as one of the agents of the rapacious exactions of Henry VII: the other, appropriately enough, was Epsom. Dudley, moreover, was known pejoratively as a 'lawyer'. And what was known seemed to account for the fact that, as Hume remarks, 'the death of Henry VII was attended with as open and visible a joy among the people as decency would permit'. It accounted also for the fact that, on the death of Henry, Dudley was arrested, accused of extortion and of constructive treason, tried, convicted, imprisoned in the Tower and executed in 1510. What more belonged to the character and career of Dudley lay hidden: the collector of revenue, the persecutor of merchants who evaded taxation, the man who enforced anachronistic feudal dues alone survived. Dudley, however, played more parts than these. He was one of the most distinguished lawyers of his day, he was Under-Sheriff of London and Speaker of the House of Commons before he became a member of the King's Council. Moreover, he wrote a book; he wrote it in prison, and it is called *The Tree of Commonwealth*. This has now been edited, with an introduction and a full critical apparatus, by Dr Brodie. It is an admirable piece of work, performed with all the necessary care and scholarship. Every student of English history will welcome its appearance.

There are two points of view from which *The Tree of Commonwealth* may be seen. First, as Dr Brodie remarks, it expresses, in the allegorical style of the time, the political ideas current among ordinary men in the late fifteenth century. It is neither original, nor perhaps very profound; certainly Dudley makes no claim to be a philosopher. But he was a politician and an observer of politics, and in the cracks of the elaborate allegory are to be found the observations of a man who understood not only the perennial principles of politics but also the shape of the politics of his day. He writes in an attractively reflective style: there is a quiet irony in his observation

---

Review of Edmund Dudley, *The Tree of Commonwealth*, ed. and intro. Dorothy Margaret Brodie (Cambridge: Cambridge University Press, 1948). First published in *Cambridge Journal*, 2 (1949), 763–4.

and a concentration of mind which, if Dr Johnson is to be believed, comes to a condemned man. When the historian has done with it, there is something here for the politician of today. But secondly, the book belongs to the literature of the education of princes; it is addressed in the first place to the King. And in this respect it is instructive to compare it with the work of Dudley's great contemporary, Machiavelli. In both writers the turmoil and disruption of the time is clearly reflected, the clash of interests, the arrogance of nobles, the greed of merchants, and the discontent of a people easily roused to rebellion by worthless and self-interested leaders. But, whereas Machiavelli wrote for a prince 'of new creation', a prince without a tradition, ruling a society composed of men whom ambition had pulled up by the roots, Dudley wrote for a prince who might be expected to recognize a tradition if his attention were called to it and the ruler of a less disintegrated society. The times might need a vigorous ruler, but not a tyrant. The strength of a commonwealth, Dudley saw, lay neither in sporadic success in subduing enemies nor in the ability of an upstart ruler to keep his people in subjection, but in the rule of law, in the maintenance of justice, in keeping faith, in honesty, humility and compassion. He shows no pious abhorrence of worldly prosperity or of the energy and enterprise which go to make it; but he sees clearly the defects of the virtues of each of the classes in the commonwealth, and in this charming medieval allegory recalls each man to his true path.

Eighty-three

Insight and Outlook

Mr Koestler has given us something to think about. It is true that there is a long-windedness about the book which is unexpected from so practised a writer; it is over-elaborate, and its argument is encumbered, not only with jargon, but also with an over-weighty apparatus of technical psychology; but I do not think anyone interested in the subject will read it without excitement as well as profit. In effect, it is a book about the psychology of what is commonly called 'creative' human activity, in which Mr Koestler includes art, science, and moral conduct. Its main hypothesis is that all 'creative' activity has at least a psychological common denominator (if not a common pattern), and that the isolation and definition of this denominator will add to our understanding of the activity. This is a reasonable hypothesis; certainly one worth exploring. And, further, there is an agreeable freedom about the method of investigation. Mr Koestler has a doctrine to propound; but instead of a direct assault upon his problem he takes us in by the 'back-door' through which he himself entered upon the enquiry. This is, perhaps, a 'literary' rather than a 'scientific' method, but it gives the reader the instructive experience of seeing the doctrine coming into being, gradually formulating itself, and making itself convincing without the misleading appearance of being 'proved.'

The back-door by which we enter is a theory of laughter and the comic. It was in working this out that Mr Koestler came upon a principle which he later conceived to be applicable to 'creative' activity in general. Thought and behaviour (so the theory runs) normally follow repetitive patterns, and are organised into homogeneous 'operative fields,' each with a logic of its own. The 'operative field' of a card-player, for example, is determined by the rules and conventions of the game he is playing. And there are as many 'operative fields' as there are definable attitudes to the world. A joke or a comic situation springs from the interpenetration of two 'oper-

---

Review of Arthur Koestler, *Insight and Outlook: an Enquiry into the Common Foundations of Science, Art and Social Ethic*s (London: Macmillan, 1949). First published in *Spectator*, 183 (1949), 20, 22.

ative fields.' The essence of the comic is simultaneous association of two habitually incompatible contexts. This Mr Koestler calls the principle of 'bisociation,' and in the first part of the book he analyses it with great care and subtlety, and investigates its application to numerous forms of the comic. But this is merely a preliminary, because it appears that the principle of 'bisociation' not only makes the comic intelligible, but affords the basis for a complete theory of 'creative' activity. 'Bisociation' is the spring of the discoveries of the scientist and the 'creations' of the artist and the poet. Merely 'associative' thought, moving along beaten tracks and keeping to the rules of the game, is the bread and butter of mental activity; but 'the brilliance of discovery, the sparkle of humour and the radiance of art' spring from 'bisociative' thought which disrupts the normal pattern and produces something new.

The third step in the argument, which the attentive reader will have been waiting for, is designed to provide a principle for distinguishing between various 'bisociative' activities and to answer the question: How is it that the intersection of two 'operative fields' sometimes produces a joke and at other times a scientific discovery or a poetic image? Nietzsche, of course, was prepared to see all 'creative' activity as 'a joke,' and understood at a profound level this no doubt is true; but most readers will be on the look-out for some help from Mr Koestler in distinguishing tragic from comic art and both from scientific discovery and moral achievement. The help comes in the form of a psychological analysis of human behaviour. There are (we are told) two opposed tendencies in human emotional behaviour, the one self-assertive (aggressive-defensive) and the other self-transcending (integrative). The exposition of this hypothesis takes Mr Koestler far afield into biology, sociology, ethics, and the history of civilisation. What he says is always interesting and often convincing; but there is too much of it to attempt a summary. Suffice it that, in general, the *outcome* of 'bisociative' activity is determined by the emotional tendency with which it is associated. In the extremes, 'bisociation' linked with a self-assertive emotional tendency is characteristic of the comic, and the genuinely aesthetic experience is linked with an impulse to self-transcendence, an impulse which is also taken to be biologically, socially, and morally progressive. But between these extremes lies the region of science—the 'neutral art' of invention and discovery, as Mr Koestler calls it—which has 'neither a pronounced aggressive nor, a markedly sympathetic emotional charge.'

Mr Koestler pursues this theme in great detail. In a chapter called 'The Eureka Process' he examines, in the light of the 'bisociative' hypothesis, the activity of the scientist. Here, in the 'exploratory drive,' logic takes a back seat; 'each original scientific achievement is a bisociative act of the same mental pattern as the creation of wit and the creation of art.' The last part of the book is concerned with art proper — what Mr Koestler calls 'the emotive arts' — and is an elaborate application of the principle of 'bisociation' to poetry and drama.

It will be clear that the reader must expect from this book, along with the excitement of following a well-constructed argument, a certain portentousness. It is to be followed by a second volume in which we are promised a deeper exploration of some of the psychological problems touched on here. Mr Koestler believes himself to have found a 'unifying formula' for all 'creative' activity, and, like most people who have discovered a formula, he is apt to ride it hard. Indeed, the main defect of the book is that it never comes out on the other side of the formula. The intelligent reader will find — as he finds in any well-thought-out formula (Coleridge's distinction between fancy and imagination, for example) — something to inspire reflection; but the inspiration will be proportional to his ability not to succumb to the formula. But if its power to tempt us to accept the formula is the chief weakness of the book, it is not the only one. Mr Koestler is not enough of a philosopher to write on aesthetics or ethics with any great confidence. His main business is with psychology, but he cannot avoid excursions into philosophy, and they are not always fortunate. He accepts without discussion the naïve view that all art is communication, and I confess that the 'natural system of ethics' he propounds leaves me puzzled, and I look forward to the more detailed exposition of it promised in Volume II.

Eighty-four

Deviation into Sense

The genuine amateur in philosophy, the unprofessional philosopher who yet is neither a crank, nor impatient of discipline, nor a man who comes to philosophy carrying all the apparatus of a foreign profession (such as politics or natural science), is a rarity. But when he appears he is usually worth listening to. Mr Wauchope is a philosopher of this kind. He is by no means ignorant of what other philosophers have thought, nor is he as independent of the history of philosophy as he sometimes suggests; and he is certainly not an incurably informal philosopher, a stranger to the rigour of the game. But it is not on account of its learning or its logical acuteness that his book will be read with excitement and delight by those interested in philosophy, but because it reflects unmistakably an *anima naturaliter philosophica*. It is at once simple and profound, clearly the fruit of many years of quiet reading and reflection, written not tentatively but with the modest dogmatism which belongs to all bold and lucid thinking, yet written with a freshness and grace uncommon in the too often tortuous literature of philosophy.

'The business of philosophy,' he writes, 'is, as it always has been, to find a standpoint from which all the variety of reality could be viewed as parts of a comprehended whole. It is to say something such that, if it were true, everything would be as it is.' Unfortunately, he continues, the business has been a failure because philosophers have fallen into the error of supposing that intellectual operations (such as understanding the world) would give their best results if the 'subjective factor,' the person who thinks, could be eliminated from the conclusion. The project of finding a world at once intelligible and 'absolutely objective' has been the evil genius of philosophic enterprise. This condemnation, fully merited by only the cruder forms of positivism, is perhaps a trifle too sweeping. And the notion that if this error were abjured, and philosophers made an entirely new start, we

---

Review of Oswald Stewart Wauchope, *Deviation into Sense: the Nature of Explanation*. London: Faber and Faber, 1948). First published in *Times Literary Supplement* (15 January 1949), 45.

human beings would be in a position to 'settle for ourselves once and for all what we are and what we are about' is perhaps a trifle too Roman in its philosophical optimism. But when Mr Wauchope begins the exposition of his own doctrine we soon leave behind the amateurish eccentricity of these early exaggerations.

'The stuff of reality is mind/matter, Self/not-self, subjective/objective' —is, in short, experience. Matter *per se* is unintelligible because it is non-entity; there are only 'events,' mind and matter in union. And the aim of philosophic explanation is to hold fast to this union and to make it intelligible. The Self in experience is 'alive.' The meaning of 'being alive' has, however, been restricted to its 'logical' meaning, 'not being dead'; the activity of living has been confined to the rational, purposeful, defensive activity of avoiding or delaying death, and the communal tactics of death-avoiding activity have (under the name of morality) engaged the main attention and loyalty of mankind. This is unfortunate because the 'logical' meaning of 'being alive' is not the most significant meaning. 'Living' is primary; 'dead' does not mean merely 'non-living', it means 'having ceased to live'. This suggests that the activity of the living Self is not merely death-avoiding, but is twofold: to 'live' and to avoid death. And if we turn to our personal experience we shall find this confirmed; much of our activity cannot be explained in terms of avoiding death. And what is more, purposeful, defensive activity is, properly speaking, subordinate to purposeless 'living' activity; we avoid death, not for its own sake, but in order to 'live.' In other words, 'living activity' is the soul's primary activity, and rational, defensive activity—sense—is a deviation from it.

Now, if we are prepared to follow Mr Wauchope to the top of this hill—and his talk on the way up is most persuasive—we shall find spread out in front of us a world, not unlike that which Blake offers us, in which the values of the 'subjective Self' (e.g., spontaneous affection) are primary and the death-avoiding values of rational and moral behaviour are secondary and derivative. But Mr Wauchope is not a Manichee; matter in union with mind is not evil, and the deviation into death-avoiding activity is legitimate so long as it is recognised as deviation. The problem of human life is not how to survive, or how to emancipate the Self from death-avoiding activity, but how to preserve a proper balance between the two activities of the Self. And the handicap from which we suffer in solving this problem is the erroneous assumption that death-avoiding activity is primary and that 'living' is secondary. In the hands of Mr Wauchope all this blossoms into a political theory for which 'the fretfulness of modern civilization, and its vulgarity, its constant plundering of the realm of spontaneity and individuality for the "general good," its bullying sociality, are the consequence of its unbalance, its morbid preoccupation with good reasons and death.' He rarely refers to other writers, but as one reads one becomes conscious of certain affinities, and among philosophers it may be supposed that Hobbes has had some influence upon his thought. Indeed, this is a philosophy such as Hobbes himself might have conceived if the fear of death had not stood in the way of his developing a more positive doctrine of Felicity. The book ends with an allegory, subtle, charming, and profound, and able to stand beside the great myths of philosophic literature.

This brief description of Mr Wauchope's argument does much less than justice to its variety and power, and the excitement with which the reader follows it. But when it is finished it will not be surprising if some doubts make their appearance. The general metaphysical position is a form of what used to be called objective idealism — a very respectable doctrine. But it is difficult to be certain that the ethical doctrine presented to us here avoids some of even the cruder errors of naturalism. The conception of 'life' and 'living behaviour' remains indistinct. There is room also for doubt whether the conception of the 'subjective Self,' the Self insulated from the not-self, upon which so much of this argument is based, is not reached too simply and too rapidly; an absolutely 'subjective' subject is as indefensible as an absolutely 'objective' object. Indeed, the 'subjectivity' of the Self, upon which so much of his argument depends, is assumed rather than demonstrated or even argued. But whatever error or incoherence in detail the reader may find to deplore, this is not the sort of book to which such error is fatal; it has enough genius, and more than enough vitality, to survive errors far more gross.

Eighty-five

The Life of Reason

This book is not merely the last work of the late Professor W.G. de Burgh, it is (and was intended by its author to be) the crown of his philosophical labours. It was left unfinished at his death, and its appearance now is due to the initiative of his wife and to the editorial exertions of several of his friends. The foreword is by Dr C.C.J. Webb, the arrangement of the chapters is the work of Professor G.H. Langley, and both the late Professor A.E. Taylor and Professor T.M. Knox have helped to prepare it for the press. In form it is a *speculum mentis*. Its project is 'to survey the forms of rational activity, both in thought and conduct, not in order to reach an abstract definition, but in order to display the nature of reason as a unity of diverse functions.' It is recognized that reason cannot be taken as co-extensive with mind, but it is contended that 'wherever in our experience there is conscious unification of diverse elements, be the unity discovered in the real, or constructed by human agency; wherever we discover or produce form in a given material, be it in sense-perception, in a work of art, in moral or economic action, in scientific, philosophical or religious thinking —there intellect or reason is at work.' The book, then, is written to expound a philosophy of reason, but it is written also to combat an error —the error, 'prevalent throughout the thought of the last three centuries in Europe and America,' which in speculation confines reasoning to logical ratiocination, and in practice to the determination of fit means to achieve non-rational ends.

The forms of speculative reason are first examined and arranged in an hierarchical order. Science, 'the speculative activity of reason as concentrated on the factor of generality,' is concerned with quantitative and measurable relations. History is knowledge of the individual. These are complementary activities of mind, but it is an 'optimistic fancy' which finds a complete knowledge of reality in their conjunction. Art is a form of

---

Review of William George de Burgh, *The Life of Reason* (London: Macdonald and Evans, 1949). First published in *Times Literary Supplement* (19 March 1949), 190.

cognitive activity which gives a more complete knowledge of the individual than history; and in philosophy there is a knowledge of the universal which carries us beyond the universals of science. But the summit of the forms of speculative reason is religion, the claim of which to give knowledge is maintained against the denials of the Logical Positivists and others. And further, the Christian faith is a form of religion which can be shown to conform to the criteria of rationality.

The practical, no less than the speculative forms of reason, compose an hierarchy. At the bottom is that kind of purpose, free, rational activity which Signor Croce called 'economic.' And above it comes activity regulated by law, and the moral life. But this hierarchy also culminates in religion — religion as *praxis* — and in Christianity as 'exhibiting on the highest plane the essential characteristics of the rational life.' To demonstrate this, 'to display religious experience as the crowning type of rational activity, as the synthesis of the highest activity of speculative reason and the highest activity of practical reason in a single form of rational life' is, indeed, the ultimate aim of the argument of this book; and not merely religion in general, but Christianity in particular. For 'if reason is taken in its full breadth of meaning as the faculty of intellectual synthesis, it cannot be restricted to the consideration of what is known as Natural Theology, but the whole *corpus* of religious knowledge, both natural and revealed, must be included within its province.' Philosophy here is seen both as *Fides quaerens intellectum* and *Intellectus quaerens fidem*. De Burgh drew his inspiration from many sources, and not least from his extensive reading in medieval philosophy. But what is perhaps most impressive about this book is its combination of religious and intellectual sincerity. It presents us with a doctrine, clearly imagined and articulated with the intellectual power of a man practised in argument. Some readers may find the doctrine at times a trifle over-formalized and the argument lacking in meditative freedom. But at the end of a long life of reflection a man may surely be allowed to display a mind made up.

Eighty-six

Matter, Mind, and Meaning

The late Mr Whately Carington was well known as an experienced investigator of those 'supernormal' phenomena which are the concern of psychical research. In this book, however, which he left unfinished, his business is not with experiments and observations, but with the conceptual framework which would make these observations (when taken at their face value) intelligible. In other words, his question is: 'What *must* the world be like if these things happen?' And his attempt to answer the question resolves itself into an investigation of the conceptions of mind and matter. The book has been edited by Professor H.H. Price, who contributes an informative preface and a number of judicious footnotes.

The project itself is a little puzzling: this distinction between the 'mass of queer facts' and their 'intelligibility' is hardly one to be insisted upon, and perhaps a better way of stating the question would be in the form of a self-examination: 'What presuppositions am I making about mind and matter when I accept these "facts" at their face value?' But, as Professor Price says, even if the result is somewhat rough-and-ready, the attempt to construct a philosophy of psychical research is a laudable enterprise. The professed object of the book—'to clean up once and for all—in principle and in outline at least—the muddle about the relation of Mind and Matter which has fretted philosophers ever since philosophising began'—is not perhaps accomplished, but something valuable is achieved by the way.

Mr Carington attributes 'the muddle' to the 'metaphysicians'; he rapidly reaches the conclusion that 'all metaphysics is nonsense,' and says so vigorously, if sometimes without any great insight. He is a positivist, and for him any statement which it is impossible to verify or refute by observation of some kind is meaningless; metaphysical statements are all of this character. 'Pure logic is all right,' but the trouble with metaphysics is that, even after all these centuries, there is no reliable text-book such as one may find on electricity or hydrodynamics. The nature of mind and matter must,

---

Review of Whately Carington, *Matter, Mind, and Meaning* (London: Methuen, 1949). First published in *Times Literary Supplement* (20 May 1949), 332.

then, be investigated without the help of the 'philosophers'. Starting from the principle (in Bertrand Russell's words), 'in dealing with any subject-matter, find out what entities are undeniably involved, and state everything in terms of these entities,' the doctrine that Mr Carington comes to favour is a form of Neutral Monism: the common constituents of mind and matter are sense-data or *cognita*. In themselves these *cognita* are neither mental nor material. 'A material object is a sequence of *cognita* or *cognitum* groups related in a particular way,' and 'if you want a more exact specification you must apply to the physicist'; a mind is the same sequence of *cognita* related according to the laws of psychology. The usefulness of such a view as this to those involved in psychical research is clear. It removes in principle the difficulty of understanding how mental and material *cognitum* systems may influence one another, how individual minds may interact, and perhaps how minds can survive death. Mr Carington's masters are Bertrand Russell and to a lesser extent Professor Ayer, and he acknowledges a debt to Messrs Ogden and Richards. But he has something to say on his own account, and the light-heartedness of his style may be taken to spring from modesty rather than from arrogance.

Eighty-seven

Barbara Celarent

Anyone, already persuaded that thinking is an admirable and profitable activity, who listens to a dialectical disputation in the scholastic manner will have the impression at once of deep seriousness and of play. If the dry pertinacity of the method reflects that profound scholastic faith in the power of reasoning to correct the inadvertencies of thought, its subtlety betrays the amateur's unspoilt delight in a good argument. The reader is likely to gain the same impression from this book; it takes reasoning seriously but does not exaggerate its place in human intercourse. It has a double purpose, and in both it succeeds admirably. First, it is a study of the dialectic of St Thomas, of the structure of the *Summa Theologica*, in which the philosophy of St Thomas is presented as an intellectual adventure and not (as it too often appears in the manuals) as a kind of staff-college doctrine. And Father Gilby's success here springs from his sure and easy grasp of his subject. Secondly, it is an account of the principles of scholastic logic and dialectic which, deriving from Aristotle, were so deeply reflected upon by medieval thinkers and transmitted by them to the modern world. The history of scholasticism is littered with handbooks on logic, many of which are dry and trivial; what we are given here is a treatment of the subject which is so humane and businesslike that the result is a book on logic that can be read with genuine pleasure as well as with profit. The logic it deals with is, of course, the traditional logic; but the view taken is that while the more modern technique of mathematical or symbolic logic has opened up new fields, a place still remains for the older study — a view which few will wish to combat.

Logic is the good manners of argument. Its concern is with the muster and arrangement of our thoughts. Its business is not with the truth of our conclusions but with their conclusiveness. To get rid of formal defects in our thinking, to avoid a bungled argument, are modest purposes, but not

---

Review of Thomas Gilby, *Barbara Celarent. A Description of Scholastic Dialectic* (London: Longmans, Green and Co., 1949). First published in *Times Literary Supplement* (3 June 1949), 369.

to be despised. The security of communication depends upon logic—not on the science of logic (men reasoned cogently before Aristotle) but on the experience from which that science derives. Incorrect statements, recklessness in enumerating contradictories, illicit inference from negatives to affirmatives, these are forms of inconsiderateness in argument which make rational talk impossible. But poise is not the whole of behaviour, and the logic which runs on rails must pass into the freer, warmer, more conversational dialectic if we are to think to any purpose. Logic is an indispensable rudder, but it operates most effectively when it is under the surface, and it cannot take hold unless we have steerage-way. In dialectic we reach out to consider possibilities, we call upon myth and analogy, we recognize that even equivocation can be benign and that all circles are not vicious. The logical censor is kept in his place, that of a servant, and the movement of the conversation is not held up unnecessarily: the game is not played for the benefit of the referee, and the friendly opposition in disputation (for dialectic is between two and is a cooperative effort to trace disagreement to its source) is as ready to understand a clumsily expressed argument as to counter with the distinctions necessary to put it right. Of course, there are dialectical as well as merely logical fallacies, sophisms, sham arguments, false or strained analogies, and these are more subtle offences against good taste in disputation, to be exorcized by a sympathy for rational argument rather than by the application of a clear rule.

Philosophy, said Ferrier, may be true but must be reasoned: this is a study of the necessary side of scholastic philosophy. It was written in the Mediterranean while the author was on active service with the Navy and had only a miniature *Summa* to consult. Perhaps the chapters on Induction and the Method of the Sciences are weaker than the rest; but the whole book is written with such good humour and grace of style that the reader has the experience of being in communication with a full, well-ordered and generous mind.

Eighty-eight

The Freedom of Necessity

As Professor Bernal remarks, the unity of this volume (in which he has collected a number of his essays published in a variety of periodicals during the last twenty years) lies in a point of view consistently expounded and reiterated. The theme is science and society; the doctrine is science as the saviour of society. He is an energetic writer, with a facile optimism which is, no doubt, encouraging to those who already believe. But the argument is too often slipshod, and the exaggerations too blatant to persuade others, or even to make much impression upon them. There is a certain carelessness in formulating antitheses; and before he has gone far the reader becomes suspicious of the word 'therefore.' What is to be made of such a sentence as: 'Isolated man is a fiction, man carries society in himself, therefore there can be no better criterion for understanding, value, and action than the collective judgment of the people'? And a writer who asserts that 'no one who has ever considered the matter would now doubt that, given the political conditions, it would be perfectly feasible to set up and get working within a few months a comprehensive, productive and distributing mechanism for the whole world' can scarcely hope to win a reputation for care and caution by turning the 'months' into 'years' on a subsequent page.

However, from the troubled verbiage of these pages a point of view does emerge. Professor Bernal has set himself the hard task of interpreting 'the forces which are moulding our time.' To write contemporary history when it is confined to diplomacy is a notoriously difficult undertaking, but when it is enlarged to a survey of the more profound movements which are afoot it is understandable that the interpreter should retreat upon a formula; and the formula here is that of Marx. The reader would, however, have more confidence in the interpretation if the knowledge displayed of modern European history generally were less superficial. But he is given to understand, in the end, that when the relics of effete capitalism have

---

Review of John Desmond Bernal, *The Freedom of Necessity* (London: Routledge and Kegan Paul, 1949). First published in *Times Literary Supplement* (17 June 1949), 400.

finally been destroyed, a society will come into being fired by the ideal of establishing 'the best possible biological and social environment for human beings.' The biological environment which is 'the common human birthright' is 'what for years it has meant for domestic animals'; the social environment is more complicated, but the prime necessity is the consciousness of a common purpose, and the most revealing example of the achievement of this is to be found in a society at war. The 'planned economy' of war presents men with an ideal for peace: 'a society is always at its best when the people who compose it are working for a common recognized end ... Except in Socialist countries, only war can bring out this consciousness of social unity in action.' And further, the experience gained in *this* war has immensely increased our knowledge of how to organize a society for the achievement of a 'clear and single purpose.' Science for the first time (outside the U.S.S.R.) was given a chance to show what it can do — not as big a chance as it should have been given, because the scientist was kept in a subordinate, advisory position and never allowed to command — but enough to show what might be done.

This, indeed, is the message of Professor Bernal's book — the inspiration of war for peace in backward societies like our own. But the reader is left in some uncertainty about the result. Is the new society to be a technocracy in which 'the ministries, as organs of State, are the servants of the people: their work begins in finding out what people need and, having found this out, they must set about discovering the best means of providing it. Scientific research is the new and sure way of doing this'? Is both 'the direction of policy' and 'the actual carrying out of policy itself' to be in the hands of the scientists? At some moments it would seem so. 'The war has taught us that we can succeed if we use science to find out what we really want and not only to get what we think we want.' And the corollary is that scientists must be organized in order to make their views prevail. Or is 'every cook' to rule the State? But whatever the solution of this problem, it seems clear that every man is to have a 'place' in society determined by his 'ability,' and that it will be of advantage to society to determine that ability and to assign the place as early as possible in a man's life.

In the 'scientific' fantasies of a generation ago the dominating figure was a megalomaniac professor whose invention had put the world in his power; his intention to destroy the world was frustrated only by the ingenuity of a schoolboy or of the schoolboy's pet dog. And this still prevails in the strip cartoon, perhaps the most revealing evidence of the impact of 'science' upon the world. This relic of capitalist individualism has disappeared from Professor Bernal's world; 'science,' or a team of scientists have taken the place of the crazy professor. Megalomania still raises its head; the invitation to power is still irresistible. But the purpose now is beneficent — to achieve 'an ever-increasing standard of material well-being and social culture.' The motive of 'private profit' has gone, but in its place appears a society in which power and profit, the project of wringing from the earth in the shortest time the maximum that can be extracted, are the sole motives to have social approval.

Eighty-nine

The Life of Reason

This is the first of a projected four-volume study of the English 'Augustans,' the name Professor James appropriates to the leaders of thought and letters in the period from about 1650 to 1780. It deals with the writings (in so far as they concern the nature of human knowledge, imagination and religious feeling) of three speculative writers who did much to set on foot and fix the intellectual idiom in which the men of this period were reared. It is not the story of the steady development of a rationalist ideology, but a study of the intellectual 'state of affairs with which the literary men of the age had to come to terms and in which they must do the best they could.' As Professor James sees it, this intellectual state of affairs was something of a handicap to the Augustan poets and dramatists; but they are not to be blamed for it — rather, admired for what they succeeded in achieving within the idiom.

The three studies which compose this book are executed in a manner both subtle and profound, and Professor James has made a notable contribution to our understanding of this period of the history of English thought. He writes in a discursive, meditative style, and the reader has the agreeable experience of watching him turn over in his mind, in a leisurely, reflective, unemphatic manner, the ideas of these writers. There is much close argument and a certain amount of repetitiveness, but there is no attempt to plug a doctrine or exaggerate a tendency. He has a genuinely philosophical mind, alive not merely to the answers which his authors provide, but to the problems they are tackling and the difficulties they encounter; he has both the temperament and the learning required of a historian of ideas. The literary man when he turns to examine a piece of philosophical writing is apt to be awake to much that the mere philosopher passes over as irrelevant — to style, mood, intention, and emotional spring. He considers not only the cogency of the argument, but also its impulse.

Review of David Gwilym James, *The English Augustans, vol. 1. The Life of Reason. Hobbes, Locke, Bolingbroke* (London: Longmans, Green and Co., 1949). First published in *Times Literary Supplement* (5 August 1949), 509.

Self-contradiction is not merely a lapse to be observed, but an effect which inspires a search for its cause. The concern of the literary man is as much with the quality of mind as with the actual argument. And when, to support this point of view, he has the necessary philosophical equipment to understand the argument, he will be able to make a valuable contribution to the interpretation of a philosophical writer. Indeed, the contemporary movement to draw philosophical writing back into its place in the history of literature has already contributed to a more profound understanding of our philosophical traditions.

There is no more promising subject for this kind of treatment than Hobbes, and Professor James's study, under the title of 'The Proud Mind', goes deeply into the subtleties of this most passionate and intuitive of English philosophers. He finds in Hobbes the unequivocal expression of that exaltation of ratiocination which was to be characteristic of the Augustans; and in Hobbes's opposition of sense, judgment and fancy he finds the 'centre of Augustan orthodoxy': chapter eight of *Leviathan* is the *locus classicus* of Augustan aesthetic. It is a crude doctrine that is to be found there, so crude that Professor James considers that Hobbes 'does not so much as begin to give a serious account of aesthetic experience'; he is without any proper appreciation, much less theory, of imagination. But, in default of anything else, this is what prevailed. Here, as at some other points in the argument, the reader may feel the absence of proper perspective; it is not, of course, suggested that Hobbes was alone in his generation in holding the theory of poetry that he did, but little is said to show that in essentials this theory and its corollaries were in fact part of the common stock of ideas of the time. And one of the few exaggerations Professor James allows himself is his assertion that 'Hobbes ... has no continuity with the past.'

Professor James is both fascinated and repelled by Hobbes; Locke, whom he studies under the title of 'The Humble Heart,' he admires and speaks of as 'the greatest of English philosophers.' What he admires is, chiefly, the piety, the fairness, the modesty, the 'mediocrity' of Locke's mind, which saved him from the rationalism of Hobbes and the extreme empiricism of Hume. In Locke Professor James finds, what he cannot find in Hobbes, the possibility of a sound and serious doctrine of imagination; but unfortunately it remained an unrealized possibility. And Locke's bequest to the Augustans, his chapter 'Of Enthusiasm' which was added to the fourth edition of the *Essay*, inadvertently inspired the rationalist deism (so foreign to Locke himself) of the Augustans of the early eighteenth century.

There is no difficulty in detecting in Bolingbroke the least philosophical of the writers under consideration. He is called here 'The Man of the World' and he earns his place not because he was a profound or even a serious thinker, but mainly an account of his direct influence upon Pope.

Bolingbroke's acknowledged master was Locke, but he was an insensitive pupil, turning into a crass formula all the tentative modesty of Locke's philosophy. 'Locke's empiricism springs from a profound sense of human ignorance … Bolingbroke's came from assurance and certainty.' And in his hands the errors of Augustan thought became a fixed and finished doctrine.

The greater part of this book is concerned with the exposition of the ideas of these writers, but not the whole of it. Professor James is critical as well as expository, and he knows that it is impossible to be profitably critical without having a point of view. Hence the pages, unfortunately scattered up and down the book, in which he suggests an aesthetic theory of his own. Enough is said for the reader to wish for more, and to wish for it to be collected into a sustained argument; until this is done criticism is difficult. There is, however, a certain uneasiness in what appears to be an unfortunate hypostatization of 'the imagination' as if it were an independent 'power' or even 'faculty,' and Professor James's doctrine of knowledge and being seems to start on the wrong foot, with a separation which he seeks to reduce but cannot succeed in abolishing; and there is sometimes an unphilosophical appeal to 'facts' as if they constituted an independent and final authority. But here, without doubt, is the suggestion of an aesthetic theory, very much in the Kantian tradition, which it is to be hoped that Professor James will later expand.

Ninety

Marxism and Contemporary Science

A man whose thought has been profoundly influenced by Marx must be allowed to call himself a Marxist, but in one who is prepared to reconsider Marxism root and branch (almost) it is puzzling to find still the urge to excuse Marx and Engels because their doctrine is not acceptable in every detail. Of all the exaggerations of Marxists, this expectation that here was something proof against time and error is the strangest: much of the history of Marxism has been a repetition of the more regrettable passages in the history of Aristoteleanism. But in spite of this oblique relic of dogmatism, this is the book of a candid man; and it would have been a better book if Mr Lindsay could have freed himself more effectively from the jargon of Marxism. He is prepared to suggest that 'Dialecticial Materialism' is an unfortunate phrase, meaning either more or less than is intended; but for the rest, what he has to say is sadly obscured by his determination to translate it into this antiquated language. There was once real inspiration in the contrast between a dialectical and a mechanical view of things, but the words have become so overladen with the dust of polemic that anyone now wishing to revive the inspiration had better find another manner of expressing himself.

Briefly, the thesis of the book is that by a 'vulgar distortion' a doctrine of human life in terms of economic determinism, of society in terms of 'structure' and 'superstructure' and of social transformation by class struggle, has been fathered on to Marx by followers who never grasped the fact that 'his great contribution is the concept of *dialectical unity*' — the idea that man, society, and the natural world compose a single whole and that it is only within this whole that change, differentiation, unbalance, contradiction and conflict take place. How successful Mr Lindsay has been in explaining, or explaining away, some of Marx's statements which seem to run counter to this view, only the pundits can decide. He

---

Review of Jack Lindsay, *Marxism and Contemporary Science; or, the Fullness of Life* (London: Dennis Dobson, 1949). First published in *Times Literary Supplement* (16 September 1949), 605.

does not deny that this 'distortion' is widespread in Marxist literature and that there is some small excuse for it, but he claims that at least Lenin, Stalin, and Dimitrov are free of it. He claims, further, that it is 'Marx's unitary outlook which for the first time in history grasps at the fullness of human life, logical, economic and cultural, in a single focus' — which is perhaps going a trifle too far. Indeed, the main effect of Mr Lindsay's argument is to remove from Marx's doctrine that element of eccentricity which was thought to distinguish it and which made it influential.

However, this is only one part of the project. The main body of the book is devoted to showing the fruitfulness of this concept of dialectical unity when it is applied to biology, psychology, anthropology, and the study of history. But, though the reader is not spared the technicalities of these sciences and is provided with many impressive lists of names and many quotations, he will not escape the suspicion that what he is being offered is not a 'critical examination of Marxist dialectics in the light of contemporary science,' but merely an account of some recent scientific enterprises in respect of their adherence to or departure from the 'unitary principle.' This is the touchstone: and, for example, Lysenko's 'genetics' seem to be approved because they adhere to this principle, and all the three schools of psychologists whose doctrines are considered are disapproved because their doctrines depart from it. And if we ask what is the authority of this principle, we are told only that it is the great discovery of Marx and that the future of Marxism lies in its elaboration and application. What is attractive about this book is Mr Lindsay's determination to be critical as well as loyal to Marxism and to seek the value in the work of others of a different persuasion. He is not a writer who helps his readers along with a clearly stated argument, but as a contribution to the now extensive library of works on 'What Marx really meant' the book has the merits of subtlety and fair-mindedness.

Ninety-one

The Origins of Modern Science

What is the activity to which we have come to give the name 'science'? That it is an important human activity, and that, while preserving a general direction for more than 2,000 years, it is an activity which in recent centuries has taken on a more precise character nobody doubts; but our question still admits of many different answers. The most general (but not the least ambiguous) description of the activity is, perhaps, 'getting to know more about ourselves and the world we inhabit'; we always know *something*, we begin with knowledge of a sort and not with mere ignorance, and the project of the scientist is to get to know more. 'The Beautiful Bosom of *Nature* will be Expos'd to our view,' says Spratt in his elaborate way; 'we shall enter into its Garden, and taste its *Fruits*, and satisfy ourselves with its plenty: instead of Idle talking and wandering under its fruitless shadows.' Obtuseness, if not ignorance, is the inheritance of mankind; the book of Nature lies open before us, our eyes travel over its pages, but to interpret what we read is a task requiring application and discipline: the aim of science is 'to repair the ruin of our first parents.'

More philosophically, the enterprise may be represented as the search for the causes of what appears before us, and the reward is the reputed happiness of those who understand, not merely things, but the manner in which things are generated. Or again, when the inquiry has been on foot for some time and a body of instructed opinion has emerged, the positivist may content himself with the view that the aim in science is to say something about the world which is convincing to the recognized experts in the matter, instructed opinion appearing as a kind of handy emblem of 'truth.'

Every man, it may be supposed, has his own private 'physiology,' and it becomes scientific when it ceases to be eccentric and is capable of convincing those whose opinion matters. Or, to make an end of examples, the activity in science may be conceived as the attempt to derive from our

---

Review of Herbert Butterfield, *The Origins of Modern Science, 1300–1800* (London: Bell and Sons, 1949). First published in *Times Literary Supplement* (25 November 1949), 761–3.

manifold experience of the world a body of knowledge which is in the highest degree communicable, not resting upon the personal idiosyncrasies of the individual scientist, but based upon the sure foundation of measurement and expressed in the impersonal language of mathematics. But if this last view of the matter is one which the contemplation of the modern history of science encourages, we should not require a historian of science to commit himself to it. Gibbon claimed to have 'described the triumph of barbarism and of religion', but he made no claim to a philosophical definition of his subject; and the historian of science is not required to have decided upon a philosophy of science before he sits down to write. And yet, he must have an eye that sees below the surface, and a standpoint from which he can look down upon the activity whose fortunes he is recording — a standpoint from which those moments of self-consciousness that have occasionally overtaken the activity are seen as part of the history itself.

Perhaps the only, certainly the chief, conceptual qualification this historian needs is the vision of scientific activity, not as a mere series of discoveries and inventions, not even as a body of knowledge, but as a manner of thinking, as a ceaseless flow of hypotheses, as the perpetual reconstruction (in whole or in part) of our experience of the world. And his enterprise will be to trace the fortunes of this manner of thinking, to disclose its character as it comes to the surface, to discover the springs of its inspiration, to reveal the subtle mediations whereby one great hypothesis succeeds another, to investigate the effect of this activity upon a society or a civilization, and then (if he is a Ranke) to consider it in the context of human activity at large — and in all this using the discoveries of science, the 'achievements,' the formulations, as mirrors in which to catch the reflection of the manner of thinking which is the true subject of his history.

Every reader has his own preferences, and he is gratified when a history of the sort he finds agreeable comes his way. But it must be understood that what is being asked for here is not a history of science of a certain sort, but for the story of the part played by science in western civilization to be treated in a genuinely historical manner. This story has had its annalists and chroniclers; the great figures and the momentous occasions in it have long ago been made familiar to us; but history only begins where chronicles leave off. And even when a writer has undertaken to endow the story with a semblance of organization, when he has not left the scale of his figures and occasions to chance, he has too often read the story backwards, finding significant in the past only that which led subsequently to positive achievement: the lost causes, the 'failures,' the unsuccessful attempts, the dead-ends have been crowded out of a story which has thus acquired the appearance of altogether unnatural 'success.' Such a writer may not lack learning in detail, and he may come to his task with enthusiasm and disinterestedness; but he is not a historian. And if it is a simple, indeed an obvious, virtue, and one that should not require remark, it is nevertheless the first and greatest virtue of Professor Butterfield's lectures on *The Origins of Modern Science* that they are informed with genuine and profound historical thinking. He has added something to our knowledge in detail, he has added more to our insight, and he has given scale and proportion, hitherto lacking, to one of the most important periods in the history of science. And he has begun to measure the potentialities in the history of science to transform our whole view of the history of western European civilization. But if, in addition to all this, his book were to persuade those who have control of this comparatively new study in our universities that the history of science should be in the hands of men who are genuine historians, it will have performed a timely service.

Professor Butterfield's theme is the coming into being of *modern* science. In the abridgements of history with which we have long had to content ourselves we have been taught that modern science is the creation of an intellectual revolution which took place in the sixteenth and seventeenth centuries; in these centuries our backward-looking historians found what they were looking for—the beginning of those methods and discoveries which have since established themselves. In history, of course, there are no absolute origins; but when the history of science ceases to be thought of as a history of discoveries, and when (with a more genuinely historical impulse) we allow our minds to proceed forward and not backward, the sixteenth and seventeenth centuries, while losing nothing of their importance, lose their appearance of being even that kind of plausible and empirical starting-place which a historian looks for. 'Modern history,' said Lord Acton, 'tells how the last four hundred years have modified the medieval conditions of life and thought'; and this is not less true in the history of science than elsewhere.

That a great revolution did take place, that its main outline emerged unmistakeably in the sixteenth and seventeenth centuries, remains true. And Professor Butterfield is not afraid to affirm it unequivocally. For him it is a revolution which 'outshines anything since the rise of Christianity and reduces the Renaissance and the Reformation to the rank of mere episodes, mere internal displacements, within the system of medieval Christendom.' It represents 'one of the great episodes in human experience.' And even to the historian (who must always be suspicious of the apparent newness of the new) it seems to possess a novelty not easily accounted for: 'there does not seem any sign that the ancient world, before its heritage had been dispersed, was moving towards anything like the scientific revolution, or that the Byzantine Empire, in spite of the continuity of its classical tradition, would ever have taken hold of ancient thought and remoulded it by a great transforming power.' But the roots of this revolution lie in a more remote past, lie deep in the Middle Ages. When the history of modern science is considered as the history of a characteristic manner of thinking, and not as a series of observations and discoveries, it is seen to spring up within an earlier manner of thinking and to derive its initial significance from the soil that nurtured it. To trace the slowly mediated changes which transformed medieval science into the science of the age of Newton is the first and most difficult task of the historian of modern science, and it is to this task that these lectures are addressed.

Modern science had a difficult birth. And when one casts around to account for this difficulty, the explanation seems to lie, not in any natural conservatism of the medieval mind, nor in any supposed deadening effect of ecclesiastical authority, but in the remarkable fact that the men of the Middle Ages found themselves endowed with an explanation of the physical universe which they had not won by the exercise of their own faculties, but had acquired as part of an authoritative bequest from an already defunct civilization. What a man has invented for himself he will be ready to criticize and to reconstruct, first in detail and then perhaps more radically, because he is aware at least of the incoherences that are merely covered up; but he lacks a similar command over what he has acquired ready-made. And because his understanding of it is inferior, his hold on it must be more tenacious. Yet the authority of Aristotelian physics in the Middle Ages seems to have been obliquely acquired; it is at least probable that had not Aristotle already been established as a master in logic, his authority in science (when his physics came to light) would have been less absolute. But what made Aristotelian physics a hurdle to be surmounted, something to be 'overthrown' before modern science could gather impetus, was as much a habit of mind as the inherent attractiveness of the Aristotelian synthesis. And here a reader would like to have found in Professor Butterfield's account some treatment of that manner of education which promoted and prolonged the life of this habit of mind: it was not so much the initial loss and slow recovery of Greek science which impeded the progress of scientific investigation in the Middle Ages, as the inheritance of that restricted ideal of education which had taken hold of the Greco-Roman world before the invasions.

But the chief task of the historian of the emergence of modern science is to show the manner in which the Aristotelian synthesis came to be broken down, and Professor Butterfield's account of it is fascinating. The progress of science, at this point as at many others, is shown to spring, not from any fresh observations of the world, but from the detection of the weak points in a prevailing hypothesis and from an effort to repair the weakness. Every scientist now knows that observation by itself, experiment and the conclusions from experiment, are never the starting-point of advance, and are never in themselves authoritative; but this seems also to have been appreciated in the early days of modern science: Galileo was in no doubt about it. There are in every great hypothesis elements of marginal coherence, and it is the part of the great scientist to seize upon these and to use them as a lever to prise open the entire system. It was Aristotle's unsatisfactory account of the movement of projectiles and the acceleration of falling bodies which made room for the development of that theory of impetus which in the end transformed physics. And it was similar cracks in the system of Ptolemy which gave a handle to the speculations of Copernicus.

In conceiving that his task as an historian is to show how great thinkers —a Copernicus, a Galileo, a Harvey, a Newton or a Lavoisier—'operated on the margin of contemporary thought' Professor Butterfield has lifted the history of science to a new and higher level. It was, perhaps, unavoidable (in this, after all, brief treatment of the history of modern science, which concentrates upon 'lines of strategic change,') that Aristotle should appear always as an enemy, as somebody to be 'overthrown', to be 'destroyed', but it is difficult to avoid the feeling that an even firmer hold upon the historian's task of providing the continuity, of revealing the mediations of change in all their detail, would result in a shift of emphasis, a translation of a negative into its positive, which would have freed this history from what appears to be a last relic of the technique of the backward look. Just as it is only from an imperfectly achieved historical outlook that Roundhead and Cavalier remain mere enemies, or that astrology is seen as merely the foe of scientific astronomy, so it is only in an abridgment that Aristotle can appear as the mere opponent of modern science.

Events as they actually happen and things as they exist have a subtlety, an absence of absoluteness, a dilution, which the historian must always be on the *qui vive* to catch. And while Professor Butterfield lays firm hold upon this conception of the science of any age as a systematic whole of hypotheses capable of indefinite expansion, he performs one of the essential offices of the historian in making his readers perceive that it is only an unfortunate abridgment which gives fixity to a system such as that of Ptolemy or of Newton. Not only are there incoherences upon the margin of every system which offer a hand-hold to the critic and which qualify the whole, but also it rarely happens that the system as it appears written down in a book corresponds to what is in the mind of its author or to what this author is understood by others to have taught. The mind, even the common mind, is always in motion; and the progress of science is not so much the replacement of one fixed or finished system by another which demands an equally unqualified attachment, as the supersession of a flowing, or at least a gyrating, nucleus of ideas by another of the same sort but different in detail. And the great change appears not when one rigid system gets the better of another but when the hidden thought of a system collapses under criticism, and the mind is set free to construct a new hypothesis with regard to the skies, the human body, the chemical composition of things, whatever it may be.

And when we have learned this elementary lesson we are ready to follow the historian as he detects the significance of the work of a scientist, not in the system he created but in the impetus he imparted to the enterprise of scientific thinking. Copernicus, no doubt, had a system; but his great influence upon the progress of science lay not in his system 'but in the stimulus he gave to men who in reality were producing something very different.' And the significance of the early and abortive self-consciousness which the scientific enterprise achieved in the work of Francis Bacon lies not in the Baconian system itself (which taken literally had greater potentialities of damaging than of advancing the enterprise) but in the piecemeal inspiration which he offered to the scientists of his time. Professor Butterfield is an austere and disciplined thinker; he scarcely needs to command his companions to bind him to the mast when the ship comes within earshot of the Sirens. And it is one of the great merits of this work that he has managed to steer a course which avoids on the one hand the merely biographical treatment of the story of modern science and on the other hand a treatment which would turn the story into a history of the rise and fall of systems.

We are apt to suppose that courage is a virtue more appropriate to a life of action than to one of intellect, but nothing is more damaging to the work of an historian than its absence. It is the main ingredient of the power to recognize a great occasion, and a historian without this power is a historian without style or significance. But history is the enemy of the lonely great, the strange and the unexpected, in persons as well as in events; and to the courage of recognition the historian must add a mole-like investigation of the composition and structure of the great occasion. Anyone (or almost anyone) can compose a story by leaping from peak to peak; so long as he does not lose his momentum he will retain his balance; but it will be an exiguous performance, in which the significance of even the peaks is lost. It is not merely one part of the task of the historian to descend into the valleys and to provide 'continuity'; it is the whole of his task from one point of view. For the 'continuity' is not something added to a story whose main lines are already fixed; it is the story itself of which the main lines are only an abridgment. And in providing the continuity the historian performs his office of interpretation, an office which the history of science is in great need of at the present time. This continuity may be found in the study of the work of that host of obscure scientific investigators who fill in the intervals between the men of genius.

As Professor Butterfield points out, it is from a study of this sort that some of the most remarkable reversals of judgment in the history of science have sprung during the last fifty years. Galileo, Kepler, Harvey remain figures of supreme importance, but they are no longer isolated, and their ideas are no longer, what they once appeared, ideas without pedigree. But, further, the historian will find himself pressed down to a level where even the names of the obscure disappear from the story.

It is never easy — if it is possible at all — to feel that one has reached the bottom of a matter (says Professor Butterfield), or touched the last limit of explanation, when dealing with an historical transition. It would appear the most fundamental changes in outlook, the most remarkable turns in the current of intellectual fashion, may be referable in the last resort to an alteration in men's feeling for things, an alteration at once so subtle and so generally pervasive that it cannot be attributed to any particular writers or any influence of academic thought as such. When at the beginning of the sixteenth century an Englishman could write concerning the clergy that it was scandalous to see half the king's subjects evading their proper allegiance to the crown — escaping the law of the land — we know that he was registering a change in the feeling men had for the territorial state, a change more significant in that people were unconscious of the fact that anything novel had been taking place. Subtle changes like this — the result not of any book but of the new texture of human experience in a new age — are apparent behind the story of the scientific revolution, a revolution which some have tried to explain by a change in men's feeling for matter itself.

Science is an activity which seems to have gained something from the mere lapse of time. This is seen to be so when, as so often happens, the conning over of ideas and observations long familiar blossoms into a new and fruitful hypothesis. But the lapse of time is perhaps most significant in the formation of what may be called a scientific opinion. Science can scarcely be said to exist where this is absent, and it has always flourished most conspicuously where such an opinion has been most lively and firmly established: the lack of it still impedes the social sciences. If science proceeded to a predetermined end, the existence of a body of scientific opinion would be less necessary; the end itself would offer the needed criticism of the current achievement. But it does not proceed in this manner, and the possibility of distinguishing between the charlatan or the eccentric and the expert depends upon the establishment of recognized scientific standards. The great contribution of the University of Padua to the scientific revolution sprang not only from the fact that circumstances combined to establish in Padua a peculiar freedom of thought, nor merely because the variety of scientific investigation which was being carried on there in the fifteenth and sixteenth centuries provided the kind of cross-fertilization among the sciences which has so often been the source of advance, but also because there gradually came into existence common practices of research and a recognized body of scientific opinion. For this scientific opinion is not an orthodoxy of doctrine, which may easily stifle the growth of new hypothesis: it is a fellowship of scientists, and consists in recognized standards and procedures of inquiry and traditions of research which cut across the different sciences and give the individual investigator a sense of support which he would otherwise lack.

In England the Royal Society did much to promote a scientific opinion of this sort; and the fact that by the end of the seventeenth century something like a common scientific opinion had come to establish itself in western Europe is perhaps the best evidence that the scientific revolution had by then passed its critical point. Nevertheless, recession is not impossible. The appeal against the opinion of the learned which is implicit in the use of the vernacular by Galileo and Descartes is understandable in the circumstances, and even the appeal of the *philosophes* to the middle classes may be regarded as an appeal from learning to intelligence; but it is not as easy to take so indulgent a view of the current confusion of political and scientific opinion in which much that has been so gradually built up seems in danger of being lost.

Professor Butterfield is concerned solely with science in the strict sense, as a manner of thinking and as a flow of hypotheses about the physical world. The history of technology, of the use men have made of scientific discoveries, is outside his theme; and since he does not mention it even to exclude it, we may suppose that it was not mere lack of space which imposed this self-limitation. It is a limitation which goes somewhat against the current view of the history of science, but most readers will agree that he has made it a convincing limitation, and that here, as elsewhere, he has struck out on a new and promising path.

Nevertheless, Professor Butterfield refuses to isolate the history of science. 'The history of science', he says, 'ought not merely to exist by itself in a separate pocket.' He is very properly critical of the notion that the historian can assign to the scientific revolution any precise 'results'. Great changes were afoot in the eighteenth century, but for the historian 'the hazard consists not in putting all these things together and rolling them into one great bundle of complex change, but in thinking that one knows how to disentangle them—what we see is the total intricate network of changes, and it is difficult to say that any one of these was the single result of the scientific revolution itself.' But when the products of scientific activity percolated down to the level of the common mind they became translated (often somewhat precipitately and usually by men who were not themselves scientists) into a new world-view: the *philosophes* of the eighteenth century were among the first to take a hand in this translation. And this new outlook as it became disseminated must be counted as one of the more important of the assignable results of the scientific revolution. This convergence of the history of European science upon the history of *moeurs* is a testing theme for an historian, and Professor Butterfield is probably wise to confine himself to a general treatment in which the relations between science and politics receive most of his attention. And yet it is disappointing to find that he has so little to say about the impact of the scientific revolution, not merely upon what may be called popular cosmology, but upon the current myth of human life and upon religion. And it is disappointing to find that what he has to say is all on one side, is designed to impress as with the loudness of the voice of science at the end of his period.

The seventeenth century did not merely bring a new factor into history, in the way we often assume. The new factor immediately began to elbow at the other ones, pushing them out of their place—and, indeed, began immediately to seek control of the rest, as the apostles of the new movement had declared their intention of doing from the very start.

All this, of course, is undeniably true: but it is not the whole story. The scientific revolution did not in fact succeed in shouting down the voices of religion and poetry, and its repercussions in the minds of men such as Pascal, Lichtenberg, Blake, and Goethe (to choose representatives to illustrate the variety of the rebound) are a significant part of the history of the impact of the scientific revolution upon European society.

Ninety-two

The Coming Defeat of Communism

To be clear-sighted in one's attitude to Communism is difficult alike for the believer and for the opponent. The believer adheres to a theory and a political programme, the one often obscure except to the eye of faith, the other dynamic but suicidal except for the few who may come out on top; and in spite of the constant efforts of acute thinkers, the theory and the programme are always on the point of falling apart.

The opponent, on the other hand, if he is to be clear-sighted, needs to know exactly what he is opposing: and this is difficult for an Englishman or an American, though it is not at all difficult for an enslaved Czech or a Pole.

It is easier for us to be either hysterical about Communism, or (like the BBC) to be ridiculously naïve.

Mr James Burnham, a distinguished American writer on politics, has written a book which, if it does nothing else, should help us to understand the precise threat to our way of life which is comprehensively indicated in the word 'Communism'.

Up to about 1939 it was possible to become and be a Communist in this country from a variety of motives, none of them entirely foolish or deplorable.

The Russian Revolution, like the French, could appear as the dawn of a glad day. And in the time of Hitler's rise or the Spanish Civil War one might join the party out of the generous impulse to side with the downtrodden; though many who did so were quickly revolted by the crooked thinking and subterfuge which comprised its theory and practice.

Review of James Burnham, *The Coming Defeat of Communism* (London: Cape, 1950). First published in *Evening Standard* (20 November 1950) as 'Stalin's Four Weak Points', headed: 'MAN WHO TOOK LASKI'S JOB ATTACKS THE COMMUNISTS. At the London School of Economics, a new professor occupies the chair of political science formerly held by Left Wing propagandist Harold Laski. His name: Michael Oakeshott. In this article for the *Evening Standard* he examines a new book which gives an American's answer to the question: Can we halt Russia without war?'

This situation belongs to the past.

The 'intellectual' or the 'emotional' Communist continues to exist, but what was once generosity has degenerated into sentimentality, and the demand for self-deception increases every year. This 'Communism', however, cannot be counted any greater menace than a hundred other pieces of foolishness.

'Communism' now is seen to stand for something else; it stands for the subjugation of the world, including the peoples of Russia, to the oligarchy which rules in Moscow.

The Communists who are significant are those who comprise this oligarchy and its agents all over the world and (in those places which are subject to the immediate pressure of Russian armed power) those who from fear or an eye to the main chance wish to be beforehand in their allegiance to their supposed future masters.

THE TYRANTS

To join the party is now to side with the tyrants.

In short, 'Communism' is a menace because it represents Russian imperialism.

And one does not need to be hysterical, the victim of a scare or to be heedless of other threats, in order to see this as a significant threat to what we regard as a civilized way of living.

In recent years several writers have come forward to advise the government of the U.S.A. on its policy in relation to Russia, and certainly Mr Burnham is more level-headed than most.

His criticism of present American policy is that it is purely defensive and that it lacks precision.

Great energy is now being displayed in military preparations to avoid defeat in a war with Russia, but he thinks that less is being done than might be done to defeat Russian imperialist designs without a war.

There is the Voice of America and there is the Marshall Plan, but the precise objectives of the opponents of Russian imperialism are not clearly thought out, and the readiest and most economical means are not being made use of.

There are some people (mostly Americans) who see the objective as the establishment of what they call a world democratic order: the only defeat of Russian Communism they recognise is the substitution for it of a political ideology of their own.

Mr Burnham does not take this view. 'Democracy' for him is a matter of degree. And we do not have to be confident that we possess the best possible institutions in order to oppose Russian Communism: all we need to know is that Russian Communism is a threat to much of what we value supremely.

Consequently, our objective must be precisely to remove that menace, and to remove it without a war.

And since the menace must remain so long as the present oligarchy is in power in Russia, our aim must be to assist in overthrowing that oligarchy by working upon the weaknesses of the regime.

The present Russian Empire, though strong, suffers from four principal weaknesses.

The great masses of the Russian people are themselves the mentally and physically enslaved victims of their government: no one of the satellite peoples composing the empire is 'reliable': the Russian government must sustain a rhythm of conquest or confess itself defeated: and there is always the liability to the sort of defection now known as Titoism.

THE ATTACK

In a series of chapters, the best of which is called the 'propaganda attack', Mr Burnham examines what he believes to be the best ways of working on these weaknesses.

He does not suppose that the Russian oligarchy can be overthrown by a spontaneous revolt—the crack must come from within the party. His aim is to enlist every possible ally inside and outside Russia, and his advice is to be unrelenting and absolutely consistent in our opposition to the oligarchy.

He considers that we are unduly nervous of provoking Russia to a shooting war. And since his object is not to destroy either Russia or 'Communism', but to remove the menace of Russian imperialism, he sees the greatest hope in Titoism—Communism-inspired defections within the Russian empire.

As a political prophet Mr Burnham has not been remarkably successful in the past: he has often shown a tendency to believe that things must go on in the way they seemed to be going when he took a look at them.

LISTEN TO HIM!

The significance of his book does not, however, lie in its assessment of the future intentions of Russian policy, but in its exploration of the most economical and most effective methods of defeating manifest Russian imperialist activities.

Some people (but without much justification) will think that he exaggerates the menace, but what makes him a writer worth listening to is his great knowledge of the theory and practice of Communism and the fact that he cannot be mistaken for a mere spokesman of American imperialism.

Ninety-three

Cambridge Conversations

It argues uncommon courage to write a book in that most difficult of all literary forms, the conversation. Success here depends upon a rare combination of imagination, flexibility of mind, and sense of character; failure can be dismal. Mr Watmough, moreover, has been bold enough to dispense with a central voice in his dialogues; there are eight speakers (six men and two women), none of whom is represented as much wiser or more in command of the situation than any other. The result is, in general, agreeable without being profound, and readable without being highly stimulating. Unfortunately it is conversation without dialectic.

The speakers in these conversations are Cambridge undergraduates — inquiring minds, but rather portentous in their seriousness. Each has a fairly clearly defined position, though none appears properly as a character. There is a high-church Tory reading history, a Liberal Nonconformist reading English literature, a proletarian Anglo-Catholic reading theology, a Socialist reading classics, and an Atheist-Communist reading economics. Of the two girls, one is reading modern languages and the other is an Anarchist reading biology — both are pretty earnest. One could wish that they had been revealed more fully as characters and less as mouthpieces of, on the whole, stereotyped points of view, so that after one or two sessions one knows roughly what each is going to say before he or she says it.

They have six meetings, each devoted to a particular topic or group of related topics. The first is entitled 'the merits of the law', and comes as an agreeable surprise. There are in fact few better entrances to the study of our civilization than that afforded by the law, and it is an entrance too seldom used. Like most of the other conversations in this book, this one does not get very far. One is not disappointed because it fails to reach conclusions, but because it ranges the subject at only a superficial level. However, it has something to say, and it goes smoothly. It is succeeded by sessions at which the problems of education, the forms of government

---

Review of Joseph Ronald Watmough, *Cambridge Conversations* (Cambridge: Bowes, 1949). First published in *Cambridge Journal*, 3 (1950), 312–13.

(and some other political topics), the subjects of university study, some moral problems (marriage, celibacy, suicide, etc.) and religion are successively discussed. There is a certain primness about the whole performance; wit is absent, there are no practical jokes, and the talk rarely rises above the commonplace. But the conversation is certainly what Dr Johnson would have called 'solid'. One's disappointment is greatest on the occasions when a speaker makes a remark which might have opened up a discussion at a more profound level, but the opportunity is missed because the characters speak so much in the idiom of their prearranged points of view. For example, the earnest Socialist says of Rugby football that 'I think it is an exciting game to watch and a powerful factor in the development of personality, but at the same time I think there is something irrational about it. I have known many accidents arise from Rugby — when I was at school, a term never passed without three or four cases of broken legs or broken collar-bones. A boy might sometimes have to remain at home for six weeks under medical care before he was fit to return. Think of the expense and trouble to his parents; think too of the retarding effect on his academic progress — all for the sake of a couple of hours "sport"!' And the only reply the high-church Tory can think of is: 'Nobody worries much about that. It is all for the good of the side, you know. Most people consider it a form of heroism.' This, from a people that (nurtured not upon oriental indifference or upon a stoic philosophy, but upon a tradition of 'nerve') has achieved a combination of love of life and indifference to injury and death more profoundly balanced than any other. Readers of this journal will note the reference to the 'Baldwin Confession' (as an example of political duplicity) which appears on p. 73 of this book.

Ninety-four

The English Utilitarians

There have been many studies of that school of political and philosophical writers who are known as the Utilitarians, and there have been many much more elaborate than this one — but I have never read one which was more to the point or one that went to the heart of the matter so simply and directly. Mr Plamenatz is concerned with what he justifiably takes to be the chief contribution of English thought to moral and political philosophy, and therefore worth study. But Utilitarianism is not so much a cut and dried doctrine as, in the first place, an attitude towards the problems of moral and political philosophy; and writers who are as diverse in doctrine as Hobbes, Hume and J.S. Mill (for example) may be seen to share this attitude. But further, Utilitarianism is a set of beliefs — but here it is difficult to find any one writer who holds them all or any writer in whom these beliefs are not contaminated by other, often inconsistent, beliefs. Mr Plamenatz formulates these beliefs in four propositions — not with the object of making Utilitarianism an exceedingly narrow and exclusive philosophy and of showing how few of the Utilitarians hold to it consistently, but in order to include all that might fairly expect to find a place. There is plenty of close argument in this book, and the author insists upon many fine distinctions; but there is nothing illiberal or piddling in his attitude. Having got clear the outline of the doctrine to be considered, he embarks upon a series of chapters on Hobbes, Locke, Hume, Bentham, James Mill, and J.S. Mill, with briefer studies of the ideas of others, such as Helvétius, Paley, Burke, Paine, Godwin and the 'classical economists'. The purpose of each of these studies is to determine the quality and individual character of each of these writers as an exponent of Utilitarianism. At the end of the volume is reprinted J.S. Mill's essay 'Utilitarianism', not because it is the least ambiguous or most mature statement of the doctrine, but because he considers that a study of its 'confusions and errors' is profitable in a

---

Review of John Plamenatz, *The English Utilitarians* (Oxford: Blackwell, 1949). First published in *Cambridge Journal*, 3 (1950), 312–13.

way in which (for example) a close study of Bentham's tangled argument is not.

This work is concerned with the history of ideas, but it should be pointed out that Mr Plamenatz is not at all interested in what Acton called the 'pedigree of ideas'. We are shown the fortunes of an attitude and a doctrine over a long period of tine, but the mediation of the changes is not anywhere examined. For the historian the main value of this work is the clarity it gives to the conceptual skeleton of Utilitarianism, and in doing this it performs an exceedingly valuable service. In detail, Mr Plamenatz has much that is his own to say, and he says it so lucidly and economically and with such fair-minded consideration and moderation that one learns even where one disagrees. Most of the writers he examines were careless and often confused: to try to understand them is usually to try to determine what they probably meant, and here Mr Plamenatz is a patient and acute guide. And most readers will, I think, be grateful for the comments on matters of political and philosophical interest which are handed out on the way; they are all very much to the point and many of them are profound observations. In short, this book supersedes everything that has been written on this scale on the subject, and, though it unaccountably stops short of Sidgwick, is as comprehensive as one could expect.

Ninety-five

John Locke's Political Philosophy

Mr. J.W. Gough has collected together eight essays, only one of which has been previously published. Between them (and with some unavoidable overlapping) they discuss the main features of Locke's political philosophy. The method of treatment neatly circumvents some of the difficulties which a sustained exposition would encounter, but it is not adopted by Mr Gough merely in order to avoid the labour of a continuous argument: it reflects a point of view which (apart from some points of detail and some novelties based upon the investigation of some unpublished writings of Locke) is the main interest of the book. What is it that holds together Locke's various views and opinions? The view has got about that, in spite of appearances, Locke's Second Treatise on Government should be regarded as a logically coherent argument, as a political philosophy unfolded in a manner which frees it from the exigencies of time and place and gives it a universal cogency. And, on the other hand, the work has been held to be nothing more than a *pièce d'occasion*. Mr Gough's contention is that we are not forced, and that it would be unwise, to choose either of these extreme alternatives. The value of Locke's work is that it states, in abstract terms, what were generally recognized to be the realities of English constitutional practice: it is less than a philosophy of politics, but it is more than a mere defence of a single moment in the English constitutional tradition. Consequently the recent investigations which have tended to detract from Locke's originality do nothing to shake the real value of what he wrote. The Second Treatise survived and owed its tremendous influence in England to the fact that it was the most cogent and level-headed exposition of what most people believed. With this approach, Mr Gough says a great deal worth saying, and says it economically and lucidly. And if, from the point of view adopted, there is any misdirection of emphasis in these essays, it is perhaps a failure to give proper weight to Locke's debt,

---

Review of John Wiedhofft Gough, *John Locke's Political Philosophy* (Oxford: Clarendon Press, 1950). First published in *English Historical Review*, 65 (1950), 550.

not only to the general outline, but also to some of the more recondite details, of the current Christian myth of politics. For example, private property antedates civil society for Locke because it sprang directly from the Fall (man *had* to work and labour creates property); civil society appeared only with Nimrod, many years after.

Ninety-six

Patriarcha

Blackwell's Political Texts aim, in general, at reprinting, with a suitable introduction and perhaps some notes, some of the more notable political writings. But on this occasion something further has been added – an edition of a seventeenth-century English writer which gives for the first time a satisfactory and reliable text. It is well known that Filmer's *Patriarcha* was not printed until many years after it was written, but that it had circulated in a number of manuscript copies among Filmer's acquaintance. It was printed on three occasions in the late seventeenth century; the first two editions (in 1680) deriving from corrupt and imperfect manuscripts, and the third (1685) less corrupt but far from satisfactory. The only other edition was that of 1884 in which the editor reproduced one of the editions of 1680. Mr Laslett, however, was fortunate enough to have discovered in the Filmer family papers a manuscript (now in the Cambridge University Library) which gave a far more authentic text than had yet been published: it is this text which is printed here, with the useful addition, at the foot of the page, of the references which Filmer omitted to give for some of his quotations. It is an admirable and important piece of work, and Mr Laslett is to be congratulated both on his good luck and on the use he has made of it. The other political writings of Filmer which are reprinted presented no such textual problems, but since most of them are available only in seventeenth-century editions, it is valuable to have them here.

If this were all, Mr Laslett would have put us deeply in his debt; but it is not all. In some forty pages of introduction he has given us the most intelligent account of Filmer and his ideas that has yet appeared. There is a brief account of the results of his considerable researches into the life of Filmer, which is followed by an admirably concise statement of the argument of *Patriarcha* and its place in the political controversies of the seventeenth

---

Review of Robert Filmer, *Patriarcha and Other Political Works*, ed. Peter Laslett. (Oxford: Blackwell, 1949). First published in *Philosophy*, 25 (1950), 280–1. Oakeshott also reviewed Filmer, *Patriarcha*, in *Cambridge Journal*, 3 (1950), 384.

century. But the most notable part of the introduction is that in which Mr Laslett deals with the place and significance of Patriarchalism generally in seventeenth-century thinking. Nobody (least of all Mr Laslett) will contend that Filmer was a powerful and impressive abstract thinker. But in this introduction he is given his correct and not insignificant place as 'the codifier of conscious and unconscious prejudice' and as an opponent of the way things were going in his day whose archaic method of argument concealed something which we, even more than his contemporaries, can understand to be worth considering.

Ninety-seven

The Concept of Mind

The hypothesis that every human being has a body and a mind (or is both body and mind) has presented philosophers with the problem of relationship and the intercourse between these two supposedly different (though in some accounts not wholly dissimilar) things. It is this hypothesis and this problem which, perhaps more than anything else, distinguishes modern from ancient philosophy; for the last four centuries they have dominated philosophical speculation. Professor Ryle is dissatisfied, not with the current solution of the problem, but with the hypothesis itself; the errors of the answers are of little account when the question is misconceived.

He is not, of course, the first to have this dissatisfaction; anyone brought upon on Greek philosophy might be expected to be critical of the hypothesis. But what he gives us here is an exceedingly acute analysis of his dissatisfaction and an identification of the kind of error which he thinks the mind-body hypothesis represents. According to his account of it, it is a category-mistake. 'It represents the facts of mental life as if they belonged to one logical type, when they actually belong to another.' Mind is represented as a kind of ghostly body, and to think of it in this manner is to make the same mistake as that of a man who thought of the 'British Constitution' as a parallel institution to the Home Office or the Church of England.

Professor Ryle's view is that, generally speaking, we know without having to be philosophers how to use and apply the ordinary 'mental-conduct' concepts (like will, emotion, imagination), but we often make grave mistakes when we classify them and put them into logical categories. And he writes in order to correct some of these mistakes. In general his doctrine is that 'when we describe people as exercising qualities of mind, we are not referring to occult episodes of which their overt acts and utterances are effects: we are referring to those overt acts and utterances themselves.' Mental activity is not the activity of a 'mind,' or activity which takes place in the hidden recesses of a mind, in distinction from the activity of a body: it is doing and saying things in a particular manner.

Review of Gilbert Ryle, *The Concept of Mind* (London: Hutchinson, 1949). First published in *Spectator*, 184 (1950), 20, 22.

Towards the end Professor Ryle remarks that 'the general trend of this book will undoubtedly, and harmlessly, be stigmatised as "behaviourist"'. Nevertheless he is not concerned with Behaviourism as a psychological technique. His book is not an attempt to give new information about the mind, but to consider the logic of mental concepts. It is a contribution to philosophy rather than psychology, though the acceptance of his doctrine would have some repercussions on psychological investigation.

It is impossible to give here any proper impression of the range and subtlety of Professor Ryle's argument, or to examine any of its parts. The reader, even if he is not in agreement with the doctrine propounded, will recognise before he is half way through that this is a piece of philosophical writing in the highest class. Philosophers will certainly find it an important 'contribution'. Among much else, the criticism of the whole 'sense datum theory' is something that has long needed to be said. But the book is more than a 'contribution': it has something of the vitality and the power of standing on its own feet which belong to the philosophical classic. What distinguishes a classic in philosophy is (among other things) its fitness to be put into the hands of a beginner; and while the beginner might soon find himself here out of his depth, it would not be on account of specific ignorance but because of lack of practice, a handicap which reading this book would greatly reduce.

Professor Ryle is sparing in his references to other writers; he is concerned with arguments not personalities. And though he half apologises for the polemical tone of the book, it seems to me peculiarly free from excess in this respect. The chief critical argument in his armoury is the *reductio ad absurdum*, the demonstration that if we take a certain view we have committed ourselves to an endless and profitless regress. But perhaps the most obvious characteristic of his manner of writing is the abounding wealth of analogy with which he illustrates his arguments.

This is at once a source of strength and a danger in a philosophical writer. While it certainly contributes to understanding, the reader is apt to think he understands the argument when all has done is to appreciate the analogy. Not until each analogy has been examined with care can we be certain that we are not being misled. I think the elaborate analogy on pp. 289–290 is misleading; the difference between the farmer making a path and the philosopher making a theory is that, while the stages of path-making are successive contributions to a final result, each stage in theory-making is itself a complete theory. I do not quite understand the confidence with which the expression 'the physical world' is used throughout the book; and there is perhaps an unfortunate abridgement in the description of what is called idealism as 'the "reduction" of the material world to mental states and processes.'

Ninety-eight

Tell Me the Next One

There are dreams that are pleasant and dreams that are potentially profitable. Any man of sense prefers the former; they can be enjoyed for the pleasure they give. But if the latter came, a man (I suppose) may be excused when he wants to tell us about them. He should, however, remember that it is easier to be boring about dreams than about anything else – even family photographs. This is an account of the circumstances in which Mr Godley had revealed to him, in a series of dreams which came to him at intervals during a period of three years, the winners of eight horse-races, to which is added a tentative 'explanation' of the experience. The dreams did not all take the same form; on three occasions Mr Godley saw in his dream a page in the newspaper giving the results of the races, on one occasion he dreamed he saw the race itself and recognised the winner by the jockey's colours, once he dreamed he heard the result of the race broadcast, and once he dreamed that he was told the name of the winner by his bookmaker on the telephone. On three occasions his dream revealed, not the name of the winner, but a name near enough to one of the horses engaged (Tubermore for Tuberose) to make him feel fairly confident. But twice his dreams let him down, once giving him an unplaced horse and once a horse that ran third. His bets gave him a net profit of £126 14s. 7d.

Mr Godley, unfortunately, is a dull man and a not very skilled writer; he is rather portentous about it all. The drama is inflated, and the style is that of a feature article in a Sunday newspaper. His elaborate calculation of the odds against his experiences is tedious, he never put his shirt on any of his visions (he seems to have been more interested in selling his story to a newspaper and in getting it investigated by the S.P.R.), there is no preface dated either from the best hotel in Ragusa or from the workhouse, too large a part of the book is taken up with demonstrating that his story is so well authenticated that he should not be suspected of perpetrating a hoax,

---

Review of John Godley, *Tell Me the Next One. On Foretelling the Winners of Horse-races from Dreams* (London: Victor Gollancz, 1950). First published in *Spectator*, 184 (1950), 734.

and his 'explanation' in terms of determinism is jejune. However, to those who may be interested (not, I think, racing men), he gives a pretty complete account of his experiences, disposing satisfactorily of the hypothesis of telepathy as an explanation. There is one point on which the reader would like further information. Were there in the races in which Mr Godley's dreams led him astray horses whose names were near enough to those he dreamed to have caused a confusion?

Ninety-nine

Beyond Realism and Idealism

An experience of excitement comes rarely enough from reading a close-packed philosophical argument to be noticed and welcomed when it appears. To convey excitement is not a meretricious achievement arising merely from a certain vivacity of style; it springs from being able to convince the reader of the importance of the problem being discussed and to infect him with the belief that this way of going about it might lead to some important or really unavoidable conclusion. And Professor Urban's book has this quality in spite of its repetitiousness and flatness of style.

Idealism and Realism come to us first as two contrasting theories of knowledge; but since each of these theories has appeared in a variety of forms, it seems sensible to try to discover the unity which in each case underlies the variety. Thus, the 'driving force' of Idealism is the belief that the known cannot be independent of the knower; and the 'resistance' of Realism is the belief that what is known must be an antecedent reality. These beliefs appear to stand in crass opposition to one another, but the remarkable thing is that neither has succeeded in refuting the other. This failure, however, in Professor Urban's view, does not spring from the incompetence of philosophers, but from the nature of the opposing beliefs; and the hope of reconciling them arises from the observation that neither is a belief concerning fact; both are beliefs about the meaning of knowledge. What is opposed is two views, not about the character of knowledge, but about its value; and oppositions between values do not necessarily have the character of contradictions. The conflict is, therefore, a dialectical conflict.

Having reached this point in his argument, and on the way made interesting excursions into the history of both Idealism and Realism, Professor Urban considers the three manners in which a theoretical reconciliation between them might be achieved. For his view is that in the actual pursuit

---

Review of Wilbur Marshall Urban, *Beyond Realism and Idealism* (London: George Allen and Unwin, 1949). First published in *Times Literary Supplement* (27 January 1950), 61.

of knowledge they *are* reconciled; what is required is a theory of this reconciliation. The theory of psychological types seems to offer a psychological reconciliation—the Idealist being the introvert and the Realist the extrovert—but this is rejected because it falls short of a 'real solution to the problem.' The 'pragmatic' solution springs from the belief that there is no real problem here at all, and is similarly rejected. The only satisfactory solution must be axiological—to show that knowledge is valueless unless the demands of both Idealism and Realism are admitted. Professor Urban achieves this in a brief exposition of a theory of communication. The last part of the book (nearly half) is given to a discussion of relevant objections to the thesis, and to illustrating the harmony between Idealism and Realism in such concrete enterprises of knowing as the physical and social sciences, history, and *Geisteswissenschaft*.

A great deal of the subtlety of Professor Urban's argument has, of course, been lost in this brief abstract. The book owes much to both Rickert and Alexander, and must be considered a notable attempt to argue out a problem to which much thought has already been given. Technically, the device of trying to determine the minimum demands of both Idealism and Realism and then seeking a manner of recognizing both the *minima* is neat, but not altogether convincing. It leaves the reader with the doubt whether what have been reconciled are permanent and irreducible attitudes or values in knowing, or whether they are, taken separately, simply mistaken theories of knowledge.

One Hundred

The Great Philosophers

Mr Tomlin is not the first to embark upon the enterprise of offering the general reader an approach to philosophy through the lives of the great philosophers, and his book may be counted among the more successful of its kind mainly because he has command of a style which is bright and entertaining without being vulgar, and because his purpose is unpretentious. This really is a book for the general reader; it is not profound or original, but neither is it a 'professorial' blunder. Nobody, having read it, will imagine that he knows all about philosophy; nobody will have wasted his time or have been seriously misled in matters of detail. The information supplied is, on the whole, accurate (though Hume should not have been credited, on two occasions, with a work called an *Essay Concerning Human Understanding*) and, with perhaps the exception of the space given to the adventures of Abélard, a good sense of proportion is preserved; there is no striking failure of judgment in what is included and what is left out. And Mr Tomlin seems to have a fairly wide personal acquaintance with the writings of the more notable philosophers from Plato to Bergson. In his brisk manner he carries us through the centuries, filling in the spaces between the great men with pages which mention the lesser, and combining biographical information with exposition of philosophical conclusion.

Of course there is simplification; there is regret for the unhappy faculty philosophers have of writing books 'making difficult problems more difficult still', and the reader comes to expect remarks such as: 'Spinoza's theory of Substance has proved a stumbling-block to philosophical students. But the idea which he is trying to put forward is really quite simple'; or Hegel's terminology and method of exposition have not been calculated to endear him to the ordinary reader. Both are difficult, sometimes aggravatingly so. But the fact to which he is endeavouring, here and elsewhere, to draw attention is a very simple one.

Review of Eric Walter Frederick Tomlin, *The Great Philosophers: The Western World* (London: Skeffington and Son, 1950). First published in *Times Literary Supplement* (24 March 1950), 189.

But there is little which could be called gross over-simplification. The mesh of Mr Tomlin's sieve is rather too large to retain much of the quality of a man's mind, but it holds something of what he thought with tolerable reliability.

These are the virtues of the book. But it is more difficult to answer the question: What sort of a view of the nature of philosophy will the reader carry away? He may be persuaded that there is nothing futile in philosophical discussion; at least he is told that it is a serious and worth-while occupation. And occasionally he will get a glimpse of a man (Berkeley, Hume or Kant) applying his mind to problems which his immediate predecessors had thrown up for consideration. But beyond this there is ambiguity. He will get nothing so simple as the idea of a *philosophia perennis*, or of philosophy as a gradually developing body of doctrine; but he may easily get the misleading impression that all these philosophers are talking about the same thing, and that there is something called 'traditional philosophy' ('reflection about the nature of reality as a whole' which is capable of providing 'a guide to life, an incentive to right action, a light to wisdom') from which certain mischievous contemporaries are leading us away. The serious and dispassionate voice of 'philosophy' usually makes itself heard without difficulty from peak to peak, but now and again (in the Middle Ages and also today) it is obscured by the 'din of logic-chopping' which rises from the valleys. Philosophy is not dogma, indeed we are told that it is an 'attitude of mind; at bottom it is nothing but that irrepressible impulse towards inquiry, that itch to probe at the meaning of things,' but somehow or other the proper course for the inquiry has become fixed and errancy is deprecated. In short, Mr Tomlin's sympathies are with metaphysics; 'philosophy' at its best is metaphysics with a message.

One Hundred and One

Mr Carr's First Volume

This opening volume is the first of three which are designed to compose together a history of the Bolshevik Revolution, 1917–23. And these three volumes are themselves the first part of a project which is to carry the history of Russia down to 1928. We have, therefore, a work in progress, and criticism must await further instalments before the value of the whole enterprise can properly be determined. Moreover, the manner in which the first three volumes have been planned makes it all the more necessary to withhold judgment until the fellows of the first instalment have appeared. For the volumes are not consecutive parts of a chronological tale: each deals with an aspect of the history of the Bolshevik Revolution and covers, from its own point of view, the whole period. The second volume is to deal with economic policy, the third with foreign relations; the volume now published is concerned with the story of the CPSU(B), the early constitutional pronouncements of the revolutionary régime, and its policy in respect of the national units of the former Russian empire. Consequently, some of what the reader may find absent from the first volume may perhaps be supplied in those which follow. But, with only the first volume before us, there are certain observations which may profitably be made and which are not likely to be falsified by what is to come.

It may be remarked, first, that Mr Carr has a profound, perhaps unrivalled, knowledge of the Russian writings, particularly Bolshevik writings, which bear upon this theme. He handles his material with great mastery and no sign of impatience: he is never at a loss for an apposite quotation. Secondly, the volume is pre-eminently readable. Its structure is clear, its details lucidly exposed and at every point there is evidence of a strong intelligence at work. Mr Carr is aware of the difficulties of his project, and he is disarmingly modest about his achievement. And thirdly, without being himself a Communist, he has so much sympathy for the

---

Review of Edmund Hallett Carr, *A History of Soviet Russia, vol. 1, The Bolshevik Revolution, 1917–1923* (London: Macmillan, 1950). First published in *Cambridge Journal*, 4 (1951), 504–6.

whole enterprise he is recounting that he is able to enter into the intentions of his subjects with remarkable success. In this volume he is dealing, in the main, with institutions, with the Bolshevik party, with the various congresses which met to discuss policy in these years, with the abortive Constituent Assembly and with the first Constitution of the USSR. But individuals appear, and particularly with Lenin Mr Carr has been to exceptional trouble to understand and expose his ideas and intentions. But there is nothing that can be called a portrait of Lenin, and in some respects the secret of his power is only imperfectly revealed. The two appendices, in which Mr Carr turns aside from the narrative to expound first Lenin's theory of the state and then the Bolshevik doctrine of self-determination, are masterpieces of understanding and lucid, economical exposition.

But to these observations must be added another, which because it concerns Mr Carr's very curious notions of how to write history, is of more general importance. It may be said at once that Mr Carr does not conceal these notions; he parades them briefly in his Preface, and they are implicit in the plan and the detail of the work. And apart from the value, in detail, of his account of the Bolshevik Revolution (which is certainly great), it is particularly interesting because it raises in an acute form some of the more teasing problems of historiography.

Everybody who has tried their hand at it, knows that there is nothing like writing a novel for revealing one's emotional limitations; inadequacies scarcely visible in ordinary speech and action are magnified and become unmistakable. Similarly, the attempt to write history shows up the crudities of one's thought: the unguarded phrase reveals and magnifies a hidden prejudice and at every turn we betray our nakedness. Both Mr Carr's powers and his weakness are fully revealed here.

Let us begin with something simple. Mr Carr (but not his publisher) disdains the intention of writing a history of Soviet Russia during the period concerned. His work, he says, 'purports to contain not an exhaustive record of the events of the period to which it relates, but an analysis of those events which moulded the main lines of further development'. In saying this he excuses himself from providing 'a vivid picture of the revolution itself' (which can be found elsewhere), but in fact he is confessing to the unfortunate enterprise of writing history backwards. And the effect of this decision is manifest on almost every page: the lost causes, the abortive attempts, the projects which came to nothing, the men who were eliminated scarcely appear, or appear only to be brushed aside by the historian in a story which can get on without them. 'The victory gained by the Marxists over Narodism and the revolutionary actions of the working class, which proved that the Marxists were right', says the official history of the

CPSU(B);[1] and though Mr Carr often improves upon the details of the story, he does not improve upon the point of view; his history is the story of those who were 'proved right' by success. On many occasions the defeated are not only squeezed out of the story, they are excluded also from giving evidence in their own persons. Of course it is not true that none but Bolsheviks appear in these pages, but it is largely true that everything that does appear is subordinated to the party which is predestined to win.

Now, that some men are defeated and others victorious, that some policies and projects go down before others, is a common occurrence, and any history which did not recognize it when it happened would be convicted of incoherence. But that lost causes are not part of history, that they should be seen only through the eyes of the victors, that defeat at the hands of events must entail defeat at the hands of the historian, and that what is victorious is predestined to victory and is insulated from what it defeats — these are strange propositions to come from an historian. A bias in favour of what is successful (or appears to the historian at the time of writing to have been successful) is far more corrupting than any merely partisan bias; and it is not to be excused here on the ground that after all this is the history of the intentions, the activities, and the fortunes of a victorious party, because these intentions and activities were not cut off from the rest of the story and were not, taken by themselves, what prevailed. History as a success story is always abbreviated history. Of course, often enough, the history of England has been written on this model — kings and statesmen being accounted 'good' or 'bad' in relation to some preconceived 'logic' of occurrences or development of events which is used as a ready-made criterion of relevance: some 'contribute', others are non-contributors, and are as if they had never been. But it is disheartening, just when we were beginning to get over this sort of thing, to find it reinstated in respect of a new tract of the history of mankind. It is, I think, Mr Carr's concern with what he calls an 'appreciation of the universal significance' of the events he is recounting which has led him astray. 'Universal significance' is difficult to observe at the longest range, and it is not surprising that the enterprise of detecting it at the range of a mere twenty-five years should have degenerated into a peculiarly simple exercise in whiggish history. If the significance Mr Carr looked for had been something more modest, something less than universal, his history would have been more genuine.

Besides the 'appreciation of universal significance', the other test imposed by Mr Carr upon himself as an historian is that of achieving 'an imaginative understanding of the outlook and purpose of his *dramatis personae.*' Here nobody will disagree. And every reader will remark upon the

---

[1] *History of the Communist Party of the Soviet Union (Bolsheviks)*, Short Course, p. 30.

outstanding achievement of Mr Carr in this respect. But there is something else to be observed — not any simple excessiveness in his sympathy, not the mere fact of sympathy outrunning itself, but the manner in which, keeping so close to his chosen task, his sympathy is replaced with total immersion. Explorers of the jungle of history, when they depart from that mean in which they remain explorers, are apt to fly to one or other of two extremes: they may insist upon all modern conveniences, dress for dinner in the jungle and never achieve a moment's real sympathy with what they are exploring, or they may 'go native'. Mr Carr has achieved the remarkable feat of 'going native' without being a Communist. He has, of course, been pushed towards this extreme rather than the other, not only by his commendable determination not to fail in sympathy, but also by his general view of the history of modern Europe with which readers of his other works are well acquainted. These presuppositions occasionally obtrude themselves in his writing about the Bolshevik Revolution; here and there, usually on the last page of a chapter when he is summing up a situation, passages appear in which they are expounded. But they lurk always below the surface, controlling the direction of his attention and the form of his analysis.

Now, if this were merely a matter of what is called 'bias' in history, there would be nothing more to do than call attention to it and commend it for its insight or observe its shortcomings. And in so far as it is a matter of 'bias', it is certainly not mere passion or prejudice: Mr Carr has a considered view of the way things have been going for some centuries, and if he fits the Bolshevik Revolution into this view and interprets it in this manner, he is doing something that Maitland would scarcely approve of, but something common enough to be excusable — particularly when no attempt at concealment is made. But unfortunately it is not a mere matter of 'bias': it is something much more important: it is a matter of style and diction. It is scarcely too much to say that 'going native' in Mr Carr's degree makes an end of anything recognizable as history.

Let us suppose a novelist who is recounting the fortunes and relations of five or six characters, each of whom is known to the others by a pet name. These pet names spring up within the world of the characters: they are invented by the characters and they compose a nomenclature the significance of which is that it helps to disclose how A thinks of B or how C and D understand the character of E. These names belong to the language which is spoken *between* the characters. But the novelist himself is not a character in his book: he is the creator of his characters. And if at any point he is engaged in disclosing the character of E, not as understood by C or D but as seen by somebody on the periphery of the world to which the characters belong, or if he wishes to disclose what E is 'really like', it will naturally be out of place, misleading, incongruous to refer to E by his pet name. Now, some such situation as this arises in writing history. The historian is the maker of his events; they have a meaning for him which was not their meaning for those who participated in them, and he will not speak of them in the same way as they spoke of them. He is the creator of his characters; and to reveal only what their contemporaries thought of them or what they thought of themselves (though this is of great importance) is to show an imperfect mastery over them. This, I assume, is what Mr Carr means when he speaks of the historian's task as the appreciation of the 'universal significance' of what he is writing about. And when the historian merely 'goes native' (resigns the task of creation and allows sympathy to become total immersion) he handicaps himself severely — unless by some miracle the characters of whom he writes had themselves an appreciation of the 'universal significance' of their own activities. I think it is Mr Carr's view that this was the happy position of the men he is writing about; but if it is, I think also that he should have elucidated the miracle at greater length.

For most of his readers, however, Mr Carr in this history is dealing with a set of people who speak an extraordinary private language. They have an idiom in which they make their thoughts known to one another. Of course this language represents, like any other language, an interpretation of the world. But the significant thing for the historian is that it is an interpretation of the world (whether or not 'true') confined to a small body of men, and that this language requires to be translated if what these men are saying is in any proper sense to be understood by anyone else. And it is on account, not of the greatness of Mr Carr's sympathy, but of its misdirection, that he entirely fails to attempt the task of translation. He has himself become so adept in the language, perhaps he has come to believe implicitly in the interpretation of the world it represents, that he has forgotten altogether that it is the eccentricity of a few. A history of the Albigenses written in the idiom of Albigensian belief would ordinarily be supposed to have been written merely for the edification of the brethren: it could mean very little to anyone else. But Mr Carr writes the history of the Bolshevik Revolution in the language of Bolshevism and yet looks for his readers (one assumes) in the world at large. It is true that in recent years, we have been bombarded to such an extent by this idiom of speech that many of its turns are familiar to us, but that it can be said to have it any clear meaning for us is an exaggeration. The way it has been used, as a jargon in which the same few phrases are repeated interminably, has ensured that it never rises above a minimum standard of intelligibility. And, above all, one would have thought, the task it imposes upon the historian is that of translation. The sceptic might suspect that the failure to translate springs from a too small faith in the intelligibility of this language, but that I think is not the case here. Mr Carr does not translate either because he believes that this is the language which reveals 'universal significance' or because he has forgotten that translation is necessary; a piece of forgetfulness all the more remarkable because on occasion he is capable of remembering.

The world, for Mr Carr, enjoys the use of two languages; the language of 'the West' (usually designated by the emotive epithet 'bourgeois') and the language of Marxist theory. His history, it would appear, is written for the instruction of 'the West', but it is written almost throughout in the language of Marxism. There are scores of passages where the reader finds himself begging the author to translate; but in vain. To begin with, the categories in which individuals are placed, the epithets used to indicate character or calling, are Marxist. We were treated in an earlier work of Mr Carr's to the classification of Burckhardt as a 'bourgeois historian', and here the idiom is unrestrained. Struve is 'a Marxist intellectual'. Molotov is 'a young intellectual from Kazan' — but what is an 'intellectual'? 'Proletarians' and 'workers' abound in these pages; men are either 'revolutionaries' or 'reactionaries'. And when the reader is introduced to 'rich peasants' and 'poor peasants', though it does not tell him very much, it is with a sigh of relief that he welcomes something that he can begin to understand. When Mr Carr wishes to describe the three leaders of the national movement in the Ukraine, one is called 'a learned professor' and another a 'self-made man' who had practised journalism, and we begin to see through the haze the kind of men we are being called upon to take notice of: but the third is merely a 'revolutionary intellectual', a term which, if it has a meaning, needs elucidation. Governments are 'bourgeois' (Finland) or 'proletarian'; revolutions are 'bourgeois', 'bourgeois nationalist', 'democratic', or 'socialist'. Parties are 'right' or 'left'. And when these categories manifestly fail to give meaning to the situation, Mr Carr follows Lenin in finding 'quasi-"proletarians"' and "bourgeois" national governments' in the eastern borderlands of Russia. And yet in observing the difference between the 'federalism' of the USSR and what we ordinarily mean by federalism, by some oversight Mr Carr does not refer to our federalism as 'bourgeois federalism', and having freed himself for a moment from the incubus of the Marxist idiom, he gives a reasoned and intelligible account of the situation. In short, Mr Carr almost invariably writes his history in the obscure, private language of the participants in the events he is recounting: there is no difference between the language of his numerous quotations from Lenin and Stalin and the language he uses to comment on them. Of course there are great difficulties. The historian has no vocabulary of his own; he is obliged in any case to use the language of morals and politics. But he should be wary of its implications. If he fails to perceive the difficulty, or surrenders to it, the 'reformer' in his pages will be opposed by the 'reactionary', 'revolution' by 'counter-revolution', and men and projects will appear only as they were thought of by their partners or opponents. For Clarendon an incident in English history was a 'rebellion', for Mr Carr,

Kornilov is the leader of an 'insurrection'. But the art of writing history is precisely the art of overcoming this difficulty — the art of understanding men and events more profoundly than they were understood when they lived and happened. Mr Carr is guilty of hubris when, in his Preface, he makes light of the difficulty of writing contemporary or near-contemporary history; its almost insuperable difficulty lies in making the translation from the language of morals and politics to the language of history. And the failure is aggravated here when the vocabulary is that of an eccentric view of morals and politics.

One of the effects of Mr Carr's surrender to the language of his characters is that he gives the appearance of accepting some of their doctrines with an uncritical readiness. The whole treatment of the much-advertised 'union of theory and practice' leaves much to be desired in this respect. And at one point an incoherence is uncovered, but not recognized, because of Mr Carr's misdirected sympathy. In the Constitution of the RSFSR, it is observed, 'the freedom of the worker was asserted, not against the state, but through the action of the state', and the 'bourgeois' notion of the individual requiring protection against the power of government was superseded in the 'autocracy of the people'. But the theory did not work out in practice. Not only did the VTsIK (as Mr Carr remarks) pass a resolution giving citizens 'a right of appeal against any neglect or violation of their rights by officials', but also a thoroughly 'bourgeois' conflict of interest appeared between the 'proletariat' and the 'peasantry'. And again, Mr Carr asserts that 'the essence of the terror [September 1918] was its class character. It selected victims on the ground, not of specific offences, but of their membership of the possessing classes'. This, no doubt, was the theory, but the brief account of the terror given in these pages shows it to have been of a different character — the elimination of 'proletarians' and their leaders who opposed the Bolshevik party.

It is not, however, to be thought that Mr Carr is universally uncritical — he can be critical, in detail, to great effect, even in respect of his hero Lenin. Inaccuracy in simple fact rarely escapes him; and he is not willing to pass over the more glaring examples of disingenuousness in the arguments of the Bolsheviks. And on the occasion when he assumes the proper role of the historian, he has some acute observations to make. For example, he points out that the principal leaders of the revolution took no part in composing the Constitution of the RSFSR, and he makes their abstention intelligible — they were engaged on more important work, the consideration of the party programme. But a more generally critical attitude is conspicuously absent. In his unwillingness to 'measure' Lenin and his partners in revolution by standards borrowed from the politics of more normal times or less disrupted societies, he comes to measure them by their own standards and endows them with a right to wreck their will in Russia whatever the consequences, approving their enterprise and applauding their 'logic'. It would have been better if he had not tried to 'measure' them at all.

Besides his prejudice in favour of success and his failure to attempt the task of translation inherent in the historian's enterprise, there is another respect in which Mr Carr's account of the Bolshevik Revolution falls short of genuine history. Indeed, he appears before us as a wizard rather than as an historian: with a wave of his wand he puts us to sleep and we are carried as if in a dream to an island in time, peopled by a race devoid of memory, a race (it appears) either without a past or with a past so obnoxious to it as to be regarded as non-contributory to its fortunes. And it is no part of Mr Carr's project to call its or our attention to what it has forgotten or rejected. Into a Russia, which has a geography (though we are provided with no map) but no history, there broke a collection of extraordinary professional adventurers, speaking a curious language and led by a man of iron determination and almost miraculous proficiency in the language, able to express himself in it with an unmatched fluency and confidence. These adventurers came with long-matured plans for the organization of this benighted people. They were not wholly at one about what they had to teach or what they had to establish, but subsequent events showed that one group was predestined to gain the upper hand and impose its ideas and policy. Consequently, we need pay little attention either to lost causes, to the context of confusion and contention from which this group emerged triumphant (it is represented as almost a sham fight), or to what they found on their appearance. We are present, it appears, not at a reformation or a revolution, but at the creation of a world *ex nihilo* by a demiurge who came from Switzerland. Consequently, the starting point of our investigation is the abstract 'idea' to be realized and the generation of this 'idea': we begin not with Russia, but with revolutionaries in conference. We are told that Lenin was 'a practical Russian revolutionary, whose revolutionary theory was framed in the light of Russian needs and Russian potentialities', and we are told something about the immediate situation when he appeared at the Finland Station in 1917, but virtually nothing is said about the Russia to be transformed. On any showing, even the most doctrinaire, this Russia could not be entirely excluded from the situation, and here and there it comes in for brief recognition, but proper consideration is given only to the revolution of 1905, which is treated as an incident in pre-messianic history. It is hinted that in the forgotten past Russia was ruled by an autocrat, that it enjoyed the advantage of a secret police, that the 'proletariat' had no legal status, and that the revolutionary task of eliminating the old bureaucracy was difficult. But Russia before the Revolution is never allowed to enter in detail into the story of the Revolution: it was merely non-contributory. Perhaps it is too early to make this complaint, perhaps in subsequent volumes Mr Carr will provide what is omitted from this;

nevertheless, it is an omission here which most readers will regret. The story, even as the story of a revolution, seems to begin in a curiously remote place.

In short, if we take the guidance given by this first volume, what Mr Carr is to provide us with is a more accurate version of the legend of Soviet history — the story of the generation of Soviet Russia as seen through the eyes of its founding fathers. In detail it differs from the official histories; in general the difference is small, except in respect of lucidity. This is something valuable; it is important for us to know how this set of people thought of themselves and what they believed themselves to be doing and to have done. But it is something to one side of what a history of Soviet Russia should be expected to supply. The nearest parallel to Mr Carr's achievement is to be found in some of the earlier writings on the history of the United States of America: his attitude towards the history of Soviet Russia is almost a replica of St Augustine's attitude towards the history of the Roman Empire.

One Hundred and Two

The B.B.C.

On its first appearance, attention naturally fastened upon the considerations which fill the foreground of the Report of the Committee on Broadcasting, and immediate comment took these as its text. But it is not less appropriate that subsequent reflection should turn to some of the questions started, but not pursued, in the Report. For, as must happen with an inquiry bound by specific terms of reference, the investigation often opened up topics which could not be explored and as often avoided what is important merely because it did not lie directly in its path; more materials were gathered than could be used, and what was used was arranged to construct a consistent argument. Consequently, with help rather than hindrance from the Report, but with some rearrangement of the information collected, the inquiring reader is able to compose for himself a picture of broadcasting in Britain today; and it is a picture which has some curious passages.

With us, broadcasting descended upon a literate population, a population which owed its education chiefly to newspapers and one accustomed to being entertained; and this, perhaps more than anything else, determined its character. In these circumstances broadcasting here could scarcely fail to be somewhat different from what it is, for example, in Russia. Chance (rather than design) made the activity a monopoly, deliberation kept it a monopoly and put it into the hands of a Public Corporation, and a masterful first Director General impressed a characteristic manner upon it. But it was a manner which, while leaving the patrons of broadcasting in some degree dissatisfied and making them in some degree rebellious, fitted tolerably their expectations. Of course, the B.B.C. began with a considerable reserve of popularity to draw upon. The wireless-set was a new toy and itself afforded entertainment, whatever was broadcast; and when the newness began to wear off, a habit of listening had been con-

---

Review of *Report of the Broadcasting Committee, 1949* (Cmd. 8116, H.M.S.O, 1951); and *Appendix H. Memoranda Submitted to the Committee* (Cmd. 8117, H.M.S.O, 1951). First published in *Cambridge Journal*, 4 (1951), 543–54.

tracted which could be disappointed only by having nothing at all to listen to. Further, the expectations were largely the creation of the B.B.C. itself, and consequently were not so difficult to satisfy. But, when all this is admitted, it remains true that among what was broadcast the listener could usually find something which was a good enough approximation to his desires for the divergencies (except in one or two respects) to pass unnoticed. It was some time before journalists began to tell listeners what they ought to think of the programmes, and until this happened the vast majority were on the whole uncritical of what they were given. A decade or more had to pass before the way things were going could be unmistakably detected.

It is sometimes said that too much is attributed to broadcasting; in itself, we are told, it is nothing more than an activity of dispersing or disseminating. It is spoken of as 'a channel for communication', a means of bringing people in touch with one another, and our attention is called to the neutrality of the instrument. And there is some significance in this observation: it reminds us that the wireless transmitter, like the internal combustion engine, is a product of human inventiveness which carries with it the unfortunate suggestion that since we have discovered a means of doing something we are well advised to do it, and the more of it the better — a suggestion which seems to separate the activity of broadcasting from what is broadcast. No doubt a transmitter, like a telephone wire, exists when it is not being used and may not improperly be called a potential means of communication, but in fact what we mean by broadcasting is an activity which does not take place until a programme is broadcast: the neutrality of the instrument is not at all shared by the activity. The B.B.C. is not, and never has been, a mere channel of communication: it is the organization of an activity in which a particular and carefully composed product is disseminated.

The original Licence in 1926 precluded the B.B.C. from broadcasting an opinion of its own on matters of public policy, and in practice it does not overtly communicate its own opinion, if it has one, on any specific topic. Nevertheless, it has a policy, and what is broadcast springs, directly or remotely, from that policy. No attempt has been made to conceal this from us, and the long B.B.C. Memorandum which is printed with the rest of the written evidence received by the Committee contains only the latest of many statements of policy. But although the policy has never been concealed and has never seriously deviated from the inspired direction given it by the first Director-General, the passage of time has carried away some of the chaff and there can be no longer any doubt about what precisely is afoot. And it is something so remarkable that it could find the ready acceptance it seems to have found only in a world grown accustomed to remarkable happenings.

Policy is often most effectively revealed, not when it is being expounded, but when it is being applied, and the discussion of monopoly in the B.B.C. Memorandum may be recognized as an occasion of this sort if we observe that much of the argument in favour of monopoly is, in fact, an attempt to show that the policy pursued by the B.B.C. would be difficult, if not impossible, for any but a monopolist organization. The foundation of B.B.C. policy, it appears, is the idea of broadcasting with a 'social purpose', broadcasting directed to the discharge of certain 'social responsibilities'. These include 'responsibility for impartiality, for the greatest possible freedom at the microphone, for the preservation of standards and the re-establishing on a broader basis of a regard for values, for the use of broadcasting as an educational medium and a means to raise public taste, for the discharge of broadcasting's duty to and in all the arts, for the encouragement of all artistic endeavour whether of creation or performance, for the use of broadcasting to develop true citizenship and the leading of a full life'; to which may be added, from another page, the responsibility for being 'a bastion against the tide seeking to submerge values in a disintegrating world'.[1] In short, it is the policy of the B.B.C. to be a standard-bearer: to inquire into and take notice of its patrons' preferences, but instead of giving them exactly what they want now, to give them what they will want when they have been baptized in the broad stream of the Corporation's 'general educational purpose'.

It might be supposed that, alongside this high social purpose, the B.B.C. would consider itself to be the purveyor of entertainment of a more ordinary character; but the conjecture is frowned upon. The Charter holds it to be desirable that the Corporation should be a means of information, education, and entertainment, and to these the tradition of the B.B.C. has added the raising of public taste. But in the policy of the B.B.C. they do not appear as disconnected activities, and it is thought pre-eminently important that the endeavour to raise public taste should never slacken or be excluded. This all-pervading purpose of the B.B.C. is articulated in three programmes, and there has been no more candid exposition of its policy than the words of the present Director-General:

> It rests on the conception of the community as a broadly based cultural pyramid slowly aspiring upwards. This pyramid is served by three main programmes, differentiated but broadly overlapping in levels of interest,

---

[1] There appears to be an unfortunate confusion of thought in this passage, arising from the ambiguity of the word 'broadcasting'. It combines the definition of social−purpose broadcasting as the observation of a duty or responsibility to use the transmitter to disseminate programmes designed to promote certain specified social ends, with the misleading suggestion that this duty is somehow imposed by the power to transmit− thus making it appear that social-purpose broadcasting is the only dutiful sort of broadcasting. But social-purpose broadcasting cannot be 'the *discharge* of broadcasting's duty to the arts', etc. (because there is no such antecedent duty); it is the *imposition* of a specific duty upon those who engage in broadcasting to use the transmitter for the encouragement of artistic endeavour, etc.

each programme leading on to the other, the listener being induced through the years increasingly to discriminate in favour of the things that are more worthwhile. Each programme at any given moment must be ahead of its public, but not so much as to lose their confidence. The listener must be led from good to better by curiosity, liking and a growth of understanding. As the standards of the education and culture of the community rise so should the programme pyramid rise as a whole.

To these general statements of policy must be added one or two important details. It is not at all the desire of the B.B.C. to create a population of what are called 'passive' listeners (or viewers, in the case of television) who merely enjoy what they are given. Indeed, those who treat listening as a 'private pleasure' and do not allow it to induce in them 'public activity' are sent to the bottom of the class; the 'good listeners' are 'serious', 'active', 'responsible' listeners. Further, it is the policy of the B.B.C. to protect this great enterprise of education from interlopers; it welcomes (or tolerates) broadcasts addressed to British listeners from foreign countries, so long, as they represent 'the people or the Government' of those countries; but it objects to foreign 'commercial' broadcasting (that is, broadcasting without a 'social purpose') reaching the British public, in the belief that it is 'bad' and that the 'bad' will inescapably drive out the 'good'. With regard to the opportunity afforded by Relay Exchanges for listeners to take a foreign programme in preference to a British, the B.B.C. has pronounced that its 'main concern is to ensure that the objectives of its broadcasting policy are not prejudiced ... It desires to safeguard its standards of impartiality, its general programme policy, and its long-term educational intent.'

In order to pursue this policy wisely and with energy, the B.B.C. has surrounded itself with advisory bodies, it broadcasts 37 1/2 hours a day, and it employs a staff of nearly 12,000. Its aim is to make each of its programmes, including television, available to the vast majority of listeners in this island, and with the shortest possible delay. The promised time is not very far off 'when it is possible every evening for every citizen of this country not only to hear but to see what has been happening in the world that day: when the great events of nations and in the international field can be remotely 'attended' by the inhabitants of almost every town and village; when the colour, the excitement, the variety and the 'worth-whileness of everyday life can be communicated to the richest, the poorest, the loneliest and the most gregarious; when harmony, design and grace can be visually as well as audibly taken into every home; then there must surely be something added which, working with all the other beneficent influences within the community, will have the capacity to make for a broader vision and a fuller life'.

Broadcasting in this country, then, is controlled by a policy: we have, first, a Corporation self-dedicated to the improvement of mankind according to a recipe of its own; and we have, secondly, that Corporation vested with the monopoly of broadcasting. We might have had neither of these things; we might have had the second without the first or (*pace* the B.B.C.) the first without the second; in fact we have both.

It is a situation so astonishing that we must be ready to listen to those who would warn us against exaggeration. We shall be reminded that, after all, the B.B.C. does not control all the sources of instruction and improvement in the country; it has the monopoly of only one of the instruments of education and entertainment. And we shall be told that, although the material broadcast is fitted to a policy, it is (one way or another) supplied by the society to which it is broadcast; the B.B.C. depends upon the current activities of society — the stage, the worlds of music, literature and learning, and the course of external events — which are independent of it, and it merely disseminates a selection from what these provide. There is, of course, truth and relevance in both these contentions; but when we consider the formidable power of the microphone, they offer little or nothing in mitigation of our situation. Both the B.B.C. and the Committee are aware of this power, but interpreting it solely in terms of 'pervasiveness', they mistake its character. For broadcasting (especially by a 'public-service' monopoly organization) is not mere dissemination, and its power does not derive merely from its range. Everything that is broadcast is unavoidably given an amplified significance; it not only travels far and wide, but it arrives at its various destinations with an immeasurably increased authority. The mere fact of broadcasting an opinion adds to the weight of its impact. The strongest argument against allowing some eccentrics on the air is not that they may give offence (which is the only argument considered by the Committee), but that the very fact of broadcasting it gives to the eccentricity an altogether false degree of importance. What was intended as an insignificant addition to the museum of popular curiosity becomes mistaken for a significant character or opinion. Broadcasting adds to whatever authority an opinion may already possess, endows with authority opinions which have none, and (without any intention of doing so on the part of the B.B.C.) unavoidably distorts our sense of proportion. It is not fanciful to suggest that there is nothing so important as to *merit* being broadcast — not even the time-signal. And it must not be forgotten that to all this must be added the fact that, in sound broadcasting, the speaker is unseen. To be chosen to speak is to acquire authority; to appear only as a voice entails a partial anonymity which obliquely acknowledges and at the same time amplifies the source of the authority.

To these heroic passages in this sketch of our situation must be added others of a somewhat different character. We need not, for the moment, consider the quality of the material used by the B.B.C. in its enterprise of evangelization, except to remark that here and there in its Memorandum the B.B.C. admits to difficulties in carrying out its policy. The material of the sought-for quality is not always available in the quantity required to fill the number of hours for which patrons now expect to be entertained or educated. But what is more important than the difficulties of the B.B.C. in maintaining its standards, is the part of the picture which concerns the audience: and here we descend from the sublime to the ludicrous.

There are now a little over twelve million licenced receiving sets. The B.B.C.'s Audience Research estimates that of those listening at any given moment in the evening 63 per cent are listening to the Light Programme, 36 per cent to the Home Service, and 1 per cent to the Third Programme (which has only a 50 per cent coverage as against the 97 per cent coverage of the two more popular programmes). For particular items the proportions may, however, be quite different. The same source of information detects the following order of preferences in the population as a whole—Variety, Plays, Light Music, Military Bands, Musical Comedy, Cinema Organs, Brass Bands, Religious Services, Discussions, Dance Bands, Talks, and so on. This suggests to the Committee that 'the types of programme most naturally suited to broadcasting as a means of communication are Plays and Light Music'; but a fairer inference than this recondite conclusion would perhaps be that the patrons of the B.B.C. prefer to be entertained while they are being evangelised. There is, however, one more piece of information which must be taken into consideration—the most sardonic passage in the picture—'the bulk of listeners treat listening as a secondary activity, a background noise while they are doing something else'. An odd situation. It is as if a benevolent newspaper proprietor were spending a fortune in an attempt to provide elevating reading-matter for mankind, only to discover that the vast bulk of those who bought his product never read a line of it, but used it for wrapping up fish and chips.

A sketch does not pretend to explore every detail, but there is another feature of our situation which is important enough to be observed: the B.B.C. is not merely convinced of the merit of its policy but, when called upon, expounds it with an altogether remarkable show of self-righteousness—a priggishness which reaches such proportions in the Memorandum submitted to the Committee as to make one wonder what sort of persons these are who control that considerable part of our life over which their monopoly presides. Even the most sympathetic reader must find this parade of 'social purpose' and 'public service' tiresomely sanctimonious: surely nothing should be taken quite so seriously as the B.B.C. takes itself. The schoolmasterish disposition towards its patrons is difficult enough to stomach, but when it descends to a deeper level, and the St. George-and-the-Dragon attitude makes its appearance, we may be forgiven (even when we exclude the more grotesque expressions of this attitude) if we reach the conclusion that here is something altogether excessive. At any rate, pretentions of this character unavoidably bring those who exhibit them upon the carpet. Those who endeavour to pass for the lights of the world must expect to attract the eyes of it, and their small blemishes are more justly ridiculous than much greater in those who are more modest. And perhaps the most curious characteristic of the Report is that it does not occur to the Committee to do anything but endorse and applaud this attitude—except, indeed, to add its own peculiar contribution of sententiousness. Glutted with 'public service' and bludgeoned with 'social purpose', the reader finds himself in the mood of the Frenchman who was so disgusted with the word *fraternité que si j'avais véritablement un frère je l'appellerais mon cousin.*

This, briefly, is the picture which emerges: to say the least, it is curious. Broadcasting in Great Britain is, in intention, nothing less than a far-reaching experiment in universal education conducted by persons whose activities are to some extent circumscribed but are virtually uncontrolled. They recognize a responsibility to the nation, but it is a responsibility for the maintenance of standards of thought and opinion and taste which they have themselves determined and in a great variety of fields. Nothing like it exists anywhere else in the world, for a similar intensity of control is matched elsewhere by a restriction of the field of interest; and one wonders whether it would exist here if we had known from the beginning what was afoot. The easy acceptance of the B.B.C. by a nation which for so long has avoided an authoritative Academy of Letters and a unified system of school or university education may be supposed to argue at least some absence of mind. Indeed, the acceptance is perhaps understandable only when we turn from the intention to the result which bulks largest, and recognize in the B.B.C. a monopoly providing a 'background noise'.

Now, if this is anything like the truth of our situation, the conclusion of the Committee, that the fundamental question for decision is the 'issue of monopoly', seems a little near-sighted. It might be thought that some room would have been found for the consideration of the much larger and more important question—whether broadcasting conducted on a policy such as that pursued by the B.B.C. is desirable at all. And it might be supposed that it would be time enough to consider monopoly when this question had been answered. Of course there must be attention to standards; but it is not unreasonable to ask whether these particular standards and this particular, over-heated pursuit of a narrowly conceived social purpose is the proper object for broadcasting, or whether what is desirable is something less highfalutin'. For if we are bidden choose between broadcasting conducted in the manner of the B.B.C. and the supposed standardless bedlam of commercial broadcasting we are offered an incomplete range of alternatives. And that the Committee did not address itself to this question is the more remarkable because the most cogent arguments against monopoly which it had to listen to were, in fact, not against monopoly itself, but against monopoly exercised by a Corporation with a severe and self-determined policy of social uplift. However, on account of a confused concern with insignificant detail, the full force of these arguments seems never to have been felt by the Committee, the majority having accepted in advance the propriety of broadcasting with the special kind of social purpose which is characteristic of the B.B.C.

When we reflect upon the desirability of broadcasting in the manner of the B.B.C., it is perhaps relevant to consider how the B.B.C.'s pursuit of its policy has worked out in practice—to consider, that is, the place the B.B.C. (not as a monopoly, nor as the provider of a 'background noise', but as a guide in matters of taste and education) has come to occupy in our society. And the Report does not leave us unprovided with information on this topic.

The impact of the B.B.C. upon school education, for example, is great and is growing: is it a happy one? Do we regard with equanimity a public corporation (whether or not it enjoys a monopoly) which invites itself into the schoolroom with the offer of stimulants, 'the voices of the outstanding men of our time', 'new facts', 'specialized knowledge' presented by 'highly skilled broadcasters', and all this accompanied with instructional pamphlets and school prayers? It is not merely a jaundiced eye which may discern in this (and perhaps in much else of the B.B.C.'s general educational effort) an encouragement of one of the less good products of contemporary education: the extensive mind, curious, interested, pseudo-sympathetic, preferring many contacts to few intimacies, preferring fact to thought and crowded with a disordered array of imperfectly realized images — the quiz mentality. Do we look forward to a uniform curriculum with ushers to turn on the wireless set and keep order? And if (with the B.B.C. and the Committee) we have no such hopes, what, we may ask ourselves, relieves us of our fears? Already the B.B.C. is applauded (by some members of the Committee) for being a 'unifying force' in education, and the educational prospects of television are said to 'seem almost boundless'. Of course, the remedy is in our hands: we may choose what seems good to us from all that is offered, or, if nothing seems good, we need not participate at all. But this is to reckon without the prestige of the B.B.C. and to neglect the laziness of mankind; to expect the worst is less foolish, all things considered, than to hope for the best. The schoolmaster need not fear to lose his job; he need fear only the ease and corruption which comes from having done for him what he should do for himself.

Or consider the News Bulletins broadcast by the B.B.C. A cloud of witnesses testified before the Committee to the high standard of impartiality; but when this is taken for granted, as it may be, there are other things to reflect upon. The world as it appears in the pages of a newspaper is a thing of rags and tatters, grim, grotesque, erratic and entertaining, and any sensible man chooses his newspaper for the quality of imagination which has gone to compose the picture it offers: truth, except in dull detail, nobody asks for. With this, of course, a B.B.C. bulletin cannot compete: the picture of the world it offers is necessarily more selective. But it is selected with a gravity which no newspaper would emulate. The world as it appears to the B.B.C. has room for trivialities, but their triviality is underlined; no listener is left in any doubt that life is earnest. 'The object', says the Memorandum, 'is to state the news of the day accurately, fairly, soberly and impersonally', but to complete the catalogue the word 'continuously' should have been added. No doubt we owe the multiplicity of news bulletins to the war, but is it in the public interest, and to what interpretation of social purpose does it belong, to keep the listening public informed, in a continuous situation report, about the dull and doubtful detail of the serious nonsense that is taking place all over the world? And when to the ten main daily news bulletins are added News Reels, days and weeks in Parliament, and the promise that before long, every evening, every citizen of this country will be able to see on the television screen what has happened in the world that day, we may wonder whether the bastion against the tide seeking to submerge values in a disintegrating world has not itself sprung a leak. Of course a news service, like a bus service, must run just in case anyone should be needing it: we cannot all listen at the same times. But this turns it into the 'sale of a popular commodity'; as a whole, its educational effect is to encourage idle curiosity: listening to the news is becoming a nervous ailment.

Or consider, to take a last example, the B.B.C. as an entertainer. It is a characteristic of the world we live in that activities which used to have their times and seasons, and were marked by a certain ceremoniousness, are now carried on continuously: we work day and night, holidays are staggered, only the ancient festivals come at their proper intervals and consequently retain a significance and power over the imagination which nothing else can acquire. Entertainment, like the rest, is splintered, and the B.B.C. as an entertainer could not expect to be an exception to the rule. But in this matter, as in others, the scale into which the B.B.C. puts the weight of its influence will go down with a bump. The Derby, which one might witness once in a life-time and retain as a brilliant and happy memory to the end of one's days, can be seen in an attenuated form every year without moving from the house; listening to a play (or seeing it) is a daily opportunity, offered euphemistically as 'theatre'; the possessor of a wireless set is never at a loss for an escape from his own thoughts or from the conversation of his companions. Of course, once again, the reply is that nobody is compelled to listen, that in fact people who listen also go to the theatre; but it is a reply which either misses the real impact of broadcast entertainment or recognizes broadcast entertainment merely as the provision of a popular commodity. The felt necessity of filling all those hours with entertainment corrupts the entertainers, because it is impossible without including a quantum of material which nobody could be happy in using; and the opportunity of turning on the tap corrupts the listener in the same manner as the ready supply of tinned food corrupts the cook. This is not, however, to say that the B.B.C. as an entertainer has done nothing to win the approval of even the severest critic. When the conversation turns to criticize the B.B.C., the *Lifeman* has an easy entrance with the gambit: 'but not the music'; and one does not require to spur one's generosity to agree that here is a remarkable achievement.

The policy of the B.B.C. in operation seems, then, to raise two main questions, one concerning quality and the other relating to quantity. And neither of these questions is properly discussed in the Report: the quality is merely applauded and the quantity scarcely considered. Our answers to both will, no doubt, be influenced by the consideration of monopoly, but neither can be reduced to this consideration. Of the first enough perhaps has been said already. The problem is not how to *improve* the standards of the B.B.C., or how to bring about a closer coincidence of performance and standard, but whether these are the proper standards to impose upon the activity of broadcasting. At any rate, the opinion of the Committee, and of the B.B.C. itself, that what alone justifies monopoly is the quality of the article at present dispensed is a proposition which calls for further reflection rather than for immediate assent. On the lowest level, it is open to question whether the antics in which the maintenance of 'impartiality' involes the B.B.C. do not suggest that broadcasting is being made to pursue a too ambitious course; and perhaps what is indicated is not the abolition of monopoly but a reduction of the activities in which impartiality is desirable.

What the B.B.C. broadcasts is, in quantity, pre-eminently suitable for the invalid, the house-bound and the inhabitant of remote places. To be able to turn it on at any moment in 17 hours out of the 24 is, for these, a benefit; for others it is a potential source of distraction. The indiscriminate competitive exploitation of the internal combustion engine has transformed our manner of life without demonstrably improving it, and there is little to show that the relentless and efficient exploitation of the power to transmit by a public service broadcasting monopoly is not having a similar result. And the opportunity which the Committee had of making recommendations which might change what has become a mere natural urge into a morally discriminating activity (so far as quantity is concerned) has unhappily been missed: the 'courage of abnegation', which the present Director-General urged upon those who devote themselves to broadcasting, finds only a distant echo in the Report, which mentions (without pursuing) the question 'whether the B.B.C. is not endeavouring to broadcast too many different programmes for more hours than is necessary'. Apart from considerations of monopoly, then, the quantity of broadcasting is something that might have received a more critical attention in the Report. But there can be little doubt that the eagerness and energy with which the B.B.C. has exploited its instrument is partly the outcome of monopoly: there was a felt necessity to show that monopoly and laziness or lack of enterprise in this case were not partners. And no doubt this is the spring of the strange assumption that broadcasting itself has somehow a 'duty' to discharge 'to and in all the arts', etc. But to suggest a continuation of the monopoly while suggesting nothing to relieve the B.B.C. from the supposed duty of ruthlessly exploiting its instrument is an unfortunate omission from the Committee's recommendations.

In short, enough evidence and argument was presented to the Committee to convince most people of the undesirability of approximating broadcasting in England to the American pattern, and of the difficulty involved in dispersing the monopoly between two or more corporations. The witnesses who favoured a move in this direction were inspired by the laudable desire for greater diversity of programme (that is, a desire to free us from exclusive reliance on the B.B.C.'s standards in broadcasting), and they seemed to think that this might spring from competing broadcasting organizations. But there is little evidence that competition itself produces diversity — rather the reverse. We enjoy a variety of newspapers, but wherever there is genuine competition there is less diversity (except in opinion) than makes no matter. And again, some argument (not very convincing and all based upon the assumed desirability of broadcasting inspired by the sort of social purpose which inspires the B.B.C.) is marshalled by the Committee itself to support its recommendation of a continuation of the present arrangements. But what does not seem to have been considered (and is consequently worth mentioning here) is the case for monopoly joined with a less grandiose purpose than that which guides the B.B.C. And this is surprising, for such a monopoly offers an escape from many of the recognized dangers and excesses which belong to the present situation. So large and so unwieldy a Corporation would be unnecessary, its position as sole employer of broadcasters would become less significant, the burden of responsibility which now alternately spurs and restrains the B.B.C. would be removed, the fortuitous and unsought authority which it now enjoys would fade away, and the enormous power it exercises over mens' minds would once more cease to be exercised by any single body. In such a monopoly there would be no danger, only convenience. And if some of the valuable potentialities of broadcasting remained unexploited, that perhaps would be a small price to pay for the removal from our midst of a concentration of power recognized by everybody, including the Committee, to be dangerous.

One Hundred and Three

Modern Capitalism and Economic Progress

A foolish objection has been taken to this book because it is the work of a scholar and at the same time does battle with the popular purveyors of economic wisdom who, having appointed themselves the guides of the people, were until yesterday considered by the less informed to be reliable guides — the Jays and the Stracheys. But we must take it for what it is — a book which 'tries to discuss practical affairs' — and be glad that the author is a competent and thoughtful economist. Mr Wilson holds strong opinions and expresses them with vigour. The advantages he has over his opponents are that even when he is vehement he does not give way to gross exaggeration, and that what he is defending is neither things as they are nor a Utopia, but what, so far as his perception goes, is taken to be the next step in the way we have been going for some long while. His objection to contemporary British socialism, as it has worked out, is that it has stepped aside from the line of advance towards a more equalitarian and more prosperous society which had already been entered upon. 'Lloyd George was on the right lines: Mr Attlee is not': 'nationalization will do nothing to reduce the inequality of capital unless the Government cheats in the payment of compensation.' He is a 'radical', and believes that, as a form of economic organization, 'capitalism' can and should be 'modernized'. As an answer to the various 'cases' for socialism, the effectiveness of his book lies in the fact that Mr Wilson has avoided taking his standards from his opponents. To some extent he is saying what they forgot to say, or suppressed, but his tone of voice is quiet, his manner is sincere, and he is not given to exaggeration. It is not an exciting book; it will not win votes; but it may help to dispel the great illusion.

The economic problem, as Mr Wilson sees it, is how to make the most profitable use of our available resources and how to increase those

---

Review of Thomas Wilson, *Modern Capitalism and Economic Progress* (London: Macmillan, 1950). First published in *Cambridge Journal*, 4 (1951), 504–6.

resources; and since everywhere this enterprise is undertaken with 'certain broad assumptions', *our* problem is how to do these things in a manner which conforms to our democratic and Christian traditions. The essence of 'capitalism' is not *laissez-faire* (which in fact never existed), but 'private enterprise' and the 'flexible mechanism of the market', controlled by law and the customs which represent our basic assumptions. Mr Wilson believes in the efficacy of these pieces of machinery (for that is how he regards them), and the book begins with a review of the social and political values which Mr Wilson believes to belong to our tradition, and with a reminder of the success which the 'capitalism' of the last hundred years has achieved — the remarkable increase in the income per head of population.

The alternative to all this, preached and practised by British socialism, is physical planning and the nationalization of industry. And Mr Wilson's carefully argued conclusion is that this alternative will do nothing to further economic progress. Physical planning in peace-time is not only dangerous to the social and political ends believed to be valuable; it is dangerous also to economic prosperity. And the widespread nationalization of industry has no contribution to make to economic progress; it is a blind alley.

But the 'capitalist' machinery of economic organization needs to be kept in trim, and at some points it now creaks. If we refuse the socialist suggestion to get rid of it and replace it by something else, we are still left with the problem of maintenance and reform. What way shall we take with our economic difficulties? Some of these difficulties are temporary, and may call for treatment which takes us to the verge of our traditions: we are a society recovering from war. These are not neglected by Mr Wilson, indeed he has a lot to say about inflation and balance of payments, but his argument goes deeper when he turns to the more permanent problems. There are three of them: inequality of income and capital; monopoly and industrial efficiency; mass unemployment.

Mr Wilson would like to see a more equalitarian society, though exactly why he does not divulge. However, it is on account of this preference that he is *not* a socialist. Specifically socialist measures have little power to reduce inequality; the remedy is taxation (of income and capital) and not the curtailment of private enterprise. It is a remedy which has been in operation in England for some generations, and what needs to be done now is to make it more rapid and more efficient. The crux of the matter is inherited wealth, because inequality of capital is much greater and less justifiable than inequality of income. Mr Wilson believes that the inheritance of wealth is justifiable if bequests are not very large and if they are not handed down from generation to generation. Consequently what he sets his face against is large estates and the means taken to avoid the taxation (death duties) which have reduced them and should further reduce them. (But why is he the enemy of the voluntary dispersal of capital before death?) He presents this as comparatively simple in operation, and likely to have no damaging results. But here, I think, he is over-optimistic. There is room for a thorough investigation of the morals and economics of bequest and inheritance: the current moral objection to it is certainly superstitious, and the economic effects of abolition are far from easy to determine. Mr Wilson does not provide this investigation, and since his position is that very large inherited capital is objectionable, it is all the more necessary for him to make clear that he is not the enemy of inheritance itself and to say why. He insists that the product of a capital tax should be used for the reduction of the national debt and for nothing else, but whether his reason is economic or moral is not clear.

In dealing with monopoly Mr Wilson is on firmer ground. It is now indisputable that 'capitalism' does not lead inevitably to monopoly, and it is equally obvious that the result of socialist practice to date has been more, larger, and less controlled monopolies than ever existed before. His suggestions about how to deal with monopolies when they arise and are impervious to the criticism of the market, are sensible; but he says nothing about monopolies of labour.

The long chapter on Unemployment and Socialism is a careful and judicious piece of writing directed again to a criticism of the socialist diagnosis and remedy for unemployment and recommending a Keynesian remedy (not physical planning) should it arise.

The book as a whole may be recommended for its accuracy and the cogency of most of its arguments. But, like others of its kind, it has an unfortunate tendency to treat economic institutions, not as ways of being active, but as pieces of machinery held in stock, to be shuffled about, selected and rejected, brought or kept in use or put by for another occasion. And this attitude appears also when Mr Wilson is dealing with politics: the 'liberty' which he takes to be the most important criterion and worthy above all to be preserved remains an abstraction: it is not 'liberty' which is 'gravely threatened by socialism' but an entire, concrete, complex way of living. Naturally an economist must 'believe in productivity', but a writer in practical affairs should make it clear that, to say the least, 'maximum productivity' is one of the most damaging of the moral superstitions of our time.

One Hundred and Four

The City of God and *Introduction to St Augustine*

St Augustine, in spite of the work of what has become a long line of distinguished scholars (mostly continental), has suffered and still suffers from being looked at backwards. He is interpreted to us as one of the 'makers of the Middle Ages', with never more than one foot in the world in which he lived. And even when a genuine attempt is made to understand him in his own world, to understand him historically, the understanding has been too often qualified by misleading distinctions: he is shown as a writer in whom a variety of disparate 'influences' converge; his world appears only as a 'background', text and context, the man and his world, are separated, are, perhaps, related to one another, but are never fully united. The process is familiar. First we form a notion of what belongs to an age, what is characteristic of it, and then, instead of using what appears to be exceptional in order to criticize and extend our notion of the character (and in this manner win a deeper insight into the character of the age), we are content to allow it to remain exceptional. It is a process which has seriously limited our understanding of the Victorian age, and not less seriously misled us in our study of those complicated and overwhelmingly important first four centuries of the Christian era. Even when passions have been laid aside, circumstances, the fact that we have been accustomed to go to those centuries with firmly insulated and narrowly formulated questions, as historians either of Christianity, or of the Roman Empire, or of the late manifestations of Greek or Judaic thought, have made them seem at best a loosely twisted strand of Greek, Hebrew, Roman, Christian 'elements', and their concrete character has been mislaid. And, among much else, the

---

Review of John Henderson Seaforth Burleigh, *The City of God. A Study of St Augustine's Philosophy* (London: Nisbet, 1949); and Reginald Hayes Barrow, *Introduction to St. Augustine, the City of God. Being selections from the De Civitate Dei* (London: Faber and Faber, 1950). First published in *Cambridge Journal*, 4 (1951), 567–8, 570, 572.

non-historical categories of orthodoxy and heresy have entered in to increase the obscurity. The Talmud, for example, is regarded as the product, not of its place and time, reflecting the whole character of this 'Hellenistic' world, but of 'Jewish thought'; and St Augustine is understood as a figure in 'Christian history' against a 'background' of 'classical antiquity'. And yet St Augustine, because of his pre-eminent coherence with his world, offers an unrivalled occasion for a study of the concrete character of that world. However, though in this respect we have still far to go (and a study of the history of these centuries is still the most testing enterprise a scholar can undertake), the situation is far more promising than it was a generation ago; and it may be taken as a sign of progress that in both the books under review a genuine attempt is made to unite text and context and to allow each to modify the other.

Professor Burleigh's book is based upon a set of lectures delivered in Edinburgh in 1944. Its sub-title is, 'A study of St Augustine's philosophy', but its strength is rather descriptive than analytical. It lays before us the circumstances and the world in which the *De Civitate Dei* was composed, the contents of the work, and the main stages of its argument. It is scholarly without being severe; sound rather than subtle; it reveals a thorough and up-to-date knowledge of Augustinian scholarship; few of its chapters are without some illuminating observation; as a whole it may be regarded as a reliable introduction and first guide to the study of St Augustine's thought, but a guide that makes, perhaps, too little demand upon those who follow. However, the class of reader who has hitherto depended upon Robertson's chapter in *Regnum Dei* (1901) is now supplied with something which not only reflects the intervening course of Augustinian studies, but embodies also a more just historical perspective. Its predominantly descriptive and historical point of view makes it complementary to Burnaby's more reflective and analytical course of lectures published under the title of *Amor Dei* (1938).

Dr Barrow's enterprise is different. The modesty of the title of his book conceals a work of exact and severe scholarship which will take its place as an original and important contribution to Augustinian studies. It consists, first, of about fifty pages of extracts (including the greater part of Book XIX) from the *De Civitate Dei*, the Latin text and the English translation being printed on opposed pages; secondly, a running commentary on the matter and the manner of these extracts; and thirdly, Appendices and Notes in which bibliographical and other concerns are discussed. The extracts from the text have been chosen and arranged to present the main line of St Augustine's argument and to avoid the many excursions and incidentals which make up the bulk of the work as St Augustine wrote it; the commentary is both historical and analytical. In composing the book, Dr Barrow had three purposes in mind: to promote a wider interest in the

De Civitate Dei by making the main lines of its argument available to those who, though they might be deterred by the bulk of the original work, nevertheless wish for a scholarly understanding of one of the masterpieces of European writing; 'to encourage a wider horizon in the teaching and learning of classics so as to include Christian writers whose debt to classics was great; and to link up once again the study of classics and the study of divinity'; and thirdly, 'to reaffirm the importance of a particular method of study, the method (*a*) of reading the actual words of an author rather than reading about him, (*b*) of reading those words in the light of the author's own day and not in the light of interpretations put upon them by later ages'. It is the third of these purposes which I take to be pre-eminently important, and in pursuing it Dr Barrow has made his own original contribution to Augustinian studies.

It has been the unfortunate illusion of some historians to think that something less than a first-class knowledge of the languages involved in their subject of study will serve their purpose, and to think that a minute and exact attention to the words of a text is unnecessary: they believe themselves to be dealing with things, not words. But the study of a text is a study of its words, and no text will reveal its meaning unless the interpreter goes to it with the questions, 'why this word and not that?' and, 'what precisely, in this literary and historical context, is the connotation of this word?' And the whole answer is never supplied by the text itself. And just as historians before now have transformed our knowledge of the course of a battle by a meticulous attention to the exact words used in the sources of information at their disposal, so Dr Barrow has illuminated our understanding of what St Augustine has to say by seeking answers to such questions as, why *civitas* and not *republica*? What precisely does Augustine mean by *iustitia, amor, pax*? These are historical questions, because though a writer like Augustine takes his liberties with language, liberties which must be examined and pinned down, he is using words which carry with them meanings of the moment, which reflect (particularly when they belong to a political vocabulary) events and situations. So Dr Barrow begins his discursive commentary: 'the first lines of this chapter (Bk I. Ch. 1) are so important that the phrases are considered one by one', and nothing will deflect him from his analysis. In short, this is not an easy 'introduction' to Augustine, it makes great demands upon the reader, but for anyone who is in earnest with the study of Augustine it is probably the best in our language.

It is impossible to notice here all the points at which Dr Barrow illuminates his subject; one only can be selected for remark—his treatment of the well-known crux in Ch. 24 of Bk. XIX. He begins with the proper observation that what St Augustine is offering us is not a 'political philosophy', and he goes on to examine the various explanations (many of them misjudged because they assume that St Augustine has a political philosophy to offer) that have been given of the apparent paradox of St Augustine's denial of *iustitia* to civil societies. His own solution is both simple and subtle and, I think, entirely convincing. It is an explanation which springs from a close attention to what St Augustine actually says and to the context of the statement. At this point, as at many others, Dr Barrow has made a real advance in the interpretation of Augustine's thought.

The shortcomings of the book are mainly philosophical: analysis of the text and historical insight are Dr Barrow's strong points; but every now and again the reader is conscious that the commentary touches what it does not elucidate. One would have liked to find a fuller discussion of what, after all, is the central subtlety of St Augustine's thought—the relation between *iustitia*, *ordo*, and *pax*; and perhaps some indication of the relation between *pax* and that most important of contemporary Roman ideas, *auctoritas*. *Pax et Princeps* is more than a mere distant background to St Augustine's thought. Now and again, as in the phrase 'Augustinianism at its best' and in the unfortunate and rash suggestion that 'the whole intellectual framework of ancient thought crashed because reason had nothing on which to base itself', an unhistorical note is heard: the crash obscures what should have been a perception of the subtle mediation by which change was taking place. Nor is it enough merely to contrast the point of view of Dante in the *De Monarchia* in respect of the Roman Empire with that of Augustine; in fact the two writers are not talking about the same thing.

Both books have useful bibliographical references, Dr Barrow's naturally fuller than Professor Burleigh's; but I miss from both any mention of F.C. Burkitt's work. He wrote nothing directly on St Augustine, but there would be considerably less light on the period and its problems if we were without the *Religion of the Manichees* and *Church and Gnosis*.

One Hundred and Five

Citizenship and Social Class

By far the most important (and the longest) of the four pieces which compose this book is that which gives it its title. *Citizenship and Social Class* is an elusive piece of writing, very compact and concise, often suggesting more than it says, and giving off an intellectual dazzle which the reader has to accustom himself to. As a lecture (a shortened form of it was given as the Alfred Marshall Lecture in Cambridge in 1949) it must have been difficult; but nobody who has given any thought to the subject will come away from reading it without the impression that here is something unusually profound and philosophical. And besides its masterly treatment of its own particular theme, it will do more than the most brilliant external account of the nature of sociology to convert those who are doubtful about the whole enterprise which goes under that name. Professor Marshall is not a voluminous writer, but when he gives us something of this quality we can resign ourselves to his long periods of silence.

His theme is the growth, in English society, of what he calls the 'status of citizenship' and its repercussions on the structure of the society and upon what he calls 'social class' and 'equality'. He begins with a brilliant piece of *histoire raisonnée* in which he traces the uneven development of the three kinds of 'rights' which compose the status of citizenship: civil, political, and social rights. Civil rights are those which put no legal obstacle in the way of a man behaving in a certain manner: he has the right to speak *if* he has anything to say, the right to enjoy property *if* he has come by it legally. Political rights give a man a voice in government and a hand in the process by which civil rights are created and maintained. Social rights are those positive opportunities and expectations a man is given, regardless of his means and his social class, to exercise his civil rights and in general enjoy a certain way of living – the right to education, to medical care, etc. Generally speaking, it is contended, these three sorts of rights were interwoven

Review of Thomas Humphrey Marshall, *Citizenship and Social Class* (Cambridge: Cambridge University Press, 1950). First published in *Cambridge Journal*, 4 (1951), 629–30.

in medieval civilization, but in the seventeenth century they parted company — developed at different speeds and, in some respects, in different directions; by 1832 an Englishman's civil rights were as complete as they are now, by 1918 his political rights were maturely established, but his social rights were slower in growth and their great period is the twentieth century. We are now in a situation in which the three have more nearly come together again and compose a coherent whole than at any period since the sixteenth century. This historical survey is preliminary to a discussion of the strains and tensions which compose and make stable contemporary English society. Elements of instability and incoherence are recognized, but on the whole we are given a picture of strength, though not of logical consistency.

I have called Professor Marshall's treatment an *histoire raisonnée* because, in spite of the great subtlety with which he traces the fortunes of these three different kinds of rights and their impact on social class, the result is something very much less than a concrete picture. In fact the three elements of citizenship never so completely parted company; and in fact they had far greater influence upon one another than Professor Marshall allows. It is too narrow a view to suggest that for a long period the Poor Law alone represented an Englishman's social rights. Social rights are the 'superstructure of legitimate expectations' which a man may have as a citizen, but expectations do not have to wait to be 'legitimized' until they are 'officially recognized'. 'Legitimization' also has its history and did not spring up suddenly and fully-armed: social rights are not the creatures of the modern state. The passage from legitimate expectation to personal right may involve a legal jump, but socially it is a slowly mediated and uninterrupted process. The church (never mentioned in these pages), which is neither a functional association nor a local community, over a long period gave men legitimate expectations. Further, Professor Marshall recognizes that when a form of activity (such as education) became a social right, the right was a claim on a minimum standard, but this characteristic should be recognized as universal: 'political journalism for the intelligentsia' may have been 'followed by newspapers for all who could read', but the quality was adapted to the market. It is not the 'components of a civilized and cultured life, formerly the monopoly of the few', which 'were brought progressively in reach of the many', how could it be? What the many enjoy is some shadowy counterpart of these components. Inequality is not so easily removed. And there are other, smaller but not unimportant, points where compression has led to historical inadequacy. The appearance of free compulsory education in the nineteenth century is spoken of as a signal departure from *laissez-faire* requiring some subtlety of view to make it seem coherent with its time and place: but this hypostatization of *laissez-faire* as the pre-eminent character of the age is surely a mistake — the same sort of mistake as that which ascribes intellectual self-confidence to the Victorian and then regards the morass of doubt and indecision which constituted the minds of so many Victorians as eccentric to the period. And does not the view that 'citizenship is based upon a set of ideals, beliefs and values' put the history the wrong way round; these ideals and values are the product of the enjoyment of citizenship, which in the first place is a manner of being active.

These are small points—and Professor Marshall's unwary use of the phrase, on two or three occasions, 'absolute natural rights' might be added to them—and they do not seriously detract from what is a modest and brilliant piece of analysis. Of course there are questions we should like to ask —why is the elimination of inherited privilege on all occasions thought to be an unquestionable advantage? How, after all that has been written, can 'democracy' and 'equality' be so naively equated? Why is the counterpart of government intervention in industrial disputes —trade union intervention in the work of government —thought to be an asset and not a questionably high price to pay? Why does Professor Marshall speak of the 'capitalist class system' when (it would appear) what he means by 'class' has little to do with the organization of industry? Why, if the 'development of democratic citizenship' is so empirical, so paradoxical a phenomenon, should we have such confidence in it as a foundation for a 'planned' society? Is there any basis for the 'personal obligation to work' which is seen to be 'attached to the status of citizenship', other than the fact that we have contracted a number of very expensive social rights? And why is Professor Marshall (who seems to be without any of the traditional beliefs which have given men confidence in the way they are going) so optimistic? But there is so much subtely and reflectiveness and so little partizanship in Professor Marshall's attitude and view of the contemporary social situation that, even if his conclusions are sometimes obscure, nobody can read him without enlightenment and the pleasure that comes from a sincere and cogent argument.

One Hundred and Six

The Discourses of Niccoló Machiavelli

This is an altogether admirable piece of work, learned, judicious, and timely, and it is possible in this review only to recommend it and to say something of its scope. *The Prince* is the best-known work of Machiavelli, but it is a book so directed to a single narrow purpose that it gives an imperfect idea of the complexity and comprehensiveness of Machiavelli's thought. For this, a study of the *Discoursi* is essential, and it is not too much to say that Father Walker has made this study possible for the first time for English students.

First, the translation has been executed with great care; it is accurate and alive: the best we have. In particular, it is the translation of one who has pondered long on the whole of Machiavelli's meaning; the greatest care has been taken in the rendering of the key words of Machiavelli's thought. And in order to carry the reader with him at every difficult or doubtful point, the translator has frequently given the original word or phrase in a footnote. It is a thoroughly candid and intelligent piece of work.

Secondly, the Introduction. This is a substantial piece of work of more than a hundred and fifty pages. But more than this, it is so learned in history, so deeply pondered and alive with thought, so calmly reflective and so full of finely noted distinctions and accurate observations, that it must be counted one of the most enlightening pieces of writing on the subject in the English language. It contains a brief account of Machiavelli's life and activities, a discussion of the relation of the *Discoursi* to Machiavelli's other writings, and an examination of Machiavelli's method and general ideas. There is absent from it any tendency to jump to hasty conclusions or to accept ready-made opinions: it is sympathetic, critical and written so lucidly and with such charm that the business of reading it becomes a pleasure. Nobody who has studied Machiavelli will fail to learn something from Father Walker's exposition of Machiavelli's ideas of Necessity, For-

Review of Niccoló Machiavelli, *The Discourses*, 2 vols, tr. and intro. L.J. Walker, (London: Routledge and Kegan Paul, 1950). First published in *Cambridge Journal*, 4 (1951), 698.

tune, and *virtù*, from his discussion of Machiavelli's alleged belief in the depravity of mankind or from the long and acute account he gives of Machiavelli's method of argument. There is, indeed, one point where Father Walker, usually so little given to wishful thinking, seems to have accepted Machiavelli's statement too much at its face-value: on pp. 79 and 117 he seems to miss the disingenuousness, or perhaps the irony, of Machiavelli's exclusion of the 'ecclesiastical principalities' from the normal rules of politics. And yet, even here, the important point is perceived—that these principalities enjoyed a political tradition which made them immune from some of the vicissitudes suffered by other states.

Father Walker's notes add enormously to the value of the translation. They are full without ever being irrelevant or garrulous; they tell the reader exactly what he needs to know, whether it is the elucidation of a piece of Roman or Italian history or of Machiavelli's argument. And the constant and apposite references, with ample quotation, to Guicciardini's *Considerazioni*, are most enlightening.

To complete the work we are given chronological tables of events in Roman and Italian history referred to by Machiavelli, four genealogical tables, a discussion of Machiavelli's sources, certain and conjectural, a list of Machiavelli's mistakes, and finally, perhaps the most useful of all the appendices, a comprehensive index of names and subjects.

One Hundred and Seven

History, Its Purpose and Method

This is an unfortunate book. Its mood is light-hearted and its overconfidence seriously qualifies it as a contribution to the discussion of the nature of historical knowledge. Everything is so obvious and simple that one wonders what all the fuss has been about. There is, of course, an intermittent contact with a more subtle view of things, but this sometimes adds to the confusion. The indiscipline appears first in a doubt whether Dr Renier's theme is the methodology of historical research or the philosophical consideration of history as a form of knowledge. In fact the book is concerned with both themes, but they are so confused that neither receives proper attention.

There is an important sense in which it is true that 'history reveals its nature through the familiarity of daily practice', and if Dr Renier had described to us how he works, the sort of problems he comes up against and how he solves them, and had told us this free from 'philosophical' reflections, he would have performed a useful service. But his remarks on the methodology of historical research are either too general (as in the chapter called 'Detecting the Traces') or too simply schematic (as in the section given to the 'divisions of history') to be of much value. There are moments when he goes beneath the surface — for example, his perception that the historian begins neither with a 'clean slate' nor with his 'sources' but with what he calls 'accepted history', and that what the historian does is to make a contribution to a story which he is not the first to tell — but they are infrequent and instead of persevering with them he darts off on another track.

Dr Renier's other theme is history as a form of knowledge; and here his treatment illustrates his contention that 'historians ... have the fullest right to adopt a philosophy'. He is engagingly candid about the philosophy he has adopted — or at least about the authors he relies upon — but what we

---

Review of Gustaaf Johannes Renier, *History, Its Purpose and Method* (London: George Allen and Unwin, 1950). First published in *Philosophical Quarterly*, 1 (1951), 284–5.

are given is illustrations of an adopted philosophy rather than an exercise in philosophical reflection. And even the adopted philosophy is so lightly grasped—it seems to be a kind of positivism—that the reader is always coming upon apparently erratic departures from it.

'The narrative of past experiences, active and passive, is for societies what memory is for their individual members', says Dr Renier. This simple view gives him a flying start, and he never looks back. History has the 'social purpose' of recalling to a society its past experiences. When it performs this service 'accurately' it does all that can properly be asked of it: and 'accurately' presents no problem which cannot be solved by reference to the known and accepted methods of historical research and criticism. There would be little objection to this view of things—simple though it is—if it were not tied up with some rather slap-dash reflections on the nature of knowledge, the heart of which is a doctrine about the relation between historical 'facts' and the 'explanation of the facts' which is an 'unavoidable concomitant' of historical narrative. In the greater part of his treatment of this problem Dr Renier holds fast to his adopted philosophy. Research puts the historian 'in possession of a large number of events' of which, when fixed by criticism, he can be certain. But these are merely the 'material' of the story he is to write; they must be given a 'shape'. And in order to do this the historian may call upon various 'principles of serialization'—time, causation, etc.—and if these are not enough he must be prepared to use his imagination. The main point, however, is that he has the 'isolated', shapeless facts first, and the process of shaping is a process of fitting together, like the pieces of a puzzle, those facts which he decides are relevant. This doctrine, no doubt, has its difficulties, and to have it put before us once again in clear outline could do no harm. But having nailed this flag securely to his mast Dr Renier inconsequentially rips it off again with the admission that 'the barest statement of fact implies the expression of a view about the fact, a theory', and the statement that it is only when he comes to write his story that the historian begins to know what his 'facts' are—a statement much closer to the experience of most historians than the naïve doctrine he has been at such pains to impress upon us. In short, this is a book in which the reader hardly knows what to expect next as he turns the page. There is some interesting information, there are some acute detached observations, there are some forcefully stated views but there is curiously little sustained argument, and even the criticism of Collingwood, which might have been valuable, peters out in irrelevance.

One Hundred and Eight

Liberties of the Mind

Most people are aware that it is only by a disingenuous revision of the meaning of the word 'freedom' that we conceal from ourselves the fact that the exercise of freedom has been greatly reduced in the last twenty-five years. The prevailing mood is one of being ready to surrender freedom: among less foolish people, for something believed to be of equal value; among others, for the mere promise of a dream. Much, says Mr Charles Morgan, has been lost (some of it well lost), but those who are still absolute for freedom must now consider the defence of the citadel — not the 'outward liberties' of behaviour, but 'the liberties of the mind itself.' The concern of these essays is the danger in which the 'core of the mind' stands of being dispossessed of its independence.

The opening essay, on Mind Control, states the theme. There are passages in it which run smoothly and whose meaning is interrupted only by the glossy mellowness of the prose; but as a whole the statement bristles with ambiguities. It would, perhaps, be a piece of philosophical pedantry to object to the way in which Mr Morgan uses the word 'mind' (as if it were a piece of sacred machinery): if we are to get anywhere with the book we must be content to suppose that we know what he means even if we should prefer another way of speaking. Nevertheless, a good deal of the confusion seems to spring from what may be called Mr Morgan's concept of mind. However, apart from this, the reader is left in serious doubt about what Mr Morgan is getting at. We seem, at first, to be invited to take note of the appearance (or near-appearance) of a scientific technique by means of which a man may be dispossessed of his 'mind' and become an automaton in the control of a technician. The evidence adduced (and admitted to be 'scant') is the behaviour of prisoners in the Soviet trials, and a conversation Mr Morgan had with an unnamed physicist whose vision extended to the possibility of being able to take possession completely of another man's 'mind'. When he is on this tack, Mr Morgan steers his readers, with

Review of Charles Langbridge Morgan, *Liberties of the Mind* (London: Macmillan, 1951). First published in *Spectator*, 186 (1951), 419.

a practised hand, on an artificially darkened course, beset with half-imagined Gothic horrors and uncanny experiences. But we are never properly frightened because the devilry is never properly revealed.

The other tack is made in broad daylight; its horrors are palpable and familiar — and consequently genuinely horrible. Here we are not being scared by the vague suggestion of some diabolically ingenious psychological technique which science has in pickle for us; we are having our attention called to the circumstances in the contemporary world which restrict the range of independent judgment and individual moral choice — the gross pressure of numbers which goes to compose a morally worthless public opinion, and the moral delusion that when we have discovered how to do something we are well advised to do it. But even here, in the full light of day, the nameless horror cannot be excluded; the whole process (following a phrase of Tennyson's) is presented as 'a mighty wave of evil' thrown up by comparatively recent events. And while the well-chosen phrase heightens the mystery of our predicament, our attention is directed to something very banal — not to the root of chaos, but merely to the *danger* of immorality when it is allied with great power. Mr Morgan seems to belong to that school of moralists which urges fear of destruction as the motive for mending our ways.

We are left, then, with some latitude of choice in the interpretation of our disease, though in one way or another 'science' is at the bottom of it. This is unfortunate, because what we look for in a moralist is a clear vision of the predicament. Mr Morgan has chosen to write at an awkward level. There is a level of diagnosis at which it would be in order to ask for the villains to be named and to demand their prosecution. And there is a profound level at which hope and fear are equally out of place, where the situation is seen to be desperate but not serious, as St Augustine, for example, saw it. Mr Morgan, however, has chosen a difficult middling station: he is remote without being profound, lofty without being confident, and he is engaged but with insufficiently identified enemies. And the confusion is carried over into the remedies he propounds. Surely it argues a want of proper consideration of the relation between this so-called 'liberty of the mind itself' and the familiar overt liberties, or a deep-rooted ambiguity of outlook, to suggest that we should 'disengage the liberty of thought as a distinct and inalienable liberty' and 'make it cognisable by positive law'.

The bulk of the book consists in short essays, each a neat variation on the imperfectly imagined theme of the Introduction. Most of them have appeared before in periodicals, and taken separately they express an agreeably sentimental, nostalgic view of life. But the collection of them here serves mainly to show up the thinness of the theme they are set to illustrate. The truth is, I suppose, that Mr Morgan's temperament is ill-fitted to deal with the theme which he handles so delicately in these pages.

There is nothing disgraceful in being nostalgic or in turning over affectionately the things one has learnt to value; but nostalgia gets in the way of precision, and to treat this theme precision is necessary. And, again, a mind devoid of irony and incapable of satire, a disposition without the energy of bitterness and without either the anger or detachment of saintliness, will seem unfitted for the task. The book does not lack sincerity, Mr Morgan really does care about the predicament as he sees it; but he fails to convince us of its reality. The style—this urbane, smoothly confidential, humourless style—meets the theme, and we are left happily splashing one another in the safety of slack water. And if an occasional ripple gets up our noses and makes us splutter—if he throws in the observation that the history of the last fifty years has been 'a steady movement towards barbarism interrupted by ineffectual idealistic swerves'—we are made to feel that it is all part of the game.

In short, Mr Morgan's theme is that of *1984*. But Orwell's precise and microscopic imagination and his ironic vision are replaced by a soft anxiety about incompletely imagined possibilities and a mannered rhetoric too nicely tuned to be effective. Nowhere have the last days of mankind been more urbanely contemplated.

One Hundred and Nine

Dominations and Powers

Human beings, who are otherwise quite used to doing two things at once (talking and drinking; travelling and enjoying the view), when they turn to reading are apt to demand something which engages them in a single activity. And when a book invites us to turn its pages and enjoy its separate scenes, and at the same time gives hints of a firm structure which encourages close study, we are apt to be suspicious. But when delight and instruction are both at a high level and avoid the suggestion that the union is synthetic, we are sometimes prepared to accept them together. This, I think, should be our attitude to *Dominations and Powers*, which is a book of this elusive and provoking sort.

The casual reader, then, may turn its pages and find in them a collection of essays. Each of these hundred chapters is a finished example of the imaginative subtlety of thought and expression which we have long ago learnt to expect from Santayana. His manner has always been to explore images rather than analyse concepts, to meditate rather than argue. And there is so much individuality about the performance that it must be counted an achievement to have escaped all these years the nemesis of writing a parody of himself. His themes here are the varieties of human behaviour, the ambivalence of human enterprise, the hindrances and servitudes we suffer, the 'false defiances of fate' and illusory escapes, and the freedom we at once enjoy and seek.

In this reading we shall observe also his loves and hates, his prejudices and predilections. Life is neither a journey nor a feast, but a predicament and a dream, to be meditated upon with a combination of sympathy and ironic detachment. In his earliest writings Santayana displayed an effortless sagacity which was open to the suspicion of being precocious; in age the dazzle may be diminished, but the wisdom is still apt and has not grown garrulous. Here he disclaims a creed, a message or the power of

---

Review of George Santayana, *Dominations and Powers. Reflections on Liberty, Society, and Government* (London: Constable, 1951). First published in *Spectator*, 187 (1951), 578.

prophecy; his attitude is at bottom aesthetic; and his sympathy lies with whatever exhibits 'harmony and strength, no matter how short-lived.' Longevity is a vulgar good, and consequently 'the folly of the enthusiast may sometimes be wiser than the wisdom of the world.'

But if this manner of reading the book scarcely needs recommendation because it will come easily to anyone who opens it and will have its immediate reward, there is something else which must be pointed out lest it escape notice. The book is not, in fact, an anthology of miscellaneous reflections strung together on the thin thread of an arbitrary attitude to the universe. It is an intellectual structure, a vertebrate and well-considered philosophy. It is true that the articulation is not obtrusive, and it is true also that the title of the book is not a very explicit signpost to the structure; but not to have detected the articulation is to have missed the proper quality of the book.

Santayana's affinity is neither with Plato nor Hegel, both of whom make their appearance, however (and though Hegel is recognisable he is barely recognised). His affinity is with Spinoza. Indeed, though there is nothing crudely derivative about his thought, to explore its convolutions is like exploring a modernised version of Spinoza's ethical and political philosophy. The human individual appears first as 'primal Will,' and in this appearance his activity is in relation to the world as 'natural.' To escape from this generative order of activity is impossible; it is our fate as animals. But in relation to their fellows the activity of human beings bifurcates into militant and rational modes. In the militant order of activity the wilfulness of the will is expressed; 'the source of militancy' lies in 'the indecision or self-contradiction of animal Will in pursuing distractedly incompatible goods.' In the rational order, on other hand, activity is animated not by a finished ideal of conduct, but by a harmony of conduct when it is appropriate to its circumstances. And here, in relation to political activity (which is always generative and may be either militant or rational), there is an echo of Burke — 'all sound reforms must be massively generative movements and not thinly militant strains' — and an even more distinct echo of Coleridge.

Writers in this tradition have a habit of bringing the argument up to a certain point and often, to this point, carrying conviction. But it is a point of uncertain equilibrium, and many questions remain unanswered; the analysis of 'circumstance' and 'expedience' is left incomplete. It is disappointing to find Santayana travelling this route with such acuteness of observation (and so much engaging talk by the way) and breaking off at the familiar point. But of the power and subtlety of the attempt there can be no doubt. *Dominations and Powers* is an achievement of philosophical imagination such as we have become unaccustomed to in these days of minute dissection.

One Hundred and Ten

The Price of Revolution

Political discussion (when it rises above the level of gossip or goes beyond the events of last week) has, for a long time, been bedevilled by abstractions. When it escapes vulgar realism, it becomes the exploration of the necessary relations between a collection of abstract nouns: Democracy, Imperialism, Communism, Capitalism, Nationalism, Freedom, Revolution, Reaction and the rest. And in shuffling these cumbersome pieces of mental furniture about, we first raise the dust and then complain that we cannot see. Half of human activity becomes incomprehensible to us, and the rest is misconceived. Anyone, therefore, who bids us desist and recalls us to concrete, if less imposing, realities, though he must appear to speak out of turn, may perhaps hope for a hearing. And when he does so with the vigour, the wit and the learning which Professor Brogan has at his disposal, the performance may be expected to attract even those who yearn for the merry din of the feast to which the ideologues invite us.

The Price of Revolution is a *tour de force*. In the present gloom of political discussion a searchlight would dazzle us; Professor Brogan has illuminated the scene brilliantly, but with a diffused light. He wastes no time criticising the current abstractions; when they appear insufferably inflated he punctures them in a footnote. His main enterprise is to throw into our dream world the precipitant of precise and detailed knowledge, and in this manner to transform it into a world of concrete activities and their probable consequences.

The range of Professor Brogan's information and the readiness of his learning are now proverbial, and here the range and readiness are displayed in all their brilliance. But there is something more; there is coherent argument and there is imagination. Hitherto, Professor Brogan's readers might be forgiven for thinking that, while his knowledge was catholic, his sympathetic understanding was fully in play only when he was writing

---

Review of Denis William Brogan, *The Price of Revolution* (London: Hamish Hamilton. 1951). First published in *Spectator*, 187 (1951), 825.

about his native place – the Clydeside. But in *The Price of Revolution* there is a well-informed imagination at work over a remarkably wide range of situations.

Professor Brogan does not claim to illuminate the whole contemporary situation. His theme is the history and significance of violent change (political and technological) in the modern world; and this theme is explored literally from China to Peru. His thesis is that for about the last hundred and fifty years we have been living in an age of revolution, but that we have not yet adapted ourselves to this circumstance. We have not accustomed ourselves to counting the cost of violent change; our political book-keeping has not kept pace with our political activity. And we are further handicapped because our present political habits of mind were formed in a period of about two generations (immediately before 1914) when it seemed probable that the era of violent change was, for the time being, over – with the consequence that our present expectations are out of touch with political realities.

A variety of conclusions emerge. All government is expensive, what *we* call good government is still beyond the means of the greater part of the world, but violent and revolutionary political methods are particularly costly and remarkably uneconomical. Their cost is to be counted not merely in the good that they destroy (that is often exaggerated), but in the very elementary goods (such as order and decency) which they endanger, and in the displacements in society which they cause, displacements which can be very little foreseen and which go on revealing themselves for generations after the event. And the uneconomical character of revolutionary remedies is revealed in their inefficiency: every revolution promised more than it was able to achieve, and what survives a revolution is often the more odious features of the *ancien régime*. But the costly and uneconomical character of revolution (when it is considered in all its concrete detail and not merely in the abridged form in which it appears in the mind of the revolutionary) should not lead us to suppose that men are not on occasion prepared to pay the price: it should lead us to make a greater effort in the exceedingly tricky business of political book-keeping.

It would be a mistake, however, to attribute to Professor Brogan the intention of persuading us to any precise course of action. He knows what he dislikes in our situation, and he can recognise what is hostile to the kind of society he thinks desirable; he does not hedge on these matters, but he is not disposed to cry over spilt milk. His main concern is that we should not be deceived about our situation. His hopes are not high and his expectations are not great. We have every prospect of remaining for some time to come in an era of revolutions and their costly consequences; 'peace, in the old sense, is probably out for a generation.' But, then, he knows also that life is nowhere, and never has been, *couleur de rose*, and that what *we* consider to be valuable—'freedom,' flexibility of government and so on—are known and desired by only a small minority of the world's population. And having a firm grasp on these simple truths, he is able to avoid the contemporary habit of exaggerating our situation into a kind of cosmic tragedy—a Predicament. For Professor Brogan it is simply a situation, perhaps a dilemma, more properly a 'pass,' to be observed and understood in its all too human and historical proportions.

In short, *The Price of Revolution* is to be welcomed and applauded as a piece of political thinking which manages to avoid the two opposed vices of most current political thinking—starry-eyed abstraction and vulgar realism. Politics are presented to us here neither as the pursuit of Utopias nor as mere 'fixing,' but as not being deceived about our situation and doing our best in almost unendurably 'interesting' circumstances. One could wish that the proof-reading had been a little more exact and that the publisher had been a little less niggardly in the matter of type and paper. But it is a book which has no difficulty in surviving such circumstantial handicaps.

One Hundred and Eleven

Psychoanalysis and Politics

The reading of human behaviour proposed by psychoanalysts is often unsatisfying on account of an element of over-elaboration. Not only is it clear that if they are right everyone else must be wrong, but general propositions which seem to contain a measure of truth are made less convincing by being insisted upon in every detail; acute observations lose their force when pressed *ad absurdum*. Consequently, even the unprejudiced student is apt to do less than justice to writers who appear to be making rather more than all that can be made of their alleged discoveries. Mr Money-Kyrle's contribution to the psychoanalytic elucidation of political behaviour is, however, welcome because, in spite of its ambitious character, it is candid, moderate, and free from gross over-simplification. His enterprise is to suggest that psychoanalysis has, first, something to offer in the determination of 'goodness' in human character and social order, and, secondly, something to offer in bringing this about. The reader must be prepared to accept the Freudian analysis of behaviour, but beyond that the argument is free from technicalities and is conducted with commendable common sense and sobriety.

A 'good' order of society (so the doctrine runs) will be one which at once encourages and springs from individuals who behave rationally; and rational behaviour is the pursuit of desires based upon 'true' or verifiable beliefs as distinct from fantasies. Thus, to behave rationally is not necessarily to be without anxiety, love, hate, inner conflict or potential conflict with others; it is to be determined only by genuine anxieties and to be contentious, not compulsively, but only with a manifest cause. Rationality is to have nothing permanently excluded from consciousness. Mr Money-Kyrle believes that this conception of 'rationality' offers a more extended and more satisfactory guide to conduct than the conceptions of 'normality' with which other psychoanalysts have worked. But it has its recognizable

---

Review of Roger Ernle Money-Kyrle, *Psychoanalysis and Politics* (London: Duckworth, 1951). First published in *Times Literary Supplement* (17 August 1951), 511.

limits. It desiderates an absence of distortion and exaggeration in belief and behaviour, but it does not itself guarantee agreement or remove conflict. However, to have confined conflict to realities and to its real proportions would be no despicable achievement; and this is precisely the result which psychoanalysis aims at—the redemption of mankind by greater self-knowledge.

But human behaviour is irretrievably ambivalent—alternating in love and hate. And in so far as they are moral beings, men are directed by the fear of a sense of guilt. This fear commonly takes either of two forms; it may be a fear of punishment or a fear of injuring or disappointing somebody who is loved. And these two forms of morality issue in two types of moral conscience, the one authoritarian and compulsive and the other 'humanistic.' The fact is, however, that in so far as behaviour is rational it tends towards the creation and maintenance of a 'humanistic' conscience, moved by love and free from merely compulsive obedience. The social order composes an environment favourable to one or other of these types of conscience, an authoritarian or over-regulated society tending to encourage a merely compulsive morality, and a 'liberal' society a 'humanistic' morality. A 'good' state will, therefore, be one which is well adapted to rational individuals and favourable to a 'humanistic' type of conscience.

The task of bringing into consciousness (and so depriving them of their malign influence) the unconscious fantasies and deceptions of men in political activity is seen to be an exceptionally difficult enterprise; but when it is recognized, not as a magic technique for lessening all social and political conflicts, but as making political behaviour more rational by removing it from the control of undetected fantasy, it is neither utopian nor impossible.

In the course of his argument Mr Money-Kyrle has some interesting remarks upon both German and English political behaviour, but he seems often to over-simplify political decisions, making them appear to spring not at all from concrete situations, but from the isolated individuals of Freudian theory determined by their infant experiences.

One Hundred and Twelve

Introduction to Politics

There is a contemporary belief that an 'Introduction' should avoid the advocacy of any specific doctrine and make the reader think for himself by presenting him with an array of problems and a summary of the available views. As an emblem of intellectual restraint this may be commendable; but it may be doubted whether it is the best manner of introduction. The range of a subject is usually better displayed in arguing an interesting case than in summarizing the views of x, y, and z: unanswered questions are often imperfectly conceived questions, and the value of an answer (from this point of view) lies not in its freedom from error, but in the thoroughness with which it is elaborated. Plato's *Republic* is the best introduction to philosophy, not because its doctrine is acceptable but because it reveals a master at work.

Mrs Pickles's book, however, conforms to the contemporary belief, and has the virtues as well as the defects of the sort of enterprise it encourages. Its object is to suggest questions without supplying answers. And in spite of a certain breathlessness in the manner in which questions tumble over one another, the problems presented for consideration are often displayed with subtlety and a wealth of illustration.

The background of the book is the conception of politics as the means to the achievement of variously denoted general ends, such as social justice, or happiness: political activity is the solution of the problem which the pursuit of such ends throws up. Some of the questions considered are of the familiar generalized kind—What is the best sort of government? Are there any general principles which ought to guide a government in exercising its power? On these Mrs Pickles usually has something interesting to say, though she is not always successful in observing the appropriate distinctions. Many of the questions are closely related to our current situation, and in considering these Mrs Pickles shows admirable good sense

---

Review of Dorothy Maud Pickles, *Introduction to Politics* (London: Sylvan Press, 1951). First published in *Times Literary Supplement* (23 November 1951), 743.

and a welcome touch of realism. She is often obliged to discuss matters of contemporary political controversy, but she manages to do so without prejudice.

Mrs Pickles warns the reader that, although she has occasion to quote from writers 'who have made important contributions to the history of political thought,' no exposition of the ideas of these writers must be expected. In a book of this sort, this is a legitimate piece of self-limitation; but even so there are some unnecessarily misleading statements. Hobbes should not have been credited with a belief in a contract between subject and sovereign. And though it is perhaps a permissible piece of shorthand to say that for Rousseau 'the sovereign is the people,' shorthand becomes parody in the few lines devoted to Hegel. And surely it would have been better to have avoided the terms 'Church' and 'State' in speaking of medieval political communities.

Indexes

PROPER NAMES

Abélard, Peter   323
Acton, John Emerich, 1st Baron Acton   200, 229, 242, 299, 312
Alembert, Jean le Rond d'   84
Alexander, Samuel   80, 322
Aliotta, Antonio   37, 39
Allen, Carleton Kemp   156, 158
Althasius, Johannes   97
Aquinas, St Thomas   80, 114, 169, 179, 182, 201
Aristotle   45, 92, 115, 121, 182, 201, 234, 249, 287–8, 300–1
Arnold, Matthew   58
Arnot, Page   101
Asia   263, 265
Atkins, Gaius   66–69
Attlee, Clement   214, 260–1, 345
Augustine, St   45, 96, 201, 333, 360
Austin, John   87, 156 n.
Australia   260
Ayer, Alfred Jules   286

Bacon, Francis, Baron Verulam   114–15, 199, 302
Bain, Alexander   142
Balfour, Arthur James   37, 39
Barclay[?]   56
Barker, Ernest   97, 99
Barth, Karl   81
Belasco, Philip   54
Bennett, Arnold   60
Bentham, Jeremy   142, 167, 193, 195, 204, 226, 311–12
Bergson, Henri   323
Berkeley, George   84, 324
Bernal, John Desmond   101
Bevin, Ernest   261
Blake, William   182, 281, 305
Bodin, Jean   109, 117, 226
Bolingbroke, Henry St John   293–4
Bosanquet, Bernard   53, 124
Bosanquet, Theodora   87
Bouquet, Alan   40
Bowie, Walter   49
Bradley, Francis Herbert   90, 140–2, 144, 190
Bristol   143
Britain   260
Broad, Charles Dunbar   125
Brown, William   39

Bryce, James   165, 168
Buckland, William Warwick   164
Burckhardt, Jacob   330
Burke, Edmund   204–5, 226, 311, 363
Burma   260
Burnet[?]   56
Burnett, James, Lord Monboddo   234
Burns, Cecil Delisle   108
Byzantium   299

Calvin, Jean   114
Carritt, Edgar Frederick   101–2
Chateaubriand, François René de   87
Chaucer, Geoffrey   239
Chesterton, Gilbert Keith   46
Chestov, Leo   91–3
China   264, 365
Clemenceau, Georges   57
Clydeside   365
Coleridge, Samuel Taylor   87, 279, 363
Collingwood, Robin George   358
Comte, Auguste   87
Condillac, Étienne Bonnot de   84
Copernicus, Nicolaus   301–2
Cripps, Stafford   214, 261
Croce, Benedetto   80, 122, 197, 284
Cromwell, Oliver   214
Curtis, Lionel   96
Czechoslovakia   306

Debussy, Claude   239
Descartes, Renée   45, 56, 89, 116, 199, 268–70, 304
Dicey, Albert Venn   149
Diderot, Denis   84, 110
Dilthey, Wilhelm   135
Dimitrov, Georgi   296
Dostoevsky, Fyodor   91, 93
Driesch, Hans   78–9

Eddington, Arthur   38
Edward I, King of England   96
Edward VIII, King of England   212
Eliot, Thomas Stearns   58, 108
Engels, Friedrich   100–1, 104, 295
England   76, 84, 86, 135, 142, 164, 186, 260, 304, 327, 344, 368
Epicurus   57, 85, 182
Erastus, Thomas   121
Europe   86, 88, 103, 105–6, 123, 137, 142, 147–8, 164, 180,   182, 190, 201, 224, 229, 244, 262–3, 283, 289,   304

Farmer, Herbert Henry 71
Feiling, Keith 63, 87
Ferguson, Adam 234
Ferrier, James Frederick 289
Figgis, John Neville 117
Filmer, Robert 315–16
Follett, Mary Parker 51
Fox, George 55
Fox, William Johnson 195
France 84
Freud, Sigmund 184, 367

Galileo, Galilei 114, 116, 301–2, 304
Gardner, Percy 50
Germany 207, 264, 368
Gerson, Jean de 114
Gibbon, Edward 298
Gierke, Otto von 97
Gisevius, Hans Bernd 214
Glehn, Marion de 140
Godwin, William 311
Goethe, Johann von 81, 305
Gore, Charles 48
Grant, Malcolm 95
Grattan, Henry 204
Greece 37, 57, 88, 123, 198, 264, 300, 317, 348
Green, Thomas Hill 125, 144, 169, 249–50
Gregory VII see Hildebrand
Groethuisen, Bernard 196

Hardy, Thomas 46
Harvey, William 301–2
Hegel, George Wilhelm Friedrich 52–3, 87, 92, 118, 125, 127, 135, 144, 165–6, 168–9, 172, 179, 190, 204, 217, 249, 253–4, 323, 363, 370
Heim, Karl 81
Helvétius, Claude Adrien 84, 311
Henry VII, King of England 275
Hildebrand 114
Hitler, Adolf 214, 306
Hobbes, Thomas 84, 97–9, 109, 110–21, 145–6, 169, 179, 182, 201, 226–7, 249, 254, 282, 293, 311, 370
Hobhouse, Leonard Trelawney 235
Hobson, Ernest 38
Hodgkin, Thomas 87
Holmes, Edmund 81
Home, Henry, Lord Kames 234
Hooker, Richard 109
Hume, David 84, 90, 234, 293, 311, 323–4
Husserl, Edmund 135
Hutcheson, Francis 234
Hyde Park 262

India 88
Inge, William Ralph 39

James, William 142
Jascalevich, Alejandro 45

Jay, Douglas 345
Jesus Christ 66–9, 96, 123
Joachim, Harold Henry 140
Johnson, Samuel 276
Judea 348

Kant, Immanuel 81, 89, 90, 98, 124–5, 165, 168, 172, 197, 227, 294, 324
Kepler, Johannes 302
Kierkegaard, Soren 136
Kornilov, Lavr 331

Laird, John 113 n., 114
Lavoisier, Antoine 301
Leibniz, Gottfried Wilhelm 110
Lenin, Vladimir Ilich 207, 296, 326, 331
Lessing, Gotthold Ephraim 139
Levy, Hermann 102
Lichtenberg, Georg Christoph 305
Lincoln, Abraham 214
Lloyd George, David 345
Locke, John 82–6, 109, 110, 117, 124, 226–7, 249, 255, 293–4, 311, 313–14
Lysenko, Trofim 296

Machiavelli, Niccolò 109, 117, 196, 226, 276, 355–6
Mackenzie, John 51–3
Macmurray, John 89, 100
Maitland, Frederick 98, 328
Malaysia 264
Malinowski, Bronislaw 37
Mannheim, Karl 206
Martet, Jean 57
Marx, Karl 100–1, 103–4, 147–8, 190, 191, 193, 271–2, 289, 295–6
McKerrow, James 122
McTaggart, John Ellis 190
Mediterranean 289
Melanesia 37
Mersenne, Marin 116
Mill, James 142, 311
Mill, John Stuart 87, 193, 311
Milton, John 109, 182
Mohammed 68
Molotov, Vyacheslav 330
Montaigne, Michel de 59, 74, 85
Montesquieu, Charles Louis de Secondat, 202, 226
  Baron de la Brède et de,
Moore, George Edward 125
Morris, William 212
Morrison, Herbert 261
Moscow 307
Murray, Gilbert 195

Needham, Joseph 38
Newton, Isaac 84, 301
Nietzsche, Friedrich 136, 148, 224–5, 278
Nimrod 314

Occam, William of 114
Ogden, Charles Kay 286
Oman, John 38
Otto, Rudolf 80
Owen, Robert 87, 195
Oxford 110

Padua 37, 303
Page, F.M.[?] 87
Paine, Thomas 311
Paley, William 190, 311
Pareto, Vilfredo 235
Pascal, Blaise 93, 120, 269–70, 305
Penn, William 55
Perry, Ralph Barton 43
Peru 365
Plato 105, 124, 127, 184, 248–9, 323, 363
Plotinus 93
Poland 264, 306
Pope, Alexander 293
Pound, Roscoe 163, 167, 178
Powys, Llewlyn 63
Prichard, Harold Arthur 125
Ptolemy 301

Rabelais, François 239
Ragusa 319
Ranke, Leopold von 298
Rashdall, Hastings 65
Reid, Thomas 234
Richards, Ivor Armstrong 286
Rickert, Heinrich 322
Robertson, George Croom 110
Rome 57, 88, 239, 333, 348, 351
Ross, William David 125
Rousseau, Jean Jacques 52, 97–8, 202, 226–7, 249, 370
Ruskin, John 195
Russell, Bertrand 76, 80, 286
Russia 241, 261, 263–5, 272, 290, 325–6, 330–2, 359

St John's College, Oxford 231
Salmond, John William 156, 175
Scandinavia 260
Schiller, Friedrich 81
Schopenhauer, Arthur 79
Scotland 234
Sellars, Roy Wood 44

Shakespeare, William 182
Sheen, Fulton 80
Sidney, Philip 109
Singer, Charles 37
Smith, Adam 234, 255
Smith, Logan Pearsall 73
Sombart, Werner 196
Sorel, Georges 191
Southcott, Joanna 262
Spinoza, Benedict 92, 117, 139, 145, 226, 254, 271, 323, 363
Spratt[?] 297
Stalin, Joseph 296, 330
Stewart, Dugald 234
Stout, George Frederick 142
Strachey, Lytton 345
Struve, Petr Berngardovich 330
Sully, James 142
Switzerland 231, 332

Tennyson, Alfred 108, 360
Thucydides 143
Tito, Josip Broz 308
Tolstoy, Leo 91, 93
Tönnies, Ferdinand 110
Troeltsch, Ernst 97, 122

Ukraine 330
United States of America 44, 206, 236, 261, 262–4, 283, 306–7, 333, 344

Vaughan, Charles Edwyn 117
Vega 57
Vico, Giambattista 228
Vorberg, Gaston 225

Walpole, Horace 83
Ward, James 142
Webb, Clement 39
Weber, Max 135, 148
Wells, Herbert George 46
Westermarck, Edward 235
Whitehead, Alfred North 80
Whittaker, Thomas 42
Widgery, Alban 46–7
Willey, Basil 112
Wilson, John Cook 90
Wood, Herbert George 122–3
Woodbridge, Frederick 45
Woolf, Virginia 239

SUBJECTS

A priori 165-6
Absolute 118
Absolutism 52, 118, 253
Action 89, 193, 257, 364
Aesthetics 43, 184-5, 269, 279, 293-4, 363
Analogy 153, 318
Aphorisms 73-5
Arrest 179
Art 93, 184-6, 239, 278-9, 283
Authority 54-5, 61, 120, 338, 351

Baptism 49
B.B.C. 149, 306, 334-44
Biology 38
Body 45, 317

Capitalism 191-2, 194, 261, 271-3, 289, 345-7, 364
Catholicism 49, 123
Change 63-4, 69, 71
Character 83, 217, 231, 233, 310, 367
Christianity 39, 40, 41, 48, 63-4, 66-70, 72, 106, 122-3, 137, 139, 222, 236, 284, 299, 314, 346, 348
Church 48, 55, 82, 109, 121, 353, 370
Civilization 105
Classics 60
Common sense 43, 83, 92
Commonwealth 96, 275-6
Communism 150, 192-3, 261, 306-8
Competition 344
Conscience 120
Consent 227
Conservatism 63-4, 203-4, 208-9, 217
Context 174-5, 348
Conversation 74, 288, 309
Creativity 277-8
Culture 58-60, 78, 106, 147, 224-5, 236, 272
Custom 88, 105, 204, 216, 222-3, 257, 346

Death 59, 281
Decadence 107, 238-9
Definition 170, 175
Democracy 86, 149, 191-4, 204, 214, 218, 220-1, 236-7, 264, 307, 346, 354, 364
Despotism 213-14
Dialectic 287-8, 309, 321
Dialectical Materialism 100-1, 295
Dogmatism 47, 101
Doubt 82
Dreams 319
Duties 78, 165, 171, 216, 218-19, 250-1, 253, 256, 258-9

Economics 61, 161, 163, 187, 207, 211, 247, 253, 283, 347
Education 52, 78, 152, 187, 195, 209, 228, 239, 240, 251, 258, 269, 276, 300, 310, 334, 341-2, 352

Empiricism 47, 293-4
Enlightenment 236-7
Equality 63, 149, 192, 242, 354
Ethics 43, 120, 125, 146, 167, 193, 269, 271, 278-9
Eucharist 49
Events 95, 132, 301
Evidence 93, 130, 230
Experience 84, 89, 91, 247, 281, 298, 303
Explanation 155, 179
   hierarchy of 176

Fabian Society 195
Facts 173, 230, 358
Fascism 150, 209, 264
Fashion 239
Fear 117, 368
Freedom 59, 106, 149, 187, 200, 213, 216, 218, 249, 258, 261, 336, 347, 359, 364, 366

General Will 52, 125
God 41, 71, 80, 94-5, 128, 153, 190

Happiness 167, 190
Hegelianism 135
History 41, 49, 63-4, 66-9, 71, 105-6, 122, 137, 143, 152, 180, 187, 189, 209, 354
   written 54, 88, 96, 103, 113, 130-4, 141, 158-60, 163, 193, 197-9, 201-2, 228-30, 283, 298-303, 326-31, 348-50, 357-8

Idealism 46, 90, 282, 318, 321-2
Identity 61, 67, 69, 131, 158
Ideology 147, 292, 307
Imagination 118, 131, 279, 293-4, 363, 364
Individualism 55, 85, 98, 117, 146, 193, 212, 216-7, 219, 249, 254-6, 290
Interest 43, 124, 240
Interpretation 155, 161, 169, 302

Jurisprudence 154-6

King 55, 276
Knowledge 37-8, 58, 83, 89, 91, 120, 133, 141, 147, 168, 172, 183, 239, 240, 253, 283, 321-2, 357, 368

Laisser-faire 191-2, 208, 255
Liberalism 84-6, 117, 196, 261
Liberty: see Freedom
Language 120, 151, 185, 330-1, 350
Law 88, 109, 120, 143, 154-83, 187, 207-8, 216, 218, 244, 253, 256, 276, 309, 360
Logic 90, 135, 148, 268, 278, 287-8, 300, 324
Love 57, 60, 75, 85, 217, 242, 367

Magic 37, 184-5
Mathematics 89, 268-9
Meaning 155
Mechanism 38, 115

Medieval: see Middle Ages
Memory 130
Metaphor 119
Metaphysics 39, 45, 73, 81, 165, 269, 324
Middle Ages 114–15, 137, 202, 218, 276, 287, 299, 300, 324, 348, 370
Mind 45, 285, 301, 317–18
Miracles 94
Misology 91, 93, 112
Modernism 50
Morality 52, 65, 78, 221, 234, 235, 245, 251, 256, 267, 272, 283–4, 304, 310, 360, 368
Mysticism 39, 54
Myth 130, 143, 167, 305, 314

Natural law 97–8, 145, 167–8, 179, 190, 203–4, 216, 218, 227, 247, 250, 254, 258
Natural rights: see Natural law
Naturalism 38, 46, 271, 282

Obligation 124, 165, 171, 249, 254
Opposition 208, 210–11, 215

Pantheism 40
Parliament 209
Peace 107, 206, 246, 252
Personality 99, 256
Philosophes 304
Philosophy 39, 42, 43, 44, 45, 46, 65, 75, 77, 78, 81, 82–4, 93, 101–2, 106, 111–13, 116, 118, 135–6, 170–4, 176, 181, 205, 248, 253, 266, 280, 292, 317–18, 323–4, 363, 369
Planning 207, 209, 211, 213, 218, 261, 346
Pluralism 52, 55
Poetry 108, 151, 180, 182, 239, 257, 278, 293
Politics 55, 61, 116, 124, 189, 196, 205, 208, 215, 217, 234, 239, 242, 260, 266, 275, 313, 356, 365, 367, 369
Pope 55
Positivism 230, 253, 284, 297, 358
Power 187, 215–16, 261, 360, 369
Pragmatism 38, 46, 50
Presuppositions 157, 165, 171, 255
Pride 117
Progress 108, 263–4
Providence 41
Puritanism 85, 236–7
Psychology 39, 45, 89, 140–2, 160, 194, 231, 240, 277–9, 318, 322, 360, 367–8

Quakers 54–5

Rationalism 110, 200, 207–8, 217, 293
Realism 44, 46, 321–2
Reason 92, 153, 235, 283, 367
Reasons 116
Reformation 67, 97, 299

Relativism 40, 148
Religion 37–9, 40, 48, 51, 55, 59, 71, 80, 88, 116, 121, 138, 250, 284, 305, 310
Renaissance 103, 137, 202, 226, 299
Revolution 86, 90, 97, 115, 170, 182, 191, 209, 236, 306, 365
Right 128, 143, 165, 171
Rights 99, 125, 216, 218, 352–3
Romanticism 85

Scepticism 82, 172, 179, 236–7, 239
Science 37–9, 43, 61, 92, 94, 106, 133, 135, 151–2, 156, 158, 170, 197, 202, 220, 234, 240–1, 243, 246–7, 268, 273, 278, 283, 289–90, 297–303, 360
Secularism 40, 200
Security 61, 192, 207–8, 213, 251–2, 256
Slavery 105, 212
Socialism 191, 194, 195, 203–4, 212, 260–1, 265, 271–3, 345–7
Society 98, 234
Sociology 43, 105, 123, 147–8, 161–3, 167, 234, 235, 278, 352
Socratic Method 172, 185
Sovereignty 55, 118, 187, 249, 370
State 52–3, 55, 61, 88, 99, 109, 143–4, 145, 190, 249–52, 254–5, 258, 303, 370
Stoicism 105
Style 83, 292, 321

Technology 244–5
Teleology 41
Text 155, 174, 350
Theism 46, 80
Theology 48–9, 65, 72, 80, 86, 101, 128
Theory 155, 161, 185, 260, 318
Thought 89, 146
Toleration 85, 237
  Toleration Act (1689) 55
Trade Unions 191, 210
Tradition 40, 130, 136, 143, 181–3, 200, 205, 237, 276, 313, 346, 356
Truth 52, 106, 128, 244, 250, 297
Tyranny 213, 215, 242, 274, 276

Utilitarianism 190, 311–12
Utopia 147, 214, 345, 366, 368

Value 43, 51, 80, 128, 137, 250, 252, 257–8, 271, 321, 354
Victorianism 85

War 205–6, 258, 263, 290, 306–8
Will 144, 146, 160, 183, 203, 249, 252, 363
World 40, 45, 60, 280–1, 298, 364
  of Ideas 70, 170, 178–9

WORKS

Alighieri, Dante, *De Monarchia* 351
Aquinas, St Thomas, *Summa Theologica* 287-8
Aristotle, *Metaphysics* 115
— *Ethics* 115
— *Politics* 115
— *Rhetoric* 115
Arnold, Matthew, *Culture and Anarchy* 60

Bassett, Reginald, *Essentials of Parliamentary Democracy* 194
The Bible 39, 49, 68, 81, 105
The Book of Common Prayer 153
Bosanquet, Bernard, *The Philosophical Theory of the State* 143, 248
Bradley, Francis Herbert, *The Presuppositions of Critical History* 140-3
— *Mr Sidgwick's Hedonism* 140
— *On the Treatment of Sexual Detail in Literature* 140
— *Appearance and Reality* 141
— *Ethical Studies* 141
Brandt, Frithiof, *Thomas Hobbes' Mechanical Conception of Nature* 115
Brogan, Colm, *Our New Masters* 261
Bulwer-Lytton, Edward, *Godolphin* 233
Burckhardt, Jacob, *Weltgeschichtliche betrachtungen* 208 n.
Burkitt, Francis Crawford, *Church and Gnosis* 351
— *The Religion of the Manichees* 351
Burnaby, John, *Amor Dei* 349

Catlin, George, *The Science and Method of Politics* 62
Chekov, Anton, *The Cherry Orchard* 64
Collingwood, Robin George, *Speculum Mentis* 184
— *An Essay on Philosophical Method* 184
Coulton, George Gordon, *Christ, St Francis and To-day* 230

Dalton, Hugh, *Practical Socialism for Britain* 192
Darwin, Charles, *The Autobiography of Charles Darwin* 152
Dostoevsky, Fyodor, *The Voice from Underground* 92

Encyclopédie 84
Euclid, *Elements of Geometry* 118

Fortnightly Review 140

Gore, Charles, *The Reconstruction of Belief* 48
Guicciardini, Francesco, *Considerazioni intorno ai Discorsi del Machiavelli* 356

Hegel, George, *Philosophie des Rechts* 87, 126
— *Geschichte der Philosophie* 110
Hobbes, Thomas, *Leviathan* 112, 293
— *De Corpore* 116
Hsiao, Kung Chan, *Political Pluralism* 51
Hyde, Edward, 1st Earl Clarendon, *History of the Rebellion* 330

International Journal of Ethics 140

Jewkes, John, *Ordeal by Planning* 207, 211

Kant, Immanuel, *Critique of Pure Reason* 92
Kautsky, Karl, *Foundations of Christianity* 123

Locke, John, *An Essay Concerning Human Understanding* 82-4, 293
— *Second Treatise on Government* 313

Machiavelli, Niccolò, *The Prince* 187, 355
Marx, Karl, and Engels, Friedrich, *Manifesto of the Communist Party* 101
Mind 42, 140-2

Orwell, George, *1984* 361

Pater, Walter, *The Renaissance* 239
Perry, Ralph, *Realms of Value* 43
Plato, *Republic* 126, 369
Pound, Roscoe, *Interpretations of Legal History* 178

Robinson, Archibald, *Regnum Dei* 349
Rochefoucauld, François de la, *Maximes* 75
Rosebery, Archibald, *Napoleon: The Last Phase* 229

Schopenhauer, Arthur, *Aphorismen* 75
Schweitzer, Albert, *The Quest of the Historical Jesus* 198
Sidgwick, Henry, *Methods of Ethics* 141
Smith, Logan Pearsall, *Trivia* 73
— *The Prospects of Literature* 74
Steiner, Rudolf, *The Threefold State* 52
Sternberg, Fritz, *Germany and a Lightning War* 262

The Talmud 349
Tolstoy, Leo, *The Diary of a Madman* 92

Voltaire, Jean François Marie Arouet de, *Lettres Anglaises* 84

Whitehead, Alfred North, *Process and Reality* 105-6